Cambridge Middle East Library

King Abdullah, Britain and the making of Jordan

Cambridge Middle East Library

General Editor
ROGER OWEN

Advisory Board
EDMUND BURKE, WALID KAZZIHA, SERIF MARDIN, BASIM MUSALLAM,
AVI SHLAIM

Also in this series

Medicine and power in Tunisia, 1780–1900
NANCY ELIZABETH GALLAGHER

Urban notables and Arab nationalism: the politics of Damascus, 1860–1920
PHILIP S. KHOURY

Egypt in the reign of Muhammad Ali
AFAF LUTFI AL-SAYYID MARSOT

The Palestinian Liberation Organisation: people, power and politics
HELENA COBBAN

Women in nineteenth-century Egypt
JUDITH E. TUCKER

Egyptian politics under Sadat
RAYMOND A. HINNEBUSCH

Nomads and settlers in Syria and Jordan, 1800–1980
NORMAN N. LEWIS

Islam and resistance in Afghanistan
OLIVIER ROY

The Imamate tradition of Oman
JOHN C. WILKINSON

The Ottoman Empire and European capitalism, 1820–1913
ŞEVKET PAMUK

Merchants of Essaouira: urban society and imperialism in southwestern Morocco, 1844–1886
DANIEL J. SCHROETER

The birth of the Palestinian refugee problem, 1947–1949
BENNY MORRIS

Jordan in the 1967 war
SAMIR A. MUTAWI

War's other voices: women writers in the Lebanese civil war
MIRIAM COOKE

Amir Abdullah, Cairo, 1920.

King Abdullah, Britain and the making of Jordan

MARY C. WILSON
Assistant Professor of History
University of Massachusetts at Amherst

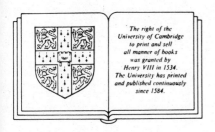

The right of the
University of Cambridge
to print and sell
all manner of books
was granted by
Henry VIII in 1534.
The University has printed
and published continuously
since 1584.

CAMBRIDGE UNIVERSITY PRESS
CAMBRIDGE
NEW YORK PORT CHESTER MELBOURNE SYDNEY

Published by the Press Syndicate of the University of Cambridge
The Pitt Building, Trumpington Street, Cambridge CB2 1RP
40 West 20th Street, New York, NY 10011, USA
10 Stamford Road, Oakleigh, Melbourne 3166, Australia

First published 1987
First paperback edition 1990

Printed in Great Britain at the University Press, Cambridge

British Library cataloguing in publication data

King Abdullah, Britain and the making of
Jordan. – (Cambridge Middle East library).
1. Abdallah, *King of Jordan* 2. Jordan –
Kings and rulers – Biography
I. Title
956.95'04'0924   DS154.53

Library of Congress cataloguing in publication data

Wilson, Mary C. (Mary Christina), 1950–
King Abdullah, Britain, and the making of Jordan.
(Cambridge Middle East Library)
Bibliography
Includes index.
1. Jordan – History.   2. 'Abdallāh, King of Jordan,
1882–1951. I. Title. II. Series.
DS154.5.W54   1987   956.94   87–6649

ISBN 0 521 32421 1 hardback
ISBN 0 521 39987 4 paperback

WV

To my mother and the memory of my father

Contents

Illustrations

Maps

Note on Transliteration

ʿAyns [ʿ] and hamzas [ʾ] are the only diacriticals included in the transliteration of Arabic technical terms, personal names, place names and sources. Commonly accepted English forms are used for some personal and place names, for example, Ibn Saud, Mecca. Abdullah is used throughout.

Acknowledgments

I should like to express my sincere gratitude to the individuals and institutions which have made this book possible. The foundation stone of most that is possible in the academic world, as in all worlds, is material support, and therefore I thank first my family, the Middle East Centre at St Antony's College, the Oxford University Chest, the Oxford University Committee of Graduate Studies, St Antony's College, the Oberlin College Graduate Study Committee, and the Social Science Research Council for their generous financial support. I also thank the Warden and Fellows of St Antony's College, the Directors of the Middle East Centre at Oxford, Derek Hopwood, Robert Mabro, Roger Owen, and Mustafa Badawi, the Director and Associate Director of the Center of Middle Eastern Studies at Harvard University, Muhsin Mahdi and Dennis Skiotis, who made those institutions happy and congenial places of study and discourse during my years of affiliation with them.

Then there are the many, often unknown persons who mind the libraries, archives, and private papers collections and who guide the lone researcher through myriad possibilities to useful information. Here I thank especially the staff at the Public Record Office in London, Mr Phillip and the staff at the Central Zionist Archives, the staff at the Israeli State Archives, Mrs Jill Butterworth at the Sudan Archive of Durham University, and Diana Grimwood-Jones, former archivist at the Middle East Centre, Oxford. Gillian Grant, current archivist at the Middle East Centre, Oxford, was the key to collecting the photographs for this volume. I would also like to thank Richard M. Douglas for his photographic work. In addition, I could have done little work at the Central Zionist Archives without the help of Suliman Bashear and Malik Qupty, who translated hundreds of documents from Hebrew to English. Frank Stewart called my attention to and translated part of Mendel Cohen's book, *be Hatser ha-Melekh Abdullah*. Hasan Kayali, in the course of his research on Ottoman–Arab relations before the First World War, found and shared with me the *irade* naming Sharif Husayn, sharif of Mecca.

I conducted many interviews and I am very grateful to those who gave so generously of their time and memories to me. Their names are listed alphabetically in the Bibliography. I am especially grateful to Crown Prince Hasan, Princess Wijdan, Suleiman Mousa, Widad Kawar, Rita and the late Mahmud al-Ghul, Moshe Ma'oz, and Munira Sa'id for their hospitality and their most kind help in arranging further interviews for me with their friends and acquaintances. I am also grateful to Zina Kawar for her assistance in Amman, to Jim Bell for digging up his original telegrams sent to *Time* magazine about Abdullah's assassination, and to Roger Louis for allowing me to see chapters of his book, *The British Empire in the Middle East 1945–1951: Arab Nationalism, the United States and Postwar Imperialism*, before it was published. I thank my brother-in-law, George Khoury, and Nadim Bibby, who patiently made all my travel arrangements, and Elizabeth Boross, John Parkin and Manka Dowling for their gracious hospitality on my numerous research trips to London. I am also indebted to my friends and colleagues who read and criticized my manuscript in whole or in part – Feroz Ahmad, Glen Balfour-Paul, Hanna Batatu, Ellen Fitzpatrick, Walid Khalidi, John Mack, Basim Musallam, Roger Owen, Paul Saba, and Bayly Winder – to my editor and sub-editor at Cambridge, Elizabeth Wetton and Hilary Gaskin, and to my typist, Melinda Glidden. Most warmly of all I should like to express my very deep gratitude to Albert Hourani and the late Elizabeth Munroe, both of whom gave unstintingly of their time, their thoughts and their friendship throughout the years – and an enormous number of drafts – of this study. Finally, to my mother, Norma Wilson, I am indebted for her support and faith in me; to my parents-in-law, Angela and the late Shukry Khoury, likewise, I am grateful for their unflagging interest in my work; and to Philip Khoury I owe a special debt of gratitude for his expert advice as a colleague, for his patience and fortitude as a husband, and for his willingness to serve as my Man Friday.

MAPS

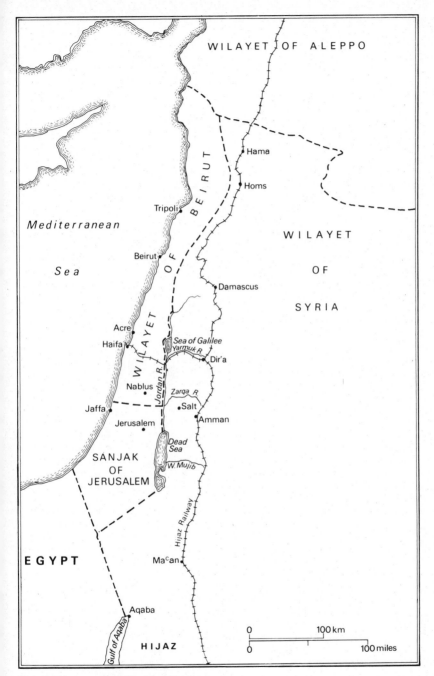

Map 1. Ottoman administrative divisions.

Map 2. The Middle East in the inter-war period.

Map 3. Transjordan.

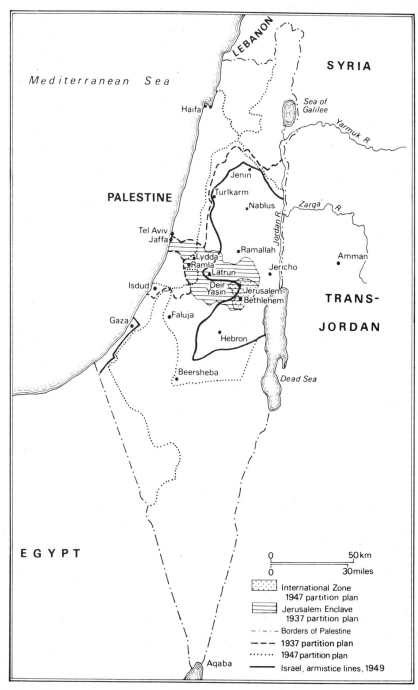

Map 4. The partition of Palestine, 1937–49.

Prologue

In January 1948, King Abdullah of Transjordan[1] sent his prime minister, his foreign minister, and the commander of his army to London. He had been invited to do so by the British government in order to negotiate some minor changes in the two-year-old Anglo-Transjordanian Treaty. At least, that was the stated reason for the trip. The unstated and primary reason was not difficult to divine, however. It had to do with Palestine.

Since the end of the Second World War, the future of Palestine had been the single most important and most difficult issue facing Britain in the Middle East. It was an issue that threatened to destroy Britain's position in the region, and one that might topple Britain's allies as well. One of these allies was King Abdullah.

The journey to London of the three officials, two of them Transjordanian and the other Glubb Pasha, the British commander of the Arab Legion, was to decide Transjordan's role in the future of Palestine. The outlines of Palestine's future had recently been hammered out at the United Nations, which had recommended partition between the hostile Arab and Jewish communities. Britain did not want to bear the responsibility for imposing and maintaining the unpopular division of territory and had consequently announced its intention to give up the mandate and withdraw from Palestine altogether by 15 May 1948. But, although Britain may not have wanted to carry out partition, it could not divest itself of all concern for the future of Palestine. For, whether Britain disassociated itself from the United Nations partition plan or not, whatever happened in Palestine would be laid at Britain's door by virtue of its twenty-five-year rule of the country under mandate.

Britain's objective in Palestine was clear. It was to withdraw without loss of life and in such a way as to retain as much as possible of its power and influence. But having declared the intention to give up the mandate and begun the process of withdrawal, the British could no longer control events as they had been able to do previously. Hence, British policy developed as a series of makeshift steps in response to circumstances as much as it was clearly planned.

Britain was especially concerned about what would be the fate of the areas of Palestine designated as Arab by the United Nations. It definitely preferred to see Transjordan take over these areas than to see the creation of an independent

1

Palestinian state, in the interests of having as smooth a transition of power as possible and of handing over the reins of power to an established ally. Therefore when the Transjordanian prime minister, Tawfiq Abu'l-Huda, excluding even his own foreign minister, requested a private conversation with the British foreign minister, Ernest Bevin was prepared to address this sensitive topic. They met on the morning of Saturday, 7 February, at 11.30. In accordance with the delicacy of both Britain's and Transjordan's position, no verbatim account of the conversation was recorded; but Glubb Pasha, who was asked to serve as interpreter and who was the only other person present, later wrote that when Tawfiq Abu'l-Huda broached the subject of Transjordan's intention to send its army into Palestine after 15 May, Bevin agreed that it seemed 'the obvious thing to do.' But he warned Tawfiq not to invade the areas allotted to the emerging Jewish state.[2]

This was very much the sort of understanding that King Abdullah wanted. He was an ambitious man, overly so some thought. And since Transjordan's army, the Arab Legion, relied on British officers in key positions and on British arms and *matériel*, and further, depended utterly on a British subsidy to pay its costs, he could hardly hope to carry out a campaign contrary to British wishes. Although the Arab portions of Palestine which he would be able to add to his kingdom were small when compared to his dreams of expansion, he viewed this acquisition not as an end in itself. Rather, he viewed it as the first step towards gathering other parts of the Arab world under his aegis and he justified it as the first step towards a larger Arab unity.

The understanding with Bevin was a departure from Abdullah's usual relations with Britain. These relations were characterized by a closeness which, although not without periodic tension, was unparalleled elsewhere in the Middle East. None the less, in twenty-seven years of relative intimacy in Transjordanian affairs, Britain had never before supported Abdullah's ambitions beyond its borders.

Within Transjordan the close association of Abdullah and Britain was a product of mutual utility. That Transjordan existed at all as a separate state was in response to Britain's strategic and political needs; and it was Abdullah's tie to Britain, his position as the keystone in the arch between British mandate authority and local society, that lifted and maintained him above the indigenous leadership of the territory. As far as British interests were concerned, Abdullah was useful as the 'native facade' behind which it was able to ensure its interests without unduly stimulating opposition.[3]

Mutual utility, however, did not mean equality. Abdullah, for Britain, was only one piece in the interlocking pattern of allies and protégés stretching from Egypt to Iran which maintained Britain's overall position of supremacy in the region. Without him the pattern might not have been so neat, but Britain would still have been able adequately to protect its interests and its position. Britain for

Abdullah, however, was the single source of significant support that had allowed him to survive the tribal revolts and attacks of the 1920s and that kept his administration afloat despite the lack of taxable assets in Transjordan itself. Without Britain, it is fair to judge that neither Abdullah nor Transjordan in its formative years would have survived.

Abdullah was fully aware of the imbalance of his dependence on Britain. It haunted him, and had, over the years, an impact upon his personality. Julian Huxley, who visited Amman in April 1948 on United Nations business, found him a man of 'peculiar shrewdness, sometimes rising to wisdom, a shrewdness compounded of native intelligence, a certain naiveté, and a rational cunning, which . . . could not have developed except in some such circumstances as his – a position of power, yet played upon by still more powerful outer forces . . .'[4] Abdullah had sought means to redress that imbalance for most of his political career. The corrective, however, was not simply independence, for Abdullah's domain, as it was created in 1921, had a population of only some 230,000,[5] no real city, no natural resources, and no importance to trade except as a desert thoroughfare. In short, it had no reason to be a state on its own rather than a part of Syria, or of Palestine, or of Saudi Arabia, or of Iraq, except that it better served Britain's interests to be so. Although its population grew and its economy expanded somewhat during the mandatory period, its human and material resource base did not change significantly. Hence, while independence might give Abdullah freedom of action from Britain, it might by the same token leave him at the mercy of his neighbors. Indeed, when Transjordan did receive formal independence in 1946, he was relieved that Britain agreed to continue its financial support of the Arab Legion even though Iraq had agreed to step into the breach if necessary.[6]

No, the corrective to Abdullah's dependence on Britain lay elsewhere. First, he had to expand his rule beyond the borders of Transjordan in order to find greater human and material resources. Second, he had to create a regional balance of forces whose self-interest, in addition to Britain's, would be served by Transjordan's continued existence and tranquility. He had, in short, to increase his internal resources and diversify his external sources of support in order to avoid domination by any one of them.

Ever since Abdullah's arrival in Amman in March 1921 his imagination had played over the territory of his neighbors, Syria, Iraq and Saudi Arabia. His goal in coming to Amman in the first place had not been Amman, *per se*, but Damascus. The alliance between his father, the sharif of Mecca, and Britain during the First World War, which had produced the Arab revolt, had not borne the expected fruit, either for his family or for the Arabs in general. An independent Arab kingdom was not allowed to emerge. Instead the former Arab provinces of the Ottoman Empire were divided between Britain and France and put under mandate.

After the war, Abdullah had marched north from his home in Mecca to challenge the divisions that were being imposed. Instead, he was made a party to these divisions by Winston Churchill, then colonial secretary, who induced him to stay in Amman in part through the vague promise that Britain itself would help him to move on to Damascus.[7] This, however, never came to pass. First the French and later the majority of Syrians themselves were adamantly against adopting Abdullah as ruler. Similarly, his dreams of unity with Iraq, ruled by his nephew after his brother Faysal's death, and of reconquering his family patrimony in the Hijaz, which had been conquered by Ibn Saud in 1924–6, came to naught. Once set up as separate hierarchies in single states, none of the other regimes in the Arab world would willingly subordinate itself to Abdullah even for the sake of Arab unity. And, owing to Abdullah's intimacy with Britain inside of Transjordan, he was not able convincingly to pose as a nationalist leader in order to appeal to the Arab public at large. Britain, for its part, had other allies in the region, and to have supported Abdullah's expansionary dreams would have hurt rather than helped British interests.

By 1948 Abdullah had not achieved any of his objectives. Transjordan, although technically independent, was as beholden as ever to Britain for financial, military and diplomatic support. And even that support was beginning to look transitory as Britain's imperial tide began to ebb world-wide. When British plans to withdraw from Palestine were announced, Abdullah began to be alarmed that Britain would soon lose the interest and the will to sustain Transjordan as well.[8] British officials were at pains to reassure him that, on the contrary, the withdrawal from Palestine rendered Transjordan more rather than less important to Britain's position in the Middle East. They were sincere, at least in the short run; but in the long run it was Abdullah who was right. Britain's imperial tide was irreversibly running out and Transjordan would not be able to count on British support forever. Although he longed to be free of British constraints on one hand, British support and the *raison d'être* of British strategic concerns could not be easily replaced on the other.

As British power waned, successor regimes, created for the most part by Britain or in Britain's favor, waited to take over in all the Arab mandated states but Palestine. Britain's troubled mandate there had allowed the creation of a Jewish Agency which was prepared and eager to step in as a state government, but not of an equivalent on the Arab side of the equation. This failure, compounded by the undermining of the Palestinian leadership in years of fruitless struggle with Britain, gave Abdullah his chance.

The 1948 agreement, then, was a real turning point for Abdullah personally, for Transjordan's position in the region, and for the Anglo-Transjordanian relationship. Abdullah was sixty-six years old. By any reckoning he had little time to achieve his ambitions. The sands of time were also running out on the regional balance of power dominated by Britain that had sustained Transjordan thus far. The ebb of British power allowed Abdullah to take Britain's place in at least part of Palestine. It also made it imperative that he do so in order to find a new constellation of regional and international forces to sustain himself and his kingdom in Britain's absence.

Britain's withdrawal from Palestine set in motion the process by which Abdullah was finally able to expand his domain. Through this expansion, Transjordan became Jordan and found a new *raison d'être* and a new regional balance of power which allowed it to survive the turmoil of the 1950s and the end of British hegemony. Although Abdullah did not live to see the development of that new order, he had, for better or for worse, laid its foundations.

Owing to the circumstances of time and place, Abdullah's life had pulsed in rhythm to the surge and diffusion of Britain's power and influence in the region. He was born in Mecca in 1882, the year that Britain occupied Egypt. He reached manhood as the framework of the Ottoman Empire gave way at last under pressure from without and within – from Britain among other forces on the outside, and from dissident and dissatisfied groups, among them Abdullah and his family, on the inside. In the aftermath of the Ottoman Empire and at the height of Britain's power in the region, he, in his middle years, became a British protégé by accepting the leadership of Transjordan under British mandate. Finally, during the twilight years of 'Britain's moment in the Middle East,'[9] when the persistence of its influence was little more than an atavism, he died in an echo of the same events in Palestine that had cost Britain its position.

The confluence of Abdullah's and Britain's interests had flowed throughout his entire lifetime. Even before his birth, the nineteenth-century expansion of British interests in the Middle East, the growing centralization and vigor of the Ottoman Empire, and the protective instinct of an Arab elite anxious to maintain its place and power within the empire had set the waters in motion. Abdullah's family in Mecca was part of that Arab elite. Hence the story of the mingling of Britain's imperial interests with Abdullah's personal ones begins in Mecca and in its developing alienation from Istanbul.

Chapter 2

Mecca and Istanbul

Abdullah is often characterized in the Middle East and the West alike as a beduin. This notion comes from the latter half of his life when his personal history became entwined with the creation of Transjordan and he came to be identified with and to identify himself with the tribal hierarchy of that country. As to his upbringing, however, nothing could be further from the truth. He grew up in two of the more important cities in the Middle East in the nineteenth century, Mecca and Istanbul. One was the holiest city of Islam and the focus of religious consciousness and practice; the other was the capital of the Ottoman Empire and the hub of political power.

Abdullah was born in Mecca in the Ottoman province of the Hijaz in February 1882. He was the second son of Husayn ibn ʿAli and ʿAbdiyya bint Abdullah.[1] His parents were themselves first cousins and both bore the title sharif, meaning noble, which denoted their descent from the Prophet Muhammad. Sharifian lineage is determined by complex genealogies which can be and have been forged, falsified and bought; yet in Mecca and in the Hijaz in general, genealogical tradition has survived in its greatest purity, making it difficult to forge false links to the Prophet there.[2] Sharifs enjoy special respect as a natural result of reverence for the Prophet, but the title itself does not ensure its bearer wealth or power and sharifs can be found at all levels of the socio-economic order. Those from Meccan lineages, however, were eligible for a special office, sharif of Mecca, which conferred on its holder religious authority, political power and wealth.[3] In the year of Abdullah's birth, his great-uncle held this office.

Abdullah, being a sharif and closely related to the sharif of Mecca was born into a privileged layer of Meccan society. He was brought up in town, although it was the custom for the sons of Meccan sharifs to be sent to nearby nomadic tribes to be raised in order to cement relations with the tribes on whose goodwill Mecca's well-being depended. His mother died when he was four, after the birth of his younger brother Faysal. After her death, his great grandmother and great aunt on his father's side took care of him.

It was at the knees of these women of the Bani Shihr tribe that he learned of tribal history and nomadic ways. They passed on to him their knowledge and love of tribal lore, songs and poetry, and his expertise in such things was often remarked upon as he grew older. Especially vivid were the tales they told him of the unsettled times at the beginning of the century, of the conquest and 'desecration' of Mecca by tribes of central Arabia acting under the impetus of Wahhabism, of its reconquest by Muhammad 'Ali of Egypt on behalf of the Ottoman Sultan, and of the accession to the sharifate by his great grandfather.[4]

Sharif of Mecca was an ancient office, dating from before the time of the Ottoman conquest of the Hijaz in the sixteenth century. Under the Ottomans the sharif retained his position of local leadership and a certain freedom of action. Indeed, within the imperial structure Mecca, the Prophet's birthplace, and Medina, where he lies buried, prospered. The two cities were the recipients of empire-wide religious taxes and alms, collected and remitted through Istanbul, and of the personal munificence and protection of the sultan, who was anxious that no problems in the holy cities should mar his standing as their overlord. Moreover, their inhabitants were not taxed, nor were they liable to conscription. In return, the sultan was able to add to his titles one that gave him primacy among Muslim rulers: *khadim al-haramayn* (servant of the two holy places).[5]

Although the sharif of Mecca had been accorded a wide range of authority at the time of the Ottoman conquest, his position and his relationship to Istanbul were not immutable. Throughout most of the Ottoman period, the Hijaz did enjoy a remarkable degree of autonomy. In the nineteenth century, however, the balance of power between Istanbul and Mecca began to change. This shift and growing British interest in the region was dramatically to affect Abdullah's life, and indeed, the history of the entire Middle East.

At the beginning of the century a rising force in Arabia upset the *status quo* in the Hijaz. The Wahhabis, followers of a central Arabian religious reformer and purist, allied with the political power of the Al Saud, a ruling family of central Arabia, occupied and 'purified' Mecca in 1803. They replaced the incumbent sharif of Mecca with one of their own choosing, thereby challenging Ottoman authority. Ottoman hegemony was re-established in 1819 through the Ottoman viceroy of Egypt, Muhammad 'Ali. He named Abdullah's great grandfather sharif of Mecca, the first of Abdullah's immediate ancestry to hold the position. Owing to this temporary but none the less frightening loss of control, the Ottomans became more vigilant in regard to the Hijaz thereafter. This vigilance, coupled with the nineteenth-century movement to strengthen the empire by reformation and centralization, resulted in the gradual erosion of Hijazi autonomy. Using to advantage the rivalry between the two leading sharifian clans, the Dhawi Zayd and Abdullah's line, the 'Abadila, Istanbul worked to bend succeeding sharifs of Mecca more closely to its own will.[5]

Ottoman control of Hijazi affairs was aided after the mid-century by new means of transport and communication, which brought Mecca closer to the center of imperial affairs. The development of steamships and the completion of the Suez Canal in 1869 facilitated movement between Istanbul and Mecca. Telegraphs and a regular postal system, set up in 1882, brought the Hijaz even more closely under Ottoman supervision. These technical innovations were double-edged, however, for they also tied the Hijaz more tightly into a world-wide network of communications and trade. In particular, the Suez Canal cut the journey by sea between Britain and the west coast of India by seventy-seven per cent, turning the Suez Canal–Red Sea route into Britain's most important imperial artery. Britain's ever-increasing interest in the Red Sea, beginning in the eighteenth century and taking a marked leap forward after 1869, strengthened Ottoman determination to rule the Hijaz with a firm hand.[6]

By the time of Abdullah's birth in 1882, the challenge to Hijazi autonomy created by modern means of communication and increased Ottoman vigilance and control had begun to be felt. In the same year a profound shock was dealt the empire. Britain occupied Egypt. This event reverberated loudly in Mecca, where Cairenes on pilgrimage reputedly dropped their offensive air of superiority and acknowledged Mecca as the true refuge of Islam, and even admitted the inferiority of their own city where unbelievers meddled in the religious affairs of the faithful. Two years later students in Mecca closely followed the uprising in the Sudan, joyfully awaiting the moment when the *mahdi* would defeat Britain and cross the Red Sea to the holy city.[7] But they waited in vain. Although Britain was defeated in 1885, its advance up the Nile was only halted for a moment. Thirteen years later British and Egyptian troops together conquered and sacked the mahdist capital, Omdurman.

Britain's occupation of Egypt rounded out its control of the outlets of the Red Sea; Aden at its southern end had been occupied in 1839. More importantly, it introduced Britain's actual presence into the Middle East in a far more profound and deeply felt manner than had the opening of the Suez Canal, though the one was prelude to the other. Britain was also concerned with the peace and tranquility of the holy cities, the facilitation of the pilgrimage, and therefore with the policies of the sharifs of Mecca, since Queen Victoria had more Muslims in her empire than the sultan had in his. Aware of Britain's interest and its ability to project its interests territorially, Ottoman authority in the Hijaz became increasingly intrusive. Istanbul even tried to stem the tide of British Indian pilgrims for fear they might become a pretext for British occupation.[8]

Britain, however, was wary of intervening directly in the affairs of the Muslim holy land. British policy was also officially committed to upholding the territorial integrity of the Ottoman Empire. Egypt, despite the British occupation, remained officially a part of the empire, but under what came to be called Britain's 'Veiled Protectorate.' So, even though the increase of Britain's interest and influence was palpable, it was not manifested by any outward change in political relations. Nevertheless, the British consul was acknowledged as the most influential foreign consul in Jidda. And because Ottoman power had at the same time become so intrusive, it was whispered locally that British protection might be preferable to Ottoman control, and that if Britain would agree to prevent Ottoman troops from reaching the Hijaz, the Turks could be expelled.[9] Rumor also implicated an Ottoman agent in the murder of the sharif of Mecca two years before Abdullah's birth, a murder supposedly committed because the sharif favored the 'Engleys.' Rumors of Britain's interest in establishing an Arabian caliphate surfaced periodically thereafter.[10]

Ottoman authority in the Hijaz was directly represented by the *vali*, or governor, who was sent from Istanbul and who resided in the provincial capital, at first Jidda, later Mecca. The bounds of authority between *vali* and sharif were not fixed and the two vied for local pre-eminence. A strong *vali* with (and sometimes without) a strong central government behind him could curtail the sharif's autonomy, while a strong-willed sharif could wield power at the expense of the *vali* and the central government.

Generally in the nineteenth century the sharifs of Mecca were more powerful than the *valis*, despite state policies of reform and centralization. 'The governorship of the Hijaz, like many other provincial governorships, was viewed as a kind of exile for losers in the game of political intrigue in Istanbul.'[11] The *vali* had an Ottoman garrison to ensure his authority in the towns of the Hijaz, but in the dreary distances in between tribal authority held sway. The lynchpin of Ottoman relations with these tribes was the sharif. By virtue of a network of marriage ties and institutionalized patronage, he was able to bind tribal hierarchies to himself in varying degrees of closeness. These ties could not be replaced by the use of force, at least not by the military organization and level of technicalization the Ottomans then had at their command.[12]

It was absolutely imperative for the empire to maintain contact with, and some sort of control over, the tribes of the Hijaz, since it was through their territory that the annual *hajj* (pilgrimage) caravan passed on its way to Mecca. The *hajj* was the greatest religious event of the Islamic year. It was also the greatest trading event, and arid Mecca's lifeline to the world. It was referred to as 'the most important of the exalted state's affairs' in Ottoman correspondence. The sultan's prestige and legitimacy rested in part on his ability to organize and ease the pilgrims' arduous journey within the empire.[13] The sharif's fitness for office was also judged in part on his ability to ensure safe passage through tribal lands as the pilgrims neared Mecca.

The *hajj* required vast powers of organization. Even with relatively primitive nineteenth-century modes of travel, it was a great communal in-gathering which brought together believers from the far-flung corners of the Ottoman Empire and from the vast Muslim communities beyond its borders in Africa, India, China, and Java. Each year, during the last month of the Muslim lunar calendar, two great streams of pilgrims gathered at Damascus and Cairo. As they flowed slowly towards Mecca the whole region along the way swung into orchestrated movement. Fortresses built to guard the way were stocked and ready to provide shelter for the passing caravan. Villages and oases gathered their yearly surplus to trade for exotic wares from afar. Each pilgrim brought goods from his native land to trade along the way for sustenance and lodging. Merchants, no less pious perhaps than simple pilgrims but traders by profession, also took the opportunity of the *hajj* to ply their wares in distant markets. Tribes offered their animals for sale or rent and their animal products in exchange for agricultural products and manufactured goods of Fez, Istanbul, Isfahan and Bukhara. The judicious distribution of cash sweeteners along the major *hajj* routes from Damascus south helped to ensure that the tribes would trade with the caravan rather than plunder it.[14]

These tens and hundreds of thousands of people, speaking dozens of languages in multi-hued dialects, their animals loaded with goods, converged *en masse* on Mecca, the birthplace of the Prophet, as it lay hot and parched in its narrow sandy valley surrounded by barren mountains. The sharif of Mecca waited to receive them, to conduct the annual rites, and to receive the subventions of goods and cash which came with the pilgrimage every year for the upkeep of the holy city and the sustenance of its population. Abdullah's birthplace, like his kingdom later, depended on external sources of support owing to its own lack of natural resources.

Mecca is hot all year round, and very dry.[15] For lack of water, little grows there although there are gardens within ten and twenty kilometres. Other fresh produce comes from Ta'if in the mountains two days to the east. Trade with the surrounding tribes provides meat and dairy products. Wheat, barley, rice, and broad beans come as subventions in kind from Egypt and Iraq. Jidda, Mecca's window on the world on the shores of the Red Sea, is sixty miles to the west. Before the advent of the automobile this was a trip of fifteen hours or two days depending on whether one travelled by donkey or camel caravan. But owing to its religious importance, Mecca is able to transcend the strictures of its temporal circumstances. Geographically remote, it none the less lies at the center of Muslim consciousness; it is towards Mecca that devout Muslims pray five times a day, and it is a religious duty to make the *hajj*. Although provincial, it is none the less cosmopolitan, for believers of all nationalities visit and many settle in the holy environs, enriching the cultural and commercial life of what would otherwise have been a little-known market town in western Arabia. Indians, Javanese, South Arabians, and Turks were the largest foreign communities. Slaves, mainly from East Africa and the Sudan, also added to the cultural and ethnic diversity of Mecca.

Everyone in Mecca depended on the traffic of pilgrims to sell their wares and services and to bring the alms and gifts which supplemented their livelihood. Most combined the service of God with trade to make a living. Gifts of cash and precious objects came from the sultan and other Muslim rulers. These gifts and the foodstuffs from Egypt and Iraq were shared out amongst the people of Mecca, who were officially divided into five groups for the purpose. At the top and receiving the largest share were the religious leaders, a group that included the hereditary clans of sharifs and sayyids (descendants of the Prophet through his two grandsons Hasan and Husayn respectively), as well as the *imams* and *khatibs* (prayer leaders and preachers) of the Great Mosque. Then came the notables of Mecca, the servants of the holy places, the general population who were born in Mecca, and finally, foreigners who had settled there. Small children, slaves, servants, merchants, employees of the Hijaz treasury, and those living in Mecca for less than five years were officially (though not always in practice) excluded from the division of gifts.

The sharif of Mecca had other sources of income in addition to the subsidies and pious offerings.[16] Although the inhabitants of Jidda and Mecca paid no taxes on their persons, homes or property, there were indirect methods of obtaining revenue. Licenses were required of shaykhs, pilgrim guides, and masters and members of the merchant and craft guilds. Duties levied at the Red Sea ports of Jidda and Yanbu‘ went to the sharif, as did a tax on all animals and provisions coming into the towns of the Hijaz from the interior, except for what came with the *hajj* caravan which passed everywhere duty free. Persian pilgrims, being Shi‘ites, were subject to a discriminatory capitation tax. Using capital gained in the above ways, the sharif could stock enough provisions to allow him to influence, if not to control, daily prices to his own benefit. Manipulation of the means and routes of pilgrim transportation also increased the sharif's income. The money thus earned was spent in part to make life more comfortable for him and his extended family, but it was spent in greater part on maintaining the respect and support of nomadic tribesmen through bountiful hospitality and lavish gifts.

As members of the ruling sharifian line, Abdullah and his family lived on an allowance befitting their status and their closeness to the reigning sharif. They also had income from property in the Hijaz and in Egypt, which they held in the form of *waqfs* (pious endowments). Coming from a religious caste in a place where learning was still the province of religion, Abdullah received a tolerably good education according to the standards of the period. He was educated at home by private tutors along with his brothers ‘Ali (b. 1879) and Faysal (b. 1886) in the traditional subjects – recitation of the Quran, reading and calligraphy. He enjoyed a vacation from his studies in the summer when his family migrated eastward to the cool hills of Ta'if. There, in what was said to be a bit of Syria transplanted by God to Arabia for the comfort of His neighbors, they and everyone else from Mecca who could afford it found relief from the intense heat of the holy city.[17]

In 1891, the long reach of the sultan touched and began to unravel the warm cocoon of Abdullah's childhood in Mecca. A dispute had flared up between the sharif of Mecca and his nephew, Husayn, Abdullah's father, which threatened to disrupt the tranquility of the Hijaz. The sultan sent a mission to inquire into and settle the contretemps. As a result Husayn was summoned to Istanbul.[18]

Husayn left Mecca for Istanbul immediately. His destination was not strange to him, for he had been born there in 1853. Nor was it surprising that the sultan invited him to stay on in Istanbul, part guest, part prisoner, under his watchful eye. Some sharifs from Mecca could always be found in the imperial capital, where they served as guarantors of the current sharif of Mecca's continued loyalty and were groomed as suitable replacements.[19] ʿAli Haydar, Husayn's chief rival for the office of sharif of Mecca fifteen years later, spent his whole life there.

Abdullah and his brothers, ʿAli and Faysal, joined their father in Istanbul a year later. They embarked from Jidda in February 1893, around the time of Abdullah's eleventh birthday, traveling in the care of their paternal grandmother, Basmajihan, and in the company of thirty-two ladies of the family and suite of their great-uncle ʿAbd al-Ilah, another sharif resident in Istanbul. It was Abdullah's first trip by sea. At Port Said he saw for the first time women unveiled, a practice he discouraged when he grew older. There, he and his brothers stocked up on heavy winter clothing in anticipation of the cold, wet weather of Istanbul. From Port Said they ran into heavy seas, but on the night of 7 March they finally arrived in the imperial capital, reaching their anchorage off Seraglio Point as dawn was breaking.[20]

The family settled into a furnished home provided by the sultan, on the Bosporus. This waterway, with its wooded slopes and its shores adorned with kiosks and Italianate palaces, fascinated Abdullah. All manner of vessels plied its waters – ferries carrying passengers from Galata Bridge on the European side to Usküdar on the Asian side, private launches delivering royal and other important personages to their palaces and villas, and small sailboats and rowboats selling fresh fruit and vegetables, meat and fish. Indeed, Abdullah thought Istanbul magnificent. In his memoirs he describes it as a home to many nationalities where none felt strange, a center of trade where anything from any country could be found, and pleasing in every season but especially in spring with its abundant fruits.[21]

During the sixteen years of Abdullah's residence, Istanbul bore the unmistakable imprint of the Ottoman sultan, Abdülhamid II. Abdülhamid was a shrewd ruler who successfully gathered the reins of power in his own hands. Unlike his immediate predecessors, the sultans of the Tanzimat period, who outwardly embraced European values, he was austere, sober and pious, setting a tone of religiosity that marked his reign. Like his predecessors, however, his aim was to centralize and strengthen the empire. To do so he adopted a pan-

Islamic ideology which depended on support and legitimization from the ranks of religious professionals. Many of these, naturally, were Arabs, and during Abdülhamid's reign the Arab provinces, the seats of Islamic learning and culture, rose to a new importance within the empire.

Abdülhamid tried to balance the power of his bureaucracy with an informal network of spies and informers which created an atmosphere of insecurity and watchfulness.[22] He also had a kitchen cabinet to offset the power of his real one. The men of Abdülhamid's camarilla were drawn from outside the traditional Turkish Muslim elite. Two of the best-known and most powerful were Arabs: Abu'l-Huda al-Sayyadi,[23] a self-made religious leader from the Aleppo region who advised Abdülhamid on religious affairs, and Ahmad 'Izzat al-'Abid, a Damascene notable, who was Abdülhamid's second secretary. It was Ahmad 'Izzat's idea to build a railway from Damascus to Mecca to facilitate the pilgrimage and draw the attention of the Islamic world to Abdülhamid. This project later became the symbol of advancing Ottoman encroachment on the customary autonomy of the Hijaz, and the focus of Husayn's strenuous opposition to such encroachment when he became sharif of Mecca.

Despite the susurrant undercurrent of Abdülhamid's Istanbul, it was enjoying a period of political and cultural renaissance during the period when Abdullah lived there. Owing to the previous fifty years of Ottoman reform and to technological advances in communications, the capital was in a position of political primacy unparalleled, perhaps, since the time of Sulayman the Magnificent. Printing presses multiplied, and newspapers, periodicals and books, though subject to censorship, increased in number and circulation. Professional schools founded in the mid-century or before on European models – the School of Engineering, the School of Medicine, the Imperial School of Military Sciences and the Imperial School of Administration – were expanded. Darülfünun, which later became the University of Istanbul, opened its doors in 1900.

Many of the students in these schools came from the Arab provinces to seek careers in the newly centralized and professional bureaucracy. A degree from Istanbul had become the surest ticket to a high post, whether in the capital or back home in the provinces. But Abdullah and his brothers were not among these ambitious youths. Their future seemed to depend on lineage rather than on a degree, and they continued their education at home. A tutor from the military academy was appointed by imperial decree to instruct them in Turkish, geography, mathematics and Ottoman and Islamic history. He later described Abdullah as mischievous in comparison to 'Ali and Faysal who were more sedate and serious.[24] None the less, under his tutelage Abdullah became proficient in Turkish, which he used in later years as an oral cypher. Arabic was not neglected: Husayn himself taught his sons the Quran, a graduate from the

Azhar taught them grammar, and one other teacher trained them in calligraphy. From these lessons Abdullah and his brothers had two vacations a year, summer and winter, during which they enjoyed hunting and fishing.[25]

Although many of Abdullah's future colleagues and rivals from all parts of the Arab world studied in Istanbul he met few of them, for his social circle was limited to the line of the Prophet and the Turkish elite.[26] The former included ʿAli Haydar, scion of the rival Dhawi Zayd line of sharifs, and Hasan Khalid Abuʾl-Huda, the son of Abdülhamid's adviser on religious affairs, who later served as chief minister of Transjordan.[27] Ties with the Turkish elite were cemented when Abdullah's father married Adilé Hanum, a grand-daughter of Mustafa Reshid Pasha (1800–56), one of the architects of Ottoman reform and a minister of foreign affairs and grand vizier under Abdülhamid's precedessors, Mahmud II and Abdülmecid. She bore a son, Zayd, in 1900, and three daughters. From among close sharifian relations, wives were also found for Abdullah and his brothers. ʿAli married the daughter of his great-uncle, ʿAbd al-Ilah. Abdullah, in 1902 at the age of twenty, married Misbah, his first cousin, the daughter of his father's brother Nasir. Faysal married another of Nasir's daughters.

It appeared that Husayn and his family had settled into life in Istanbul. He was appointed to the council of state, an advisory body to Abdülhamid. But it was in Mecca that his political future lay and to Meccan affairs that he kept his ears attuned. There, in 1905, the sharif of Mecca died. Husayn put forward his name as a candidate for the vacant office, as did two other sharifs resident in Istanbul, ʿAbd al-Ilah, Abdullah's great-uncle, and ʿAli Haydar of the rival Dhawi Zayd clan. But a fourth candidate, ʿAli ibn Abdullah, Abdullah's maternal uncle living in Mecca, was chosen instead. (It was rumored that he paid seventy thousand pounds for the honor.)[28] But within three years Husayn had another chance at the office owing to political upheaval in Istanbul.

In the summer of 1908, a rebellion of junior Ottoman officers of the Third Army in Macedonia triggered political changes in Istanbul. The rebellion in the army was seized on by the Committee of Union and Progress (CUP), a secret political society in Macedonia, to force Abdülhamid to reconvene parliament along the lines of the constitution of 1876. This 'Young Turk' revolution, as it came to be called, succeeded in curbing the unbridled authority of the sultan by reimposing the constitution and introducing parliamentary procedures. Abdülhamid remained on the throne for eight months thereafter, but was finally deposed and replaced by his brother when an attempted counter-revolution failed.

These events caused confusion and consternation in the provinces. In the Hijaz, there was a mutiny in the Seventh Army Corps and the Ottoman governor was recalled. Disturbances broke out in Mecca against the supposed intent of the new regime to curtail the privileges and powers of the sharif of

Mecca. Accused of fomenting this unrest, he was subsequently removed from his position.[29] 'Abd al-Ilah, Abdullah's great uncle, was named the new sharif of Mecca, but as he was preparing to leave Istanbul for Mecca he suddenly died.

It was at this moment that, according to Abdullah's memoirs, he made a decisive intervention. Amid rumours that 'Ali Haydar was about to be appointed, he urged his father to put his claim to the office of sharif of Mecca in writing. He then took this note by hand to the grand vizier, Kamil Pasha. Dissatisfied with his reception at the Porte, he fired off telegrams to the *shaykh al-islam* and the first secretary of the palace, hoping that one of them might intercede with the sultan. The next day Husayn was invited to Yildiz; he came away the new sharif of Mecca.[30]

In the murky political waters of the Istanbul of 1908, where the struggle for power between the CUP, the sultan and the grand vizier was not yet resolved, the configuration of circumstances and influences which led to Husayn's appointment is not clear. Husayn was not a Unionist, nor was he sympathetic to the constitution. Indeed, the CUP was reported to be displeased at his appointment. Certainly when disputes between Mecca and Istanbul developed later, the CUP supported his rival, 'Ali Haydar, and attempted, without success, to depose Husayn. The sultan may have seen in Husayn a future ally against the Committee, though at the same time he was said to fear Husayn's extreme ambition. Abdullah credited the first secretary, 'Ali Cevat, with providing the key to his father's appointment, and he may have been important behind the scenes, but most historians and some contemporary evidence point to the influence of Kamil Pasha, the Anglophile grand vizier, as decisive.[31]

Beyond the immediate struggle for power in Istanbul, Britain's hand can be discerned in the balance and counterpoise of interests which tipped in favor of Husayn. Although Britain probably did not intervene directly, it was a power that Istanbul had to conciliate. Therefore, Britain's tacit approval of any new sharif was important. Some months before his appointment Husayn had sent the British ambassador a 'very friendly message expressing his feelings of gratitude to England for her sympathy towards the Ottoman constitutional movement.' Hence the ambassador was able to describe him, at the time of his appointment, as 'an upright man, who is unlikely to connive at or condone the extortions on pilgrims or other malpractices of his predecessor under the old régime.'[32] However the impact of British opinion might be measured, Britain's approval of Husayn is chiefly important in retrospect. It shows the general advance of British intrusiveness in Hijazi affairs and a confluence of interests between Husayn and Britain well before their decisive wartime anti-Ottoman alliance.

Husayn set off for Mecca towards the end of November. As he was about to embark, he was given a written assurance by the grand vizier, Kamil Pasha, that the traditional rights of the sharif of Mecca would not be affected by the introduction of constitutional government in Istanbul.[33] With such an assurance in his pocket, the new sharif was expected to quell the cries of 'down with the red tarboushes' by which Meccans had expressed their fears that Ottoman bureaucrats of the new regime intended to supersede Meccan privileges.

Abdullah accompanied his father back to Mecca, along with his youngest, half-Turkish brother Zayd. His other two brothers, 'Ali and Faysal, stayed behind to tidy up the family's affairs in Istanbul and to see to the packing and moving of the womenfolk and their effects.

Abdullah's adolescence and youth in the imperial capital were formative. Although British administrators in Transjordan were later to describe him in moments of exasperation as having been trained in the 'Ottoman school of intrigue,' what this meant in a non-pejorative sense was that he was thoroughly familiar with the indirect exercise of power in circumstances not of his creation and not wholly in his control. What he learned in Istanbul was reinforced when his father became sharif of Mecca.

Abdullah admired Abdülhamid for not imitating Europe and later kept his own distance from European fashions and modes of thought despite his dependence on Britain. He defended Abdülhamid to posterity: the sultan, he wrote, 'acted in good faith and sincerity, and if he had faults it was the fault of diligence.' By Abdullah's lights Abdülhamid was not tyrannical, but cautious and careful, and compared with what came after him, his was a just reign. Although life in Istanbul had not been of his choosing, it was an honorable existence, an exile of respect which in later years Abdullah looked back on with nostalgia. For him, no spectacle of British pomp and pageantry, even the coronation of George VI, matched the richness and intricacy of Ottoman spectacles.[34]

Husayn and his two sons arrived in Jidda on 3 December. Met by a delegation which welcomed the 'constitutional amir [prince],' Husayn immediately let his feelings about constitutions be known. 'The constitution of the country of God,' he said, 'is the law of God [*shari'a*] and the sayings and doings [*sunna*] of His Prophet.'[35] He had arrived at the beginning of the pilgrimage on a steamer carrying eight hundred pilgrims,[36] and the single most important duty of his office – ensuring a smooth and properly-conducted *hajj* – was upon him as he set out by camel for Mecca.

Husayn's first pilgrimage as sharif of Mecca was not without difficulties. Shi'ite pilgrims disagreed with his ruling on the new moon which signalled the beginning of *Dhu'l-Hijja* and delayed their pilgrimage by one day. Tribes around Medina, unhappy with their loss of revenue caused by competition from the newly built Hijaz railway (completed from Damascus to Medina in September) and with the failure of the Turks to pay their annual stipend, attacked the railway, destroyed telegraph lines, and harassed pilgrims.

Although Husayn concluded a two-month truce with the tribes in an effort to assure the pilgrims' safe passage, the tribes continued their interference and obstruction to such an extent that he publicly expressed his regret to the Egyptian caravan. In the meantime the *amir al-hajj* (commander of the pilgrimage) of the Syrian caravan, fearful of tribal restlessness around Medina and perhaps acting on behalf of the CUP to discredit Husayn, announced that the traditional land route was unsafe and ordered the Syrian caravan to return to Damascus by sea, from Jidda to Haifa.

This was a direct challenge to Husayn's ability to fulfill the duties of his new station and he acted forcefully to assert himself. The use of the sea route would have deprived him of revenue and of the goodwill of the bedouin between Mecca and Medina, who stood to profit by the passage of the caravan through their territory. He consigned the caravan to the care of Abdullah and of his brother Nasir, who accompanied it, safely, by land to Damascus. The *amir al-hajj*, 'Abd al-Rahman al-Yusuf, returned by sea alone.[37]

At the head of the great *hajj* caravan Abdullah had his first sight of Damascus – the city which the Prophet had likened to paradise and which, in the twentieth century, was the cradle of Arab nationalism. The journey by caravan from Mecca to Medina and by train from Medina to Damascus had been uneventful. All of Damascus turned out at the railway station to welcome the pilgrims and to celebrate the completion of their sacred duty. After the customary welcoming speeches and poetry recitations, Abdullah and his uncle paid a courtesy call on the Ottoman *vali* and then proceeded to the home of 'Ata Pasha al-Bakri, where they had been invited to stay. The Bakris were an aristocratic landowning family who claimed descent from the Prophet and thus, however distantly, kinship with Abdullah and his family. 'Ata Pasha had been an influential member of the Damascus Municipal and District Councils since the 1890s, during which time he was invited to Istanbul to receive the title of 'pasha'. There he had first met Husayn and his sons.[38]

Abdullah spent seven days in Damascus, where he discovered, among the Damascene elite, a certain restiveness and dissatisfaction with the new order in Istanbul. In the wake of the Young Turk revolution, the configuration of power within this elite had begun to change. Some families had lost power as Abdülhamid's network of provincial officials in Damascus was dismantled and replaced by CUP adherents and sympathizers. Others had lost influence when their friends and allies in high positions in Istanbul, closely identified with the Hamidian regime, fell from power. Notably, the Bakris had lost their important link to central authority when Ahmad 'Izzat al-'Abid, Abdülhamid's closest political confidant, was ousted by the CUP. Damascus witnessed both pro- and anti-CUP demonstrations, but elections to the new parliament in the autumn of 1908 showed the anti-CUP faction to be the stronger.[39] In his memoirs Abdullah wrote of this disaffected elite as being on the verge of 'splitting the bonds,'[40] but it is a phrase written from the vantage of hindsight. In 1909 the aim of the Bakris and others like them was to turn the clock back to a former time of prestige, prosperity and shared power for the Arab elite within the empire. It was only gradually perceived, after the failure of the April counter-revolution, that the clock could not be turned back and that the Damascene elite would have to blaze new paths to power.

Abdullah and his uncle returned to Medina by train and stayed there ten days to settle some local tribal affairs. When they arrived in Mecca, tranquil after the bustle of pilgrimage, they found that ʿAli and Faysal had returned from Istanbul with the women of the family. Nine months later, Abdullah's wife presented him with his first son, Talal. A daughter, Haya, had been born some years previously.

With his new office Sharif Husayn inherited two palaces in Mecca. One was recently built and sumptuously furnished: this was where his wife lived and where he slept. The second was larger than the first, but older. It was five stories tall with three or four divisions and more than one hundred rooms. Known in Mecca as the *dar al-hukm* (house of justice) or *saray sayyidna* (palace of our master), it was where Husayn spent his days and the early part of the evening, conducting the affairs of the sharifate and meeting friends. An imposing building, it was approached by a wide and deep stairway leading to a huge iron door which was opened every day at dawn and closed four hours after sunset. Beyond the door was a short corridor leading to a spacious courtyard enclosed on four sides by the buildings which made up the *dar al-hukm*. The buildings on the north and west side were taller than the rest and contained the apartments used by Abdullah and his brothers.[41] There was another palace in Taʾif where the family could escape the summer heat of Mecca.[42]

The new sharif of Mecca, like his predecessors, worked to extend his power locally amongst the tribes while fighting the rising tide of Ottoman centralization. In his first four years of office, he was quite successful in doing so. He saw, in succession, the appointment and recall of seven titular or acting *valis*. Getting Abdullah elected to the Ottoman parliament was one step in the consolidation of his power.[43]

Mecca, like other Ottoman towns, had elected its complement of representatives to parliament in the late autumn of 1908, following the Young Turk revolution. But Mecca's two deputies had not gone to the opening session – the unrest in the Hijaz at the time had made them cautious. Soon after Husayn's arrival he set about replacing them with representatives of assured loyalty to himself.[44] A new election was held in January–February, when Abdullah and Shaykh Hasan al-Shaybi (whose family traditionally held the keys to the Kaʿba) were chosen by a select group of electors. Abdullah received 144 votes and Shaykh Hasan ninety-eight, defeating two CUP candidates and twenty other local Arab candidates sympathetic to the 'Arab Liberal Party', presumably part of the broad coalition known as the Liberal Union which had formed in opposition to the CUP throughout the empire.[45]

From 1910 to 1914 Abdullah spent winter and spring in Istanbul in order to attend parliament, and summer and fall in the Hijaz, regularly breaking his journey in between to visit the khedive of Egypt, ʿAbbas Hilmi, with whom he had become friendly during the 1909 *hajj*.[46] Political life in the capital had quickened since the downfall of Abdülhamid. Despite the imposition of martial law after the defeat of the counter-revolution in April 1909, the CUP did not hold a monopoly of authority. Rather, it was engaged in a triangular power struggle with the army on one hand and a broad and growing opposition coalition, the Liberal Union, on the other. Arabs, as Ottomans and citizens of the empire, were in each of the three groups vying for power. But it was to the Liberal Union with its ideas of decentralization that the majority of Arab provincial politicians were drawn, and within the Liberal Union that they began to express their interests self-consciously as Arab interests. At the same time smaller groups, exclusively Arab in membership, were formed to define Arab interests within the empire. These included both public organizations and secret societies. The former included *al-Ikhaʾ al-ʿArabi al-ʿUthmani* (the Ottoman Arab Fraternity) founded in Istanbul in 1908 and suppressed after the counter-revolution, *al-Muntada al-Adabi* (the Literary Club) founded in Istanbul in 1909, and *Hizb al-Lamarkaziyya al-Idariyya al-ʿUthmani* (the Ottoman Party for Administrative Decentralization) founded in 1912 in Cairo. The secret societies were *al-Qahtaniyya* (the Order of Qahtan), *al-Fatat* (the Young Arab Society), and *al-ʿAhd* (the Covenant).[47]

Abdullah was certainly opposed to the CUP and sympathized with the Liberal Union. Nevertheless he did not add his name to its roster of members or play an important part in parliamentary politics. He characterized his first two terms as 'terms of examination and exploration,'[48] but his later terms gave evidence of no increased participation. Press accounts of parliamentary activities did not mention him, nor do any memoirs of the day. Remarks of British observers were negative: 'the two members for Mecca are understood to have done nothing in Parliament.'[49]

Likewise, there is no evidence that Abdullah was a member of any of the Arab societies before 1914.[50] However he was aware of the growing body of interests articulated as Arab. The pressure of Arab concerns in the empire made itself felt on Ottoman policies in various ways. For example, a project, agreed to by the cabinet, to amalgamate the Ottoman Hamidieh navigation company in the Euphrates with the British Lynch company was strongly opposed by Arab deputies, who feared British expansion in Iraq. Demonstrations erupted in Baghdad and Basra and the grand vizier was forced to resign to make possible the revocation of the Lynch concession by his successor.[51] Arab deputies also expressed concern in parliament about attempts by Zionist organizations to buy land in Palestine for the settlement of Jewish immigrants, leading to the enforcement of laws restricting land sales to foreigners.[52] But the greatest sign of the Arabs' importance was when the empire joined battle with Italy over Libya in 1911, because the 'Government . . . which is already being accused of being too Ottoman and too much inclined to neglect the interests of the other races of the Empire, especially the Arab, could never agree to relinquish an Arab province to a Christian Power. It would mean a rising *en masse* of all Arab Provinces of the Empire against the Government.'[53] Territorial losses in the Balkans in 1912 and 1913 served to underline the importance of the Arabs in the shrinking empire.

The period just before the First World War was a period both of increasing Arab importance in the empire and of increasing Arab discontent and self-conscious organization. Abdullah had seen the first signs of discontent in Damascus in 1909, and his friend, the khedive of Egypt, ʿAbbas Hilmi, reminded him of an Arab body of opinion in 1911. That spring, the Ottoman government had asked Husayn to join in a campaign against the rebellious ʿAsir district just south of the Hijaz. Husayn, seeing a chance to spread his own influence at the behest of the empire, agreed and sent for Abdullah, who was in Istanbul attending parliament, to join him. On his way to Mecca, Abdullah stopped as usual in Egypt to visit the khedive. ʿAbbas Hilmi tended to support the rebels and warned Abdullah that Arab opinion would be against him in a campaign against fellow Arabs. He advised Abdullah to put off the campaign, using the extreme summer heat as a pretext, but Abdullah refused.[54]

Sulayman Pasha, Ottoman *mutasarrif* of ʿAsir, was also against Husayn's interference, but for different reasons. He believed, and informed the Sublime Porte of his belief, that Husayn was interested in ʿAsir for personal reasons and would pose as the restorer of Ottoman control in order to establish his own presence there.[55] But his fears were over-ridden, if not entirely dismissed, because Husayn's help was badly needed.

Husayn, accompanied by Abdullah and Faysal, arrived in Qunfudha on the coast of ʿAsir at the beginning of May. His task was to open the way to Abha, the capital of the province, where Sulayman Pasha was besieged. The news from Abha was grave, and a relief column of three regular battalions under an Ottoman officer and 400 Arab cavalry under Abdullah set out immediately. Six hours inland from Qunfudha, at the village of Qawz, the relief column was surprised by a force of 600 rebels. The Arab cavalry under Abdullah panicked and bolted. The Turkish infantry left behind lost four officers and one hundred men in the field; others died of thirst on the retreat. Of the three Turkish battalions only seventy men made it back to Qunfudha.

The failure of the Arab cavalry to stand by the Turkish column caused a breach between Turkish and Arab forces and increased Turkish distrust of Husayn. Sulayman Pasha blamed the rout on Husayn's lack of preparation:

Husayn had no knowledge of the country or its terrain, he had not reconnoitered rebel forces and had no knowledge of their strength, and, most disastrously, he had not secured a water supply for the Turkish infantry. Abdullah's shortcomings as commander of the cavalry in ʿAsir revealed a lack of military acumen and skill which would cost him dearly in the future.

It took twenty-five days for Ottoman troops, including new battalions from Istanbul and Yemen, to regroup to Qunfudha. Towards the end of May they set out as before, for Abha via Qawz. This time the sharifian cavalry was led by a distant sharifian relative, Zayd ibn Fawaz, under whom Abdullah served. As before they met rebel forces near Qawz, but this time the Ottoman troops and their Arab allies were victorious. Once Qawz had been secured, Husayn, who had stayed behind in Qunfudha, joined the troops to order their advance on Abha.

Abha was reached in mid-July. The supplies and fresh troops were a welcome relief, but the military situation in ʿAsir remained fundamentally unaltered and the rebels did not capitulate. Husayn took a different route home, through the mountains to Taʾif, where he made a triumphal entrance with Abdullah, Faysal and the Arab cavalry on 17 August. Yet he had failed to make his mark in ʿAsir. As the Ottoman *mutasarrif* reflected, the sharif's campaign was like 'a ship in the water, its prow cutting waves in the front and the water returning to harmony behind it leaving nothing but a faint trace which soon passed away.'[56]

Nevertheless, after the foray into ʿAsir Husayn became, in the words of the British consul, 'exceedingly independent, and . . . likely to give much trouble to the Government.'[57] In Husayn's eyes, however, it was the government that was inexorably closing in on his sphere of activities. The summer before the campaign in ʿAsir, the Ottoman *muhafiz* of Medina, ʿAli Ridaʾ Pasha al-Rikabi, had announced that the Sharif Husayn's deputy in the city no longer had any function, implying that Medina was no longer considered to be under his authority. Abdullah, acting for his father who was busy with tribal problems on the border between the Hijaz and the central Arabian region of Najd, wired Istanbul requesting clarification. The Porte replied that Husayn was responsible for pilgrims in the Hijaz from Madaʾin Salih (north of Medina) south, but not for the administration of Medina. Since the telegraph and the Hijaz railway had ensured speed of communications between Medina and Istanbul, the *muhafaza* of Medina would be considered separate from the Hijaz for administrative purposes and bound directly to the ministry of the interior.[58] In short, modern communications enabled Husayn's administrative duties to be divorced from his religious duties, the former being taken over directly by the central government. After the ʿAsir campaign there was much trouble among the tribes in and around Medina, and it was suggested that Husayn looked favorably on this insubordination as a means of discrediting the new administrative arrangement and forcing Istanbul to ask him to intervene.[59]

Between the 'Asir campaign in 1911 and the outbreak of the First World War in 1914, relations between Mecca and Istanbul were tense. The empire, however, was preoccupied with the Balkan War and the campaign in Libya and so did not press its will upon Husayn. But by 1914 Libya and the Balkans had been lost, and Istanbul began to consolidate its hold over what was left of the empire and particularly over the Arab provinces. Early in the year a new *vali* was appointed to the Hijaz, and was sent out with orders to apply the new (1912) Law of Vilayets to the Hijaz and to secure Husayn's agreement to the extension of the Hijaz railway to Mecca. Both orders threatened Husayn, the first because it implied that the prerogatives of the sharifate would be abolished in the interest of administrative uniformity, and the second because it would give the government easy access to and greater control over Mecca. Even more threatening to Husayn were the troop reinforcements dispatched with the new *vali*, which signalled a new determination on the part of Istanbul to see its will prevail.

Abdullah was at the time on his way to Istanbul via Cairo for the opening of parliament, delayed that year until May because of elections. In the Red Sea he passed the ship, bristling with troops, carrying the new *vali* to the Hijaz. The sight made a distinct impression on him.[60]

Abdullah stayed in Cairo as the guest of the khedive, as was his custom. There, on 5 February, he met Lord Kitchener, British consul-general and minister plenipotentiary in Egypt.[61] With the recent developments in the Hijaz very much on his mind Abdullah asked 'whether in case this friction became acute and an attempt was made by the Turkish Government to dismiss his father . . . you [Sir Edward Grey, the British Foreign Minister] would use your good offices with the Sublime Porte to prevent any such attempt.' Abdullah also, according to Kitchener,

. . . stated very decidedly that in case the Turkish Government dismissed his father the Arab tribes of the Hedjaz would fight for the Sherif . . . [and] . . . hoped in such circumstances that the British Government would not allow reinforcements to be sent by sea for the purpose of preventing the Arabs from exercising the rights which they have enjoyed from time immemorial in their own country round the holy places.[62]

Although Kitchener's and Abdullah's[63] accounts differ as to who initiated the meeting, both accounts agree that Kitchener evaded the suggestion that Britain might support the sharif of Mecca by taking refuge in Britain's traditional policy of upholding the territorial integrity of the Ottoman Empire.

While Abdullah was in Cairo, Husayn and the new *vali*, Vehib Bey, clashed. The *vali* ordered the arms of Husayn's Arab police force to be turned over to his own uniformed Turkish force, and restricted Husayn's powers of judgment and punishment in local affairs. The tribes around Mecca rose in revolt at the instigation of Husayn, cutting the road between Jidda and Mecca. The chief representative of the CUP in Mecca was killed. The pretext of the revolt was tribal opposition to the extension of the Hijaz railway which would deprive the tribes of their camel transport profits.[64] The crisis was temporarily averted by a telegram from the grand vizier confirming Husayn's rights in the Hijaz and putting off the final decision on the extension of the railway. At the same time Abdullah was summoned from Cairo to Istanbul to negotiate a compromise on the railway issue.[65]

Abdullah arrived in Istanbul in mid-March, apprehensive about what awaited him there. But the grand vizier, the minister of war and the minister of the interior, with whom he met, were lenient. The Law of Vilayets was virtually repudiated – it had not been passed by parliament yet and only existed on paper in any case – and they offered Husayn concessions for his co-operation in extending the railway. Husayn would be granted his position for his lifetime and it would pass to his sons after him, he would be given 250,000 gold pounds to buy tribal allegiance and one-third of the annual revenue of the railway to spend as he wished, and he would have command of the security forces sent to protect the railway during construction.[66]

With this message Abdullah was sent back to the Hijaz. He was warned not to travel via Egypt, or, if that was unavoidable, not to see Kitchener or any British representative. But he stopped in Cairo anyway, where he met Ronald Storrs, the Oriental secretary of the British consulate, to plumb further British attitudes towards the Mecca–Istanbul dispute. He told Storrs he had been instructed by his father to discuss the possibility of obtaining an agreement with Britain which would guarantee the *status quo* in Arabia against 'wanton Turkish aggression.' Storrs was unable to promise anything.[67]

Abdullah delivered the Porte's offer to his father along with the negative results of his meetings in Cairo with British representatives. Husayn temporized and delayed, neither accepting nor rejecting Istanbul's terms. In July, Abdullah was again summoned to Istanbul. He went armed only with a strategy for delay – the suggestion that a committee should be formed to study the matter – which he duly presented to the grand vizier.[68] But he had arrived in Istanbul two days after the assassination of Archduke Francis Ferdinand at Sarajevo. Events in Europe postponed further haggling over the extension of the Hijaz railway. Abdullah hastened home to watch the unfolding of the war from afar.

Two months later, Husayn and his sons Abdullah and Zayd were at dinner at the palace in Ta'if when a stranger was announced.[69] The stranger was a messenger to Abdullah from Ronald Storrs in Cairo, and his message was to ask what might happen in the Hijaz if, as seemed likely, the Ottoman Empire joined the war on the side of Austria and Germany.

The implications of such a question were vast. The response, hammered out in family council, was friendly. Abdullah replied that 'the people of the Hedjaz will accept and be well satisfied with more close union with Great Britain . . . owing to the notorious neglect by Constantinople of religion and its rights . . . Great Britain will take first place in their eyes so long as she protects the rights of our country . . . and its independence.'[70] This answer, relayed by Storrs to London, prompted another message. Like the previous one, it was addressed to Abdullah. It suggested that Husayn ally himself with Britain, promising in return to respect and protect his position as sharif of Mecca and to support the Arabs in general in their struggle for independence. It also hinted that Britain would look with favor on Husayn's accession to the caliphate.[71] Abdullah replied in general terms conveying his father's friendship for Britain, but stating his need for more time to prepare for such a step.[72]

Britain was not disappointed with this exchange. As Sir Reginald Wingate, governor-general of the Sudan, remarked about Storrs' efforts, 'His dealings with Mecca are good auguries for the future, and I think it only requires a few severe defeats to get the Arabian Arabs to take the law into their own hands.'[73]

Chapter 3

The Arab revolt

Wingate's few decisive defeats did not soon follow, and Abdullah's father was, in any case, a far more cautious man than Wingate imagined. Sharif Husayn did not take revolt against the Ottoman Empire lightly, in spite of his recent difficulties with the Unionist government. Only when he felt that all avenues through Istanbul towards his ambitions were closed did he cast his lot with Britain. Even then, contact with Turkey was never completely cut off.

Husayn's ambitions were quite simple and constant. Since 1908 he had not deviated from his desire for an autonomous, hereditary amirate in the Hijaz, one that would be safe against Ottoman administrative encroachments on one hand, but that would enjoy Ottoman favor over neighboring principalities on the other. Of all his sons, Abdullah was the most ambitious on his behalf. The 'spur' of his father, if not the brains behind him, was T. E. Lawrence's assessment of him on their first meeting in 1916: 'He is obviously working to establish the greatness of the family, and has large ideas, which no doubt include his own particular advancement.'[1] Abdullah had been Husayn's chief go-between with the Ottomans between 1908 and 1914. It was he who had first brought his father's position and ambitions to Britain's attention. And, just before the war broke out, he had reputedly concocted a plan to take pilgrims hostage in hopes of securing either an Ottoman or a European guarantee of autonomy in exchange for their release.[2] The war disrupted the plot by cutting off the stream of pilgrims.

At the same time the war created new opportunities for Sharif Husayn, with Abdullah behind him, to achieve autonomy in the Hijaz and predominance in Arabia. When the Ottoman Empire joined Germany and Austria in October 1914, his support in the war effort became a bargaining chip in his negotiations to win his long-term aims. The Turks, intent on holding the empire together, were unwilling to offer what Husayn wanted for his loyalty which they claimed as theirs by right. They feared that giving in to Husayn might cause a chain reaction of similar demands which would ultimately weaken the fabric of their empire. Britain could offer more and from Britain Husayn demanded more, not out of greed, but because the risks involved in tearing down the carefully built Ottoman structure of identity and legitimacy were much higher. For a Muslim leader to seek an alliance with a Christian power in order to cause the break-up of the foremost Islamic state of the period needed impressive justification. It was not enough to challenge the Ottoman Empire for the sake of personal ambition, and in particular it was not enough for the sharif of Mecca, who depended on the support and approbation of Muslims the world over.

In these dangerous circumstances Husayn needed to find a new, non-Ottoman identity, one which could command the support and the sympathy not only of Hijazis, but of a larger community of souls. He also needed a justification, a large sweeping historic cause whose moral imperative would be able to drown out criticism. An Arab, of the line of the Prophet, he found such an identity and such a cause in the nascent ideology of Arab nationalism. This movement, born and nurtured in Damascus, Beirut and Cairo, provided both the legitimacy of purpose and a large framework of endeavor to justify and ennoble Husayn's dynastic ambitions.[3] Hence, the man who had acted on behalf of the Ottoman Empire against Arabs in ʿAsir three years before the war now became the champion of Arabs against the Ottoman Empire. The price he demanded from Britain for his rebellion was no less than an independent Arab kingdom.

By all accounts it was Abdullah who was most eager for an alliance with Britain.[4] Of his family he was certainly the best known to British officials owing to his pre-war meetings with Kitchener and Storrs in Cairo. It was to him that Britain had addressed those first messages exploring the possibility of a wartime alliance in the autumn of 1914, and to him that Britain paid £13,000 seed money in the spring of 1916 just before the declaration of the Arab revolt.[5]

But it was Abdullah's younger brother Faysal who had the best contacts with Arab nationalists. In the spring of 1915, while Husayn was mulling over Britain's initial proposals, Faysal had been sent by his father to Damascus and Istanbul to spy out the lay of the land. In Damascus he made contact with the nationalist society, *al-Fatat*. When he returned to Mecca it was agreed in family council to resume the correspondence begun by Britain the previous fall, with the aim of cementing an alliance against the Ottomans.

Once that decision had been made, Abdullah and his two brothers, ʿAli and Faysal, divided duties amongst themselves. Faysal was sent back to Damascus to consolidate nationalist support there. ʿAli, Abdullah's older brother, went to Medina to organize the tribes, who, since 1908, had been at odds with Istanbul over the issue of the railway. Abdullah took on the task of rallying the tribes in the Mecca-Taʾif area, conveniently close to home where he could continue to encourage and advise his father.[6]

On 14 July 1915, Sharif Husayn initiated what has come to be known as the Husayn–McMahon correspondence. This exchange of eight letters between him and Sir Henry McMahon, the British high commissioner of Egypt, from July 1915 to January 1916, laid down in general terms what he could expect from Britain on behalf of the Arabs in return for rebelling against the Ottoman Empire. The British accepted Husayn as a spokesman for the Arabs because it suited them to do so at the time. Owing to the number of Muslims under British rule in India and Egypt, Britain feared that a call to *jihad* (holy war) by the sultan might trigger an anti-British rebellion within Britain's empire just when Britain needed all its strength to face external enemies. The sharif of Mecca, by allying himself with Britain, could effectively split Muslim loyalties and render a call to *jihad* meaningless.

The Husayn–McMahon correspondence was intended to establish spheres of territorial interest between Husayn on one hand and Britain and its established allies on the other. Husayn began by outlining a future Arab kingdom stretching west to east, from the Mediterranean and the Red Sea to Iran and the Persian Gulf, and north to south, from roughly the thirty-seventh parallel to the Indian Ocean, except for Aden where he recognized Britain's established presence. Britain wanted to avoid a discussion of territorial boundaries at the outset, but, when pushed, it excepted from Husayn's vast sweep of territory the coastal areas west of Aleppo, Hama, Homs and Damascus, and of Mersin and Alexandretta, which 'can not be said to be purely Arab,' and the *vilayets* of Baghdad and Basra, where Britain claimed special interests. Britain, rather vaguely, also excluded any area where France might have special interests. Husayn, naturally, did not accept Britain's definition of what was or was not 'purely Arab', although he did agree to the exclusion of Adana and Mersin, but not of Alexandretta. In the interests of reaching a basis for mutual action as soon as possible, the remaining points of disagreement – the *vilayets* of Baghdad and Basra and the area west of the Damascus–Aleppo line – were not belabored. Rather, they were left for future discussion 'at the appropriate time,' or 'when the time comes for the conclusion of peace.' Finally McMahon wrote in his last letter to Husayn that the basis of an alliance had been reached. With that, he left it to Husayn's 'discretion to choose the most suitable opportunity for the initiation of more decisive measures.'[7]

At the same time that Husayn was corresponding with McMahon, he continued to maintain, so far as possible, normal relations with Istanbul. Sitting on the fence had some benefits. For example, in the spring of 1916 he was the happy recipient of £50,000 sterling from London and of some 50,000 to 60,000 gold pounds from Istanbul.[8] However, although Istanbul sent him money, it would not raise its price for his allegiance to include the political concessions demanded by Husayn in the Hijaz.

Refraining from decisive action one way or another grew increasingly difficult for Husayn as the war progressed. Istanbul pressed him to send Hijazi recruits to help with the war effort, and it wanted him, as sharif of Mecca, to confirm the call to *jihad*. At the same time the Ottomans stepped up their persecution of Arab nationalists in Damascus and Beirut, the very ones amongst whom Faysal was working. Finally, when Britain suspended food shipments to the Hijaz from Egyptian and Sudanese ports in order to prevent contraband from reaching Turkish forces,[9] Husayn was forced to declare himself. On 10 June 1916 the Arab revolt was proclaimed.

Within days of the declaration of the revolt, Mecca and Jidda fell to Husayn. The easy and virtually bloodless victories owed everything to the season, for the Turkish garrison had already withdrawn to its summer billet in Ta'if. The capitulation of that city to Abdullah after a three-month siege marked the first substantive victory of the revolt.

Abdullah, for all his eagerness to declare the revolt, was remarkably easy-going about its prosecution. British onlookers remarked that Ta'if would have fallen quickly if the Arabs had been more aggressive. They noted, with a whiff of disapproval, that Abdullah had decided to lose time rather than lives.[10] Indeed, the siege was a desultory affair.[11] Every morning at dawn the Egyptian artillery battery with Abdullah pounded the city walls, and when this was over, 4,000 beduin cavalry put on a display of horsemanship within sight of the city, but just beyond the range of Turkish fire. After this daily ritual, the Turks had the rest of the day and night to repair any damage in the walls, unmolested until the next morning's barrage.

Abdullah's camp was well stocked with fresh fruit and vegetables from the gardens outside Ta'if's walls. As food stores dwindled within the city, its inhabitants were allowed to leave peacefully, crossing Abdullah's lines to wait in nearby villages or in Mecca for the Turks to capitulate. When Ta'if at last surrendered on 23 September, its Turkish garrison of eighty-three officers, seventy-two civilian officials and 1,982 troops was treated with scrupulous honor and respect. Abdullah might be officially at war with the empire, but he was determined to maintain correct relations as a hedge against the unknowable future.

After the surrender of Ta'if, Abdullah returned in triumph to Mecca. From there he went to Jidda to discuss the next steps of the revolt with Ronald Storrs, Oriental secretary at the British high commission in Cairo, who had come from Egypt for the purpose with T. E. Lawrence in tow. Having been warned that there was fever in town, Abdullah camped four miles outside. His camp consisted of six large tents, four of Damascene work and two from the Indian Muir Mills. His personal habitation was a double Damascus tent of eight sides, one of which formed the entrance and another the door into the sleeping chamber. The walls were decorated with brilliantly colored and intricately patterned appliqué work of birds, flowers, and texts prescribing virtue and deprecating tyranny. A square trellis grill let in the cool breeze. For convenience a telephone line was run out to him from Jidda.

28

Storrs called on Abdullah first. He found him unchanged since they had last met in Egypt two and a half years before. Dressed in a yellow silk *kuffiyya*, a white silk *thawb*, a camel hair *abaya* and patent leather boots, Abdullah welcomed him to his tent and invited him to be seated on a 'deplorable' bent-wood, cane-bottomed chair. He served him a European-style lunch and surprised him by reading aloud the words 'Muir Mills' printed on the wall of the dining tent, explaining that he knew the Frankish alphabet, but none of its languages. Conversation revolved around the war, the death of Kitchener, and the fate of Abdullah's good friend, ʿAbbas Hilmi, who had been deposed as khedive of Egypt by Britain in 1914. Abdullah hoped that Britain would 'Do Something For Him'. The meeting was purely social, business being reserved for Abdullah's return call at the British residency in Jidda later that day.

The return meeting was not so pleasant as the first, for Storrs had to tell Abdullah that Britain had decided not to send troops or airplanes to the Hijaz and that he did not have the £10,000 which Abdullah had personally asked for to help win over the tribes of the northern Hijaz. In Storrs' words,

Abdullah took the blow like a fine gentleman, and asked to be allowed to state his case . . . He gave a fairly accurate historical summary of the negotiations, quoting several times HMG's promise that we would do Everything Possible to help the Arabs, and citing textually a phrase in a letter from [Major General Sir John] Maxwell (which I had never seen) placing at their absolute disposal, so far as I could gather, very considerable portions of the British Army.

Abdullah concluded the evening by imploring Storrs and the British consul in Jidda, C. E. Wilson, to send a telegram to London urging reconsideration of the matter of British troops for the Hijaz, 'with a pathetic belief in our power to affect the decision of the War Council.'

The next morning at ten, discussions were resumed at the residency, but they were of no immediate use so far as Abdullah was concerned, for Storrs could not produce the desired troops out of thin air. Storrs was, however, favorably impressed by Abdullah. 'He has intelligence, energy and charm,' he wrote, and when he got back to Cairo he succeeded in getting Abdullah the ten thousand sterling.[12]

T. E. Lawrence was also, on the whole, favorably impressed by Abdullah, whom he was meeting for the first time. He sent a vivid portrait of him back to Britain's Arab Bureau in Cairo:

Aged 35, but looks younger. Short and thick built, apparently as strong as a horse, with merry dark brown eyes, a round smooth face, full but short lips, straight nose, brown beard. In manner affectedly open and very charming, not standing at all on ceremony, but jesting with the tribesmen like one of their own sheikhs. On serious occasions he judges his words carefully, and shows himself a keen dialectician . . . The Arabs consider

Figure 1. Amir Abdullah, seated; standing, left to right: Saʿid Bey ʿAli, Colonel C. E. Wilson, ʿAziz ʿAli al-Masri, Ronald Storrs, Jidda, 1916.

him a most astute politician, and a far-seeing statesman: but he has possibly more of the former than of the latter in his composition.[13]

Lawrence's opinion of Abdullah later changed for the worse.

Abdullah and his father were alarmed that their new ally had not lived up to their expectations. Disappointed with the lack of material backing, they decided to seize the moral initiative by creating an independent government in the Hijaz on a European model. Abdullah was appointed foreign minister, ʿAli became grand vizier, and Faysal minister of the interior. Abdullah's office was the most important one and clearly indicated his unique position, standing between his family and those they claimed to represent, on one hand, and their European allies on the other. To maintain a hand in local affairs he had himself appointed president of the legislative assembly, although that institution never took hold. ʿAli, the eldest brother and his father's presumed heir, stayed very much in his father's shadow as grand vizier, and Faysal, the youngest of the three, was given a position with no clear function.

The creation of such august offices was but the background for Husayn to adopt an equally august title. On 29 October, the ʿulamaʾ and notables of Mecca gathered at the *dar al-hukm* to acclaim him king of the Arabs. It was Abdullah's job, as foreign minister, to sell him as such to Europe. A clever ruse, 'doubtless evolved in the fertile brain of Emir Abdulla,'[14] drew French Muslim officers to the scene, which they, not comprehending Hijazi Arabic very well, believed was a celebration of the Muslim new year which happened to fall at that time. Congratulating Husayn on the new year, they unwittingly implied French recognition of his new title. In fact, neither Britain nor France recognized the title owing to their relations with other Arab leaders who would not look kindly on Husayn's overlordship. After several months of dispute, during which Abdullah strenuously put forward his father's case, Husayn was informed that he could be recognized as king of the Hijaz only.

Husayn responded by saying he attached no importance to titles anyway.[15] Abdullah, however, did, and he was quite clear about his reasons for doing so. By telephone with the British consulate in Jidda, he ticked off other Arab leaders one by one: Ibn Saud was a shaykh and Husayn did not propose to interfere with his work or his land. The Idrisi of ʿAsir was not recognized by anyone to be anything. The imam of Yemen could rule his land, but he would not deny that the sharif of Mecca should be the ruler of the Hijaz and king of the Arabs. As for the Arab tribes, none would oppose the sharif's becoming king of the Arabs since the history of the sharif of Mecca went back to the time of the Arab kingdom of the Abbasids.[16] In short, Abdullah was not primarily thinking of Arab lands further north, which had been the main subject in the Husayn–McMahon correspondence, when he encouraged his father to adopt the title; rather, he was thinking of the balance of power in the Arabian peninsula itself, where he longed to make his family predominant. Indeed, Abdullah's concern for peninsular politics dominated his wartime activities, for it was there, in Arabia, that his own ambitions lay.

Of the four brothers, only Abdullah and Faysal were taken seriously by Britain. The eldest, ʿAli, was judged physically weak and possibly consumptive. He had neither the 'go' of Faysal, nor the charm and shrewdness of Abdullah. In kind moments he was excused as 'bookish', and in unkind ones damned as a 'rotter'.[17] For these reasons it was Abdullah whom Britain considered to be Husayn's true heir and whom they thought Husayn himself preferred.[18] (Since Abdullah was at this time Britain's chief link with the family and the revolt, there may have been a degree of wishful thinking involved.) The youngest brother, Zayd, besides having a Turkish mother which automatically rendered him suspect, was simply too young to carry much weight. Abdullah and Faysal were both esteemed as better soldiers and politicians than their brothers. However relations between the two were not easy. Lawrence, for example, had noticed their rivalry immediately: 'The clash between [Abdullah] and Feisal will be interesting,' he had written upon first meeting the brothers.[19] Abdullah appears to have been his father's favorite; Faysal was closer to his other two brothers. For Abdullah this lack of sympathy grew into bitter jealousy over the years as Faysal, younger than Abdullah by four years, took his place as chief go-between with Europe and outstripped him in Arab favor.

Abdullah had agreed, in his meetings with Storrs and Lawrence in the autumn of 1916, to join his brothers in preparation for an attack on Medina. In November he left his father's side and marched northward. By mid-January he had set up a permanent camp in Wadi ʿAys, sixty miles north of Medina on the Hijaz railway line. There he threatened Turkish communications to Medina, making possible Faysal's advance up the coast to Wejh and eventually on to Aqaba and Damascus.

When Abdullah arrived in the neighborhood of Medina in the winter of 1917, he was highly regarded by the British, but there his reputation began to flag. Medina was a well-fortified city with a Turkish garrison of some 7,000 troops under the Turkish general, Fakhri Pasha. Abdullah's task was to cut off its communications from the north, by cutting the railway, and from the east, by stopping caravans from Haʾil, Najd and beyond. His headquarters in Wadi ʿAys consisted of four officers and one hundred trained men, two howitzers, two mountain guns, and thirteen machine guns. He also had varying numbers of rifle-bearing beduin, sometimes as many as 5,000.[20] Detailed to advise him were one French officer (a very French Algerian named Captain Raho, whom Abdullah taught Arabic in an attempt to make him an Arab again), several other French officers who visited from time to time,[21] and a team of British officers from the Arab Bureau, who took turns staying with him.

Abdullah's camp, nicknamed by the French 'le camp du Drap d'Or,' was not a very business-like place.[22] Lawrence, who spent ten days there in March 1917, discovered that Abdullah passed his days in his luxuriously carpeted tent, 'in reading the Arabic newspapers, in eating and sleeping, and especially in jesting. . .' He played William Tell, using a rifle instead of a crossbow, with one of his entourage, paying him well for his risk, and whiled away the rest of his time with Arabic poetry and more conventional forms of rifle practice. Access to his camp appeared to be almost completely limited to his intimates. He spent little time with visiting shaykhs and deputations, and less overseeing supply and military arrangements. He was, however, greatly interested in the war in Europe and in European politics generally, and he astonished Lawrence by his command of the intricate family relationships of the royal houses of Europe and of the names and characters of the members of their governments.[23] That Abdullah may have had reason to restrict access to his camp or the discussion of Arabian politics owing to the presence of an Englishman did not occur to Lawrence.

Abdullah appeared at best lazy and at worst stupid for not pressing his attack at Medina and for not even carrying out his siege very well. (After the surrender of Medina, Fakhri Pasha remarked that he often felt grateful to Britain for issuing supplies so freely to the beduin, who sold their surplus to him with little hindrance from Abdullah.[24]) Behind his seemingly resolute avoidance of activity, Lawrence judged, lurked jealousy of Faysal, 'as if he wished ostentatiously to neglect military operations to prevent unbecoming comparison with his brother's performance.'[25] Yet his position, though too passive for Lawrence's taste, did aid Faysal; by tying down a 7,000-man Turkish garrison in Medina, he did make possible Faysal's better-known exploits further north.

Abdullah, moreover, had good reasons for acting as he did, but his reasons were not ones to win British sympathy or its approbation. As he candidly told Lawrence, he looked southward towards Yemen for his future and intended, as soon as he was set free from the boredom of besieging Medina, to conquer 'Asir and compel the imam of Yemen into a position of vassalage.[26] He had other concerns as well, concerns that he did not divulge to Lawrence. These had to do with the growing power of the tribal chief, Ibn Saud, in central Arabia.

Problems between the Abdullah's family and Ibn Saud had begun in 1910, when Sharif Husayn, anxious to expand his domain eastward, had claimed sovereignty over the district of Qasim and over the 'Utayba tribe which Ibn Saud considered his. Leaving Abdullah in Ta'if to rule in his stead, Husayn mounted an expedition against Ibn Saud.[27] The results, though inconclusive, slightly favored Husayn. In 1915, Abdullah had ventured into the interior as a peacemaker between Ibn Rashid of Ha'il and Ibn Saud in an effort to create a *pax Arabica* under the aegis of the sharif of Mecca. Ibn Saud had just suffered defeat at Ibn Rashid's hands and Abdullah sided with him as the weaker and less threatening of the two. For a short while a truce reigned between Mecca and Ibn Saud.[28] Since then, however, Ibn Saud's fortunes had been on the upswing. He had signed a treaty with Britain at the end of 1915 which recognized his independent rule in Najd, al-Hasa, Qatif and Jubayl and by which he promised to remain neutral in the war. He was also beginning to consolidate his position with the tribes of central Arabia.[29]

To Abdullah, as he sat at Medina watching and waiting, Ibn Saud was 'a son of a dog,' whose ambitions to unite and rule Arabia challenged his own.[30] Most of Abdullah's forces were 'Utayba tribesmen, of the very tribe whose allegiance was in question between himself and Ibn Saud. Lawrence had found these tribesmen little interested in the war and had been irritated to see Abdullah in his camp claiming to be a beduin and an 'Utayba. Abdullah, for his part, had been annoyed by Lawrence's presence, fearful that it would inspire criticism amongst the conservative tribe.[31] Concern for the sensitivities of the 'Utayba may also have contributed to his passivity at the gates of Medina, the burial place of the Prophet. Indeed, Medina did not surrender until well after the armistice in Europe had been signed, and then it surrendered only because of a mutiny amongst the Turkish troops inside, not because Abdullah forced it to do so.

Although Abdullah may have been ineffectual at Medina for reasons not directly related either to his military skill or to his commitment to the Arab revolt, his standing in British eyes slipped. In comparison with Faysal's activities in Syria, which culminated in the entrance to Damascus with allied forces in October 1918, Abdullah looked distinctly second-rate. From that time on, Faysal replaced Abdullah as Britain's main Arab intermediary.

The change of their relative positions did not worry Abdullah at first. As long as he had hopes of a kingdom in the south, Faysal's activities in Syria did not inspire the corrosive jealousy that later characterized his feelings for his brother. Although his own personal ambitions lay in Arabia, he hoped to see the expansion of his family's power under Faysal in the north as well. He was consequently disturbed when he learned of the British occupation of Baghdad in the spring of 1917.[32] And when Mark Sykes was making the rounds of the Middle East later that spring to gauge Arab attitudes towards a post-war division of Arab territory, Abdullah let him know in no uncertain terms that if Syria were not to be in the new Arab kingdom, the revolt would have been in vain. In Abdullah's estimation the Arab kingdom must be large enough to impress Muslim opinion, to justify the destruction of the Ottoman Empire, and to support the Hijaz, itself without resources except for the annual *hajj*.[33]

And so Abdullah stayed on at Medina, carrying out periodic raids against the Hijaz railway for which Britain provided money and arms,[34] but losing Britain's esteem and growing increasingly impatient for the war to end. In the meantime he stockpiled British weapons and gold and tried to woo nearby and distant tribes in preparation for the coming struggle with Ibn Saud. Though Britain's support was undoubtedly a boon for Abdullah, Ibn Saud had one asset he could not match. This was the ideology of Wahhabism, a reformed and puritanical Islam, which captured the imagination and passionate advocacy of some of the tribesmen of Arabia. Welded into troops of *ikhwan* (brethren), these tribesmen were, for a time, the most effective and feared fighting force in Arabia.

As Ibn Saud waxed stronger and more menacing in the spring of 1918, the delicate balance that Abdullah had tried to strike at Wadi ʿAys between fulfilling his undertaking to Britain and seeing to his interests in Arabia began to tip heavily towards the latter. Britain, in turn, started to complain vociferously that he was doing nothing for the revolt and had squandered his resources on concerns other than British ones. There was much talk of financial mismanagement: He was throwing away his monthly stipend of £50,000 on distant tribes while letting his own troops go without pay; he had diverted funds to build up his personal wealth; gold sovereigns had been melted down by the thousands in Mecca and converted into fancy swords and daggers for distribution to 'paltry Sheikhs and slaves, and as sops to potential enemies.'[35] Faysal attempted to defend his brother, admitting that Abdullah's head and heart were bound up in the problems of Najd, but insisting that he was fighting for Britain in Najd as well as for familial interests, since 'Great Britain will not profit by the Arab revival, if the tomb at Medina and the Haram at Mecca are destroyed, and the pilgrimage prevented.'[36] (This was an allusion to the Wahhabi sacking of the holy cities in 1803–4.) British officers who complained to Husayn about Abdullah's misdeeds got no satisfaction. He responded to their complaints by hinting at the possibility of a 'Civil War' in which he expected Britain to come to his aid.[37]

Husayn's prediction of imminent conflict was soon proved right. In the spring of 1918 Ibn Saud levied taxes on the Sbay tribe, whose tribal lands were centered around the Khurma oasis on the eastern border of the Hijaz. This tribe had previously been taxed by Mecca, which meant it had accepted the overlordship of Mecca. When King Husayn's tax collectors arrived in turn, they were imprisoned by the local ruler, Khalid ibn Luwa'y.[38] Khalid, himself a sharif, had been appointed by Husayn to be his representative in the district of Khurma some time before the First World War. He had joined the Arab revolt and was with Abdullah at the siege of Ta'if and at Wadi ʿAys. There they had a falling out, and he returned to Khurma and allied himself with Ibn Saud.[39]

The imprisonment of the king's tax collectors was tantamount to a declaration of war. Abdullah responded by diverting half of his troops from Medina to the new battlefield. The British consul at Jidda admonished him in a manner which passed, among Englishmen, as Arab – 'Let us keep our eyes fixed on the larger issues beside which the question as to whether Khurma is occupied by the King's adherents or the Akhwan is like a mosquito to an elephant'[40] – but to no effect. To Abdullah and his men the Khurma crisis was the over-riding concern in the final months of the First World War. Abdullah sent his closest friend and most trusted lieutenant, Sharif Shakir, a distant cousin, to lead the battle. As the war in Europe ground slowly to a halt, Shakir stayed in the vicinity of Khurma skirmishing with Khalid bin Luwa'y. No decisive victory was gained by either side.[41]

* * *

The war in Europe came to an end with the signing of the armistice on 11 November. Faysal, who was trying to sort things out in Damascus, asked Abdullah to come to help him, and, in particular, to take his place while he was at the Paris Peace Conference.[42] Britain was against the idea, for Abdullah was seen as stronger, less straight, and more anti-French than Faysal. His presence, it was felt in British circles, would make Britain's task 'infinitely more difficult,' and so he was encouraged to stay at Medina.[43]

Despite the armistice, Medina had not yet capitulated. Fakhri Pasha, the Turkish commander, offered numerous excuses to delay his submission: he recognized neither Abdullah nor the British advisers with him as allied commanders to whom he could honorably surrender; he was responsible for the Prophet's tomb and could only be relieved of his duty by a personal order from the sultan and caliph; he had had a vision of the Prophet encouraging him not to submit.[44] The real motive for his resistance is still clouded in rumor and speculation. Abdullah believed that Fakhri Pasha was acting in collusion with Ibn Saud and Khalid ibn Luwa'y to keep him and his force from joining Shakir at Wadi Khurma.[45] Others speculated that Fakhri refused to surrender to an enemy who had not beaten him, or that he held out in order to secure free passage for himself and his troops to Turkey.[46]

In the end, Fakhri Pasha was forced to submit by his own men.[47] He offered his surrender to Abdullah, who treated him with the same courtesy and respect he had shown to the Turkish garrison at Ta'if two and a half years earlier. Indeed, Abdullah reportedly told him that he had never been against the Ottoman Empire, but only against the Committee of Union and Progress. Influenced perhaps by earlier Turkish warnings that Britain and France had secretly divided up Arab lands between themselves, Abdullah now suggested to Fakhri Pasha that it was time for a *rapprochement* between Arab and Turk.[48]

Abdullah made a triumphal entry into Medina. ʿAli arrived in the city shortly thereafter, on 2 February 1919, freeing Abdullah at long last for battle against Ibn Saud.

Abdullah went first to Mecca to regroup his forces and discuss strategy with his father. Three months later he set out eastward, to settle the territorial dispute between his family and Ibn Saud. The long-awaited engagement between the two forces was decisive – it changed Abdullah's life and the history of Arabia.

On May 21, Abdullah and his forces captured Turaba, a small market town to the south of Khurma. In response, Ibn Saud sent *ikhwan* reinforcements to aid Khalid ibn Luwa'y. Several days later the *ikhwan* attacked, with catastrophic results. Before the rise of the morning star, Khalid and his men silently crept up on Abdullah's unguarded camp. Abdullah's men were startled into wakefulness, but too late to save themselves. The *ikhwan* were already among their tents

Figure 2. The Turkish commander Fakhri Pasha surrendering to Amirs Abdullah (back to camera) and 'Ali, outside of Medina, 1919.

and those who were not killed in their beds were killed before they could reach their mounts and flee. Thirty-five of Abdullah's slaves died fighting at the door of his tent while he and Shakir slashed a hole in the back and escaped in their night clothes. Both were wounded in body and in pride as they made their getaway with the insulting epithet '*shurayf*' (meaning little *sharif* and referring to Abdullah's diminutive height) ringing in their ears.[49]

The battle at Turaba was a turning point in Abdullah's life and in the history of Arabia. From that time on, Husayn and his sons were on the defensive while Ibn Saud grew inexorably more powerful. The king of the Hijaz did not have the authority of the sultan and the Ottoman Empire to back him up, and his new British ally later proved unwilling to support him against Ibn Saud. For Abdullah, many of his comrades of the 'camp du Drap d'Or' were left dead on the battlefield. Jokers and poets, poor soldiers by British standards, but full of life, they now lay strewn in the desert. Captain Raho, Abdullah's French Algerian adviser, died with them.[50]

Abdullah's Arabian ambitions died at Turaba as well. The reverberations of the dreadful rout echoed throughout Arabia, diminishing his stature and his family's prestige. In a single night his dreams of an Arabian empire had turned to nightmares. But his own words perhaps best express his loss: 'I have unfortunately escaped from amongst the very dear people who were killed in a most abominable manner. All my attendants and staff were killed before I left them while I myself was surrounded by the enemy but I managed to escape

. . .'[51] Abdullah remained ambitious, but he was forced to look in new directions for an outlet. Inevitably he looked northward, and it is from this time that his relations with Faysal, who had replaced him in British esteem and who was vaulted on to the world stage at the Peace Conference at Versailles, grew especially bitter.

Chapter 4

The creation of Transjordan

The First World War saw the demise of four empires. The multi-ethnic Ottoman and Austro-Hungarian Empires were divided amongst their chief ethnic groups, Germany was forced to disgorge its colonies, and Russia was embroiled in civil war and eventually reconstituted on wholly new grounds. Of the three empires on the losing side of the war, the Ottoman Empire was dealt the harshest hand at the Paris Peace Conference. Not only was it partitioned amongst ethnic groups, but its divisions were to be subject to direct and indirect domination by the powers on the winning side of the war.

Britain and France, the major powers on the winning side, emerged from the war with their colonial empires intact – indeed solidified and about to be expanded – but the face of imperialism began to change after the First World War. Both powers lacked the men and money to maintain empires in the grand old style of Queen Victoria and Jules Ferry. They were mortally fatigued, and the post-war wave of popular sentiment to 'bring the boys back home' was resisted with difficulty by statesmen who continued to think in terms of imperial assets and routes of communication.[1] At the same time, two ideas emanating from opposite ends of the globe assured the world that the peace settlement would be different in form and content from the imperially acquisitive treaties of the nineteenth century. From Moscow, the successful revolutionary Lenin predicted the rebellion of all colonial people against their colonizers. From Washington, the prophet–moralist Woodrow Wilson declaimed his Fourteen Points, throughout which ran the principle of self-determination.

And yet, despite the currency of anti-imperialist ideas and the immediacy of severely restricted resources, Britain and France had interests in the Middle East and the ability to sustain them. Britain's interests were to safeguard the route to India, to secure cheap and accessible oil for its navy, to maintain the balance of power in the Mediterranean to its advantage, and to guard its commercial and financial interests. France's were to preserve its centuries-old tie with the Catholics of Syria, to gain a strategic and economic base in the eastern Mediterranean, to ensure a cheap supply of cotton and silk, and to prevent Arab nationalism from infecting its North African empire.

During the Peace Conference, a bargain was struck between what Britain and France perceived to be their vital interests on one hand, and the internationalism and anti-imperialism then in vogue on the other. This compromise was the principle of mandate by which an 'advanced' state was to tutor another, less advanced state in the complexities of democratic self-government until the latter was ready to rule itself. The mandate principle allowed the Middle East to be divided between Britain and France according to their interests in time-honored imperial custom, but, in the spirit of the times, it qualified imperial domination by providing for eventual self-government. Thus the mandate system served both to render British and French imperialism palatable at the Peace Conference, and to make it possible for at least some sections of Arab society sometimes to acquiesce in and co-operate with European rule.

The war had left Britain in predominant control of the Middle East. British forces occupied not only Palestine and Iraq, where Britain claimed special interests, but also Syria, which had been promised by Britain to both Sharif Husayn, representing the Arabs, and France. The problem facing Britain at the Peace conference was to choose which of these two conflicting promises to honor. The Arab case was presented at Paris by Husayn's son, Faysal, who, since the end of the war, had been setting up an Arab administration in Damascus with British support. He claimed Syria on the strength of the Husayn–McMahon correspondence, Arab services to the Allies during the war, and his existing administration. France clung tenaciously to its own wartime understanding with Britain, the Sykes–Picot agreement, which had promised France a Syrian sphere of influence.

France eventually won its case, because Britain judged that Anglo-French solidarity in Europe was too important to be jeopardized over Arab affairs. In September 1919 Britain agreed to withdraw its troops from Syria in favor of French troops. In April 1920, the division of spoils in the Middle East was settled at the San Remo Conference. Contradicting the spirit of disinterest embodied in the idea of mandate, Britain and France were awarded mandates precisely according to their interests in the region. Britain got Palestine and Iraq. The one gave Britain a base in the eastern Mediterranean guarding the Suez Canal; the other was within India's orbit of trade and communications and almost certainly had commercial oil reserves. France got Syria and Lebanon, where most of its Middle Eastern financial and cultural concerns were located. Faysal remained in control of Syria for the time being, but his days were clearly numbered.

In the Hijaz the diplomatic struggle for Syria was observed with misgivings. Since Abdullah's defeat at Turaba, Husayn had been more anxious than ever to secure Syria, for he well understood that the Hijaz with its meager resources could hardly stand alone. But he began to mistrust Faysal, fearing he would strike a bargain with Britain and France at the expense of his own over-arching ambition to be king of the Arabs. When he learned of the 1919 Anglo-French agreement over Syria and of Faysal's consequent efforts to reach an accommodation with France, he felt his suspicions were justified.[2]

Abdullah, smarting from his humiliation at Turaba, regarded Faysal's activities in Europe with extreme jealousy. He felt that his younger brother had usurped his own position as chief interlocutor in Euro-Arab affairs. Playing on his father's suspicions, he arranged to go to Egypt on the eve of the San Remo conference. Ostensibly he was returning the visit of the high commissioner of Egypt, Lord Allenby, to the Hijaz earlier that year; in fact, he had secured his father's permission to replace Faysal as his representative in Europe. Within these layers of purpose lay an inner and very personal motive, which had to do with Iraq.

After Abdullah's defeat at Turaba his ambitions, thwarted in Arabia, had fixed on Baghdad. In March 1920, a general Syrian congress held in Damascus had elected Faysal king of Syria. Twenty-nine Iraqis present had taken the opportunity to proclaim Abdullah king of Iraq.[3] He now wished to present his case for Iraq in person to the British in Egypt and he hoped to go on to Europe from there. He did not succeed, however. Although his trip to Cairo was outwardly a happy one – he was awarded the Grand Cross of the Most Excellent Order of the British Empire – Allenby rebuffed his pretensions and sent him back to the Hijaz rather than on to Europe.[4]

Abdullah did not know it, but his name had already been discussed and discarded in connection with the Iraqi throne. The future government of Iraq had been a topic of heated debate between London, Cairo, Baghdad and Delhi since the end of the war. Barely two weeks after the armistice, the Eastern Committee, made up of high-level officials from the Foreign, War and India Offices, laid down guidelines for British policy in Iraq. The Committee agreed that the government of Iraq, though in form an Arab government, should be controlled by Britain. Who would best serve as a figurehead was a more difficult problem. Abdullah's name, raised by T. E. Lawrence, was discussed with interest. In the bad habit of the period and place, he was described in disdainful terms. Lord Robert Cecil, under-secretary of state for foreign affairs, had never met Abdullah but felt he 'would do tolerably well if we have the right man to control him. He is a cleverish fellow . . . a sensualist, idle and very lazy.' Although the stereotype that was presented did Abdullah an injustice, it did not make him unfit for British purposes in Iraq. As Edwin Montagu, secretary of state for India, explained: 'If Abdullah is the lascivious, idle creature he is represented to be, he is the ideal man, because he would leave the British Administrator to govern the country wholly.'[5]

Abdullah's candidature for a titular position in Iraq, however, was opposed by the top British officials in Baghdad, A. T. Wilson and Gertrude Bell. Both at this time favored a system of direct British administration. They claimed that the inhabitants of Iraq did not want an Arab government, although Bell later revised her opinion, causing a significant breach between herself and Wilson.[6] Wilson felt that a son of Husayn was unacceptable for reasons connected with Persian Gulf and central Arabian politics.[7]

Lord Curzon, chairman of the Eastern Committee, was not satisfied with the negative response from Baghdad, so he asked other British officers in the Middle East for assessments of Abdullah's 'character, capacity and fitness' to be head of an unnamed Arab state 'whose prince would not govern.' C. E. Wilson, British consul in Jidda throughout the war, replied without elaboration that Abdullah's abilities and character would qualify him for the position of titular amir. Kinahan Cornwallis, director of the Arab Bureau, considered Abdullah to be cleverer than his brothers, but also unscrupulous, extravagant and very ambitious, and therefore not likely to be content for long as a mere figurehead. Ronald Storrs, at that time military governor of Jerusalem, was less concerned with Abdullah's fitness for such a post than he was with the qualifications of the British officer who would be Abdullah's adviser. Of Abdullah, Storrs commented merely that he was the most intelligent of Husayn's sons. Finally, the *éminence grise* of the Arab Bureau, D. G. Hogarth, though he had not met Abdullah, wrote a voluminous answer based on three years of second-hand knowledge. He assessed Abdullah's qualifications with less caution and more contempt than did those who actually knew him. In sum, he felt Abdullah was the best Britain could do for Iraq: although he was 'indolent, pleasure loving and . . . vicious . . . he would make a presentable titular ruler and [was] intelligent enough to grasp real facts and conform to them.'[8]

In the meantime, A. T. Wilson had been instructed to conduct a poll as to whether the population of Iraq would accept Abdullah as amir. Wilson's report confirmed his own opinion – that no one wanted an Arab amir because there was no suitable candidate. Against the hard rock of Wilson's opposition, Abdullah's candidature came to rest. It was later discovered that his method of gauging popular opinion had precluded a positive response.[9]

By a strange twist of fate Faysal succeeded where Abdullah had failed. After France had been awarded the mandate for Syria it embarked on a course designed to set its new house in order. In cleaning out the cobwebs, it cleared out Faysal and his administration as well. For, beyond its fear of Arab nationalism, France also believed that through 'l'élégant émir de Berkeley square' British influence would be re-introduced into Syria. On 14 July 1920, the French high commissioner of Syria and Lebanon, General Gouraud, presented Faysal with an ultimatum which demanded, among other things, the recognition of the French mandate, the demobilization of his army, and the punishment of 'the criminals who have continuously shown enmity towards France,' in other words, of the nationalists who had supported him. In spite of Faysal's last minute acceptance of the ultimatum, French forces advanced on

Damascus ten days later. After defeating a hastily organized resistance at Maysalun on 24 July, they occupied Damascus.[10]

After the defeat, Faysal fled southward to Dir'a on the border between the British and French zones. When France then threatened to bomb Dir'a he hurriedly left for British Palestine and from there to Europe. Some of his supporters fled to Cairo and Palestine. Others stayed nearby in southern Syria (Transjordan) which France did not occupy. From there they sent messages to Husayn asking for men and arms and for another of his sons to come to lead the national struggle.[11]

In a surprising *volte face*, as soon as A. T. Wilson heard of Faysal's expulsion he cabled London:

Feisal alone of all Arabian potentates has any idea of practical difficulties of running a civilised government . . . He can scarcely fail to realise that foreign assistance is vital . . . He realises [the] danger of relying on an Arab army. If we were to offer him the Amirate of Mesopotamia not only might we re-establish our position in the eyes of [the] Arab world, but we also might go far to wipe out [the] accusation which would otherwise be made against us of bad faith both with Feisal and with [the] people of this country . . .[12]

Thus the demise of Faysal's government was considered an invaluable lesson in *realpolitik* which served to render him eminently suitable for British purposes.

While Faysal, in defeat, became a convenient candidate, Abdullah remained anathema to Wilson. He added in his cable endorsing Faysal, 'Nothing that I have heard during the last few months has led me to modify my views of [the] unsuitability of Abdulla . . .' Exactly what Wilson had heard and from whom is unclear, although he professed to have been offended by a rumor that Abdullah had already appointed his Syrian supporters to posts in his projected government in Iraq.[13]

British sympathy for Faysal was immediate and tangible. When he passed through Haifa on his way to Europe, the British high commissioner, Sir Herbert Samuel, was instructed to inform him that Britain hoped in the future to be able to reward his loyalty.[14] Within a week that reward was rumored to be the throne of Iraq.[15] On 17 August the Beirut newspaper *Lisan al-Hal* printed a story implying that Faysal's friends in London would compensate him for his loss of Syria with the throne of Iraq.[16]

These rumors reached Abdullah's ears in Mecca, making him uneasy and bitter. He complained to Major Batten, the acting British consul in Jidda, that Faysal appeared to be Britain's man now and that he alone of the three brothers had no prospects in spite of the part he had played in the war and afterwards.[17]

In August 1920, despite the rumors concerning Faysal and Iraq, the political future of Husayn and his sons looked dim indeed. Husayn's grand design to become king of the Arabs had been whittled down to a throne in the Hijaz alone. Abdullah's ambitions in Arabia had been throttled. Faysal had lost Syria.

Except for his brief trip to Cairo, Abdullah had been immured in the Hijaz for over a year, far from the European corridors of power where the immediate future of the Middle East was being decided. He had been as obliging as possible towards the British, intervening on their behalf with his increasingly irascible father in disputes over monetary reform, communications, and the quarantine. But, although the British consul in Jidda was 'convinced that he is loyal to our interests,'[18] no room had been made for him in the British scheme of things further north. Rather, he appeared about to lose Iraq to his brother.

As a result Abdullah abruptly changed his tactics. He agreed to an armistice with Ibn Saud, whom he nevertheless continued to denigrate privately as 'that worthless man' and 'a mere Bedu.'[19] And, turning his back momentarily on Arabia, he set his sights northward. The messages from the nationalists gathered in Amman had invited him to lead the movement to restore Syria to the Arabs, and this he set out to do in a desperate attempt to bring himself forcefully to Britain's attention.

Abdullah left Mecca by camel caravan on 27 September. His troops were reported at between 500 and 1,000 tribesmen. His budget was estimated at £90,000: £70,000 from Jidda customs and £20,000 in forced loans from local merchants.[20] In Medina he boarded the Hijaz railway, bound for Ma'an on what was officially announced as a tour of inspection.[21]

Ma'an, a dusty oasis town, was ideal for Abdullah's purposes. It lay in disputed territory between the Hijaz and Britain's sphere of influence further north. It was also a market place and watering hole for tribes who roamed the area from the Jordan Valley in the west to Wadi Sirhan in the east. From there he could rally tribes in his support. Equally important was its situation on the Hijaz railway and its telegraph office through which he kept in touch with events further afield.[22] He stayed there for three months while he waited for the situation further north to grow clearer.

Since the end of the war the territory north of Ma'an had been ruled from Damascus as a province of Faysal's Kingdom of Syria. Although it fell within the British zone according to the Sykes–Picot agreement, Britain was content with this arrangement because it favored Arab rule in the interior and Faysal was, after all, Britain's protégé. However, when France occupied Damascus the picture changed dramatically. Britain did not want to see France extend its control southward to the borders of Palestine and closer to the Suez Canal. It suddenly became important to know 'what is the "Syria" for which the French received a mandate at San Remo?' and 'does it include Transjordania?'[23] The British foreign secretary, Lord Curzon, decided that it did not and that Britain henceforth would regard the area as independent, but in the 'closest relation' with Palestine.[24] Wary of French interest, which had already set off a campaign of gift-giving among tribal leaders in Transjordan,[25] Britain began to make plans to administer the territory.

By the time Abdullah arrived in Ma'an only the most rudimentary British presence had been established. Indeed, Britain had taken on Transjordan with notably less relish than either Palestine or Iraq. Palestine overlooked the Suez Canal, Britain's umbilical cord to India; Iraq promised oil. Transjordan, however, had only slight strategic interest and absolutely no natural resources. In later years Transjordan did come to be valued as a contiguous land and air corridor between Iraq and Palestine, and as a buffer zone between Palestine, where Britain undertook to foster a Jewish national home, and the tribes of Arabia. But on the eve of shouldering the white man's burden there, Britain did so half-heartedly, more to prevent France from extending its influence southward than because of any value intrinsic to the area itself.

At the outset there were three trends of thought in British official opinion regarding Transjordan. The first, emanating from the Foreign Office, favored avoiding a commitment as far as possible by setting up Zayd, Husayn's youngest and least important son, as ruler.[26] The second was articulated by Sir Herbert Samuel, the high commissioner for Palestine, who wanted to incorporate Transjordan, or at least its fertile western edge, directly into Palestine. Although he cited popular demand and strategic and economic considerations as the basis for his opinion, he was strongly influenced by his sympathy for Zionism and his desire to add to the territory that would be available for Jewish settlement.[27] Since the Balfour declaration, promising the Jews a national home in Palestine, had been incorporated into the terms of the British mandate, whatever territory could be brought under the mandate would, he thought at the time, be subject to Jewish colonization. The third trend, decreed by exigencies at the War Office which was over-extended in putting down an anti-British revolt in Iraq, ruled out the use of any troops for the occupation of Transjordan.

Britain's initial policy towards Transjordan, hammered out between the lukewarm interest evinced at the Foreign Office, the occupation urged by Samuel, and the denial of military support ordained by realities at the War Office, was a stopgap measure designed to establish a British presence in the area that would not be so fixed as to prevent later mutations, such as, for example, eventual inclusion in Palestine. The use of troops was ruled out not only by limited resources at the War Office, but by the chance to win a propaganda victory over the French; instead of duplicating France's harsh policy of military occupation in Syria, Britain would merely extend a benevolent helping hand. Thus Samuel was authorized to send a few political officers to the districts of 'Ajlun, Salt-Amman, and Karak. Their duties were confined to encouraging local self-government and to giving advice. Kindness, influence, and propaganda were to be their means of authority, and caution and tact their primary virtues, for it had apparently been decided that 'it was better to lose a few officers than to involve an Army.'[28]

Although the Foreign Office advised Samuel that 'the immediate inclusion under the Palestine administration as such of Trans-Jordania . . . might give a handle to Nationalist agitators,' a gradual process leading to the eventual incorporation of Transjordan by Palestine was not ruled out. London hoped that through the political officers, the people of Transjordan would come to realize the benefits of British administration, which happy experience, so the Foreign Office rhapsodized, was 'the best means of securing a genuine and lasting desire for any extension of British administration towards the East.' The officers were also to encourage trade with Palestine and to emphasize Palestine's position as a natural outlet for Transjordan, so that material interest could be brought to bear where moral interest might lag.[29]

Of his instructions, Samuel wrote: 'I have at last arrived at a settlement with the F.O. about Trans-Jordania – less than I wanted, but 'twill serve. (I am referring not to extent of territory but to manner of occupation.)'[30] Although not completely satisfied, he none the less set about his task with energy. His first step was to secure some sort of local acquiescence since, if troops were needed initially, any occupation of Transjordan at all might be scuttled. So, in recognition of Faysal's recent status and continued influence in the area, Samuel informed him of Britain's plans. Faysal, in Haifa en route for Europe, gave his qualified approval, provided that the new government be only temporarily separated from Syria, subject to reunification 'when the French army evacuates the occupied districts.'[31] Samuel then organized a meeting of Transjordanian leaders at Salt on 21 August, at which he would announce British plans.

On 20 August Samuel and a few political officers left Jerusalem by car, headed for the Jordan river, the frontier of British territory at that time. 'It is an entirely irregular proceeding,' he noted, 'my going outside my own jurisdiction into a country which was Faisal's, and is still being administered by the Damascus Government, now under French influence. But it is equally irregular for a government under French influence to be exercising functions in territory which is agreed to be within the British sphere: and of the two irregularities I prefer mine.'[32] Across the river where the road ended, Samuel and his party mounted horses and, accompanied by a fifty-man cavalry escort, climbed the twelve miles to Salt. They arrived in the late afternoon, and Samuel made his way to the home of Yusuf al-Sukkar, a wealthy Christian merchant, where he received deputations prior to the public meeting scheduled for the following afternoon.

The meeting, held in the courtyard of the Catholic church, was attended by about 600 people. Seated in a lone armchair on a dais covered with carpets, Samuel presided. Sentence by sentence his speech describing British policy was translated into Arabic: political officers would be stationed in towns to help

Figure 3. Sir Herbert Samuel at Salt, August 1920.

organize local governments; Transjordan would not come under Palestinian administration; there would be no conscription and no disarmament. In a final, crowd-pleasing gesture Samuel agreed to amnesty two Palestinians who had been accused of instigating anti-Zionist riots in Jerusalem in April and had sought refuge across the Jordan.[33] One, Amin al-Husayni, later mufti of Jerusalem and president of the Supreme Muslim Council in Palestine, became the leader of the Palestine nationalist movement and Abdullah's particular *bête noire*. The other, 'Arif al-'Arif, subsequently served briefly in Transjordan's bureaucracy as chief secretary, but grew critical of Abdullah's policies and intentions.

On balance, Samuel's statement of policy was unobjectionable. Three things feared by the Arabs of Transjordan – conscription, disarmament, and annexation by Palestine – were abjured, and two youthful leaders were allowed to return home. The presence of a few British agents, unsupported by troops, seemed a small concession in return for the protection Britain's presence would afford against the French, who, it was feared, might press their occupation southward. Moreover, in the confusion and disarray which followed Faysal's expulsion, no one among the inhabitants or the political refugees had sufficient stature or local backing to defy what Samuel had so mildly proposed. Therefore,

Samuel returned to Jerusalem well pleased with the success of his mission. He left behind several officers to see to the administration of Transjordan and the maintenance of British influence.

Abdullah's arrival in Maʿan on 21 November threatened to disrupt Samuel's cozy arrangement. According to reports, Abdullah had a force of 300 men and six machine guns – hardly enough to challenge Britain or France in a pitched battle, but a healthy guerilla force similar to those operating at the time in northern Syria under Shaykh Salih al-ʿAli and Ibrahim Hananu.[34] Indeed, French intelligence reported that Abdullah was in contact with these leaders, as well as with their main supplier, the Turkish nationalist leader Mustafa Kemal, who was fighting for the territorial integrity of Turkey against French designs in Cilicia.[35] But although Abdullah's presence was a nagging worry to Samuel, his posture was hardly threatening. He stayed put in Maʿan, where his activities were confined to composing poems and appeals for support, which were printed on a hand press in his tent, and to discussing strategy with those who made the trip to Maʿan to meet him. Meanwhile his agents in Amman and Salt drummed up local support and Nabih al-ʿAzma in Jerusalem kept him informed about British reactions to his activities.[36]

Those who came to meet Abdullah in Maʿan can be divided into two distinct groups: traditional leaders and nationalists.[37] The traditional leaders were from the general area of Transjordan and were shaykhs of tribal segments of various size and importance, community leaders, and other local notables.[38] Their positions of leadership were based on a combination of inherited familial prestige, personal merit and wealth. Few had been formally educated and none belonged to any nationalist organization. The nationalists were from the towns of Syria, Palestine, and the northwest corner of Transjordan.[39] All had received sound secular educations, except for one who had had religious training, and most were professionals – lawyers, officers or bureaucrats. The most important characteristic of this group, however, was that its members were all ideologically motivated to some degree. Many belonged to nationalist organisations and most had been politically active, either with Faysal in Syria or against Zionism in Palestine.

Both groups had a distinct function for Abdullah. The nationalists had organizational skills and experience and they were familiar with British and French goals, military power, and political susceptibilities. More importantly, they had an ideology which could attract followers across regional, confessional, and class lines. The traditional leaders were in control of Transjordan south of Amman, the territory in which Abdullah first had to establish a base. If they were openly hostile, his claims to leadership would ring hollow.

Abdullah spent three months of uncertainty in Maʿan, weighing his next step.

For Britain and France, these months were a period of rising tension. Samuel, fearing Abdullah's advance and still hoping for Transjordan's immediate inclusion in Palestine, increased pressure for a military occupation.[40] London, however, persevered in its resolution not to send troops. Hubert Young at the Foreign Office commented acidly on Samuel's campaign for troops: 'I remain unconvinced by the various, and in some cases contradictory arguments put forward for the military occupation of Trans-Jordania . . . Sir H. Samuel fears that Palestine is not to get her proper boundaries on the North, and casts longing eyes across the Jordan to make up for it.'[41] The War Office likened the geographical position of Transjordan to that of the northwest frontier of India, which had proved to be a bottomless pit in its need for an ever greater commitment of British troops.[42] Meanwhile, M. de Caix, the French *délégué* in Damascus, privately accused Britain of avoiding the occupation of Transjordan in order to direct Arab hostility toward France in Syria.[43]

While Abdullah was waiting in the wings in Ma'an, Faysal was in London representing his father in Anglo-Hijazi negotiations. Britain viewed these talks as a way to get King Husayn to be a party to the decisions taken by the allies at San Remo which divided Arab lands into separate states and put them under British or French mandates. To this end Britain was prepared to offer the leadership of these states to Husayn's sons.[44] Called the 'sharifian solution,' it was the method by which London hoped not only to conciliate Husayn, but also to create an interlocking political grid whereby pressure on one state could win obedience in another.

The territories under consideration were Iraq and Transjordan. Faysal presented Abdullah's claims to Iraq as superior to his own, but he agreed to accept the Iraqi throne himself under certain conditions: that Britain must reject Abdullah and ask him to take Abdullah's place, and that the people of Iraq must want to have him as king.[45] London predictably plumped for Faysal, and it was left for Sir Percy Cox, high commissioner for Iraq, to arrange his acclamation.

Abdullah had lost Iraq. However, his lack of position was considered a problem by London. The future of Transjordan was also a problem and so London decided to try to settle the two together. Britain had resolved the question of Transjordan's legal status by fiat. Unwilling to raise again in the League of Nations the question of the division of the Middle East, it simply decided to assume that Transjordan formed part of the as yet undefined area covered by the mandate for Palestine which had been awarded to Britain at the San Remo conference ten months before. However, since Britain was anxious to conciliate the Arabs by fulfilling what was convenient of the wartime promises, it was further decided that Transjordan would be exempted from the Zionist clauses of the Palestine mandate. What sort of administration would be created had not yet been decided. By January the Foreign Office had conceded that Transjordan might have its own Arab ruler. By February they acknowledged Abdullah by name for the position.[46]

Rumors of the trends in British thinking may have reached Amman, for a high-level delegation of nationalists went to Ma'an at the end of February, intent on bringing Abdullah back to Amman with them. The delegation was composed of four members, Shaykh Kamil al-Qassab, Amin al-Tamimi, 'Awni al-Qudamani, and 'Awni 'Abd al-Hadi, and one unexpected addition, Mazhar Raslan, who had previously sent Abdullah a telegram suggesting it would be better if he returned to the Hijaz.[47] Mazhar's change of heart was significant since he was currently acting as *mutasarrif* of Salt in co-operation with British political officers. 'Awni 'Abd al-Hadi's presence was also crucial. He had come to Ma'an from Jerusalem where Samuel had informed him that Britain did not intend to rule Transjordan directly, as it ruled Palestine, but rather intended to help the inhabitants to organize their own government.[48] This news apparently convinced Abdullah that a move further north would not cause a confrontation with Britain, and within a few days he once again boarded the Hijaz railway, to complete the last leg of his journey to Amman. 'Abd al-Hadi's information also emphasized the importance of conciliating local leaders within Transjordan, a factor which in the future was often at odds with nationalist aims.

Abdullah arrived in Amman on 2 March 1921. It was, as one of the British officers described it,

quite big for this part of the country & built along the bottom of a narrow valley with houses up the side of the hill. The houses are mostly one-storey & extraordinary in shape, many of them giving the idea of a Swiss Chalet, and others very like Irish peasant cottages and quite as ugly with white-washed outer walls . . . There are a tremendous amount of [Arab] soldiers here.[49]

After the months of anticipation and uncertainty, his arrival was somewhat of an anti-climax. In Karak, the southernmost district to which Britain had sent a political officer, Alec Kirkbride met and welcomed him.[50] They took an instant liking to each other and in later years their friendship served Anglo-Transjordanian relations well. On arrival in Amman, Abdullah immediately dispatched 'Awni 'Abd al-Hadi to Jerusalem with a letter to Samuel conveying his desire to maintain friendly relations with Britain and explaining why he had come to Amman. He came, he explained, as the representative of his brother Faysal to restore order and government to Transjordan, which had fallen into a state of anarchy since his brother's exile. Samuel, despite the months of stress, responded amicably.[51]

Abdullah's timing was propitious and probably not accidental. Following the consolidation of British Middle East concerns in a new Middle East department under the jurisdiction of the Colonial Office,[52] Britain's Middle East policy was up for a complete review. There was also, coincidentally, a new secretary of state for the colonies: Winston Churchill.

Under a new department with a new chief, British Middle East policy was to be centralized, if not set in new directions. The showpiece of this process was to be a gathering of Britain's Middle East experts at Cairo. But before they met at Cairo, several key decisions had already been taken in London, namely, that Faysal was to go to Iraq, Transjordan was to be in some degree separate from Palestine, and Abdullah might figure in the arrangements for Transjordan. It remained for those gathered in Cairo to come to an agreement with Abdullah.

The Cairo Conference opened on 12 March 1921.[53] Iraq was the first item on the agenda, and, as expected, it was decided to proceed with the plan to put Faysal on the throne. On 16 March the Palestine mission arrived, headed by Sir Herbert Samuel, and the attention of the conference turned to the affairs of Palestine and in particular to the problem of Transjordan. There was no overt dispute about the basic policy that some sort of Arab administration should be set up in Transjordan under British auspices; rather, reservations about that policy were expressed by questioning the suitability of Abdullah. Samuel was uncertain as to his desirability, while Wyndham Deedes, civil secretary to the government of Palestine, opposed his appointment without elaboration. Like Samuel, he was sympathetic to the goals of Zionism and he felt that 'No Eastern is reliable and Abdullah is no exception.'[54] T. E. Lawrence hoped that Abdullah might be invited by France to rule Syria, and feared that he might then take Transjordan with him into the French orbit.

These vague sentiments gave way before Britain's reluctance to use armed force to dislodge Abdullah and in the absence of any other suitable candidate. Therefore, on 18 March, Churchill was able to inform London that the conference was proceeding to make arrangements for Transjordan on the assumption that a satisfactory agreement with Abdullah would be reached. He anticipated that either Abdullah would become governor under the high commissioner of Palestine, or that someone agreeable to Abdullah would take the position.[55] London replied with some reservations of its own: the French would certainly protest all the louder if two sharifian regimes were set up simultaneously in two areas bordering on Syria, and Abdullah himself was likely to think Transjordan too paltry a prize for the compromises he would have to make if he took it on.[56] Thus cautioned, Churchill went to Jerusalem to talk to Abdullah.

Churchill's arrival in Jerusalem on 26 March came as no surprise to Abdullah. He had been prepared for such a meeting by 'Awni 'Abd al-Hadi, who counselled him on how to conduct the negotiations.[57] At this time nationalists like 'Awni were not necessarily against making deals with Britain, for they recognized the need for a base of action and a refuge and they wanted to avoid alienating both Britain and France at the same time. Moreover, it seemed

Figure 4. Winston Churchill, T. E. Lawrence and Amir Abdullah in Jerusalem, March 1921.

important to Arab nationalists that Transjordan, a part, as they saw it, of Faysal's kingdom of Syria, remain free not only of French occupation but of direct British administration as well.

Lawrence was sent to Salt to fetch Abdullah by car. On the way back to Jerusalem he prepared him for what Churchill would offer.[58] Intent on his conversation with Lawrence, Abdullah offended many Palestinians by ignoring the welcoming receptions they had organized along the way.[59] The offense was recalled in later years as a harbinger of Abdullah's treatment of the Palestinian leadership and of his disregard for Palestinian aspirations. The accusation certainly rankled, for Abdullah, in his memoirs published twenty-five years later, bothered to blame Lawrence for not allowing him to stop.[60]

The talks between Churchill and Abdullah lasted for three days. Besides the principals, Samuel, Deedes and Hubert Young attended. T. E. Lawrence translated for Churchill and ʿAwni ʿAbd al-Hadi for Abdullah. Since ʿAwni did not know English, the negotiations took place in French. Abdullah began by suggesting the unification of Palestine and Transjordan under an Arab ruler, or the unification of Transjordan and Iraq. Both ideas were firmly squashed. In the end he agreed to take on responsibility for Transjordan alone for a period of six months. He promised to keep the territory clear of anti-French and anti-Zionist agitation to the best of his ability, and was promised in return a stipend of £5,000.[61] It was further agreed that no British troops would be stationed there.

However, the most persuasive of Britain's offers was Churchill's suggestion that if Abdullah 'succeeded in checking anti-French action for six months he would . . . greatly improve his own chances of a personal reconciliation with the French, which might even lead to his being instated by them as emir of Syria in Damascus.' Churchill said that he had made it perfectly clear to Abdullah 'that while they would do everything they could to assist towards the attainment of this object, His Majesty's Government could not in any way guarantee that it would be achieved.'[62] Others thought Churchill had been less than straightforward. George Antonius, for one, believed that 'What Churchill did in fact do was . . . to trick Abdullah into remaining in Amman as ruler of TJ on the promise of a real settlement which was never realized.'[63]

With this agreement, the division of the Fertile Crescent into separate states dominated by either Britain or France was completed. Despite the short term nature of the arrangement, Transjordan proved to be a lasting creation. For Abdullah himself, his six months stretched to a lifetime.

The carving up of geographic Syria, which included Syria, Lebanon, and Palestine as well as Transjordan, severely disrupted normal economic, political, and social ties wrought by centuries of habit and usage. Under the Ottoman Empire, the territory that came to be known as Transjordan had been marginal.[64] Since it contained no great urban centers and few taxable assets, protection of the pilgrimage route was the focus of the empire's concern there. Trade and the political ties were for the most part organized along the north–south axis of the *hajj* route from Damascus to Medina and Mecca. A series of fortresses had been built in the sixteenth century stretching from Damascus to the Hijaz at such places as ʿAjlun, Salt, Karak, Qatrana, and Maʿan. The Ottoman government supplemented its armed forces by paying subventions to tribal shaykhs along the route, and tribesmen serving the state for pay were an integral part of the pilgrimage administration. Damascus was the nearest *entrepôt* and political center.

Ottoman control over the caravan route and over Transjordan ebbed and flowed in the following centuries. The seventeenth century was a period of decentralization and neglect, while the first half of the eighteenth century saw an improvement in communications between Damascus and Medina via the route through Transjordan. The latter half of the eighteenth century was another period of decline in security along the *hajj* route, but this ebbing of the Ottoman tide was reversed in the nineteenth-century period of imperial reform and revitalization.

At that time, aided by technological innovations in transport and communications, the empire gradually centralized its effective rule and expanded it into hitherto marginal areas. In 1851 the area of northwest Transjordan from the Yarmuk to the Zarqa' rivers was organized as the *qada'* of 'Ajlun with its capital at Irbid and attached to the *mutasarrifiyya* of the Hawran. Ottoman authority was extended further southward in the late 1860s into the area known as the Balqa', which stretched from the Zarqa' river to Wadi Mujib. The *qada'* of Belqa' was incorporated into the *sanjak* of Nablus and had its capital at Salt, which was mentioned by travellers of the period as the only settled village in the area. It was a flourishing town with shops selling local and Manchester cotton cloth, local woolen goods, foodstuffs and iron implements. Before the establishment of an Ottoman garrison there in the 1860s, Salt had paid a large annual tribute to the 'Adwan tribe for protection. Ten years afterwards, the garrison had succeeded in turning the situation around so that Salt was able to collect taxes from surrounding pastoral tribes.

In the 1880s the Balqa' underwent a demographic change with the arrival of Circassian immigrants fleeing Russian rule, which had been gradually extended southward through the Caucasus in the nineteenth century. The immigrants, who had appealed to the sultan for asylum, began to arrive in the *qada'* in 1878.[65] An estimated 500 settled first among the Roman ruins at Amman (uninhabited since Roman times) and then spread to several nearby sites. Granted land and tax concessions by the sultan to facilitate their settlement, these hardy and self-sufficient peasants held their own against the beduin and even introduced large-wheeled carts and a system of dirt roads into the area. The expansion of settlement and cultivation was not, however, exclusive to the Circassians: during the same period several Christian families from Karak moved to Ma'daba and settled among the deserted ruins there and the Abu Jabir family of Salt started cultivating a sixty-feddan farm two miles south of Amman.[66]

With the British occupation of Egypt in 1882 Transjordan gained strategic importance, for the Ottomans feared the extension of British control eastwards and down the Red Sea. In 1893 Istanbul dispatched a garrison and a *mutasarrif* to Karak, which, until that time, it had been content to rule simply by investing the locally accepted strongman (a Majali) with the title of governor. The new district of Karak included Ma'an, Shawbak, and Tafila.

The Hijaz railway[67] further strengthened the hand of the Ottoman government in the newly organized districts of 'Ajlun, Balqa', and Karak. In 1903 the line was opened from Damascus to Amman; by 1904 it reached Maʿan, and by 1908, Medina. Trains ran from Damascus to Maʿan three times weekly in each direction, leaving Damascus at 1.00 p.m. and arriving at Maʿan the following day around 11.00 a.m. The railway brought increased employment, trade and security, along with greater contact with the central government. Circassians at Amman were employed as laborers on the line and in positions of lower management. Goods bought in Damascus for resale in Transjordan were sent south by train and transported in Circassian carts from the station to their point of sale. Maʿan, where the German engineer Meissner Pasha built depots, repair facilities and even a home for himself, became one of the most important stations along the line.

This period of burgeoning trade, population, and cultivation owing to the extension of Ottoman authority was brought to an end by the First World War and the Arab revolt. Traffic on the railway was disrupted during the war, and with it the concomitant blessings of trade and security. Nomadic tribes that had begun to diversify their economies by establishing and controlling farming communities, cultivated by their own tribesmen or by peasant tenants, appear to have returned to a more nomadic way of life.[68] After the war the marginality of the territory was emphasized by British and French preoccupation with surrounding areas to the north, east and west. Trade and cultivation resumed, but were changed by the erection of borders and the imposition of new and different foreign interests.

Population figures for Transjordan before 1920 are unreliable and vary widely from source to source. Of three major sources, Ottoman figures for 1915,[69] British estimates in 1921[70] and figures from a contemporary Arabic document,[71] the latter seem to be the most realistic and are presented in the following table. These figures leave out the districts of Aqaba and Maʿan.

The territory was far more homogeneous than any of the other Middle Eastern mandated states. The most significant split in the ranks of future Transjordanians was based on mode of life and economy, whether pastoral or peasant, rather than on ethnic or religious diversity. As shown in the following table, the total population of Transjordan, excluding the district of Maʿan and Aqaba, was around 225,000: fifty-four per cent of which was classified as settled and forty-six per cent as nomadic. The division itself was not absolute. Many nomads engaged in part-time agricultural activities; peasants were also seasonal pastoralists. The main non-Arab ethnic group was the Circassians, who constituted less than five per cent of the population. Their ethnic difference, however, was mitigated by their religion, Sunni Islam, which they shared with the vast majority of Arabs in Transjordan. The chief religious split was between Muslims and Christians, with the former greatly outnumbering the latter. The Christians, less than ten per cent of the population, were split among Greek Orthodox, Greek Catholic, Roman Catholic and Protestant rites, in order of

Population of Transjordan in 1922

TOTAL POPULATION			225,380
Settled population			

district	number of villages	major villages and their populations		total population
ʿAjlun	101	Irbid	3,500	69,330
		Ramtha	4,500	
		Kafrinja	3,200	
		Suf	3,200	
Balqaʾ	15	Salt	20,000	39,600
		Amman	2,400	
		Wadi Sir	3,200	
		Maʿdaba	2,400	
Karak	8	Karak	3,000	13,500
		Tafila	2,500	
TOTAL SETTLED POPULATION			122,430

Nomadic population

tribe	number of tents	population
Bani Sakhr	5,500	27,500
ʿAdwan and Balqaʾ Tribes	10,400	52,000
Banu Hamida, Hajaya, Salit	1,500	7,500
Tribes of Karak and Tafila	3,190	15,950
TOTAL TRIBAL POPULATION		102,950

numerical importance. Circassians lived in exclusively Circassian settlements, except for Amman which had begun to attract a more diverse population. Christians formed a large minority in Karak and Salt, inhabited Maʿdaba exclusively, and were scattered among the numerous villages of the ʿAjlun district. Some relied chiefly on pastoralism for their livelihood while others were cultivators. Relations between Muslims and Christians and between Circassians and Arabs were generally good. When these groups came into conflict it was, at base, less a matter of religion or ethnicity than a facet of the competition between pastoralists and peasants for control of land.

Although nineteenth-century travellers across the Jordan river were lavish in their descriptions of dense forests and undulating fields of wheat and barley, the cultivated part of Transjordan did not extend much beyond the Jordan valley and the narrow strip of land on the ridge abutting it. Scarcity of water accounted for the cultivation pattern. The Jordan river and its tributaries, the Yarmuk and Zarqa' rivers, are the only sources of riverine water, while rainfall ranges from a yearly average of sixteen inches in the north to less than two inches in the eastern desert. The 'Ajlun district is the most fertile area, and in the early twentieth century it produced wheat, barley, lentils, peas, grapes and olives. Corn, wheat and barley grew in the Balqa', although the grapes of Salt (sultanas) were the most famous produce of the region. The district of Karak produced wheat and barley, but much of its land lay uncultivated for lack of water. The oasis towns of the southern district had little more than kitchen gardens, except for Aqaba which had date palms.[72]

Virtually everyone in Transjordan was identified by family, clan, and tribal affiliation. This social organization reflected the territory's low level of urbanization and marginal relationship to centers of power. Damascus, the natural regional economic and political capital, was too far distant to have a profound impact on the forms of social organization in the hinterland that formed Transjordan. In the absence of state security, tribal forms of protective social and economic affiliation expressed through kinship and usually associated with nomadic animal husbandry extended into agricultural regions and villages. Hence, tribalism in Transjordan was not limited to nomads; rather, the tribes of Transjordan filled every economic niche from nomadic camel breeders to settled farmers, forming a complex web of integrative social alliances. By the 1920s, and in some cases before, landowning came to be perceived as a source of social power and wealth, but landownership did not necessarily weaken the social meaning of tribalism. The most successful men to emerge thereafter in terms of independent political power were those who could combine the leadership of a large tribe with vast, personally held estates.

The most important tribes in Transjordan were the Huwaytat, the Bani Sakhr, the 'Adwan, and the Bani Hasan.[73] They were important and potentially threatening to Abdullah because they were large and because they were armed. The Huwaytat, whose range extended from Tafila southward, were enriched during the war by British gold and by high camel prices. Consequently, farmlands under their hegemony had been either neglected or leased to fellahin while the tribe itself reverted to an entirely nomadic existence. After Transjordan was created, half of the tribe under 'Awda Abu Tayih became Wahhabi and swore allegiance to Ibn Saud. The other half under Hamid Ibn Jazi remained in Transjordan, but in a weakened position. The Bani Sakhr, whose tribal lands were further north and almost entirely within Transjordan, were likewise largely nomadic. Throughout the nineteenth century this tribe had gradually moved northward out of Arabia. By the twentieth century they controlled most of the Balqa' and in winter ranged as far south as Wadi Sirhan. They herded sheep and camels, and received rent in kind from peasant clients who farmed their extensive estates. In the 1880s, Sattam Ibn Fayiz, the first of the Bani Sakhr shaykhs to become interested in securing cultivable land, personally supervised farms at Umm al-Amad, south of Amman, although he and his tribe maintained a nomadic lifestyle. After the war two other leading families of the Bani Sakhr similarly became interested in agriculture, but found that the Ibn Fayiz clan had already laid *de facto* claim to the most fertile land. During the mandate period the Ibn Fayiz emerged as the strongest section of the tribe. Its leader, Mithqal Ibn Fayiz, though illiterate, became the largest landowner in Transjordan. The 'Adwan were, by 1920, semi-settled in the Balqa' and the Jordan valley. Over the previous century this tribe had lost its position of paramountcy to the encroaching Bani Sakhr; none the less, in 1923 it mounted a major challenge to Abdullah's rule. The 'Adwan–Bani Sakhr rivalry continued to dominate internal tribal politics well into the twentieth century, with the lesser tribes allied to one or the other. The Bani Hasan, numbering an estimated 860 tents in 1917, inhabited territory north of Amman on the Zarqa' River. Allied with the 'Adwan they opposed the Bani Sakhr.

There was nothing of a cultural or economic nature to distinguish particularly the inhabitants of Transjordan from their neighbors on any side. Their tribal organization was marked, but this was a function of distance from a dominant urban center rather than a special quality emerging out of Transjordan itself. In the northwest, which had sufficient water for perennial agriculture, village life predominated. Although villagers may have been organized into tribal groups, they had similar interests to their Palestinian and Syrian neighbors and closer ties to them than to the tribes further south. Nor were there any outstanding geographical features to mark Transjordan off from its neighbors. The only wrinkle in the earth's surface that might pass as a natural border was the Jordan valley – Wadi 'Araba rift, the deepest valley in the world, beyond which lay Palestine.

What chiefly distinguished Transjordan was a matter of political distinction imposed by Europe rather than one of geography, culture or ethnicity. Syria, to the north, was under French mandate, while Transjordan was under British. Palestine, to the west, was under direct British rule and was subject to Jewish colonization. Transjordan was indirectly ruled and not subject to colonization. Towards Iraq, similarly under British indirect rule, Transjordan projected a hand across the desert so that Britain would have a continuous land corridor from the oil fields to the Mediterranean coast. To the south of Transjordan lay what to Europeans was the threatening tribalism of central Arabia, free of European domination.

Transjordan's existence hinged on European interests rather than on a local or regional rationale. Owing to these interests, what had once been a marginal area – part of the Ottoman political fabric and of an Arab and regional social and economic fabric – suddenly stood apart from its neighbors. However its separateness was not at first absolute or necessarily longlasting. Tribes in its southern half continued to be involved in tribal politics emanating from even further south. Villagers in the north continued to be involved in political events in Syria and Palestine. For several years British statesmen continued to entertain notions of its further integration into Palestine. For Abdullah, Transjordan was but the threshold to greater power. He expected, at first, to move on to Damascus. In later years he hoped to unite Transjordan with any willing neighbor.

Chapter 5

Settling in

As soon as the Jerusalem meetings between Churchill and Abdullah were over, the two men headed in opposite directions. Churchill returned to London to get official approval for his Transjordan policy. Abdullah went back to Amman to establish himself in his new domain.

Churchill's was the easier task. His plan was readily accepted by Whitehall because it required no troops and it was tentative enough not to prejudice other, perhaps better, arrangements that might be possible in the future. He described Abdullah's position as 'informal', and added that 'no question either of governorship or sovereignty is raised.' He urged that his new protégé be regarded with some leniency: 'The same latitude must be given to [Abdullah] in speeches that he makes as would be given to a Member supporting the Government, but with a shaky seat.'[1] A monthly stipend of £5000 was settled on Abdullah.

The final form British rule would take remained a subject of discussion. Some British statesmen continued to contemplate Transjordan's total incorporation into Palestine, but over the next four years the political and strategic worth of a Transjordan separate from Palestine gradually became more apparent. In the meantime Britain's goal was to keep Transjordan quiet while the mandatory regimes of its more important neighbors were firmly established. Consequently British directives in Transjordan initially concerned matters of security rather than methods of governing.[2]

Abdullah's position in such a situation was insecure, dependent on his own, and Transjordan's, yet to be proven worth in Britain's structure of regional security. He had accepted a six-month agreement because, to him, it suggested better things in the near future, namely a move to Damascus; but as that possibility receded, he grew correspondingly more anxious to secure his position where he was. To do so he moved away from the nationalist group that was his original ally in Transjordan and closer to Britain. Since this group was not, for the most part, native to Transjordan such movement caused minimal internal repercussions. Yet his shift towards Britain eventually had a dramatic effect on his larger, regional ambitions.

The Amman that Abdullah returned to after his meetings with Churchill was a

Figure 5. Amir Abdullah and Sharif ʿAli ibn Husayn al-Harithi in front of Abdullah's tent at Amman, 1921.

village of between 2,500 and 5,000 inhabitants.[3] Its population had been enlarged by the recent influx of Arab nationalists following Faysal's ouster from Damascus, but its core was the group of Circassian settlers that had been there since the 1880s. A small minority in the region, they welcomed Abdullah and came under his protection. He set up temporary headquarters in the home of Saʿid al-Mufti, a prominent Circassian.[4]

Throughout his reign Abdullah lived a peripatetic existence. In the early years, before his palace was built in Amman, he lived in various places in the Balqaʾ. The summer of 1921, for example, found him first in the home of the Christian Abu Jabir family in Salt and later in his tents at Maʾdaba. In the area of Amman his favorite camping spot was outside of town, where the old airport was later built. The makeshift manner of his living arrangements encouraged a certain lack of formality, reminiscent of the atmosphere of the 'Camp du Drap d'Or.' For example, Abramson described coming upon him in his camp playing blind man's bluff, tug-of-war, wolf and lambs and the like with his retinue and visiting tribal shaykhs.[5] Later his movements became more regular, between Amman in the summer and Shuna Nimrin in the Jordan valley in winter, although his taste for games did not abate.

Despite its primitive facilities and small size, Amman gradually assumed a position of central importance in the country. It was here that Faysal's supporters had gathered in 1920. It was on the Hijaz railway and so had the best communications then available with Damascus, Haifa (the major port in the eastern Mediterranean) and the Hijaz. It also lay on the edge of the desert half-way between the northern, more settled region and the southern zone. Salt, the old Ottoman district capital, was the largest town of Transjordan at the time. But it was too close to Palestine and had a long history of strife with the nomadic tribes of Transjordan's desert hinterland. Amman, in a sense, was more neutral ground. To seal matters, when Abdullah was in Salt in the summer of 1921 his beduin retinue clashed with local men. Abdullah's cronies got the worst of it and were forced to get out of town.[6] His subsequent relations with Salt were never very good.

Abdullah began his administration by forming a government of grand proportions. He appointed a cabinet entirely of nationalists who had previously served Faysal in Syria. It was headed by Rashid Tali'a, a Druze from the Shuf region of Lebanon who was under sentence of death in French Syria. Under Rashid Bey were, Amin al-Tamimi from Nablus, Mazhar Raslan of Homs, Hasan al-Hakim from Damascus, and 'Ali Khulqi al-Shara'iri from 'Ajlun, the only cabinet member from Transjordan.[7]

This cabinet looked like a government in exile and aptly symbolized Abdullah's ambitions to move on to Damascus. Rashid Tali'a, Amin al-Tamimi and Mazhar Raslan were members of the *Hizb al-Istiqlal al-'Arabi* (Arab Independence Party), a post-war and public outgrowth of the pre-war and secret *al-Fatat* society. The Istiqlal, as it was commonly called, was the best organized, most widespread (with branches throughout geographical Syria and Iraq), and most radical of the post-war nationalist parties. Its goals were two: the unification of geographical Syria into one Arab state, and independence for the states of Greater (geographical) Syria and Iraq. Foreign tutelage was rejected, as was Britain's Zionist policy in Palestine.

On the British side of the equation, Albert Abramson, formerly military governor of Hebron and currently president of the land commission in Palestine, was appointed chief political officer. His duties were to act as the liaison between the high commissioner in Jerusalem and Abdullah and to make sure that Abdullah remained faithful to his promises. He had come highly recommended by Samuel, Deedes and Lawrence, though London knew little about him.[8] The other British officers put in place by Samuel six months earlier

Figure 6. Amir Abdullah with some of his supporters and officials, Amman, 1922. Front row from left: Muhammad Muraywid, unknown shaykh, Ghalib al-Sha'lan, Amir Abdullah, Mazhar Raslan, Rashid Tali'a, Amin al-Tamimi.

were to stay at their posts, and, in particular, Frederick Peake was to continue his assignment of raising a local reserve force.

Arab nationalism and British imperialism were ultimately to collide in the Middle East. In the early 1920s, however, despite the disappointments of the Peace Conference, this ultimate collision was not wholly obvious: mutual need, mutual misrepresentation and mutual misapprehension had created the illusion of certain shared interests between the two. The end result of making a deal with Britain was both partially obscured and open to modification, since it was British policy to conciliate Arab nationalists as far as possible in order to co-opt them into the mandate system. Many nationalists, moreover, sensed Britain's disapproval of French methods and mistakenly thought that this disapproval could be turned into backing for their own cause.

In the circumstances, Abdullah was briefly able to create a middle ground for himself between his nationalist supporters and his British overlords. By naming a nationalist cabinet he satisfied nationalist aspirations for a role in government. By taking little part in administration himself, he ensured that his advisers and administrators took the blame for any excesses on the nationalist side of the equation as far as Britain was concerned. Another stratagem he used was to

63

cultivate his 'languidity', so that, rather than refusing British demands outright and causing a potentially non-negotiable confrontation, he could appear compliant, but fail to carry out certain orders. British complaints about Abdullah reflected his success: they dubbed him lazy, languid, and ineffectual, but never unco-operative or recalcitrant, at least in this early period. A deeper purpose to Abdullah's superficial characteristics was suspected, however. Abramson described him as 'loveable, considerate and generous, possibly simple and frank, but more probably extremely deep and purposeful.'[9]

Although these were effective short-term ploys, they did not protect Abdullah for long. A series of minor conflicts and a number of subtle pressures clearly demonstrated Britain's superior strength. Lack of consistent support from Abdullah ultimately alienated most of his nationalist supporters.

The first open conflict between British and nationalist desires arose in May, over the size of the local reserve force. Britain wanted a small one, Abdullah's nationalist advisers a large one. To discuss the matter, Abdullah was invited to Palestine as a guest on board HMS Iron Duke docked at Haifa. Pleased with his invitation and 'cram full of the Iron Duke,' Abdullah deferred amicably to British wishes regarding the size of the force, intimating that the larger figure had been put forward at the instigation of his Syrian followers, and excusing himself by calling attention to his difficult position.[10]

The clash between British policy and nationalist goals, and Abdullah's growing deference to Britain's superior power, was not always so direct, however. At times the struggle was played out amongst the natural divisions of the population of Transjordan and against the background of their confusion, given the rapidity of recent political events, as to where their future lay. For example, Kura, an area within the ʿAjlun district, refused to pay an animal tax to officials at Irbid in June. The trouble stemmed from local rivalry between the tribes of Kura and the town of Irbid, and the resentment of the leading Shuraydi family towards Abdullah's administration.[11] Eventually the Shuraydi family stronghold at Tibna was bombed by the RAF to quell their rebelliousness. Abramson, however, insisted on blaming Amin al-Tamimi, the *mutasarrif* of ʿAjlun, for the incident. While his report acknowledged that the local reason for the revolt was that Kura had already paid that year's tax to the previous administration in Irbid, he added his own embellishment: 'The inhabitants of Trans-Jordania resent the presence in highly paid positions of Syrian exiles and object to paying taxes to provide posts for these exiles.'[12] In this manner he pressured Abdullah to remove al-Tamimi, a nationalist from Nablus and a member of the Istiqlal, from his administration.

In addition to attributing a false rationale to local upsets, British officials seem to have attempted to create a real indigenous opposition to what they called 'rule by Syrians,' in order to rid Transjordan of 'troublesome elements.' The evidence, although only circumstantial, is highly suggestive. In April 1921,

Rufayfan al-Majali, the strongman of Karak and a man to be reckoned with in Transjordanian affairs, visited Jerusalem to meet with British officials. He did so without Abdullah's prior knowledge or approval.[13] Less than a month later he, Mithqal Ibn Fayiz of the Bani Sakhr, and some other local leaders reportedly decided to tell Abdullah that unless the Syrians acted more circumspectly and took a greater interest in improving conditions in Transjordan, they should be removed.[14]

The conflict between local personalities and outsiders from Damascus, Nablus and the like was not itself peculiar, but the national terms in which the rivalry was expressed rings of British rather than of Arab sensibilities at the time. A further hint of British prompting was evident in Lawrence's boast, 'It would take no time to work up public opinion and [turn] them out.'[15] Later, British advisers would speak approvingly of a movement called 'Transjordan for the Transjordanians.' It was a nationalism more wishful than actual at the time, but it was useful for Britain in combatting the wider and more threatening Arab nationalist movement. It is significant that such a slogan did not survive into the thirties when the Transjordanian administration came to be peopled by co-operative Palestinians, although echoes of it could be heard in the very different circumstances after 1948.

After the Kura troubles, which had the dire consequence for British interests of destroying the local reserve force that had been created under British auspices by Frederick Peake,[16] Britain's dissatisfaction with Abdullah's administration, or lack thereof, began to mount. Abdullah, Samuel complained, was preoccupied with ideas of a wider bearing and greater ambition. His 'Syrian entourage' was a source of embarrassment to Abramson and was disliked in Transjordan and regarded as expensive and incompetent.[17] General Congreve amplified these comments a few days later with the observation that 'In Trans Jordania Abdulla is a fraud: he spends his subsidy on himself and his friends. He cannot rule for lack of force, ability and energy – we are wasting our money on him and the country is going to wrack and anarchy.'[18]

Lawrence defended Abdullah back in London by recalling British policy: 'I think we felt that Trans-Jordan must hang in suspense, till its neighbours settled themselves. We asked Abdullah only to keep peace with his neighbours, not to run a good administration . . . his regime prejudices us in no way, whatever eventual solution we wish to carry out, provided that it is not too popular and not too efficient!'[19] However his timely reminder could not mitigate the reaction over the next crisis to rock Abdullah's regime.

On 23 June 1921, General Gouraud, the French high commissioner for Syria and Lebanon, was ambushed while on tour of inspection near the Transjordanian border. He escaped, but a French officer with him was killed. Almost immediately Samuel was informed by the French consul general in Jerusalem that suspicion for the attack fell on Transjordanians and Syrians living in Transjordan. For over a month nothing further was heard. Then, suddenly, Paris took up the matter directly with London, asserting that the culprits were not only resident in Transjordan, but that they were members of Abdullah's entourage.[20] Thereafter Abramson and his successor intermittently pressured Abdullah to deliver up the suspects. Abdullah avoided complying with the demand by protesting that it contravened his honor and Arab laws of hospitality, and by dispatching gendarmes who always arrived a little too late to catch any of the suspects. Britain actually felt French accusations to be extreme and defended Abdullah outside of Transjordan; inside, however, the case served British interests as a convenient lever to push from time to time, to remind him of the dangers of being associated with nationalist activity. He never did turn in any of the suspects, and the case dragged on for two years until Gouraud was replaced by General Maxime Weygand.

Other sorts of upsets also provided opportunities to increase pressure on Abdullah. In September 1921 a silly mistake made by Abramson led to demonstrations in Amman. The incident began when Ibrahim Hananu arrived in Amman. For the previous two years Hananu, one of the most respected nationalist leaders, had led an armed revolt against French troops in the Aleppo region. When the revolt was eventually supressed, Hananu, like other national-ists before him, fled to Transjordan. His arrival went unnoticed by British officials in Amman, who apparently had no idea who he was. Encouraged by the lack of reaction, Abdullah asked Abramson to provide Hananu with a letter of introduction to the British administration in Palestine. Abramson did so. Armed with that letter, Hananu travelled on to Palestine. There he was arrested by better-informed officials and extradited to Syria.[21]

News of Hananu's fate electrified Amman. An angry crowd gathered spon-taneously in the center of town, seized Frederick Peake, who happened to be walking through the market place at the time, and threatened him with death if he did not produce Hananu. Hananu's fate equally outraged Abdullah, who accused Britain of a breach of faith. In the end, Peake was rescued by one of his officers (Fu'ad Salim, who a year later was abruptly dismissed from the reserve force by Peake for being a member of the Istiqlal), and Abdullah climbed down and agreed to arrest three 'Syrians' accused of fomenting the trouble.[22]

The problems in Amman that September capped what Britain summed up as an unsatisfactory six months. Since July, almost everything about Transjordan had been up for review – its status, its ruler, even its chief political officer, who, as London laconically put it, 'is not the best possible man as British adviser to Abdullah.'[23] While nothing more was heard of Abramson's shortcomings, plenty was aired about Abdullah's, centering on his 'languid' participation in the administration of the country and on his lavish spending.[24]

The general feeling in London was that Abdullah should somehow be eased out of Transjordan. The preferred British solution was that he should be invited north to rule in Damascus and that Transjordan, with a governor of lesser status, should become a province of Palestine. France, however, had made it clear that Abdullah was not welcome in Damascus. Moreover, Palestine had not become the stable state with which, in the British scenario, Transjordan would automatically desire unification. And so in September Britain faced much the same problem as it had six months earlier: how to get Abdullah out of Transjordan and what to do with the territory once he had left.

For the nationalists, the six months had also been a period of disillusionment. It was becoming increasingly obvious that Abdullah was unable and perhaps unwilling to provide consistent support or protection. In August 1921 the cabinet of Rashid Tali'a fell and was replaced by an advisory council headed by Mazhar Raslan.[25] The tone of Mazhar's council was less aggressively nationalistic than that of Tali'a's cabinet. Mazhar himself, though a member of the Istiqlal, was regarded with distrust by some of his peers.[26] Tali'a stayed on in Transjordan for another year or so, but was never offered a post again owing to a virtual British ban on his presence in government. Meanwhile, amnesties in Syria and Iraq allowed the majority of nationalist refugees to return home.

For Abdullah the six months was a period of frustration as he came to the gradual realization that Damascus was farther away than he had originally thought (or had been led to believe). To add to his frustration, he was tortured by jealousy of his brother, Faysal, who had been crowned king of Iraq in August.[27] Abramson described him as 'very often depressed and at other times very impatient.'[28] Pressed one time too many to arrest Gouraud's assailants, he finally burst out in an emotional invective against his fate:

I came over to Trans-Jordania determined to make a bid for Syria; In Jerusalem I agreed to Mr. Winston Churchill's policy, because I did not wish to do anything to cause trouble to Great Britain, it having been my policy during the war to work in with Great Britain; I was mainly responsible for bringing the Arabs in with Great Britain; I refused to allow Feisul to agree to the offer from the Turks; I might have had Irak; when in Jerisalem [sic] I pointed out that six months inaction in Trans-Jordania after going there and telling the whole Arab world that I intended to make a bid for Syria, would mean the loss of Syria and the alienation of the Arabs; I understood that there was a good chance of means being found by the end of the six months to install me in Damascus. I have now lost everything . . . I have had enough of this wilderness of Trans-Jordania where I am surrounded by these hateful Syrians who think of themselves only . . .[29]

If this outburst was intended to arouse feelings of commiseration or guilt in British circles, it failed to hit the mark. Instead it confirmed Britain's wishful thinking that, apart from any British desire to remove Abdullah from Transjordan, Abdullah himself was eager to go.

T. E. Lawrence was sent to review the situation first-hand. He was coming from the Hijaz where he had failed to get King Husayn to sign an Anglo-Hijazi treaty.[30] Britain's sharifian policy appeared to be coming apart at the seams. Just prior to Lawrence's arrival, the Transjordan situation was assessed as follows:

What we have got to face is either continued expenditure on Abdullah, whose influence has gone down almost to vanishing point, and who is no longer a substitute for even a section of Infantry, or to take our courage in both hands and send a small force over, if only temporarily, in order to set Revenue collection on a proper footing, and to make sure of getting rid of the Syrians and Hedjazis.

Of course if Lawrence can manage to screw Abdullah up to deposing these people, and to appointing a suitable Regent to take his own place we may be able to avoid . . . sending troops, but if, as we are warned here, Abdullah proves too difficult, I can see nothing for it but to remove him and appoint in his place an Arab Governor . . .[31]

Lawrence also anticipated that he would have to usher Abdullah out of Transjordan, and was confident in his ability to do so. Only Hubert Young in the Middle East Department sounded a cautionary note: '. . . one cannot lose sight of the fact that all the plans that were made in Cairo in March about Trans-Jordania were upset when Abdullah himself was consulted, and it is possible that the same thing may happen again.'[32]

Young's remarks proved prescient. Presented with the possibility of having to leave Transjordan, Abdullah proved eager to stay on. Lawrence, who had shared the generally held low opinion of Abdullah's administration when he left London, found when he arrived in Amman that Britain was as much at fault as Abdullah for ongoing security and administrative problems.[33] He tackled British deficiencies of supply and organization with his customary energy while London set about appointing a new representative to Amman.

The name under discussion in London as Abramson's replacement was that of H. St John Philby. Philby, a member of the Indian civil service, had most recently served in Iraq. There he had come into conflict with the British administration over Faysal's installation as king, the manner of which he disapproved. His attitude was such that the high commissioner of Iraq, Sir Percy Cox, had been forced to ask him to leave. Despite being stubborn, contrary and opinionated,[34] Philby was a good administrator, strong-willed, and fluent in Arabic.

On hearing of his appointment, Philby confided jubilantly to his diary, 'we are to have another run for our money.'[35] What he meant was that he would have another chance to promote Arab independence, as he defined it. Although he had objected vehemently to Britain's behind-the-scenes machinations in getting Faysal put on the throne of Iraq, he accepted Abdullah's position without cavil. After passing muster with Abdullah and Lawrence in Amman, Samuel in Jerusalem, and Churchill in London, he returned to Amman in November 1921 as the chief British representative.

As for Abdullah, owing to Lawrence's assessment it had been quietly agreed that he would stay on in Transjordan for the time being. No formal announcement was made, for Britain wanted to keep its options open in Transjordan and to avoid arousing the French, who still disliked the idea of sharifian governments being set up on the borders of Syria.

On 29 November 1921, Philby, Lawrence and Abramson called on Abdullah at his headquarters in Sa'id al-Mufti's modest home, which was unchanged save for the addition of sentry boxes on either side of the gate painted in the green, white, black and red sharifian colors. Philby had come to present his credentials, Abramson to take formal leave. They were invited to stay for lunch, a comfortable masculine affair with talk of horses, guns and the like. Philby's excellent Arabic and his interest in tribal lore stood him in good stead with Abdullah, although his admiration for Ibn Saud made him something of a curious choice for a post in Transjordan. When the topic of Ibn Saud's recent conquest of Ha'il came up, Philby noted that it was 'an event which has obviously impressed Abdullah and given him food for thought.'[36] Later, to Abdullah's annoyance, he kept a picture of Ibn Saud on his desk.

By putting Philby in Amman, Britain had instituted a new regime of sorts, but its long range intentions towards Abdullah and towards Transjordan were still unclear. Still unresolved was the fundamental question, 'Do we or do we not wish to see Abdulla settle himself firmly in the Trans-Jordanian saddle, and come to be regarded as the permanent sovereign of the country?'[37]

Philby's instructions were consequently sketchy. He was told that the governing factor in Transjordan was 'not so much encouragement of national aspirations . . . as protection of Palestine from anti-British and anti-Zionist activities and of Syria from propaganda against the French.'[38] In other words, little had changed since the Cairo Conference. Internal affairs, as long as they did not reverberate across the borders, were left to his discretion.

For Philby, with his indomitable independence of mind, the dearth of instruction was a boon. It left him free to indulge his own ideas of proper government, which included what he called Arab independence. What he meant by the idea in the context of Transjordan was independence from the Palestine administration rather than absolute freedom from European interference. Indeed, Philby took his duties as a colonial administrator very seriously, and his idea of Arab independence did not include a tolerance for nationalist activities which might impede the fulfillment of his duties. Like his predecessor he did his best to get rid of Arab nationalists in Transjordan on the grounds of their 'foreignness.' In order to promote the sort of independence he had in mind, Philby set out to create democratic institutions and to put Transjordan finances in order with the eventual aim of financial self-sufficiency. Both goals brought him into conflict with Abdullah. Two other of Philby's major concerns, ones which he had more success in achieving, were to better Abdullah's relations with the French administration in Syria and to delimit Transjordan's boundaries to the south and east.

During the first year or so of Philby's tenure, relations between Abdullah and himself were particularly felicitous. Abdullah gave Philby Sa'id al-Mufti's house.[39] Both men enjoyed playing chess, although in Philby's opinion Abdullah played 'too rapidly and [did] not think out a scheme.'[40] Both men had suffered disappointments over Iraq and neither wished Faysal well. When Hubert Young passed through Amman with a glowing report of Faysal's administration, Abdullah became extremely upset, ate no dinner, and retired early in spite of Philby's attempt to cheer him up with some *Weekly Times* chess problems.[41] Philby at first also considered Abdullah 'an ideal constitutional monarch, taking no active part in the administration except when referred to for a decision or for advice either by the Local Government or by the people.'[42] His opinion soon changed, causing a disastrous rift between the two men.

In the first flush of getting to know one another, Abdullah and Philby made a happy trip to Palestine together. The purpose of the trip was to bring Abdullah and the high commissioner for Palestine, Sir Herbert Samuel, together to make sure that Abdullah understood his obligations and to reassure Samuel that Abdullah would be a co-operative neighbor and vassal. The discussions between the two were not official in the sense of further defining Abdullah's position or the future of Transjordan. Britain still wished to leave these matters open for revision. Rather, the trip was planned mainly to create good feelings. It was filled mostly with social engagements: lunches, teas and dinners with British officials and Arab notables, enlivened by music and games. Abdullah played chess with Philby (one all to date), Storrs (eight games after dinner while the rest of the conversation flagged), and Samuel (Samuel won). He also visited Haifa, Acre and Hebron in order to meet local dignitaries and politicians. On the return journey he was permitted by the French to travel by train incognito via Dir'a, a concession which gave him hope that the French attitude towards him was softening.[43]

Yet Britain's intentions in Transjordan could not be left in abeyance forever. Shortly after Abdullah's trip to Palestine, Churchill had expressed the desire to let things in Transjordan 'pursue their present course' (that is, remain fluid and undefined), 'at any rate until the constitution of Palestine is definitely promulgated.'[44] This statement gave voice to the general feeling held by the Middle East department that, once things in Palestine settled down, Transjordan would more easily be administered as an Arab district of Palestine. However, Palestinian affairs did not proceed as hoped. The limited constitutional government that Britain offered the Palestinians was rejected out of hand, since it allowed for the creation and protection of a Jewish national home. Britain's failure to enlist the co-operation of the Arab community of Palestine foiled the succeeding step that had been envisaged – that Transjordan would, in turn, fall into line under an orderly Palestine administration. When the League of Nations ratified the British mandate for Palestine in September 1922, Transjordan was excluded from the Zionist clauses of the mandate, but Transjordan never became an Arab province of Palestine.

Concurrent events on other borders of Transjordan also encouraged British statesmen to think of Transjordan as a useful entity in and of itself. Philby worked hard to foster good relations with the French in Syria. Owing to his skill in doing so, France came to regard Abdullah's position in Transjordan with less hostility. Although M. Robert de Caix, Gouraud's secretary-general, explained to Philby that his government had definitely and finally decided never to involve itself with sharifians, he said France would be willing to recognize Abdullah's position in Transjordan once the Gouraud culprits were turned over.[45]

On Transjordan's southern side, Ibn Saud had consolidated his hold in north central Arabia, pushing northward to Jawf. Jawf was an especially important oasis town, for it lay at the southern end of Wadi Sirhan, a long and comparatively well-watered valley that served as a major route north, ending some fifty miles southeast of Amman. From Jawf, on 15 August 1922, a stunning raid was launched by tribes loyal to Ibn Saud against two Bani Sakhr villages only twelve miles south of Amman.

The expansion of Ibn Saud northward affected Abdullah's position in Transjordan and his relationship to Britain in two ways. First, Saudi expansionism through the vehicle of Wahhabism gave Transjordan a new value in British strategy in the region. This value was based on its continued separation from Palestine. With the conquests of Ha'il and Jawf, the tribes of central Arabia moved geographically nearer to the mandated Arab states and spiritually closer to a unity which posed a potential threat to the mandatory regimes. Britain was particularly anxious about Palestine where it was committed to a policy of Zionist colonization inimical, in the eyes of Wahhabi purists, to Islam. From Jawf, Ibn Saud stood in a good position not only to launch attacks against Transjordan and Palestine, but those areas became far more vulnerable to 'infection' by the ideology of Wahhabism. Although Transjordan itself was not immune to infection or attack, it was a bulwark against Wahhabism as long as Abdullah, Ibn Saud's enemy, was its ruler and as long as its inhabitants did not have a strong grievance against British authority or against Abdullah.

Transjordan did not gain much in British eyes: 'We regard Trans-Jordania more as a buffer to Palestine than as a country capable of development in itself, and at present at any rate, money spent in that territory is only justified by the fact that it reduces what might otherwise have to be spent on military measures in Palestine.'[46] It did, however, gain recognition as a geographical barrier whose distinct political circumstances served Britain's interests. For just as the British were discovering the depth of Palestinian opposition to the mandate, they became acutely sensitive to the extent which Wahhabism might magnify and galvanize anti-British sentiment. Arab nationalists in Palestine were already in contact with Ibn Saud and articles which looked favorably on Wahhabism and on Ibn Saud were appearing in Palestinian papers. Although it was acknowledged that the strict tenets of Wahhabism would not normally be attractive to Palestinians, who were generally better educated and more sophisticated than Arabs of the peninsula, yet in the unique circumstances of the Palestine mandate it was felt that Wahhabism might be a compelling and potent ideology.[47]

The second effect of Saudi expansionism was that it made Abdullah more than ever dependent, and conscious of his dependence, on Britain's military might. He had already been disastrously defeated by Ibn Saud once, at Turaba, with loyal tribes in his command. In Transjordan there was not yet a strong bond between himself and the tribes or among the tribes themselves. There was certainly no bond in any way comparable to Wahhabism, which welded Arabian tribes together in a spirit of religious militancy and righteousness and hurled them against other tribes in campaigns of conquest and proselytization. He had begun to forge links with the tribes in Transjordan, especially with the Huwaytat and the Bani Sakhr, who were directly in the path of Wahhabi expansion; but his only tools were tax benefits, land, cash handouts, and the like.[48] Ibn Saud, however, had the ideology of a reformed, purified and activist Islam to galvanize the loyalty of the tribes under his aegis. Against this superior tribal force, Abdullah was dependent on Britain's superior technology.

As Abdullah grew increasingly aware of his dependence on Britain for protection against external enemies, so in his internal affairs did his deference to British wishes increase. Philby followed his predecessor's footsteps in easing nationalists out of positions of responsibility and out of the country altogether. In March the advisory council headed by Mazhar Raslan was changed. The new chief adviser, 'Ali Rida' al-Rikabi, had recently arrived in Transjordan from Damascus. Though a Syrian, he was not one of those Syrians whose 'foreignness' was grounds for exclusion from a career in Transjordan.

Al-Rikabi's political history was checkered. During the war he had served the Turks as head of the municipality of Damascus. On the defeat of the Turks in 1918 he passed smoothly into Faysal's administration and was appointed military governor. He became, at that time, a member of the leadership of the nationalist society, *al-Fatat*. After the French conquest and occupation of Damascus in 1920, al-Rikabi remained openly in the city, unlike the rest of Faysal's nationalist supporters, who fled. By April 1921 he was reported to have made his peace with General Gouraud, to be receiving a fifty-lira subsidy per month, and to be a likely candidate for a ministerial post. Indeed, his relations with the French were such that in October 1921, Abdullah had written to ask him to sound them out with a view towards *rapprochement*.[49]

The British administration in Palestine mistrusted al-Rikabi as 'corrupt and possibly bought by the French.'[50] As Samuel commented, 'even his best friends feel themselves obliged to express the most complete reservations as to the integrity of his moral character.'[51] It was perhaps owing to that very lack of integrity that Philby and his successor found him to be a very effective instrument against former friends and political allies. Within a month of his becoming chief adviser, two of the most prominent nationalists in Transjordan, 'Adil Arslan, the chief secretary, and Nabih al-'Azma, the chief of police, were forced out of office. His appointment also helped to improve relations with the French, who considered him 'the best man in Syria.'[52]

Against this background of unrest in Palestine, religious hostility in Arabia and increased docility in Transjordan, the British government finally invited Abdullah to visit London. Abdullah had been anxious for such an invitation for months. However trouble in Iraq had claimed Britain's attention. Faysal and Britain had locked horns during negotiations for an Anglo–Iraqi treaty, and the altercation had caused the outwardly felicitous relationship between Faysal and the British administration in Iraq to give way to one of suspicion and mistrust. It was even suggested at the time that 'perhaps if Abdullah could take Feisal's place, Iraq would be easier and Trans-Jordania would drop into its place as a province of Palestine.'[53] Faysal's fortuitous attack of appendicitis in August averted a showdown and cleared the way to London for Abdullah. In a wire which Philby described as 'lamentable . . . breathing parsimony in every syllable . . .', the high commissioner was instructed to invite him to London.[54]

Abdullah left for England on 3 October 1922. His chief goal was to have the status of Transjordan defined officially with himself as amir – after all, he had not reached any formal agreement with Britain beyond the handshake with Churchill eighteen months previously. Subsidiary to that basic desire he had a number of other requests. Some, like his demand for a port on the Mediterranean, were rejected outright; others were disposed of by sleight of hand. For example, his desire that Transjordan be totally dissociated from Palestine was accomplished by the fine distinction of making Philby responsible to the high commissioner in his role as representative of the mandatory power, but not in his capacity as head of the Palestine administration. (Privately, London held the reservation that 'the door would not be closed to a possible rapprochement between the two administrations in the future.')[55]

Borders were also on the agenda. The major problem concerned how much territory to concede to Ibn Saud. Sir Gilbert Clayton, chief secretary for the government of Palestine, convinced Abdullah to give up Jawf oasis at the bottom of Wadi Sirhan, but promised that Kaf, at the top, would be secured for Transjordan. (Britain did not keep this promise.) In the north and west

Abdullah accepted the existing borders with Syria and Palestine, which had yet to be demarcated on the ground. The Iraqi border on the east he felt could be easily arranged. The Hijaz border on the south he preferred to defer until he could speak with his father.[56]

A financial settlement set British financial assistance to Transjordan at the amount of £150,000 for the year beginning 1 April 1923. Tied to that assistance were certain conditions, both financial and political.[57] The conditions relating directly to the budget were that the cost of the reserve force and the expenses of the chief British representative's establishment be the first charge on the revenues of Transjordan, that complete financial information be made regularly available to London, that internal taxation be reformed, and finally that Abdullah's civil list be fixed at £36,000 a year, doled out in equal monthly installments. The political string attached to the grant-in-aid was that the security forces in Transjordan – the reserve force created by Peake, the police and the gendarmerie – were to be united in one force with a total strength of 1,300 and put under Peake's command. This measure handily reduced the number of positions open to Arab officers and put Peake in unchallenged control of the whole security apparatus.

On Tuesday 14 November Abdullah left London. He had been met half-way in his desire for a formal acknowledgement of his and Transjordan's status by a carefully qualified written 'assurance'. But at the last moment there was a slight hitch in making the assurance public – the foreign office requested a delay of ten days while it was squared with the French. Ten days stretched to two weeks and then to three. Finally the Foreign Office announced that it needed some gesture of good will towards France on Abdullah's part before the assurance could be announced. It was suggested that the arrest of at least one of those accused of taking part in the attack on General Gouraud or the arrest of Sultan al-Atrash, a Druze leader who had fled to Transjordan recently following an anti-French uprising in Jabal Druze, would serve.[58] Abdullah, to his chagrin, therefore returned to Amman empty-handed.

The withholding of the assurance spurred Philby on to redouble his efforts to squash nationalist activities in Transjordan. As soon as he got back from London, he visited Damascus. He took Peake with him and they discussed with the French the possibility of military co-operation on the Syrian–Transjordanian border. Commandant Arlebosse, head of the political section in Damascus and 'the most hated man in Syria,' then visited Amman to discuss the joint military venture. Abdullah gave Peake *carte blanche* to work with the French, impressing them with his co-operativeness. According to Philby, Arlebosse appreciatively commented about Abdullah, 'Si ce type-là avait été à Damas à la place de Faisal, il serait là jusqu'à maintenant.'[59] Joint military exercises took place in the second week of March 1923.

Within a month of this demonstration of united strength and purpose, Sultan

Figure 7. Sir Herbert Samuel delivering the assurance at Amman, May 1923. To Samuel's left are Amir Abdullah, Sharif Shakir ibn Zayd and Peake Pasha (facing camera in kuffiya and uniform).

al-Atrash surrendered, and the Foreign Office agreed, finally, to release the assurance. At about the same time, the successful Arab boycott of elections in Palestine killed any lingering hope that the Palestine situation would settle down in the near future, removing an unspoken reluctance to solidify further Transjordan's separation from Palestine. The last local obstacle to the announcement was safely overcome when Abdullah, over the objections of some of his advisers, agreed to implement the unification of Transjordan's security forces under Peake's command as had been agreed in London. The unified force was christened the Arab Legion.

With these points of dispute out of the way, the result of Abdullah's trip to London six months earlier was finally announced amidst a day of celebration:

Subject to approval of the League of Nations, His Britannic Majesty's Government will recognise the existence of an independent Government in Trans-Jordan, under the rule of His Highness the Amir Abdullah ibn Husain, provided such government is constitutional and places His Britannic Majesty's Government in a position to fulfil their international obligations in respect of the territory by means of an agreement to be concluded between the two Governments.[60]

The assurance, characterized by its conditional nature – 'will recognize . . .

provided that,' was not, in fact, very reassuring. It placed the burden of fulfillment on Abdullah, who had to institute a constitutional regime before recognition would be validated by some sort of 'agreement' between Britain and Transjordan. Abdullah had dug in his heels over the matter of a constitution until now, and unless London forced one upon him, the promised agreement would be a dead letter. It was in London's power, therefore, to let the idea of a constitution and hence of an 'independent' Transjordan die of inanition. And what, finally, was Britain prepared to recognize? The independence envisioned by the assurance was not independence from Britain; rather, by independence Britain meant maintaining a government in Transjordan separate from the government of Palestine, but still under British control.

This is what Philby had set out to achieve, and he was justifiably pleased to be one step closer to his goal. Abdullah was also pleased, but his pleasure was qualified. Judging from his actions (rather than from his statements), he intended to put off introducing a constitution for as long as possible, but he was happy, for the present, to be mentioned in writing as 'His Highness the Amir,' ruler of Transjordan. His speech on the occasion encouraged his subjects to believe that the assurance was a declaration of independence and to regard Britain as a friend of the Arabs,[61] but he certainly knew himself that little had changed in his relationship with Britain.

The announcement of the assurance was the high point of Abdullah and Philby's working relationship. In the ensuing months tension between the two mounted over the issue of a constitution, leading in the end to a confrontation and an irreparable break.

Ever since taking on his position in Amman, Philby had pushed for a constitutional regime with an elected legislative assembly. Abdullah's unwillingness to establish an official representative body of any sort led Philby to conclude that he was nervous about the general acceptability of his government. According to Philby he was justifiably so because of the large number of 'Syrian' officials who were unpopular with the local inhabitants. Philby proceeded to press Abdullah to get rid of the Syrians, by which he meant Arab nationalists. Useful Syrians like al-Rikabi were welcome. However, although Arab nationalists, whether Syrians, Palestinians, or Iraqis, were gradually leaving Transjordan, there was no movement in the direction of democratization. Abdullah was reluctant to cede any of his already circumscribed power to democratic institutions.

Following the announcement of the assurance, Philby, impatient and more certain than ever of the rectitude of his ends, stepped up his campaign. Faced with Abdullah's continued inaction he took whatever opportunities came to hand to add weight and leverage to his case. In June 1923 such an opportunity arose. At that time Amman had no proper mosque and Abdullah was anxious to build one. Philby supported the idea to the extent of setting the proper direction for the *qibla* himself, but when Abdullah ordered the destruction of a sixth-century Byzantine basilica to make way for the mosque (and to provide building materials for a house being built 'for one of the Amir's minions,' according to Philby),[62] Philby was enraged. He was an avid amateur archaeologist and he protested in very strong terms. Abdullah's retort, 'And who shall punish me?' infuriated Philby further.[63]

After this explosion the two were no longer on speaking terms. Both appealed to higher authorities for support and vindication. Abdullah informed Clayton that he and Philby could not work together and that one or the other of them must go.[64] Philby used the event to expound on the merits of creating a representative assembly which would 'either force the Amir into constitutional and reasonable channels or into flight from the country,' and went on, 'I am convinced that his absence would be less harmful than his presence in his present frame of mind.'[65]

To bolster his case against Abdullah, Philby opened up another front of criticism, one which struck a more responsive chord in London: financial mismanagement. Until the summer of 1923, Philby had noted Abdullah's extravagant spending, but had been sympathetic to his financial needs and difficulties. After the basilica incident, Philby revealed everything he knew about Abdullah's irregular financial dealings. Chief among these was the giving of expensive gifts to favorites and the giving away of state land to pay back creditors and to bind the indigenous leaders of Transjordan, mainly tribal shaykhs, to him more securely.[66]

Gilbert Clayton was sent from Jerusalem to smooth down the ruffled feathers. He effected a reconciliation of sorts which at least permitted the two men to keep up a front of co-operation, but he advised the Colonial Office that at a convenient time Philby should be transferred (though not immediately so that Abdullah would not feel he had scored a triumph).[67] In the meantime Abdullah was permitted to correspond directly with the high commissioner in Jerusalem, rather than through Philby as before. Philby stayed on in Amman for another nine months, but the basilica incident ended his effectiveness along with the friendly games of chess, the jokes and riddles, and the discussion of Arabic proverbs that had tempered his relationship with Abdullah.

Shortly after the argument, which everyone in tiny Amman knew about since neither Abdullah nor Philby was able to hold his tongue, Abdullah faced the most serious internal threat of his entire career in Transjordan. This was the rebellion of the ʿAdwan tribe. Owing to the recent falling out between Philby and Abdullah, Amman gossip laid the rebellion at Philby's doorstep.

The crisis, rooted in the historical rivalry between the ʿAdwan and Bani Sakhr tribes, was set off by a rumor that tithes collected in the Balqaʾ from the ʿAdwan and others were to be given to the Bani Sakhr shaykhs. This was not implausible given Abdullah's partiality for the Bani Sakhr, which stemmed from the juxtaposition of Bani Sakhr lands and Wahhabi controlled territory. Because the Bani Sakhr were the primary target for Wahhabi aggression and proselytization, Abdullah lavished attention on them to keep their loyalty. His attention took the form of granting Bani Sakhr shaykhs huge tracts of land and assessing their taxes at a fraction of what the 'Adwan and other residents of the Balqa' paid.[68] However necessary Abdullah's policy may have been to bind the Bani Sakhr to himself, it could not but kindle resentment and rebellion among the 'Adwan.

The 'Adwan revolt began to simmer towards the end of August 1923.[69] Unequal taxation and tribal jealousy were its basic causes, but the 'Adwan also made demands for a representative assembly and for increased Transjordanian participation in government. It was the inclusion of these demands which led some to see Philby's hand in the affair.[70] Philby himself accused 'certain effendis' (educated town politicians) of egging on Sultan al-'Adwan.

The crisis escalated until, on the morning of 16 September, Sultan al-'Adwan began to march towards Amman at the head of his tribal forces. He had written to Philby informing him that the rebellion was an internal matter and not anti-British, and that if Philby intervened on Abdullah's behalf, he would report him to the Colonial Office. This dictum so irritated Philby that he responded with an ultimatum to the 'Adwan: disband or be attacked. When the 'Adwan began to move from Suwaylih towards Amman, they were met by the Arab Legion and two armored cars. Owing to a series of mistakes, fighting broke out.[71] The rebels suffered eighty-six casualties (including thirteen women) and their leaders fled to Jabal Druze in Syria.

Abdullah did not emerge from the 'Adwan crisis stronger than before. Ominously, the 'effendis' whom Philby accused of instigating the rebellion came from Karak, Amman and Irbid and could not be easily dismissed as Syrian agitators. His throne had been preserved by British rather than by local support, reminding him of his dependence on Britain. As Philby commented at the time: 'the Amir and his Government have been driven by the Adwan rebellion . . . into a sense of dependence on British help and I feel confident that they will now be less inclined to disregard well-meant counsels . . .'[72]

Certainly, local British officials were bolstered by the spectacle of their military superiority and by the belief that Abdullah now better understood his position. On the strength of this belief, Philby and Peake decided it was time to rid the Arab Legion and the Transjordan government of remaining Istiqlalis. Three officers, all belonging to the Istiqlal, were discharged from the Legion. Abdullah was then prevailed upon to expel them from the country along with two other well-known Istiqlalis, 'Adil Arslan and Subhi al-Khadra. By the end of December the Palestinian Istiqlali Ahmad Hilmi had been deprived of his post in the council of advisers as well. His fellow Palestinian, Ibrahim Hashim, was allowed to stay on only after promising faithfully to cut all his ties with the Istiqlal.[73]

With these expulsions, Transjordan was cleansed of most of the prominent Arab nationalists whom Britain considered to be troublemakers. It had taken merely two and a half years. During that time Britain had seen, or had pretended to see, Arab nationalists behind every local upset and every failure of Abdullah and the local administration to follow British dictates. Abdullah had, in a sense, connived in this misinterpretation. By allowing the nationalists to be held responsible, he avoided any direct confrontation with Britain over his own unwillingness or inability to carry out British policy, but the thinning out of nationalist ranks and nationalist influence in Transjordan brought Abdullah himself face to face with British policy. A constitutional regime did not immediately follow the departure of the 'Syrians' because it was Abdullah, for his own reasons, rather than the nationalists or their presence, who had worked against the idea all along. And Abdullah continued to merit charges of financial mismanagement even after the departure of the 'Syrians' whose salaries, in Britain's thinking, had been the cause of Abdullah's indebtedness. Hence, without the nationalists as a buffer, Abdullah himself was held responsible for the shortcomings of his administration. The resulting tension between Abdullah and Britain gradually came to a head.

The coming confrontation was held off by interference of another sort in the affairs of Transjordan: familial. In January Abdullah's father, King Husayn of the Hijaz, paid him a visit. The tone of his visit was set the moment he disembarked at Aqaba. Though sixty-eight years old, he disdained the luxurious Mercedes provided by Abdullah and travelled instead by camel and donkey to the railhead at Maʿan. Just as he upset Abdullah's transport arrangements, so did he upset affairs generally in Transjordan for the duration of his two month visit. It was a trying time for all, in spite of Philby's facetious remark that his visit 'brought the Amir's Administration to an almost complete standstill – an incalculable boon to the country.' Abdullah was relegated to a secondary position while Husayn assumed virtual control of the country. Britain momentarily lost something of its control, for it had to deal more circumspectly with Husayn than with Abdullah.[74]

King Husayn's presence made Amman a focus of political attention, similar to the hustle and bustle of Abdullah's first days there. Individuals and delegations came from Palestine, Syria, Lebanon and Egypt. From Jerusalem came British mandate officials and even a Zionist delegation.[75] All aims, claims, programs and resolutions were listened to politely, but in the end he offered little guidance or inspiration. Only Britain succeeded in getting him to do

Figure 8. King Husayn of the Hijaz (right), with the president of the Palestinian Arab Executive Committee, Musa Kazim Pasha al-Husayni (center), Amman, 1924.

something. He agreed, after much persuasion, to send his youngest son Zayd to a British-sponsored conference in Kuwait which was being held at that time to discuss Hashemite–Saudi borders.

The major event of Husayn's visit was his assumption of the caliphate. On 3 March 1924, the Turkish National Assembly deposed Abdülmecid, the last Ottoman caliph, and within twenty-four hours he was bundled out of the country to exile in Switzerland. This bolt of lightning was followed immediately by the thunder of the announcement from Shuna, where Husayn was enjoying the warmth of Abdullah's winter camp, that he would take on the position of caliph himself. Since Britain had talked about the caliphate more than any other power in recent years, his claim to the title may have been directed at London as much as at the Arab or the larger Muslim world in a final attempt to regain British support in his struggle with Ibn Saud.[76] In the event his action backfired badly, ending in his deposition eight months later to the day.

Husayn took on the caliphate, he claimed, in response to the many telegrams of acclamation which arrived from the countries of the Fertile Crescent and the Hijaz. It was suspected, however, that the flood of telegrams was at least in part engineered. The Hijaz, according to the British consul there, was particularly sluggish in its response to his declaration.[77] Nevertheless, the official story, as told by Abdullah to the correspondent of the *Manchester Guardian*, was that the mufti of Mecca had proclaimed Husayn caliph before the pilgrims and that they, representing all of the Muslim world, had approved. Abdullah was described as delighted with the new glory accruing to the Hashemite house, while Husayn, in contrast, affected a modest and subdued manner consonant with the responsibilities of his new position.[78]

In fact, Husayn's bid for the caliphate won support only in Transjordan, Palestine and Syria. Reaction in the Hijaz and Iraq was mixed. In Syria it became an act of nationalist defiance to proclaim the name of Husayn in the Friday prayers since the French administration had forced the mufti of Damascus to forbid the mention of any name at all.[79] As such, proclaimed support for Husayn was a symbol more meaningful to Syrian politics than to Husayn's ambitions. In Palestine, support of Husayn was likewise a political matter, and was tendered on condition that he defend the Arab cause and consult the people of Palestine before deciding any question affecting their country.[80] Support for Husayn on nationalist grounds was not unanimous, however, as many considered him too tainted by his association with Britain to be eligible for the highest office in Islam.[81] Britain remained totally aloof from Husayn's assumption of the office, although in the past, in the Husayn–McMahon correspondence for example, it had dangled the office before him. Outside of the Fertile Crescent he had almost no support. Indian and Javanese Muslims remained loyal to Abdülmecid and in Egypt King Fu'ad had his own ambitions for the office.[82] Husayn's most immediate and most dangerous opponent was Ibn Saud who professed himself deeply offended at Husayn's arrogance in appropriating the office for himself. Ibn Saud did not suffer the offense quietly and he began to make final preparations for the conquest of the Hijaz. Indeed, the lack of support which Husayn's proclamation elicited perhaps encouraged Ibn Saud to think that the Arab and Muslim worlds would do little to save him in the event of a Saudi attack on the Hijaz.

Husayn left Transjordan shortly after assuming the caliphate. Philby, whose relations with Abdullah had never been fully repaired after their argument over the destruction of the basilica and whose position had been further eroded by successive disagreements with Samuel, had handed in his resignation in mid-January. Cantankerous to the end, he explained to the officials in Transjordan with whom he worked that he had quit because he saw no hope for Transjordan's future owing to the failure of Abdullah and his government to make good.[83] Abdullah was happy to see him go. Years later, on hearing that Philby had converted to Islam, he remarked, 'Islam has gained little, and Christianity has lost even less.'[84]

Philby's successor was Lieutenant Colonel (later Sir) Henry Cox, who had served in the Sudan before the war and had most recently been district governor for Nablus. Like Philby, he had a strong sense of duty and the will to see his duty done. Unlike Philby, he fitted into the British colonial hierarchy and did not suffer from a sense of moral rectitude in conflict with the norms of the Colonial Office. In contrast to Philby's exuberance at taking on Transjordan, Cox reflected grimly, 'I will make Transjordan or else Transjordan will break me.'[85]

The premises on which Cox took up his position in Transjordan were fundamentally different from those on which British policy had previously been based. When Abramson and Philby had been posted to Amman, Whitehall was more concerned with Transjordan's neighbors than with Transjordan itself. Consequently a heavy emphasis was put on security, the aim of which was to sever Arab nationalist ties between the different mandated territories. Transjordan stood at the crossroads between Syria and Palestine and between Palestine and Iraq, and was itself a haven for political refugees from these territories. Correspondingly little attention was left over for internal affairs not directly related to security.

During Philby's term of office the emphasis had begun to shift. First, the borders of Palestine and Syria became less of a worry. France in particular was settling down to its task in Syria and had less to fear from the British–sharifian entente. Nationalist activity from Amman had also decreased significantly. Second, Britain had gradually been forced to give up its secret hope that Transjordan would in the near future come directly under Palestine as an Arab province. The threat of Ibn Saud and Wahhabism had endowed Transjordan with its own strategic worth. Hence, by the time Cox took over, the guiding idea behind British policy had become 'that [Abdullah's] administration should be of a character that we, as Mandatory Power, can justify to the League of Nations and to the World at large.'[86]

Cox stepped into a virtual nightmare in Transjordan. Without consulting the Colonial Office, Treasury had decided to cut off Transjordan's grant-in-aid as of 1 April 1924. Instead, financial assistance for Transjordan was to come under the budget for the government of Palestine. The consequent loss to Transjordanian coffers from the previous financial year was £90,000.[87] Abdullah's response to this news was to ask whether he could then consider himself free from all previous obligations to Britain, adding that necessary funds could be got from the Hijaz but not without the virtual annexation of Transjordan to that country.[88] Thus when Cox arrived, Transjordan was in a very difficult financial situation and Britain and Abdullah were at loggerheads.

Cox's primary duty was to impose stringent financial controls. His first act in this regard was to impose a change of government on Abdullah. He reasoned that the existing government had been a party to the financial fiasco by not supplying Philby with a statement of accounts which Philby could have presented to Treasury as proof of Transjordan's need for and justifiable claim to a grant-in-aid. 'Ali Rida' al-Rikabi, who had just returned to Jerusalem after losing his bid for French patronage in the Syrian elections for a federal council, once again became chief minister in place of Abdullah's friend from Istanbul days, Hasan Khalid Abu'l-Huda.

Abdullah intensely disliked being saddled with al-Rikabi again, not, as the British seemed to believe, with the hatred of a weak man for a strong one,[89] but for the same reasons that almost everyone (except those who found him useful) disliked al-Rikabi – his untrustworthiness, his extreme ambition, and his arrogance. With al-Rikabi, Abdullah had at a most critical moment a chief adviser who would not shield him, and whom he could not blame for the failure to fulfill British desires as he had Rashid Tali'a or Mazhar Raslan. Nor had al-Rikabi any feelings of personal friendship or loyalty towards Abdullah as had Hasan Khalid. Al-Rikabi was only too willing to agree to whatever Britain wanted in the way of financial control, making it appear as if it was only Abdullah who stood in Britain's way.

Abdullah was certainly not insensible to the threat posed by al-Rikabi. In one of his first interviews with Cox he did his best to charm him, saying that the past was beyond recall but that for the future he desired nothing but happy relations with Britain and would accept financial control and a constitutional government as long as Britain honored the terms of its 1923 assurance, that is, as long as it recognized Transjordanian independence under his own rule. Indeed, with a great deal of foresight (or with inside information), he even mentioned his fear that while he was on pilgrimage Britain would decide that his return was undesirable and replace him with al-Rikabi.[90]

Cox, however, was unmoved by Abdullah's attempts at conciliation. On the contrary, within a month of his arrival in Amman he wrote to London about Abdullah, describing him as a disease which was rapidly destroying the country.[91] Since he had barely had time to marshall his own evidence for such a diagnosis, he must have been influenced by those with whom he worked most closely – Peake and al-Rikabi. Two weeks after Cox's arrival Peake, the British officer with the longest experience in Transjordan and whose word thus carried a great deal of authority, had submitted a very damaging report on the history of Abdullah's administration. In it he stated unequivocally that no government would suceeed in Transjordan as long as Abdullah remained and suggested that an excellent opportunity to get rid of him would occur soon with his departure for the pilgrimage.[92] Al-Rikabi, meanwhile, in these few months when Abdullah had lost – or rather had never succeeded in gaining – the ear of the chief British representative, stepped into the breach. He told Samuel, for example, that his difficulties in enforcing the budget were greatly increased by the *presence* of Abdullah.[93] Like Peake, Cox suggested that Abdullah should not be allowed to return from the Hijaz.[94]

Abdullah, therefore, seemed to be delivering himself up on a silver platter when he left as planned for the pilgrimage at the end of June. In his absence an ultimatum was framed, and it was decided not to allow Abdullah to return unless he agreed to it. To the original financial grievances were added other demands concerning military inspection and control, the expulsion of undesirables, the conclusion of an extradition agreement with Syria, and the abolition of the department of tribal administration. Gilbert Clayton, the author of the ultimatum, closed it with a scarcely veiled threat: 'I trust that Your Highness' definite acceptance of the above conditions will render it unnecessary for his Majesty's Government to reconsider the whole position in Trans-Jordan.'[95]

On 14 August 1924, Abdullah was due to arrive at Aqaba. Cox was instructed to deliver the ultimatum to him personally. As a precautionary measure one squadron of the 9th Lancers was sent to Amman from Palestine. On the same day, however, just as had happened two years previously, Wahhabi tribes conducted a fierce raid on Bani Sakhr villages just south of Amman. RAF airplanes and armored cars swung into action and bombed the Wahhabis into retreat. This incident provided the perfect cover for the troop movements related to the delivery of the ultimatum.[96] More importantly, it forcibly reminded Abdullah, in case he had forgotten the lessons of the ʿAdwan revolt and the other massive Wahhabi attack of 15 August 1922, that he could not rule Transjordan without British military support.

In the event, the delivery of the ultimatum was something of an anti-climax. Abdullah read it, protested his innocence and good faith with tears in his eyes, and submitted.[97] His acceptance marked the real end of the provisional period which Churchill and he had initiated at the Cairo Conference three and a half years before. It also marked his own understanding and acceptance of his position *vis à vis* Britain. He continued to chafe against Britain's control, but the chafing was more plainly for personal reasons than before.

Chapter 6

Discovering the limits

Abdullah's acceptance of the British ultimatum marked a new phase in his relations with Britain. It made it explicit that power lay, finally, in British hands, and that Britain was prepared to impose its power. It also focussed British attention, for the first time really, on Transjordan's internal affairs. British power had not only become obvious, it was about to be directed to the minutiae of Transjordanian affairs – an uncomfortable prospect for Abdullah. At the same time, events in Arabia and Syria contributed to the political atomization of the Middle East, especially from the sharifian point of view, and to Abdullah's isolation in a Transjordan dominated by Britain. Although increasingly isolated, he did not grow any less ambitious. Indeed, his awareness of Transjordan's limitations was the springboard of his ambition.

The ultimatum cleared the way for Britain to impose its will in financial and military affairs. Cox energetically pursued the advantage he had gained. A British financial adviser, Alan Kirkbride (the younger brother of the later British resident, Alec Kirkbride), was appointed to help him and to oversee the work of the department of finance. A program of enforced economy helped to decrease Transjordan's deficit but did not alter its financial dependence on Britain. Britain continued to shore up Transjordan's financial position with a grant-in-aid amounting to about one third of total yearly revenue until the Second World War.[1]

One of the biggest budget cuts, and clearly the most onerous one for Abdullah, concerned his civil list, which dropped from £36,000 in 1923–4, to £20,000 in 1924–5, to £13,000 in 1925–6. Because he was about £10,000 in debt, the civil list was subsequently augmented to help him pay back his creditors. In return, Kirkbride assumed control of civil list disbursements.[2] Kirkbride was able to pay off Abdullah's debts 'by screwing him down to the last piastre and at the risk of our having a serious row with him.'[3]

Abdullah survived the lean years by selling some of his belongings and by using the wealth of his first wife.[4] When the debts were paid off the civil list was dropped back to £12,000, and even Cox, who had earlier been highly critical of Abdullah's spending habits, was moved by his penury to intercede on his behalf. Cox's idea was that he should be given some land by the state which would not only generate income, but provide an occupation for his younger son, Nayyif, as well.[5] It was this idea, rather than a raise in the civil list directly, which eventually caught on.

With regard to military affairs, Peake was already in undisputed control of the unified local force, the Arab Legion. But before the ultimatum, his position was difficult. 'The Amir, the Government (except the new Prime Minister [al-Rikabi]) and the Istiqlal hate the Arab Legion. Their hatred is caused by different reasons, but they all agree on one point and that is the presence of a British Officer . . . With regard to the officers and men their support will last exactly so long as I am able to pay them.'[6] Afterwards, his government critics, at least, were intimidated. In 1925, the Legion numbered 1,472 including police, legionnaires and prison guards, officers and ranks.[7]

There were no Legion posts east of the Hijaz railway, and in 1926 the Transjordan Frontier Force (TJFF) was created as part of the Imperial Forces in Palestine under British command, with the duty of tribal control in Transjordan. With the TJFF taking over desert patrol duties, the Legion was reduced to 855 men and lost its semi-military character, becoming a 'dismounted urban and a partly mounted and partly dismounted rural constabulary.'[8] In this way, Transjordan lost, for a brief period, even the semblance of its own army. Despite the reduction in ranks, three more British officers were appointed to the Legion in the respective capacities of financial secretary, inspector of police, and controller of stores.

The creation of the TJFF reopened what had become a perennial bureaucratic dispute amongst the various departments of the British government: what was Transjordan's relation to Palestine. The TJFF suffered the confusion of having a name and duties which identified it with Transjordan, but of being part of the Imperial Forces in Palestine which made it a Palestinian responsibility. The result of this lack of clarity was that the TJFF got embroiled in the financial haggling between London and Jerusalem as to who was to foot the bill for the Transjordan deficit. Although almost everyone in London in 1926 had accepted the separation of Transjordan and Palestine, the Treasury, in an effort to decrease its own liability, persisted in seeing Transjordan as 'exclusively a Palestinian interest,' and one for which Palestine should be made to pay.[9]

The high commissioner, Lord Plumer, strenuously objected to paying for the TJFF, however.[10] With even more vehemence he refused to make up Transjordan's civil deficit. He considered that Palestinian control of Transjordan, which he felt would naturally result from such an arrangement, was contrary to British policy. He became so incensed over the whole matter that he threatened to resign. In the end the Treasury arranged that Palestine's share would be five-sixths of the cost of the TJFF only, following the line of reasoning that security in Transjordan contributed to security in Palestine.

Plumer grudgingly agreed and completed his tour of duty. In any case, the TJFF proved incapable of patrolling the Transjordanian desert. When John Bagot Glubb was brought over from Iraq in 1930 to create a desert force as part of the Arab Legion, the TJFF retired back across the Jordan river to duties in Palestine.

Britain's close control of Transjordan's financial and military affairs could not have come at a worse time for Abdullah's stature in the region. While his dependence on Britain was being hammered into him in Transjordanian affairs, events on his borders worked to exclude him from the wider Arab arena.

The Wahhabi attack on Transjordan in August 1924 was not, as some liked to believe at the time, undertaken in collusion with Britain in order to force Abdullah to accept the ultimatum.[11] Rather, the raid was part of Ibn Saud's strategy aimed at conquering the Hijaz. Three weeks afterwards, his forces took Ta'if. On 3 October Husayn abdicated in favor of his eldest son 'Ali, and ten days after that Mecca capitulated. 'Ali hung on in Jidda for another year before following in his father's footsteps.

The road to Mecca and Ta'if had lain open to Ibn Saud since he had defeated Abdullah at Turaba in 1919. In the five years that had passed since then, he had not pressed his advantage against the Hashemites; instead, he had consolidated his position elsewhere in Arabia. The spring of 1924 found him in the north central part of the peninsula, which would be at his back during an attack on the Hijaz. The raid on Transjordan that summer coincided with a massing of Wahhabi forces on Iraq's border. Both maneuvers were designed to keep Husayn's sons at bay during the conquest of the Hijaz. It was by chance that one of the by-products of his strategy ensured Abdullah's unconditional acceptance of the ultimatum.

The Saudi conquest, although it took a year owing to religious sensitivities, was not difficult. Since the end of the war, Husayn's position had declined.[12] The Arab revolt had not culminated in the creation of a larger Arab state, but in the division of Arab territory and its subjection to European domination. Husayn did not become king of the Arabs, but simply king of the Hijaz. Freed from Ottoman suzerainty, his new independence was a mixed blessing. In the place of Ottoman largesse, he now received a dwindling British subsidy. For lack of an imperial framework, the pilgrimage also declined. The post-war upheaval had disrupted pilgrim traffic from Turkey and Syria, and political rivalry between Husayn and Ibn Saud and Husayn and King Fuad caused him to bar pilgrims from Najd and Egypt. To make up for the loss of revenue coming with the pilgrimage, he raised local taxes and charged the pilgrims who did come exorbitant fees. The final pilgrimage presided over by him was a 'scandal', owing to water shortages and extreme fees, and this failure to maintain an orderly pilgrimage cost him support in the Islamic world. The loss of outside revenue and rising taxes cost him internal support, especially among the tribes who were the military backbone of his regime.

Abdullah was an impotent bystander as his father's kingdom of the Hijaz tottered and fell. He had done what he could to smooth relations between his father and Britain, without success. Above all Britain had wanted a treaty with Husayn which it believed would help to moderate opposition to its Middle Eastern policies, especially in Palestine.[13] Abdullah had urged his father to sign such a treaty, and had negotiated one which he felt would be acceptable when Lawrence was in Amman in 1921, but Husayn refused to sign it. Britain then hoped that the threat of Ibn Saud would force him to soften his position. Sir Herbert Samuel voiced a common belief when he wrote, 'It is possible that the increasing menace to the Hijaz of Wahabite aggression may render King Hussein more amenable and more likely to subscribe to terms which would meet the needs of our policy in Palestine.'[14] However he was unbending, and in 1924 Britain withdrew its subsidy.

In the end, Husayn faced the Saudis and their forces of *ikhwan* virtually alone except for a few rickety planes bought from the Italians and manned by White Russian pilots.[15] Abdullah sent off some hundreds of tribesmen, Hijazis who had come with him to Transjordan, but these made no difference to the outcome. He also pleaded with Britain to intervene, but to no avail. After six years of worsening relations with Husayn, Britain did not lift a finger to help its old ally.

Unlike his sons, Husayn had not been able to make a successful transition from the old Ottoman framework to the new regional order dominated by Britain. Abdullah had made the necessary compromises and had got, in return, a throne, more or less secure. Faysal had made similar compromises and had also got a throne. (Owing to the structure of Iraq, he was able to counter the weight of Britain's imperial interests with local ones, thus creating a greater sense of independence for himself than Abdullah was ever able to do.) Husayn, however, never gave up trying to justify and legitimize his initial act of breaking away from the Ottoman Empire. Even after it became politically impossible to create the Arab kingdom he had hoped for, he continually strove to impose his moral hegemony, which was the only way left for him to win the approbation of Arabs and Muslims divided into rival states for the most part dominated by Europe. To this end, in part, he had assumed the caliphate. To this end also he had supported Arab demands in Palestine, refusing to conclude a treaty with Britain which would imply acceptance of Britain's Jewish national home policy. His refusal, in Abdullah's analysis, cost him his throne.

To Abdullah's chagrin, Britain prevented him from offering his father sanctuary. When Husayn left the Hijaz he headed up the Red Sea for Transjordan. Britain did not want the ex-king of the Hijaz to settle there, and asked him to remain in Aqaba until his future had been decided. Abdullah, in sullen compliance, sent tents to Aqaba for his father to live in while he continued to appeal his father's fate. In the meantime a fierce rivalry ensued between Palestine and Iraq as to which mandate was to avoid having Husayn.[16] Clearly he could not stay for long in Aqaba, since his presence there would be a magnet for disaffected Hijazis and a target for Ibn Saud. Ten months later Ibn Saud threatened to attack Aqaba and Husayn was quickly put aboard a British steamer bound for Cyprus. He lived there with his second wife, a Turk and the mother of Zayd, and their daughters until he fell mortally ill in 1930. At that time he was allowed to go to Amman to be close to his sons. He spoke and ate little for six months, and died on 4 June 1931 at the age of seventy-eight.[17] He was buried in Jerusalem in a small mosque abutting the *haram al-sharif*. A window was opened in the wall of the *haram* to connect the tomb with the sacred space. Hajj Amin al-Husayni, mufti of Jerusalem and later one of Abdullah's bitterest enemies, facilitated the funeral arrangements and delivered a eulogy at the ceremony in al-Aqsa mosque. Present at the burial were Arab and British dignitaries and uninvited emissaries from the Chief Rabbinate and the Jewish Agency.[18]

Husayn's fate seemed to confirm Abdullah in his path of least resistance. The lesson of the fall of the Hijaz, for him, was that common interests between himself and Britain had to be maintained at all cost. It was a lesson that was fresh in his mind when a revolt against the French broke out in Syria.

In the summer of 1925, events in Jabal Druze sparked a rebellion which spread to all of Syria and into Lebanon.[19] Jabal Druze lay just across Transjordan's northern border. In the past, Abdullah had had close relations with the Druze leader, Sultan al-Atrash, who had found refuge in Transjordan during the 1922 Druze uprising; in 1925, however, Abdullah was notable for his lack of response. The revolt lasted for almost two years. It called down upon Syria massive French retaliation – Damascus was bombed twice – and it attracted armed participants and financial support from surrounding states. It was, in short, the most important anti-mandate rebellion in the Middle East until Palestine erupted in the late thirties. Yet the man who only four years earlier had left Mecca to re-establish an Arab kingdom in Damascus stood aloof from the struggle.

Abdullah's standing in Syria plummeted thereafter. His aloofness was attributed to his desire to win France over to the idea of putting him on the throne. There were in fact other, better reasons. He was preoccupied with the final throes of the Hijaz, and Britain now had a tight grip on Transjordan's finances and military. With Britain's sanction, Druze non-combatants were permitted refuge in Transjordan, but, owing to French complaints, they were eventually hounded southward into Ibn Saud's domain.[20]

Abdullah's lack of support for the rebels came as something of a surprise.[21] Although Arab nationalists, many of them Syrian, had become disillusioned with him since his arrival in Transjordan, their disillusionment was not yet complete. He was still considered a useful symbol of Arab nationalism, representing the continuity of Arab demands from the time of the Husayn–McMahon correspondence and the subsequent non-fulfillment of British promises. After the suppression of the revolt, however, the grounds and goals of Arab nationalism shifted subtly. After the revolt, some Arab nationalists in Syria stopped seeing their future in terms of rectifying the broken promises of the past. Instead of looking backwards to Faysal's kingdom of Syria, they began to work within a new framework, one which concentrated more on Syria and less on pan-Arabism, and which was republican rather than monarchical. There was no place in this framework for Abdullah.

The failure of the Syrian revolt confirmed the regional trend, evident since 1921, towards the dissolution of pan-Arab nationalism. Arab nationalism now came to be organized in and focussed on each Arab mandated state, replacing the earlier emphasis on unity. The problem for Abdullah, based in Transjordan, was that Transjordan did not have the demographic or social structure to sustain a nationalist movement on its own. It lacked cities, the centers of learning, trade and wealth, which were the fountainhead of nationalist organization and ideology during the inter-war period. It lacked a sizeable middle class – the disgruntled professionals, merchants and clerics – whose interests were the first to be adversely affected by European interference in trade and finance, laws and government, education and religion. It lacked the numbers – the urban dwellers who could be quickly organized in demonstrations – to make an effective manifestation of popular feeling. It lacked the resources – Transjordan was dependent on a British subsidy – to make real independence believable. Hence Abdullah, confined to Transjordan, was unable to distance himself from the pressure of British interests.

The dearth of local pockets of independent power was both good and bad for Abdullah. On one hand, his relationship with Britain was never seriously challenged; on the other, he did not have the complex play of forces which would have allowed him to create an area of independent action for himself. While the leaders of the other Arab mandated states were not strangers to compromise with Europe, they were able to deal with Europe from a certain position of strength, from their position as leaders who, using nationalist ideology, could mobilize popular support to make things difficult for Britain or France. The concessions they gained were won in a complex process of manifesting political strength and leadership through strikes and demonstrations on the one hand, and negotiating with the mandatory power on the other. Concessions gained by Abdullah, however, were rewards for good behavior. Hence over the years he came to be seen in the region as a British puppet rather than as the Arab nationalist he considered himself to be.

Transjordan, standing alone, looked more like the amirates and shaykhdoms of the Arabian peninsula than its mandated neighbors to the north, west and east. Power was shared, unequally, between Britain and Abdullah. In 1927 the title of the chief British representative was changed to British resident, a title with a distinct imperial tradition. The commander of the Arab Legion was British, as were the chief officers under him. Besides Abdullah, the top Arab official was the chief minister, who, until the late 1940s, was always a naturalized Transjordanian with no local base of power independent from Britain or Abdullah. Without connection to a viable nationalist movement, the chief minister had to get along with both Britain and Abdullah. He was changed when he lost the confidence of the former and when the latter decided more would be lost by fighting for him than by giving in. The men who filled this post were, by definition, politically colorless individuals who rotated in and out of office without greatly affecting policy. The bureaucrats who were appointed to the executive council under the chief minister were more often than not naturalized citizens as well. No one had to answer to a politically motivated popular constituency on a regular basis, and each was able to make compromises to stay in office. The sum of individual compromises redounded to Britain's benefit.

British and Palestinian officials seconded from the Palestine administration helped to shape the new bureaucracy. In 1924 two British officers filled the posts of financial and judicial adviser and four Palestinians were appointed to the offices of civil secretary, postmaster general, and directors of public health and works. Later the number of seconded officials, both British and Palestinian, increased. In addition, Palestinians and Syrians served as medical officers, surveyors, teachers and agricultural officers, because there were no trained Transjordanians to fill these posts. Other Palestinians, for example the future chief ministers Ibrahim Hashim and Tawfiq Abu'l-Huda, dated from the earlier period but had been allowed to stay on after severing their nationalist connections. Samir al-Rifaʻi, another future chief minister, came to Amman from Palestine originally as a member of the RAF civilian staff.[22]

Syrians and Hijazis fleeing the current unrest in their own lands also added to the population of Amman in the mid-1920s. They did not move into the Transjordanian administration as readily as did the Palestinians, however. A group of Syrian merchants arrived following the French bombing of Damascus during the Syrian revolt.[23] These Syrians were more welcome than their politically-motivated predecessors had been – they were traders, and needed regional tranquility to ply their wares, mostly cloth and foodstuffs. British economic policies in Transjordan, which focussed on land settlement and land tax, did not threaten them, and duty was not charged on goods of Syrian manufacture. They settled easily into Amman life, becoming a prosperous community.

After the Saudi conquest of the Hijaz, numbers of Hijazis travelled to Abdullah's court. From among their ranks came Abdullah Sirraj, who served briefly as chief minister in the 1930s. Some, being skilled in tribal relations, helped Abdullah with tribal affairs. Others later joined the Arab Legion.

Specially escorted from the Hijaz came Abdullah's immediate family,[24] which by 1925 consisted of two wives and five children. His first wife, Sharifa Misbah, was the daughter of his uncle (Husayn's brother) Nasir. They had been married in 1902 and had two children, the Amir Talal (b. 1909), Abdullah's eldest son and heir, and a daughter, Haya. Abdullah's second wife, a Turk of Tatar origin, had originally been employed in Husayn's household in Istanbul. In 1908 when Husayn returned to the Hijaz as sharif of Mecca, she came with the family and Abdullah married her around 1912.[25] She subsequently bore three children, a son, Nayyif (b. 1914), and two daughters, Maqbula and Munira.

Abdullah's first duty in his family was to his eldest son. Talal was sixteen years old when the family moved to Transjordan. In the Hijaz, he had been educated by tutors at home as Abdullah had been in his time. After he arrived in Amman it was arranged that he be sent to England to be coached for the university entrance exam, aiming at admission to Oxford or Cambridge in two to three years' time.

Talal arrived in England for the summer term in 1926.[26] During his two years of private tuition, he stayed with two different tutors who regularly took on four or five live-in pupils for three eight-week terms a year. Although both of his tutors spoke highly of him, his general educational background before coming to England was soon discovered to be so deficient that it was decided to give up on university and aim for the Royal Military Academy at Sandhurst instead. In the fall of 1928 he enrolled as a cadet.

Although Talal may not have been an exceptional scholar, Mr F. Ezechial, who supervised and facilitated his educational and living arrangements in England, praised him as 'a lad of quiet and contented disposition' and 'an exceptionally nice fellow.'[27] He appeared anxious to please his father, and, like him, was an avid chess player. By December 1929, Talal, at age twenty, had finished his course at Sandhurst and was at a loose end. Altogether, he had spent three years in England with only one visit home in the summer of 1927.

Talal had never spent much time in his father's company and after returning to Amman it became apparent that the two did not get along. British advisers deemed it desirable to remove him from Amman for several more years and so he was sent to Cyprus to be attached, in an honorary capacity, to Sir Ronald Storrs' staff.[28] Soon after his arrival, his grandfather, Husayn, fell ill. He accompanied his grandfather to Amman and then went on to Iraq where he enrolled in the Iraq Army Military School. He returned to Amman for his grandfather's funeral and stayed on there afterwards, doing nothing and living on a small income from lands in Egypt and a £15 monthly allowance from Abdullah.

It was during this time that the problems between father and son became a matter of consternation to British onlookers. The high commissioner in Palestine, Sir John Chancellor, wrote in 1931: 'Talal must be removed from Trans-Jordan. His father bullies him intolerably and the poor boy is now completely cowed. The next thing will be that the malcontents will try and get him to intrigue against his father.'[29]

In February 1932 Talal was attached to the Middlesex regiment in Jerusalem, but his attachment barely lasted six months. His British superiors complained that he preferred to associate with Arabs rather than with 'brother officers.'[30] Colonel Cox, who sympathized with Talal and was concerned for him, recommended that he should get away from the palace either by getting married, in which case he would have to have a house of his own, or by undertaking another period of training in England. Talal's name was linked with several of his first cousins, the daughters of 'Ali and Faysal, but in the spring of 1934 he was engaged to Sfyneh, the daughter of 'Ali Haydar, Husayn's old rival for the sharifate. That summer, however, while Abdullah was in England, Talal's mother peremptorily broke off the engagement in favor of one with her niece, Talal's first cousin, Zayn.[31] Despite Abdullah's annoyance over the disruption of his own arrangements, Talal married Zayn in November 1934. The following November their first child was born, a son, who was named Husayn after his great grandfather.

Abdullah was fonder of his other son, Nayyif, by his Turkish wife. He had a jovial disposition, more like Abdullah's own than Talal's serious mien. Born in 1914, Nayyif was eleven when he came to Amman. In 1927 he was enrolled at a government school in Jerusalem.[32] While in Jerusalem he roomed at the Arab College under the supervision of the director of the college, Ahmad al-Khalidi, and was tutored privately in Arabic, English and religion by the college staff. Khalidi pronounced Nayyif 'ineducable' and word in the Colonial Office had it that he was 'backward and inclined to be lazy,' and that Talal, 'a very nice young man . . . [was] a better type than his brother.'[33] Although Abdullah wanted Nayyif to go to England for further education, the most that could be arranged was a course at Victoria College in Alexandria, a school modeled along the lines of a British public school, which he entered at age fifteen in the fall of 1929. After Victoria College, he enrolled for police training in Palestine. Here his education ended.[34] In later life, he was repeatedly characterized by British observers in terms recalling Ahmad al-Khalidi's blunt assessment.

In the summer of 1934, both boys met Abdullah in Jerusalem on his way home from England. Neither was in fact a boy at the time – Talal was twenty-five and Nayyif was twenty – though the impression they made at the British residency where they stayed was quite otherwise.

. . . they wore swords and spurs and one heard them rattling at the far end of the passage, like Punch ghosts, before they came into the room. The larger one had been to

Sandhurst . . . and was moderately friendly: the smaller could only snigger . . . behind his hand. They played hide and seek with their father along the passages until midnight – or that was the sound they made at any rate – and were up at half past four in the morning to have the Koran read to them by Dad.[35]

The women of the family lived lives largely hidden from public view. On arriving in Amman they took over Abdullah's newly built palace, Raghadan, which was divided into two apartments, one for each wife and her children. The windows were protected by wooden shutters which were usually closed in keeping with the customs of the Hijaz and Abdullah's ideas regarding the modesty of women.[36] His daughters, insofar as they were educated at all, were educated by tutors at home. For amusement they went on outings in a heavily curtained car and occasionally saw films from a secluded gallery at the RAF cinema. It was only under pressure from Lady Cox, the wife of the British resident, that a telephone was installed for Abdullah's wives. Zayn, Talal's new wife, who had been brought up unveiled in Egypt, was constrained to adopt the veil by her conservative father-in-law. Although their public lives were circumscribed, the women of the family managed property and wielded influence from behind the scenes.[37]

The arrival of Abdullah's family was symbolic of the settling and consolidation of Amman and Transjordan which was then beginning to get under way. Before 1925, little had been done to give substance to the handshake by which Churchill and Abdullah had created Transjordan. Afterwards, the creation of political institutions, the erection of borders, and the gradual in-migration of diverse communities began slowly to fill in the contours of Transjordan's political and social structure. An unofficial estimate (probably high) put the population of Amman at 20,000 after the influx of Syrians in 1925–6.[38] Although the permanent population was certainly less, a building boom resulted. Abdullah had begun to build himself a palace in 1923, the main streets were realigned and widened in 1925, and new shops and houses began to line the new streets. In the following two years offices for Abdullah and a British residency were built. Communications remained rudimentary: the telegraph system needed to be reconstructed, a bi-weekly motor service connected Amman with Baghdad, and portions of the Hijaz railway connected Amman to Ma'an, Haifa and Damascus. Amman published its first telephone directory in 1926, the postal service was regularized, and two newspapers appeared in 1927.[39] The earthquake of 1927 destroyed or damaged some Amman buildings which were then rebuilt with the aid of kibbutzniks from Palestine, and concrete.[40]

Raghdan Palace was modest but dignified in its sandstone simplicity. For Abdullah there was, on the first floor, a library, a small reception parlor, and an official dining room with a balcony from which bagpipers entertained dinner guests. On the second floor in front there was a large throne room for

Figure 9. Raghdan Palace, Amman, mid-1920s.

ceremonial functions. He held his weekly *salamlik* (men's reception) there on Friday mornings. The entrance hall to the official rooms was lined with distortion mirrors, and the effect of high commissioners and other august visitors growing tall and thin or short and fat, tickled his fancy as much as it disconcerted his guests.[41] A tent was erected on the palace grounds where he could relax.

Abdullah, however, continued his mobile lifestyle. He did so partly for political reasons, camping for weeks at a time in various parts of Transjordan to cement relations with tribes and villages, and partly for his own enjoyment. He always spent the winter months in the Jordan valley, refusing for many years to build a house there so that his wives could not join him.[42]

The addition of communities of Syrians, Hijazis and Palestinians provided

Abdullah with some diversity of forces which enhanced his local ascendancy, even if it did not allow him effectively to challenge Britain. He was able to keep Transjordanians at arm's length, away from formal institutions of power, as if he feared that their influence, rooted in local society, might supplant his own in the British scheme of things. Although he relied on local notables in the day-to-day business of informal government, with few exceptions he resisted formalizing their positions and bringing them into direct contact with Britain – at most they served on district administrative councils. He also put off for as long as possible the introduction of a constitution and an elected Legislative Council, fearing that democratization would erode his already limited power. Created in 1928, the Legislative Council proved to be an entrée for native-born Transjordanians to the Executive Council.

The introduction of constitutional government was the one condition, established by the 1923 assurance, for signing a formal agreement with Great Britain. And, with the completion of the Anglo-Iraqi treaty in 1927, Abdullah became very anxious to keep up with his brother Faysal by completing his own agreement with Britain.[43] It was in this context that he finally agreed to promulgate a constitution. In the event, the Anglo-Transjordan agreement formalized Britain's control of Transjordanian affairs stipulated in the ultimatum and expanded since that time. The constitution, however, with its creation of a Legislative Council, unexpectedly provided some play in the taut ropes that bound Abdullah to Britain.

For two years, from 1926–8, an agreement with Britain and the formal documents of constitutional rule had been in preparation. In the meantime such niceties of distinction as changing the appellation of Transjordan from *mantaqa* (district) to *amara* (amirate) and separating the Palestinian and Transjordanian functions of the high commissioner, so that in dealing with Transjordan he might be called simply the high commissioner for Transjordan, were meant to add to the substance of Transjordan's existence.

However, when the Transjordan paperwork was finished in 1928, the result was a disappointment to most who had been led to believe that an agreement with Britain would mean independence. Instead, the agreement detailed Britain's rights and duties in Transjordan.[44] These were extensive, having to do with foreign affairs, armed forces, communications and state finances. There was no express mention of Transjordan's independence in the body of the agreement, and Britain retained control of all crucial governmental activities. As before, Transjordan was made to bear the cost of the British resident and his staff as the first item on its budget. What Transjordan got in return was a continuation of Britain's yearly subsidy.

The constitution too was a limited document.[45] Its main innovation was a twenty-one-man Legislative Council of fourteen elected members, two appointed tribal representatives, and the chief minister and four other appointed

Executive Council members. The duties of the council were mainly advisory. Legislation could be introduced only by the chief minister or a head of department for approval by simple majority vote, 'subject always to the treaty obligations of His Highness the Amir.' The chief minister, who acted as the president of the Legislative Council, did not normally vote on matters in council, except to break ties, tipping the scales in the government's direction. The chief minister continued in form to be responsible to Abdullah, but it was Britain who ultimately rang the changes of chief minister.

The ratio of appointed to elected members and the method of election meant that the Legislative Council could be constructed to pose little trouble to either Abdullah or the British. The fourteen elected members came from three electoral districts: 'Ajlun (three Muslims and one Christian), Balqa' (three Muslim Arabs, two Circassians and two Christians), and Karak (three Muslims and one Christian). The minorities were over-represented. These members were elected by franchise for males of eighteen and over, in a two-stage election process. In the first stage electors were chosen at a ratio of one secondary elector to every 200 primary electors. The secondary electors who finally voted on the members of the Legislative Council were subject to persuasive manipulation since they were both identifiable and limited in number. The two tribal representatives were appointed from two tribal districts, north and south. The northern district included the Bani Sakhr, the Sirhan, the Bani Khalid, the 'Issa, and the Slayt, and the tribes and sub-tribes under their protection. The southern district included the Huwaytat, the Mana'iyun, and the Hajaya, and tribes and sub-tribes under their protection. Abdullah appointed a commission of ten for each district; the commission then chose the representative for the district. Those defined as beduin were thereby excluded from the franchise.[46]

Demonstrations erupted over the Anglo-Transjordan agreement.[47] Local leaders who expected to be elected to the Legislative Council exploited this unusual manifestation of popular will in an attempt to expand the powers of the legislature, and threatened to boycott the elections unless the Executive Council was made responsible to the Legislative Council. But the boycott was not pursued wholeheartedly, for these leaders were not about to give up their chance to participate in the formal politics of the central administration.[48] Indeed, members of the erstwhile opposition were elected to the new Legislative Council without winning their point, and they then proceeded to ratify the agreement.

None the less, the Legislative Council did give Abdullah some leverage with Britain. For example, it refused to pass the 1931 budget, apparently with his encouragement. The British resident then told him to dissolve the Legislative Council and change his Executive Council as well. He did so, but participated actively in the elections for a new Legislative Council to get men elected who would 'influence the other members to resist any measure against the will of the

Mandatory Power which he and his government could not resist openly.'[49] Although the budget was finally passed, Cox described what he thought Abdullah had hoped to accomplish thus:

His point of view . . . is that the Mandatory Power should believe that it is he alone who can make the wheels run smoothly and that whenever anything is to be done or whenever any mistake is to be rectified we should run to him for help. To this end . . . he likes to have a party . . . which under his orders will make difficulties and under his orders will clear them out of the way again.[50]

Abdullah, for his part, would have liked to get rid of the domineering Cox. At about this time he hinted to officials at the Jewish Agency that perhaps their influence in London could help in this direction.[51]

While Abdullah was playing politics with an emerging Transjordanian elite, Britain had embarked on programs which rationalized the landownership and tax structure of the country.[52] Such programs narrowed the discretionary powers which Abdullah had enjoyed in the early twenties to dispose of state lands and assess taxes in ways that were politically useful to him. A Department of Lands and Surveys was created for the purpose and put under a British director. Between 1928 and 1933 a fiscal survey was carried out, from north to south, and as a result of its findings land taxes were re-assessed and made uniform and equitable throughout the country. In 1933, the huge task of determining individual holdings and breaking up land held in common began, based on Ottoman and other written records, oral testimony, and arbitration. ʿAjlun, the most settled district, was the only area finished before the Second World War.[53] Some tribal land was broken up into individual plots. For example, some 5,000 title deeds were distributed to the Bani Hasan in the ʿAjlun district. Other tribes got some agricultural lands in individual holdings and some grazing lands held in common. In general, Britain's aim was to discourage the formation of large estates as had occurred in Iraq and to create a stable class of small- and medium-sized peasant landowners.[54] Some large landowners did emerge, however, notably the tribal shaykhs, Mithqal Ibn Fayiz of the Bani Sakhr and Sultan al-ʿAdwan of the ʿAdwan, the Karak notable, Rufayfan al-Majali, and Abdullah himself, who was awarded a grant of state lands at Britain's suggestion in 1931.

Regulating land tax and establishing a reliable land registry curtailed Abdullah's use of such resources to extend and cement his patronage networks. Starting in 1930, with the arrival of John Bagot Glubb, some of the tribes who had been the object of his patronage were removed from his reach as well. Throughout the 1920s Sharif Shakir had been Abdullah's chief tribal intermediary. He was the head of the Department of Tribal Administration, abolished by the 1924 ultimatum because its jurisdiction had crept into the settled areas,[55] and later head of the Beduin Control Board. Such special bodies were created to administer 'nomadic and settled Beduin,' who came under 'tribal law' instead of the *sharīʿa* and civil courts of the towns. (Who was considered beduin and why is not clear. By the time of Glubb's arrival the jurisdiction of the Bediun Control Board may have covered those tribes which were included in the northern and southern tribal areas for purposes of representation in the Legislative Council.)

Glubb was brought to Transjordan to eliminate raiding after completing a similar assignment in Iraq. As with land settlement, the elimination of raiding was meant to reduce friction and causes of discontent amongst the Transjordan population. Starting with a few recruits who came with him from Iraq, he created a desert patrol of about 150 men. Aided by armored cars, modern weapons and radio communications, the desert patrol was able to bring raiding to an end by 1932.

As commander of the desert patrol and second in command of the Arab Legion, Glubb became the chief intermediary between the 'beduin' and the government, replacing Sharif Shakir who died in 1934. He became the chief arbiter of tribal law;[56] during drought he organized relief from Amman, and during times of trouble he was given special sums to dispense to ensure the tranquillity of the tribal areas.[57] Although the desert patrol was only twelve per cent of the entire Legion establishment at the outset, as the Legion expanded in response to the Palestine rebellion of 1936–9 and the Second World War, the 'beduin' component grew to over half, giving the Legion its distinctive ethos. Through Glubb, Britain circumvented Abdullah in dealing with the tribes, and created a force distinctive, in the mandate period and later, for its imperviousness to Arab nationalism.

Glubb's desert force was formed just as Transjordan's borders were being formalized and demarcated. Britain guided negotiations in all frontier matters; what belonged to whom was determined mainly according to British interests. Because raiding complicated Britain's relations with Transjordan's neighbors, the French in Syria and Ibn Saud, and jeopardized its territorial interests, one of the purposes of the Legion was to halt raiding into Syria and Arabia. Borders with Palestine and Iraq, countries similarly under British control, did not present equivalent problems, although with the intensification of opposition to British policy in Palestine in the 1930s, the Legion helped to curb access to Palestine across its border with Transjordan.

Britain had been trying to settle the borders between Arabia and Transjordan since before the fall of the Hijaz. At the ill-starred Kuwait Conference, held during the winter of 1923–4, Britain had sponsored a plan whereby Abdullah was to give up his claims to Kaf at the upper edge of the Wadi Sirhan to Ibn Saud, in return for which Ibn Saud would give up Khurma to Husayn, who would then complete the circle by giving up Aqaba and Maʿan to Abdullah.[58] No one accepted the idea, and Husayn, in particular, had made a point of thwarting Britain's desire to get Aqaba and Ma'an for Transjordan when he reaffirmed his administrative control over the area during his visit to Transjordan in 1924.[59] But shortly afterwards, with the Saudi conquest of the Hijaz imminent, the disposition of Ma'an and Aqaba suddenly became important to Abdullah as well.

At first Britain offered to protect the Aqaba–Ma'an district as an inducement to Abdullah to secure its cession to Transjordan. Aware of Britain's motive, Abdullah agreed on condition that Britain mediate the Hijaz–Saudi war.[60] Britain refused, and Husayn abdicated and fled to Aqaba. His presence there made it a target for Ibn Saud, and Britain became more anxious than ever to secure it for Transjordan. Finally, when Ibn Saud complained that Husayn was aiding the Hijaz army from there and threatened to send forces northwards, Britain dislodged him.[61] After he had gone, Abdullah proceeded to Ma'an to announce the new administrative arrangements for the district. 'Ali acquiesced in the takeover which he could not prevent, commenting that he was too concerned with territory being annexed by his enemies to worry about that being taken by his friends.[62]

Even before the conquest of the Hijaz had been completed, Sir Gilbert Clayton had been sent to negotiate frontiers between Najd and the mandated states Iraq and Transjordan.[63] The Transjordan–Najd settlement, known as the Hadda agreement, was signed on 2 November 1925. A borderline was drawn, very nearly the present border between Saudi Arabia and Jordan, whereby Ibn Saud gave up his demand for a territorial link to Syria, but received free rights of passage to Syria through the Iraq–Transjordan corridor required by Britain for strategic purposes. All of Wadi Sirhan, including Kaf at its northwest end, was included in Ibn Saud's territory. Aqaba and Ma'an were not on the agenda of the Hadda negotiations, but in 1927 when Britain itself sought a treaty with Ibn Saud, the subject was broached. The Colonial Office was determined to get the territory for Transjordan, not so much because it was Transjordan's only outlet to the sea, but because Britain feared that if the Hijaz shared a border with Palestine and the Sinai, British control of Palestine and Egypt might be weakened.[64] At that time Ibn Saud acceded to Transjordan's temporary administration of the area, but refused to give up his claims outright.

The Syrian border had become a concern during the Syrian revolt. Before that time there was general agreement between Britain and France on the division of territory according to the terms of the Sykes–Picot agreement; during the revolt, however, the movement of Druze refugees across the border and the desire of the French to bring the Druze back under their jurisdiction encouraged the French to regard any place in Transjordan with a Druze population as a part of Syria. By 1927 the French interpretation of the border differed from the British by as much as twelve miles at some points. Identity cards issued by the Syrian state of Jabal Druze listed some domiciles as al-

Azraq, Jabal Druze, thus laying claim to the Azraq oasis well inside Transjordanian territory.[65] In 1931 the border was worked out on the ground. Britain made some concessions to the French, but secured what it needed in Transjordan for a projected Baghdad–Haifa railway (never built) and for the Iraq Petroleum Company pipeline.[66]

The borders, especially that with Arabia, were not especially to Abdullah's liking, but, according to Clayton, Abdullah knew his limitations: 'It is obvious to him . . . that he cannot hold territory beyond that which HMG is prepared to defend for him . . .'[67] Indeed, Abdullah did understand the limitations not only of his dependence on Britain, but of the structure of Transjordan that made his dependence all the more absolute. It was because of this basic understanding that he entertained throughout his life ambitions to expand his rule and thereby to alter in his favor the structure of his dependence. His dreams of expansion, in contrast to the daily reality of Transjordan, had no limits.

In particular, Abdullah dreamt of a Syrian throne. This ambition was one of the constants of his life to which he always returned, regardless of political reality. The Syrian revolt had shifted Syrian politics in such a way as to make his dream increasingly remote. After the revolt the question of monarchy so divided nationalist ranks that it became an embarrassment to be avoided as far as possible. In these circumstances it was the French, not the nationalists, who in times of stress and during elections drew the red herring of a throne across the nationalist path in hopes of splitting nationalist solidarity and deflecting nationalist pressure.[68] While fewer and fewer Syrians entertained a monarchical vision after the revolt, some continued to play politics with the various Arab monarchs and contenders for the hypothetical throne. Over the years, the list of candidates grew in length, but diminished in seriousness.[69] Abdullah's ambitions were kept in play, but their realization grew increasingly chimerical.

The Hijaz, after Ibn Saud's conquest, became another target for Abdullah's ambitions. In 1932 he was implicated in an unsuccessful tribal uprising there, and almost paid for his involvement with his throne since the adventure violated the Anglo–Transjordanian agreements of 1928, but Britain decided that a cast iron case had not been made against him. Within two months rumor had it that he was connected with yet another anti-Saudi movement, this time in 'Asir. This rebellion too was short-lived and his complicity never proved beyond doubt.[70] Soon thereafter Britain finally got him to sign a treaty of friendship with Ibn Saud which helped to reduce future adventurism. The negotiations were peculiar, being dominated on the Transjordanian side by Colonel Cox and the British minister in Jidda, Sir Andrew Ryan. Ibn Saud considered his relations with Transjordan to be 'in reality . . . relations between ourselves and the British,' and following his logic to the end, he insisted that Britain guarantee Abdullah's fidelity to the treaty.[71]

In the 1930s two new fields of endeavor opened up to Abdullah: Iraq, owing to the death of Faysal, and Palestine, owing to Britain's growing problems there.[72] Abdullah saw himself as unfairly deprived of Iraq by Faysal and the British in 1921. He was intensely jealous of Faysal and the two saw each other infrequently between 1921 and Faysal's death. He then tried, unsuccessfully, to establish himself as King Ghazi's mentor. After ʿAli's death in 1935 he began to put forward ideas of the unity of the Fertile Crescent under himself by reason of seniority. In geographical terms, however, Palestine was the more natural outlet for his ambitions. Britain's inability to work with the Palestinian leadership after 1936 created an *entrée* for Abdullah, who by reason of his dependence on Britain, would be a more malleable mediator between British interests and Palestinian aspirations.

Transjordan after 1924 resembled a patch of desert after a sandstorm. The wind of Arab nationalism had momentarily whipped up the dust devils of political change and had then moved on. The landscape left behind was familiar, but different. Abdullah looked less of an Arab nationalist than he had before 1921, while Britain looked less of a partner and more of a boss.

External events had unwittingly conspired with internal ones to validate the picture. The meaning of the 1924 ultimatum – the overt expression of British power in such a transaction – had barely sunk in before the Hijaz tottered and fell, partly for lack of a treaty with Britain. Abdullah's non-participation in the Syrian revolt further distanced him from nationalist politics, the universal counterweight of the period to British control. These events, while pushing Abdullah ever deeper into Britain's embrace, also reminded him that this embrace was not forever welcoming. An alliance with Britain was necessary, but conditional, and in 1928 it was Britain that laid down the conditions. The Anglo-Transjordanian agreement, with inequality written into every clause, was the price of his position and one that he was willing to pay. He expressed this vividly when, on receiving a ratified copy of the agreement, he seized it and fervently kissed George V's signature.[73]

This act, however, was in a sense deceptive. Abdullah had needed an agreement with Britain and was pleased to have it, but he did not necessarily like the circumstances he found himself in. Indeed, it was largely to escape the fixity of his internal position, marked most prominently by his relationship of dependence on Britain, that he so persistently indulged in adventures beyond his borders.

Chapter 7

Abdullah and Palestine, 1921–39

Palestine was never the sole or even the chief focus of Abdullah's ambitions, at least until 1947. Yet the unsettled future of that land and its shared subjection to British mandate gradually drew him into its affairs.

Geography and British political and military strategy dictated a close relationship between Transjordan and Palestine. Their particular governments were different, but the two fell under the same mandate, causing administrative overlap and certain common cares. The high commissioner for Palestine was also the high commissioner for Transjordan. In Palestine he was himself the head of government in a system which had no mediating 'native' bodies, at least for the Arabs. In Transjordan he was the repository of mandatory authority while Abdullah was the symbolic head of government.

The long border between Transjordan and Palestine was very permeable. Papers or passports were not generally needed to pass from one to the other. Trading ties had been encouraged ever since 1920 and the two territories shared the Palestine pound after its introduction in 1927. Transjordan served Palestine as a reserve of unskilled seasonal labor. Palestine provided Transjordan with trained men for its new bureaucracy. Economic problems in one reverberated in the other; political problems too resounded across the Jordan valley.

From the beginning, Abdullah's public utterances and actions with regard to Palestine were shaped by his need to get along with Britain. When he met Churchill at the Cairo Conference in 1921 he avoided criticizing Britain's Jewish national home policy.[1] He was accused in Palestine of 'having sold himself to the Zionist,'[2] but Britain was prepared to pay him for his trouble. As one British officer remarked at the time, 'Nothing was too bad for Abdalla till he came to Jerusalem and expressed himself favourable to Zionism, of course he isn't, and then nothing was too good for him.'[3] A year later he and Raghib al-Nashashibi, mayor of Jerusalem and a future ally, broke the Arab boycott of Samuel's swearing-in ceremony and were the only Arabs of rank to attend.[4] To express its appreciation, the mandatory administration urged the Colonial Office to indulge Abdullah's financial desires.[5] Thus a system of prompt material rewards was instituted to assure his co-operation in Palestinian affairs, and operated throughout his lifetime.

The Zionist movement was also interested in Abdullah. This was not because

103

he was felt to be influential in Palestine itself – rather, Zionist interest in Abdullah stemmed from the Zionist doctrine that Transjordan was a part of Palestine and ought, therefore, to be a part of the Jewish national home.

Just before the Cairo Conference, Weizmann had made plain the Zionist case for Transjordan. It rested, as did the claim to Palestine proper, on economic and strategic arguments dressed up in Biblical garb:

> . . . it is only through a permanent settlement of a peaceful population upon the Trans-Jordanian plateaux that the problem of the defence of the whole Jordan Valley can be satisfactorily solved . . . the fields of Gilead [ʿAjlun district], Moab [Balqaʾ and Karak districts] and Edom [Tafila and south], with the rivers Arnon [Wadi Mujib] and Jabbok [Zarqaʾ], to say nothing of Yarmuk . . . are historically and geographically and economically linked to Palestine, and . . . it is upon these fields, now that the rich plains to the north [south Lebanon] have been taken from Palestine and given to France, that the success of the Jewish National Home must largely rest. Trans-Jordania has from earliest time been an integral and vital part of Palestine. There the tribes of Reuben, Gad and Manasseh first pitched their tents and pastured their flocks.[6]

When Britain decided to set up a separate administration in Transjordan, Zionists were furious. Colonel Meinertzhagen for one described himself as 'foaming at the mouth with anger and indignation.'[7] The separation was accepted as a matter of temporary expediency, but the 'reunification' of the two banks of the Jordan remained a Zionist goal.[8]

It was Weizmann's policy that 'the road to Allenby Bridge along which we shall cross over to Trans-Jordan will not be paved by soldiers but by Jewish labour and the Jewish plough.'[9] Doctors from Tel Aviv were made available to Abdullah and his family. Colonel Kisch, the head of the Zionist Organization in Palestine in the 1920s, made regular visits. Kibbutzniks helped to rebuild Amman and Salt after the devastating 1927 earthquake.[10] In the early 1930s, several joint projects were discussed, for example, electricity, drainage, and paved roads for Amman.[11]

Abdullah was familiar with Zionist economic arguments in favor of co-operation. On the steamer which had taken him from Haifa to Trieste on his way to England in 1922, he had shared passage with A. M. Novomeysky, a Russian Jewish chemical engineer interested in extracting chemicals from the Dead Sea. Novomeysky accepted Zionist dogma that Transjordan was a part of Palestine, and during the voyage he expounded on the advantages to Abdullah of co-operation between the two territories.[12] These conversations were followed by a meeting in London with Chaim Weizmann, where Abdullah offered to guarantee the development of a Jewish national home if the World Zionist Organization would use its influence to help him become the king of Palestine.[13] His offer was rejected.

Novomeysky's case for economic co-operation later bore fruit for some

Jewish entrepreneurs. In 1927 the Palestine Electric Company under the chairmanship of Pinhas Rutenberg was allowed to buy 6,000 dunams of land in Transjordan at Jisr al-Majami' to build a plant at the confluence of the Zarqa' and Jordan Rivers. Abdullah ceremonially started up the turbines at the official opening of the plant. Despite his imprimatur, however, some Transjordanian consumers boycotted the electricity produced at the Jewish-owned plant by buying their own generators. In 1929 Novomeysky's company, the Palestine Potash Company, succeeded with co-operation from Transjordan in winning a concession to extract potash from the Dead Sea. Such schemes usually hid hopes that through them Jewish colonists might be introduced into Transjordan. For example, Rutenberg found his company did not need 6,000 dunams, and tried to arrange to sell the land to Jewish settlers. In 1936 he put forward another development scheme which would provide for the economic development of northern Transjordan and the settlement of Jewish colonists north of the Zarqa' River, the most fertile part of the country.[14]

In spite of Zionist claims, Zionist interest in Transjordan (and Abdullah's knowledge of this interest) was little more than a subtle undercurrent in Middle Eastern affairs throughout the 1920s. It was not until the 1930s that it became an irresistible undertow which dragged Abdullah out to sea. The reason for the intensification of Zionist interest in Transjordan lay in the aftermath of the 1929 Wailing Wall riots.

The riots led to a careful study of the effects of Jewish immigration in Palestine and to a reconsideration of British policy. The resulting Passfield White Paper established tight mandatory control of both land sales and immigration. Immigration was made specifically dependent on the capacity of the whole economy, Arab and Jewish, to absorb new immigrants.

This policy precipitated a renewed interest in Transjordan among Zionists. Although the White Paper was never put into effect, Zionist leaders had been badly frightened. They consequently sought a territorial safety valve to add to the area open to Jewish colonization or to be a spill-off area for the dispossessed Arabs of Palestine, and to bring down the price of land in Palestine. This safety valve was Transjordan.[15]

The sign of revived Zionist interest in Transjordan was the growing volume of contacts between Jewish settlers in Palestine and Transjordan Arabs. The possibility that these contacts would actually yield the desired fruit – the acquisition of land – had been improved by the settlement of title at that time being carried out in Transjordan which contributed to the 'ease with which a landowner can mortgage his property.'[16] Large landowners were the target of Zionist initiatives. They were considered doubly attractive, for they 'control the Legislative Council and sway public opinion.'[17] Zionist political strategists reckoned that if this group could be shown the virtues of Jewish capital investment, indeed if they themselves received the benefit of this investment,

Figure 10. Amir Abdullah starting up the turbines at the Palestine Electric Corporation plant at Jisr Majami'. Pinhas Rutenberg is standing directly behind Abdullah.

then they would bring the Transjordan government around to approving land acquisition and settlement by Jews.

This desire to expand land acquisition into Transjordan was matched by the need of the new class of large landowners for liquid capital to pay registration fees and taxes in order to secure their new landholdings. Two new tax laws, passed in 1932 and 1933, redistributed the land tax burden in Transjordan by district, in particular revising upwards the valuation of land in the Karak district. The new tax laws also changed the principle of taxation in the Balqa' district, where it had been a tithe based on actual production, to a flat rate per dunam, which had to be paid whether the land was cultivated or not.[18] Since land was virtually the only local outlet for investment, most large landowners sought to lease or sell part of their holdings to get capital to pay their taxes and develop the rest. Eagerness to sell or lease marginal land was aggravated by drought, which in 1933 was in its third year.[19]

The first to offer land to Jewish investors was Mithqal Ibn Fayiz. He owed the Transjordan treasury £P2,396 for 34,000 dunams (one dunam is about a quarter of an acre) which he had bought at Jiza, a village on the Hijaz railway south of Amman.[20] Unable to pay his debt, he contacted a Jewish investor, acting on behalf of the Palestine Land Development Company, in December 1930. He asked one pound per dunam for land which had cost him ten piastres per dunam, and an advance of £P2,500 since he could not sell the land until he paid his debt to the Treasury.[21] The Jewish Agency naturally baulked at such a large sum, and as his desperation for cash increased, so did his enticements. On top of the original offer he proposed to sell other lands in the vicinity of Jiza amounting to 100,000 dunams. Then he suggested getting together with other Bani Sakhr shaykhs a larger area of a half million dunams. Later he threw in the Azraq oasis, making a total offer of one million dunams.[22]

In the meantime other Transjordan notables came to the attention of Jewish investors. In 1932 two agricultural experts from Petah Tikva visited Transjordan to inspect the lands of Rufayfan al-Majali and Husayn al-Tarawna near Karak. Rufayfan also took them to a tract of land in the Ghawr al-Kibd which had recently been granted to Abdullah by the state. He 'said that the Emir had told him that he would be very happy if they would take the trouble and inspect the land also, and give necessary advice and help.' The verdict on the al-Majali and al-Tarawna lands was that they were suitable for citrus cultivation. Later, orange and banana groves were planted for both men in the interests of fostering good relations. As for Abdullah's land, 'they did inspect that land very superficially, but intimated to [Rufayfan] that when the time was ripe, good use could be made of the same . . .'[23] By the end of 1932 half a dozen other Transjordan landowners were on the Jewish Agency's list of possible contacts.[24]

Despite these promising beginnings, the Jewish Agency was only able to move very slowly. In order to capitalize on its shaykhly contacts the Agency needed two things: money, and a change of British policy which would allow the free and clear purchase of land in Transjordan. Contrary to the belief of many Arabs, Zionist finances were tight. The Jewish National Fund was reported to have little surplus over and above the sum needed for the payment of past purchases in Palestine. Justice Louis Brandeis was interested in the Transjordan project, however, and gave some money to Emanuel Neumann to further the cause. American Zionist interest in Transjordan was so vociferous that Chaim Arlosoroff, the head of the political department of the Jewish Agency, warned Brandeis that it might scare off potential Transjordanian sellers.[25]

Securing a change of policy was equally difficult. The discussion of the Passfield White Paper in London had raised the question of opening Transjordan to Jewish land acquisition for the settlement of Jewish colonists or displaced Palestinians. Weizmann and Lewis Namier (the noted historian, who, at that time, was the political secretary to the Zionist Organization in London) took up the issue directly with the Cabinet and the Middle East Committee. British officials were extremely cautious, however, claiming that the 1928 Anglo-Transjordan agreement prevented them from interfering in Transjordanian affairs. They counseled that a Zionist footing in Transjordan could be made only by coming to terms with Abdullah. Rebuffed in London, the Zionist front moved to Jerusalem. Weizmann and the Baron Edmund de Rothschild tackled the high commissioner, Sir John Chancellor, in turn, both without success. Nor was there any luck to be had with the new high commissioner, Sir Arthur Wauchope, who took up his duties in mid-1931. The most that British officials in London and Jerusalem would say was that the eventual opening of Transjordan to Arab and Jewish settlers was not ruled out, but the present was not the proper time.[26]

There remained the possibility of getting around British caution by coming to terms directly with Abdullah. To understand how this was done, it is necessary to return to the 1929 Wailing Wall riots.

During the riots, as during other disturbances in Palestine, Abdullah was expected to keep the peace in Transjordan and to prevent his subjects from entering the fray. Although Transjordanian tribes did threaten to cross the Jordan and demonstrations did take place in the towns, the lack of organization in and between these movements meant that Abdullah's efforts to keep Transjordan quiet were highly successful, allowing most of the Imperial Forces stationed there (the RAF and the TJFF) to be moved to Palestine.[27] In reward for his services, it was decided to give him a private estate of state lands, an idea proposed by Cox several years earlier as a way for Britain to increase Abdullah's income at minimal cost to itself. The idea had the additional attraction of further tying his interests to Transjordan and of possibly inspiring his younger son Nayyif to take up the occupation of gentleman farmer. Since Britain did not itself have the authority to give away Transjordanian land, the matter was put through the Legislative Council, which duly passed a law granting Abdullah the land. Later he was exempted from taxation on his new estates and the Colonial Office gave him £P3,000 to help him start his agricultural enterprise.[28]

The land was in three tracts: 3,000 dunams at al-Humar (or 'Ayn Humar), 2,000 dunams in the Zawr al-Kattar, and 60,000 dunams in the Ghawr al-Kibd. Al-Humar was at that time the most valuable. On high ground about twelve miles west of Amman, it had a spring and could be partly irrigated. At the time it was given to Abdullah it was leased by Turcoman peasants from the government at £P102.600 a year. In 1933 Abdullah leased it to Zayd al-Atrash, brother of the Druze leader Sultan Pasha al-Atrash, and 'Uqla al-Kitani, a Greek Orthodox Christian and close adviser to the Atrash clan, at an annual rent of £P150. When it was assessed to see how much the government would forfeit by exempting Abdullah from taxation, the potential income of the estate was calculated at £P660, meaning an annual revenue loss of £P66. The Zawr al-Kattar estate was adjacent to the Jordan river immediately to the north of the Allenby bridge. In 1930 it was uncultivated, though it was judged to be readily irrigable and suitable for oranges and bananas. By 1933, when it was assessed for taxation, it was still uncultivated. At that time it was estimated that only 1,000 dunams would be arable after clearance and reclamation, yielding a potential annual income of 50 mils per dunam. The Ghawr al-Kibd land was by far the least immediately valuable. It lay in the Jordan valley bounded on the north by the Zarqa' river. Although it was potentially arable if water could be got to it, in 1930 it was worth practically nothing since none of the waters of the Zarqa' were available for its irrigation and the cost of pumping water from the Jordan river was prohibitive. When it was assessed for taxation in 1933 it was assumed that there would be no income from the land for some time to come.[29]

As a landowner, Abdullah joined the ranks of the landowning tribal shaykhs and town notables. Like them he had land, but neither the know-how nor the capital to do anything with it. Like them he was also a target of Zionist interest, on account of his property and his position. Zionist representatives could now appeal to him to allow Jewish purchase of land and immigration, not only for – as they maintained – the general good of his country, but for his personal profit. He had been approached, in the general sense, by Lord Reading (chairman of the board of the Palestine Electric Corporation) and by Chaim Arlosoroff, but nothing concrete had been achieved. He told Lord Reading that he personally had no objection to Jewish colonists, but that his people might, and he repeated to Arlosoroff that he personally did not fear Jewish immigration, but added that such a fear did exist in Palestine and neither he nor the Jewish Agency could ignore it.[30] Something concrete was achieved, however, when Emanuel Neumann and Joshua Farbstein, representing the Jewish Agency, approached him with the intent of leasing his lands in the Ghawr al-Kibd. They did not get a lease outright – rather, they signed an option which reserved the lease for them at a cost of £P500 for six months. The lease affixed to the option was for thirty-three years, renewable twice for a total of ninety-nine years at £P2,000 a year plus five per cent of the net annual profit. It was assumed that the lease would go through as soon as political difficulties had been cleared up. The cost of the option was to be subtracted from the first year's rent.[31]

Abdullah's deal with Farbstein and Neumann was not the first time he had tried to lease the Ghawr al-Kibd lands. Earlier in 1932, through the intercession of his old friend, 'Abbas Hilmi, he had made a similar but more lucrative deal with the Compagnie Agricole Industrielle et Commerciale d'Orient in Lucerne. At that time he received a £2,000 deposit for the lease of the Ghawr al-Kibd pending a study of its utility. If the lease was not taken up, and it was not, he did not have to pay back the deposit.[32]

Financially, Abdullah had made quite a killing. For land deemed valueless by British tax assessors, he had received £P2,500 from the Compagnie and the Jewish Agency. In March 1933, when he extended the option with the Jewish Agency for another six months, he received another £P500.[33] Three thousand pounds, unbudgeted and unaccounted for by Britain, was for him a considerable windfall (his civil list for the year was £P14,481). And, since he had not actually leased the land, he got it seemingly for nothing. There were hidden costs, however.

News of the option got out immediately. After a loud and adverse reaction, especially in Palestine, Abdullah published an official disavowal,[34] but it was in fact a sham. Secretly, he wrote to reassure his prospective leaseholders that the option remained operative.[35] His later extension of the option confirmed his intention.

Ongoing rumors of Abdullah's dealings with Jewish settlers had serious repercussions for his reputation, especially in Palestine; yet it is not clear that Abdullah had Palestine in mind when he embarked on the deal. At the time, he was suspected of fomenting tribal revolts in the Hijaz and 'Asir and he may have felt that money to support these revolts was more important than his reputation in Palestine. Sir George Rendel, head of the Eastern Department, described Abdullah's analysis of the Saudi situation in 1932 as follows: 'At this date he was firmly refusing to recognize King Ibn Saud of Arabia on the ground, as he explained to me, that Saudi Arabia was in a state of anarchy (which we knew to be untrue) and that Ibn Saud's rule was crumbling (obvious nonsense). I was unable to shake him on either point . . .'[36] The revolts were easily crushed, however, and shortly afterwards Britain finally got him to sign a treaty with Ibn Saud.

During the spring and summer of 1933 the controversy over the option grew more heated. At a time of rising Jewish immigration, it was not easily glossed over or forgotten. Indeed, it took on a life of its own in Transjordanian politics and in wider, pan-Arab politics.

Locally, Abdullah could count on the support of the small group of large landowners who hoped for similar financial gain. In April the Jewish Agency held a banquet at the King David Hotel attended by several Transjordanians.[37] Several days later Mithqal mortgaged 750 dunams at the village of Barazin against a loan of £P650.[38] With Abdullah's urging, these landowners formed a 'party' in his support, first the *Hizb al-Tadamun* (Solidarity Party) under Mithqal Ibn Fayiz, later the People's Party under Majid al-'Adwan. Both were ephemeral.

Against Abdullah was ranged popular feeling, kept alive to the issue by the Palestine press, and a diverse group that came together in an opposition 'party.' It was composed of a wide array of political activists and bureaucrats who had a larger vision of forces at work in the Arab world, and who, in addition, did not have the landed interests of those who supported the option. The figurehead of this group was Husayn al-Tarawna, who himself had been in touch with the Jewish Agency regarding his land near Karak. His antipathy to the option appeared to be rooted less in anti-Zionism than in the local politics of Karak, where the al-Majalis had the upper hand while the al-Tarawnas were their chief rivals. Since the al-Majalis were outspokenly in favor of economic transactions with the Jewish Agency, Tarawna necessarily took the other side of the argument regardless of his previous conduct. Yet the opposition was not wholly opportunistic. It included men as widely different as the Hijazi, Abdullah Sirraj, the current chief minister; the Palestinian, Tawfiq Abu'l-Huda, the current chief secretary; and the Syrian pan-Arabists, 'Adil al-'Azma and Subhi Abu Ghanima, both members of the Legislative Council. They were motivated by a variety of considerations, some of local and regional political strategy, others of principle.

Because of the regional implications of the option, pan-Arab parties also became involved, foremost among them the newly reconstituted Istiqlal party based in Palestine.[39] Like the old Istiqlal it professed a pan-Arab ideology which aimed at eliminating local and personal jealousies and confessional differences in the common struggle against foreign domination in all Arab countries. Its founders were old Istiqlalis like 'Awni 'Abd al-Hadi, 'Izzat Darwaza and Subhi al-Khadra, to whose ranks had been added Palestinians too young to have been active in the original Istiqlal. Besides ideology and membership, the new Istiqlal inherited two other characteristics from its predecessor: an internal split between supporters of the Hashemites and supporters of the Saudis, and, among Hashemite partisans, a proclivity for Faysal rather than Abdullah.

The involvement of the Istiqlal with the Transjordan opposition and a visit by Faysal to Amman in the summer of 1933 brought the political temperature to the boil. Behind the turmoil, on one side, lay the fear that Transjordan was about to be thrown open to Jewish colonization. It was rumored that the opposition was demanding the unification of Transjordan and Iraq to prevent such a step. On the other side, Abdullah's reaction was rooted in defensiveness and intense alarm at the amount of criticism levelled against him. Bristling with his old jealousy and resentment of his brother, he suspected that Faysal himself was a party to the demand for unification. Indeed, so sure was he of nefarious carryings-on that he dispatched his eldest son Talal to the desert to keep him from meeting Faysal and falling into some conspiracy. He also had a severe argument with his old friend and comrade-in-arms, Sharif Shakir, whom he accused of supporting Faysal.[40] He then launched a general offensive against the Transjordan opposition and against the Istiqlal in particular. Both sides organized congresses and various other public forums to air their differences. Feelings ran extremely high, with both groups, loyalists and opposition, freely abusing each other. One prominent member of the opposition was thrashed in the main street of Amman, naturally Abdullah's stronghold.[41]

The shock of Faysal's untimely death in early September knocked the wind out of the rising political passions. Abdullah immediately sought a reconciliation with the Istiqlal, and the pro-Hashemite Istiqlal leaders 'Adil al-'Azma and 'Awni 'Abd al-Hadi travelled in his suite to the funeral in Baghdad.[42]

111

*   *   *

Faysal's death left a void at the pinnacle of the Arab national movement. Ever since the short-lived Arab Kingdom of Syria, he had been regarded as the symbolic leader of the pan-Arab movement and the heir to the throne of a united Arab kingdom, and despite the dissolution of pan-Arabism in practice, it remained an ideologically potent ideal.

Abdullah had always been jealous of his younger brother's pre-eminence, and, when he died, Abdullah hoped to take his place. But, the gift of land which Britain had intended would tie him to his country had done so in unexpected ways. He was now identified with a small group of Transjordan landowners[43] and more remote than ever from larger regional concerns. His attempts to strike a pose of regional leadership on the heels of his recent transaction with the Jewish Agency were at best not taken seriously and at worst suspected of masking treachery.

The occasion for Abdullah's major campaign to assume a position of Arab leadership was an invitation to visit London. In the six months before his departure in June 1934, he exerted himself to the utmost to get a mandate from Palestinian leaders to speak on their behalf to the British, but his efforts fell flat. He was not accepted as a spokesman by any of the major Palestinian leaders or parties. So great was their distrust of him that it was even suggested that ʿAwni ʿAbd al-Hadi arrange to be in England at the same time to keep an eye on him. The only figure of any stature who encouraged Abdullah's pretensions was Raghib al-Nashashibi, who had been at Abdullah's side twelve years previously at the first high commissioner's inauguration. But he carried little weight compared to the majority Palestinian sentiment against Abdullah voiced by the Istiqlal Party and by Hajj Amin al-Husayni, who, as *mufti* of Jerusalem and president of the Supreme Muslim Council, was the most powerful Arab politician in Palestine.

Abdullah's attempt to enter the arena of Palestinian politics brought him into direct conflict with Hajj Amin. Relations between the two had never been warm. Their mutual antagonism was obvious as far back as 1921, when, one day after lunch at Government House in Jerusalem, Hajj Amin pointedly suggested that Abdullah take a nap so he could talk to the high commissioner alone.[44] However it was not until the mid-1930s, when Abdullah began to compete for the position of chief intermediary between Britain and the Palestinians, that relations between the two began to show the open rancour that, in 1951, led many to lay Abdullah's assassination at Hajj Amin's door.

Before Abdullah left for London, Wauchope warned the Colonial Office that 'any representations he may make will be purely on his own and without the support of any body of opinion.[45] Any lingering uncertainties about his acceptability as a spokesman for Palestine were graphically dispelled the moment his ship weighed anchor. Within the hour proclamations were

Figure 11. Amir Abdullah and King Faysal at the Haram al-Sharif in Jerusalem, July 1933.

published in Palestine and Transjordan denouncing any negotiations he might carry out in London on behalf of Palestine.[46]

In the event, Abdullah's trip to London had very little political content and was arranged instead for good will purposes. He made a loop tour to Edinburgh by way of Oxford, Stratford and the Lake District, returning to London through York and Cambridge, and he attended such diversions as Ascot, the International Horse Show, and the British Empire Polo Trophy Meeting, a program which catered to his well-known love of horses.[47] When he got back home he described all of it enthusiastically to the high commissioner:

. . . how he saw over the Humber factory, how he went to the House of Commons and sat in the distinguished strangers' gallery and got a wave from Sir Herbert Samuel, how he went to the aeroplane display at Hendon and watched men coming down from aeroplanes in parachutes and had to hide his eyes till the parachutes opened; how he went to Edinburgh and was met by the Lord Provost, and to Peebles and stayed at the best hotel: he told all this like a boy of 14 just back from Wembley, trying all the time to think what was the next most exciting thing that he had seen: he had a beautiful childish power of description – especially when he began to imitate the aeroplanes and the fizz of the bombs

113

Figure 12. Amir Abdullah, ex-King 'Ali of the Hijaz, Hajj Amin al-Husayni and delegates to the Jerusalem pan-Islamic Conference, Shuna, 1931.

as they dropped hitting the ground: he had brought presents for H. E. in the proper oriental way – photographs of himself in a striking attitude, cigars, tuffets, and (his best present) an iced cake in the shape of a mosque from McVities – to remind H. E. of the Dome of the Rock whenever he ate it I suppose – but unfortunately the dome had been smashed completely on the way, and the walls of the Rotunda were badly caved in on the east side.[48]

But he had been unable to use his relationship with Britain to seek a settlement in Palestine and to vault himself into Faysal's vacant position. His land dealings with the Jewish Agency had cost him too much in credibility amongst his own.

Abdullah had no one but himself to blame for his predicament. He had been too eager to make some easy money – and too clever – and he seemed to have little idea of the principle involved and no conception of the political conse-quences for one in his position. But Britain bore some of the responsibility for bringing him to his present pass. In a sense, Britain had provided the rope and Abdullah had hanged himself, in the matter of land deals with the Jewish Agency.

Ever since Transjordan had re-emerged as a focus of Zionist lobbying efforts in the wake of the Passfield White Paper, Britain had given out contradictory signals regarding its attitude towards Zionist ambitions in Transjordan. Rather than sticking by the terms of the mandate, which clearly excluded Transjordan from the area of Jewish settlement, British officials in London and Jerusalem had adopted the formula that eventual Jewish settlement was possible, though the present was not the proper time. The high commissioner, for example, used his influence in Transjordan to prevent the Legislative Council from passing a law forbidding the sale or lease of lands to foreigners, because, as Moshe Shertok understood him, 'he was definitely in favour of Jewish settlement activities being extended to Transjordan in the future. . .'[49] Yet the law on the books which allowed foreigners to buy land subject to the permission of the government was sufficiently protective that when Mithqal leased his lands, Britain felt constrained to warn that there was 'no guarantee that the lender will ever see the colour of his money, or obtain its equivalent in land.'[50]

In such a situation the Jewish Agency naturally did what it could to make the present the proper time for Jewish settlement in Transjordan. Getting Abdullah's support through the option was an important part of its effort. Even though the high commissioner had disapproved of the option as damaging to Abdullah's prestige and therefore to his effectiveness as an ally, he none the less helped to draw up a set of conditions, which was accepted by Weizmann, to govern future Jewish settlement in Transjordan.[51] However in succeeding years, when the option came up for annual renewal, Britain grew more reticent about settlement possibilities owing to rising tensions in Palestine. The alternative, that Arabs from Palestine might settle in Transjordan if Jews could not, was rejected vehemently by the high commissioner as even more politically explosive than Jewish settlement itself, because 'it would be looked upon as tantamount to expulsion . . .'[52]

By 1935, the continuation of the option had assumed the character of a political subsidy to Abdullah. The Jewish Agency had always been aware that for Abdullah and other Transjordan landowners, the Jews were 'a milch cow,' but it was apparently worth the investment to keep Abdullah friendly. Even though the opening of Transjordan to Jewish settlement was not likely in the near future, the option was renewed in January 1935 for four more years at a cost of £P3,500.[53]

Britain had made possible Abdullah's transactions with the Jewish Agency, but Abdullah paid the price for them in political frustration. If Faysal's death created an opening on the pan-Arab stage, Abdullah's dealings with the Jewish Agency underlined his unsuitability to fill it. Yet his adventures in Palestine were by no means over. In 1936, accumulated tensions there reached flashpoint. The resulting explosion caused Britain to rethink its Palestine policy. In the process, new possibilities and new pitfalls presented themselves to Abdullah.

Nineteen thirty-six was a year of unusual turbulence throughout the Middle East. At the turn of the year massive popular strikes and demonstrations paved the way for the return to parliamentary government in Egypt and for the resumption of Anglo-Egyptian negotiations. In January and February a fifty-day general strike in Syria ended when a nationalist delegation was invited to proceed to Paris to begin negotiations for a Franco-Syrian treaty. In April, Palestine exploded.

Immediately behind the explosion in Palestine lay three years of very high rates of Jewish immigration fueled by the precipitate rise of fascism and anti-Semitism in Europe. By 1936 it had become obvious to the Arab population that if something were not done immediately to stem this tide, their country would soon be changed beyond all recognition and beyond all hope of reasserting their rights therein. At the same time the idea of a strike, popularized by the success of the general strike in Syria, was in the air. And so in mid-April, when the desperation and frustration of the Arab community boiled over in a series of murders of Jews by Arabs and was met by retaliatory killings of Arabs by Jews, mass meetings in the towns of Palestine called a strike and named local committees to organize it. The aims of the strike, formulated by the heads of the diverse Palestinian parties which came together in a national steering and co-ordinating committee, the Arab Higher Committee, under the presidency of Hajj Amin al-Husayni, were the cessation of Jewish immigration, the prohibition of land transfers from Arabs to Jews, and the introduction of self-governing institutions.[54]

For Abdullah, the strike was another opportunity to do what he had been prevented from doing two years earlier: carve out a role for himself in the Arab world by mediating between Palestine and Great Britain. Indeed, he was at the moment in a better position than most Arab leaders to do so since he had good relations with Britain and was not enmeshed in disputes and negotiations of his own with Europe, like Egypt and Syria, or preoccupied with internal unrest like Iraq. He was also anxious to work out a compromise lest the growing gulf between Britain and the Arabs become too wide to straddle. The Arab Higher Committee itself decided to enlist Abdullah's support in order to prevent him from working at cross purposes. To that end, members of the committee visited Amman. He urged them to call off the strike and send a delegation to London, but they refused.[55]

Britain's response to the strike was to propose sending out a Royal Commission to study the situation as soon as the strike was called off. On hearing this news, Abdullah again met with the Arab Higher Committee and again advised it to call off the strike. As before, the committee refused, but it did make plain the minimum concession necessary to stop the strike: a temporary cessation of Jewish immigration for the duration of the Royal Commission's visit. Abdullah's task then became clear. If he could not convince the committee to call off the strike unconditionally, he had somehow to bring about a temporary suspension of immigration.

Abdullah first approached Britain, but without success. He then turned to Zionist leaders in Palestine. He hoped to convince them to declare a moratorium on immigration voluntarily, or at least to take the pressure off Palestine by redirecting settlers to Transjordan. In this way a semblance of stemming immigration might be achieved which would allow Britain and the Arabs of Palestine to compose their differences. His appeals rested on the premise that 'the land is burning under their (the Arab Higher Committee's) feet and some help must be given to the leaders to regain some of the people's confidence,' and presumed that Jewish leaders would rather not have to cope with a fully mobilized Palestinian population.[56] But the Jewish Agency did not agree to take such a step, and, at the beginning of June, Abdullah summoned the Arab Higher Committee to Amman to urge once again that the strike be ended unconditionally. Once again he was refused.

It was not until the end of July that a faint breeze from Britain suggested that the diplomatic doldrums might break. On the 29th the Secretary of State for the Colonies, William Ormsby-Gore, was scheduled to announce the terms of reference and the composition of the Royal Commission. A week before he had been asked in Parliament to assure the House that there would be no change in immigration policy until after the commission had completed its investigation and reported its recommendations. He gave the required assurance, but appeared to suggest that a temporary suspension of immigration was still possible if the strike were called off first.[57]

This possibility stirred Abdullah to new activity. He approached the Arab Higher Committee again, this time in a manner originally suggested to him by the Jewish Agency.[58] He offered to make a public appeal to the committee, 'as a Hashemite and a guardian of Arab interest,' to end the strike. In the appeal he would praise the committee for 'their persistence and sacrifice' and promise to speak to the Royal Commission on their behalf. In reply the Arab Higher Committee would publish a declaration praising the strike effort but asking Palestinians to respect Abdullah's wishes. This suggestion, remarkable for its similarity to the strategy that finally brought the strike to an end in October, was discussed for hours. But, of the committee, only Raghib al-Nashashibi supported Abdullah. The rest baulked at giving him such authority in Palestinian affairs, and Hajj Amin ended the debate by making Abdullah's intercession conditional on Ormsby-Gore's statement to Parliament. If Ormsby-Gore made certain promises, then the committee would empower Abdullah to appeal to the nation to end the strike and would endorse his appeal.[59]

Not content to sit idly by, waiting for Ormsby-Gore's pronouncement, Abdullah sent off his confidence man, Muhammad al-Unsi,[60] to the Jewish Agency with a report about his meeting with the Arab Higher Committee and a request for help in getting the Secretary of State to 'say something nice' to the Arabs in his speech. Moshe Shertok (later Sharett), head of the Political

Department, agreed and visited the high commissioner, who in turn promised to wire London that Mr Shertok, 'while reiterating the opposition of the Jewish Agency to any form of suspension of immigration . . . suggests that in tomorrow's statement the Secretary of State should include an appeal to the statesmanship of the Arab leaders to stop violence and help restore normal conditions.'[61] Unfortunately for Abdullah, Ormsby-Gore's much-anticipated statement contained no special messages or promises for the Arabs, although it left open the question of a temporary suspension of immigration.

Abdullah, encouraged by Wauchope, continued to believe that Britain would suspend immigration during the commission's investigation. On 5 August he again invited the Arab Higher Committee to Amman in hopes of convincing them of his belief. To improve his chances he packed the meeting with Palestinians not included in the committee, partisans of his ally Raghib al-Nashashibi. His tactics misfired, however. The committee refused to make Abdullah's leap of faith, and demanded written guarantees before calling off the strike – guarantees which he was unable to secure. Worse, his action accentuated a growing split in the committee between those led by Hajj Amin, who continued to hold out for the suspension of immigration, and those more ready to compromise on the point, represented by Raghib al-Nashashibi. A temporary increase of disorders in Palestine following Abdullah's intervention demonstrated Hajj Amin's superior power.[62] Two weeks later, the Arab Higher Committee sent a letter to Abdullah thanking him for his efforts to find a solution to the crisis.[63] It was in fact an abrupt dismissal.

No sooner was Abdullah discarded than a new mediator appeared, Nuri al-Sa'id, the foreign minister of Iraq. Nuri's was not a new presence in Palestinian affairs. From the beginning of the strike the Arab Higher Committee had asked Arab rulers to speak up in support of the Palestinian Arabs and most had done so. Nuri al-Sa'id, Ibn Saud and some Egyptian leaders had all directed appeals and offers of mediation to British officials in their respective countries or in London, and Nuri and Muhammad 'Ali Alluba (a leader of the Liberal Party in Egypt) had also spoken to Zionist leaders along lines similar to Abdullah's approach. But none of these could take part in the daily political bargaining that was current in Palestine with the same degree of intensity and intimacy as Abdullah. Nuri's arrival in Jerusalem on 20 August dramatically changed all that. In Jerusalem, Nuri took over the field of face-to-face negotiations with the Arab Higher Committee, the Jewish Agency and the British administration, a sphere that previously had been uniquely Abdullah's.

Abdullah was angry about the way the Arab Higher Committee had brushed him off and about Nuri's subsequent intervention.[64] He refused to attend a reception at Government House in Jerusalem for Nuri and pointedly told Cox that he did not see how Nuri's effort could succeed since it depended on his securing the same promises from Britain which had so far eluded himself. He was especially piqued because his own ally on the Arab Higher Committee, Raghib al-Nashashibi, had welcomed Nuri's mediation with open arms. But he did not interfere except to ask London to keep him abreast of developments. He was mollified to hear that Nuri got no concessions.

Nuri's initiative failed, and in early September 1936 London announced its intention to end the strike by force. However, in the time that it took for the legal details of martial law to be worked out and for more British forces to reach Palestine, attempts to find a diplomatic and peaceful resolution were intensified, culminating in the appeal by the Arab kings and amir which ended the strike just as the machinery of martial law was ready to go into operation.

Abdullah felt that the collective approach was meant to neutralize the effects of his personal mediation and he took no part in framing the appeal. Indeed, he worked to undercut the joint appeal in a final attempt to get London to guarantee concessions to him in confidence, which would allow him to regain control of mediation. At the last minute, however, his name was associated with it through the insistence of Raghib al-Nashashibi.[65]

On 9 October the kings of Saudi Arabia and Iraq, the imam of Yemen, and Amir Abdullah sent the prepared declaration:

Through the President of the Arab Higher Committee to our sons the Arabs of Palestine: we have been deeply pained by the present state of affairs in Palestine. For this reason we have agreed with our brothers the Kings and the Emir to call upon you to resolve for peace in order to save further shedding of blood. In doing this, we rely on the good intentions of your friend Great Britain, who has declared that she will do justice. You must be confident that we will continue our efforts to assist you.[66]

This statement was published two days later along with one from the Arab Higher Committee calling on the Arabs of Palestine to end the strike. In response they put down their arms with relief and resumed their normal economic activities after the long siege. The Royal Commission could now proceed on its mission.

Abdullah celebrated the end of the strike by taking a vacation in Egypt. The preceding six months had been both busy and stressful. Although Transjordan did not manifest the political effervescence that had characterized neighboring Arab countries in 1936, it was affected by it, and especially by the events in Palestine. Communications installations, oil pipelines and government offices in Transjordan were sabotaged, and solidarity strikes and demonstrations took place in Transjordan towns. Among activists two schools of thought developed: those who wanted to organize Transjordanian levies to join the struggle in Palestine, and advocates of local rebellion to divert British troops from Palestine. Neither course of action materialized, although some Transjordanians did join the growing bands of guerillas in Palestine and arms were smuggled across Transjordan's border into Palestine. Political unrest was compounded by economic hardship. Rainfall the preceding winter had been low and the summer harvest was consequently poor; pasturage for nomadic herders was also sparse. Palestine, which in normal times served as a labor market, was closed by the strike.[67]

Both force and incentives were used to dispel these clouds in the sunny skies of Transjordan's tranquillity. Arab Legion and TJFF troops were stationed in Amman to protect the political heart of the country. Before the strike was over the Arab Legion had been increased by two hundred regulars and a reserve force had been created to back it up. Two new laws were passed providing for the collective punishment of villages near sites of pipeline sabotage and for the expulsion of Palestinians, and schools were closed before the end of term to prevent student demonstrations. On the incentive side, money was disbursed liberally to key tribal leaders. By the end of August Colonel Glubb had handed out £P1,050 and Abdullah £P1,590. In addition some £P16,225 was spent on organizing relief work, mainly road building, which went 'a very long way towards keeping people in the distressed areas quiet.'[68] Some of Abdullah's largesse came from the Jewish Agency.[69]

Although the strike was over, sailing was not yet smooth for the Royal Commission. On 5 November, the very day the commission left England for Palestine, the new immigration schedule was made public. It was deliberately low, but to the Arab Higher Committee which had continued to hope for a temporary cessation of immigration, the announcement had the impact of a public slap in the face. Taking the position that the continuation of immigration prejudiced the commission's approach and implied that Britain did not intend seriously to review and re-cast its policy in Palestine, the Arab Higher Committee decided to boycott the commission proceedings.[70]

In this new crisis Abdullah again tried to act as a mediator between Palestine and London. He decided that the boycott, for Palestinian leaders, was justified and put himself forward as the representative of the Arabs of Palestine to the Royal Commission instead.[71] It was perhaps to forestall such an eventuality that the Arab Higher Committee finally accepted the counsel of Kings Ibn Saud and Ghazi and called off the boycott at the beginning of January.[72]

Nevertheless, Abdullah was the first Arab to see the Royal Commission officially: three of its members visited him in Amman several days after the boycott had been called off. He told them that the solution to the Palestine problem could be found in the terms of the mandate itself – that Britain should fulfill its promises to the Arabs as it had its promises to the Jews and that this could be done by creating representative government in Palestine. To the commission's protests that since there were many more Arabs than Jews in Palestine such a government would necessarily negate Britain's promises to the Jews, Abdullah replied that a representative government could be set up which would abide by the general political outlines of the mandate, much as the government of Iraq had taken over from the mandatory power while continuing to operate within guidelines guaranteed by the Anglo-Iraqi Treaty. He also said he would welcome Jewish immigrants to Transjordan once the trouble in Palestine had been settled, provided they came as ordinary citizens and did not claim preferential treatment. The commission was favorably impressed with Abdullah and he too was pleased with the attention he had received.[73]

The Royal Commission was back in London by the end of January. For the next seven months the future of all Palestine, and of Abdullah as well, was caught in the coils of imperial decision-making. The wait was relieved by the coronation of George VI, which Abdullah attended. He took the opportunity to do some lobbying at the Colonial Office.

At the top of Abdullah's list of worries was money. Here London was able to give him some satisfaction, for a decision had already been made to increase the grant-in-aid. He also wanted some slight modifications in the Anglo-Transjordan agreement, but Whitehall wanted to keep things as they were until the Royal Commission came out with its report. For his personal coffers he wanted compensation for – as he claimed – forgoing his plans to lease his lands to the Jewish Agency in obedience to Britain's wishes. This request fell on deaf ears, even though the Colonial Office did not seem to know that the option was still, in fact, operative.[74] He also met some Zionist representatives and discussed settling Jews in Transjordan in return for financial help.[75]

Abdullah made up for disappointments in London by stopping in Turkey on his way home. It was his first visit there since 1914. Atatürk was very friendly, if eccentric. He arrived at a reception in Abdullah's honor after Abdullah had retired and most of the guests had gone home. Abdullah returned from his rooms and spent the rest of the night conversing with Atatürk 'without yielding to Presidential pressure to drink wine.' At the end of this all-night session Atatürk had a highly flattering message sent to London advising Britain that 'to widen the powers of His Highness by making him a King would be a great service not only to the Arabs who adore him, but also to the British government . . .' The value of this statement was, unfortunately for Abdullah, discounted by the wine, which 'explains the rather crapulous tone of [Atatürk's] message.'[76]

Atatürk was mistaken about Arab adoration for Abdullah. Indeed, Arab sentiment was so much the contrary that Abdullah had to reroute his journey home. His visit had taken place at a time of great stress in Turkish–Arab relations, owing to Turkey's growing encroachments in the Syrian sanjak of Alexandretta. Nationalists in Syria suspected that in order to get Turkish support for his Syrian ambitions, he would agree to the cession of the sanjak. The ire his visit aroused among Arabs was such that, rather than going home by train through Syria as had been planned, the British ambassador in Ankara insisted that he go by sea to Haifa and by special train from Haifa to Jerusalem.[77]

Back in Amman Abdullah denied any harmful intent in visiting Turkey. He also vigorously denied the rumors then current that he supported the partition of Palestine: 'anything ascribed to me in connection with the question of partition is an intentional lie. The worst sin is falsehood.'[78]

The report of the Royal Commission was made public on 7 July 1937. In two sections it outlined the history and administration of the mandate, while in the third and final section it offered 'drastic treatment' for the 'irrepressible conflict between two national communities within the narrow bounds of one small country.' The treatment was partition. One of the successor states was to be 'an Arab state consisting of Transjordan and the Arab part of Palestine, and the other a Jewish state.' The report also raised the possibility of the transfer of populations, meaning, for the most part, moving Arabs from coastal Palestine.[79]

Neither the Foreign Office nor the Colonial Office had been pleased with the report when it was reviewed before publication. Compounding the doubtful viability of partition itself was the corollary that Abdullah should gain the part of Palestine left to the Arabs. It was not that Abdullah was disliked in London, or that his services in years past were not appreciated. Rather, the report's tepid reception was because Britain knew that Abdullah's accidental gain would inevitably antagonize other Arab leaders, jeopardizing their acceptance of the idea of partition itself:

> The proposal that the new Arab state should be incorporated in Transjordan, while no doubt sound in principle, is open to the somewhat accidental objection that this will presumably mean that it will come under the rule of the Amir Abdullah, who is regarded by most of the Arab world as very doubtfully loyal to the Arab cause, and who has further, quite recently, compromised his position by the close relations which he has established with the Turks. The Amir Abdullah, though possessing many virtues, is politically short sighted, and a good deal given to petty intrigue. It may be then that to hand over large areas of Palestine to a new state under his rule will lead to difficulties of a new type between Transjordan . . . and other Arab states, such as Syria and Saudi Arabia . . .[80]

The Colonial Office fantasized that there was the possibility of 'buying Abdullah out.' Wauchope was told to warn Abdullah that any attempt 'to push his claim or count his chickens before they are hatched would only prejudice his chances both with His Majesty's Government and with Arabs in Palestine and elsewhere.' He was to tell Abdullah that Britain favored a scheme of partition, but that it was not committed to any point of detail.[81] The suggestion that the Arab portion of Palestine might be added to Transjordan was too tempting for

Abdullah to ignore, however. He immediately declared himself in favor of partition,[82] the only Arab leader publicly to do so.

In the following weeks the thunderheads of protest gathered force over Palestine. The Arab community of Palestine unanimously rejected the partition plan proposed by the Royal Commission. Abdullah, for his precipitous acceptance, became a political leper. He attempted and failed to win Hajj Amin to the idea by offering him the post of prime minister in the new state.[83] His old allies were no less dismayed: Raghib al-Nashashibi and his National Defense party publicly dissociated themselves from him. His supporters in Haifa and Acre were horrified that he could accept a partition which relegated them to the Jewish portion of Palestine. Others of his partisans were forced to flee Palestine in fear of their lives.[84] Denunciations of partition and of Abdullah's acceptance also rang out from the other Arab capitals. As London had feared, opposition to partition stemmed from antagonism to Abdullah as much as from dislike of the idea itself. Damascus had a score to settle with Abdullah for his trip to Turkey a month earlier and for his repeated interference in Syrian politics in favor of a Hashemite monarchy there. Ibn Saud naturally opposed any enhancement of his life-long adversary's power. The strongest and most ferocious attacks, however, came from an unexpected source, Abdullah's kinsmen in Iraq. Iraq's violent rejection of partition, of which the colonial secretary remarked 'No more unfriendly act, or one more personally embarrassing to me, could have been committed,'[85] included a bitter campaign against Abdullah personally in the Iraqi press. Like other Arab reactions to Abdullah's acceptance of partition, Iraq's reflected accumulated grievances. It also reflected the growing insecurity of the Iraqi regime, which could little afford too close an identification with the increasingly disliked Abdullah.

Ever since the Bakr Sidqi coup of October 1936, Abdullah had followed Iraqi affairs closely. He was naturally upset by the implications of the coup – the loss of power for his nephew Ghazi, king of Iraq, and the challenge to the legitimacy of Hashemite claims that had been fostered since the Arab revolt. His anxiety was such that Ghazi invited him to Baghdad in December to see for himself that the situation was not as grave as he imagined. And indeed, Abdullah was relieved with what he found and particularly with the isolationism of the new government, which left the field of pan-Arab politics open for his own activities.[86] Nevertheless, in the spring of 1937 his anxiety for the safety of Ghazi's throne mounted. His interference knew no bounds as he tried to get Ghazi to meet him outside the borders of Iraq, or tried to pass messages to him through the late King Faysal's mistress. He called Baghdad so often that the Iraqi exchange adopted the expedient of telling him that the line was out of order.[87]

After months of such harassment, which Ghazi intensely resented and which the Iraqi government had tried unsuccessfully to get Britain to curb, Abdullah's acceptance of partition provided the perfect opportunity to discredit him, to neutralize any effects his intrigues might have had, and to release pent up frustration. It also offered the government a chance to broaden its appeal by rejoining, at least rhetorically, the ranks of pan-Arabism.

Thus, in the summer of 1937, Abdullah stood alone in the Arab world. Assassination plots, emanating from Syria and Palestine, were in the wind and some arrests were made. His own subjects were divided on the issue of partition, and some, it was reported, were prepared to act as a fifth column against him should Ibn Saud agree to invade Transjordan.[88] So extreme was his sense of isolation that he sent Muhammad al-Unsi to Jerusalem to make sure that the Jewish Agency did not desert him as well, to deal with other, more popular Arab leaders.[89]

Why had Abdullah, alone, embraced partition? His contemporaries had no trouble in assigning a motive. He alone stood to gain thereby. Palestinians overwhelmingly rejected the idea; a two-year-long armed rebellion which broke out some months after the Royal Commission's report graphically illustrated their rage and frustration. It also helped to convince Britain that partition was no way to straighten out its problematic policy in Palestine.

The rebellion did do one thing for Abdullah, however. It cleared out the nationalist leaders who were his rivals in Palestine. He had advocated their removal by Britain ever since the general strike.[90] As opposition grew more intense and more dangerous after the partition plan was announced, Britain finally decided to arrest the Arab Higher Committee. Hajj Amin escaped arrest in Palestine but was caught in Lebanon and placed under house arrest. Those who escaped arrest altogether fled to Damascus, Cairo and Baghdad. From Damascus they directed the rebellion in Palestine. Unfortunately for Abdullah, in the circumstances of the rebellion he was unable to capitalize on their absence to increase his influence in Palestine.

The very nature of the armed rebellion excluded Abdullah from participation whether as a figurehead, a spokesman or a mediator. It 'straddled the fence between a peasant war, and a people's revolutionary war,'[91] and began to expose the substructure of Palestinian society, setting its various components openly against one another and casting doubt on the assumptions that had held political hierarchies in place till then. It also exposed the iron hand of British domination. Mediation was excluded by Britain's determination to crush the revolt first and talk about the future of Palestine later, and Abdullah had in any case disqualified himself from such a role by his outspoken advocacy of partition.

For the two years of the armed uprising, Abdullah kept a very low profile. He did not travel outside Transjordan, even to Jerusalem; his contacts with the Jewish Agency were pared down, though never cut. He kept British officials in Transjordan at a distance, and limited his official pronouncements on the situation.

Abdullah tried to make himself nearly invisible during this troubled time. Transjordan, however, because of its geographical position, was the lifeline of the armed guerillas in Palestine. Arms and men from the Hijaz, Syria and Iraq reached Palestine via Transjordan, and Transjordan served as a haven for fighters when British military pressure in Palestine mounted. The rough terrain and lush vegetation of the 'Ajlun district in the northwest corner of Transjordan was one of the main thoroughfares of men, arms and messages from Damascus and beyond, and one of the safer places for rebels to meet. Moreover, the peasant population of the area had always been of dubious loyalty to Abdullah, feeling more akin to the peasants of the Hauran and the Galilee than to the tribal elements favored in Amman. Like the majority of peasants of Palestine, they provided the rebels with cover and provisions as needed.[92] Estimates of the numbers of Transjordanians that joined in the fighting varied between fifty and 250.[93] Within Transjordan itself communications, the oil pipeline, and government offices were regularly sabotaged.

Abdullah was protected against such internal reverberations by the Arab Legion, and he also encouraged villagers in the north to organize for self-defense against the rebels. This idea was similar to the one behind the creation of the so-called peace bands in Palestine, the anti-rebel armed bands organized to prevent villagers from supporting the rebels. Indeed, Abdullah was rumored to have contacts with Fakhri al-Nashashibi and Fakhri 'Abd al-Hadi, the chief organizers of these groups.[94]

Although Britain was determined to crush the rebellion and committed a large proportion of its standing forces to do so, the idea of partition had never been warmly embraced in Whitehall. Almost as soon as the Royal Commission findings had been made public, Whitehall began to distance itself from the idea. A Partition Commission under Sir John Woodhead, which was later sent out to look into the actual working out of partition on the ground, provided a path for retreat. The resulting report offered three plans of partition and indicated the most reasonable of these, but it concluded that viable states would not result from any of the plans put forward. The statement of policy based on the commission's findings buried partition and announced that Britain would seek a solution based on an understanding between Arabs and Jews. To find this solution Palestinian and other Arab leaders and Zionist delegates would soon be invited to London to confer with the British government and, if all went well, with one another.[95]

Abdullah had met with members of the Partition Commission despite the unanimous Palestinian boycott of its work. He presented a written statement suggesting, as an alternative to partition, that Palestine be united to Transjordan under himself and that within the larger state Jewish areas be guaranteed autonomy. He also proposed to retain the British mandate for ten years. After that, the mandate would be replaced by a treaty on the lines of the

Anglo-Iraqi Treaty. Immigration, the thorniest problem, would continue in the autonomous Jewish areas. Later, 'Should the Arabs experience good faith and willingness on the part of the Jews to combine with them and should they see no harm in the immigration of a suitable number to the lands of the United Arab State (outside the Jewish areas) the decision on such a question will be left to the discretion of the Arabs.'[96]

Abdullah's plan was not new, although some of its details were. Arab critics called it a 'miniature scheme of partition' and resented his interference over the heads of the exiled Palestinian leaders. On the popular level, shops were closed in several Transjordan towns to demonstrate solidarity with Palestine and opposition to Abdullah.[97]

As soon as Abdullah learned that the Woodhead findings had torpedoed the partition plan, he let London know that he expected compensation. 'He regards His Majesty's Government as bound in honour to make good the loss of expectation involved because he supported their policy and kept Trans-Jordan quiet.'[98] London responded with alacrity. He was immediately voted a non-recurring grant of £1,500, and his chief minister, Tawfiq Abu'l-Huda, was invited to come to London ahead of the other Arab delegates to the proposed round-table negotiations on Palestine in order to discuss Transjordan's status.[99]

The St James' Conference, which was to be the vehicle for shaping a new Palestine policy, was assembled with haste owing to the by now unmistakable advent of war with Germany. Already in September 1938, during the Munich crisis, plans for the disposition of the Middle East in the event of a European war had been considered. It had been decided at that time, well before the report of the Partition Commission was completed, that partition would be suspended and immigration stopped in the event of war, and a proclamation to that effect had been cabled to all British posts in the Middle East to be held in readiness against the sudden outbreak of war.[100] Although hostilities were temporarily averted, Chamberlain's 'peace in our time' was soon seen to be no more than a postponement of war. In the respite, one of the many tasks facing Britain was the squaring of accounts in the Middle East for the purpose of strengthening imperial defense. It was for this purpose that the St James' Conference was called.

The conference assembled, on the Arab side, members of the Arab Higher Committee (although not Hajj Amin) and of the al-Nashashibi organ, the National Defence Party (including Raghib al-Nashashibi), representing Palestine, and representatives of Egypt, Iraq, Transjordan, Saudi Arabia and Yemen. On the Jewish side there were representatives of the Jewish Agency in Palestine and of Jewish communities in Britain, Europe, South Africa and America. The two delegations met once, informally, but the conference was in essence two conferences since the Arab and Jewish delegations conferred with Britain alone. The Transjordan representative, Tawfiq Abu'l-Huda, took a back seat in the proceedings, conforming to general Arab sentiments on all points.

By the end of the conference, Britain and the Arabs had reached greater understanding than Britain and the Jews. The resulting White Paper reflected the degree of their agreement. A constitutional government would be established in Palestine gradually over the next ten years; Jewish immigration over the next five years was set at 75,000, which, it was estimated, would bring the Jewish population up to roughly one-third of the total population of Palestine; no further immigration would be permitted without Arab acquiescence after that period, and land sales would be regulated.[101] The eventual independence of Palestine was predicated upon good relations between Arabs and Jews, an ambiguity disliked and distrusted by the Arab Higher Committee.

Abdullah embraced Britain's new policy. Some of the sting had been taken out of his disappointment over partition by the concessions Tawfiq Abu'l-Huda had been able to win for Transjordan in his prior discussions with the Colonial Office. These discussions were interesting for what they revealed about Abdullah's position in Transjordan. Abu'l-Huda affirmed that Transjordan would not ask for its independence before it had the financial resources to support itself, and added that Transjordan ought to be united with Syria and Palestine to enable it to 'stand on its own feet.' He also made a strong pitch for discretionary funds for Abdullah to spend on gaining greater support in the country:

The people, the Bedouins and all the Sheikhs of the different villages are strongly bound to [Abdullah] personally because he is a Moslem and he is the grandson of the Prophet and because he is very democratic with them and they always find his doors wide open . . . This in itself is not quite enough and . . . some times the Emir incurs debts so as to be able to spend on such activities as would keep the people bound to him . . . The Arab Legion and the other administrative authorities have some special secret fund for expenditure of this kind . . .

and he went on to make a case that Abdullah should have access to similar funds. The concessions were announced a day before the new Palestine policy, 'to give it a day's start on the Palestine White Paper, so that Amir Abdullah would receive good publicity for the concessions he has gained.' They concerned the appointment of consular representatives to certain neighboring Arab countries, the liberalization of Abdullah's powers to raise and maintain military forces, an increase in his civil list to £18,000 a year, a decrease in financial and administrative supervision, and the replacement of seconded officials with Transjordanians when possible.[102]

Other Arab reactions to Britain's new Palestine policy were mixed. Like Abdullah, Raghib al-Nashashibi welcomed it, and the two were reconciled after their two-year estrangement.[103] Hajj Amin rejected it and publicly carried the

Arab Higher Committee with him, although some members looked on it with more favor. Similarly the Arab states publicly rejected it, but Egypt and Iraq privately urged acceptance. The White Paper thus helped Abdullah to find his way back into the Arab fold at the same time that, by causing a split in Arab ranks both inside and outside of Palestine, it contributed to the decline of the Arab Higher Committee.

The outbreak of the Second World War five months later also contributed to the decline of Abdullah's rivals in Palestine. With the onset of war, the hopes and dreams of the last war revived. Even though the Arab world had been let down by the arrangements following the First World War, nevertheless war, with its insecurities and fluidities, seemed to open all sorts of possibilities for peoples and countries only marginally involved. Diplomatic expectations replaced political organization among the Arabs of Palestine and for the five years of the war a fatal paralysis gripped the Palestine national movement. The British were in overwhelming military control of Palestine. Hajj Amin spent much of the war in Germany. During this time, Abdullah positioned himself with care to be able, at the end of the war, to take part in settling the unfinished business of Palestine.

Chapter 8

War and politics

The news that war had been declared reached Amman on the afternoon of 3 September. Abdullah immediately wired a message of support to King George VI and that evening all German residents were taken into custody. The next day Emergency Regulations were put into effect, instituting such extraordinary powers as censorship and administrative detention. He also offered Britain the use of the Arab Legion and was disappointed that no local theater of hostilities initially provided the opportunity for him to prove his zealous loyalty.[1]

Of all the Arab states with treaty or mandatory ties to Great Britain, Transjordan switched gears to the wartime exigencies of those alliances with the least resistance. In contrast, Egypt would not do more than declare itself a non-belligerent ally, and King Faruq and Prime Minister 'Ali Mahir were widely believed to harbor Axis sympathies. The Iraqi government tried to maintain a neutral position in the conflict. Its ambivalent feelings towards Britain were evident in its narrow interpretation of the Anglo-Iraqi Treaty, an interpretation so different from Britain's that it led to war between Iraqi and British forces in 1941. But whatever the individual expressions of loyalty or lack thereof, war in Europe signified one thing to the Arab states – the chance to complete the process of liberation begun in the First World War. Whether this was to be achieved through alliance with Britain or by hoping Britain might be defeated was largely a matter of historical circumstance. Abdullah, whose position in Transjordan had been created by Britain and whose government relied on a hefty British subsidy, had little choice but to hitch his wagon to Britain's star and hope for the best.

There was little opposition to Abdullah's pro-British policy within Transjordan. In the twenty years of the British mandate, no structures of independent political organization had emerged, nor had the demographic or economic structure of Transjordan changed sufficiently to allow effective nationalist politics. The total population of Transjordan in 1938 was estimated at 300,000; its largest towns were Amman and Salt, with populations of roughly 20,000 each.[2] The Arab Legion was firmly controlled by Britain and was not a conduit of political influence as was the army in Iraq. Education available in Transjordan was still rudimentary and had not created an indigenous intelli-

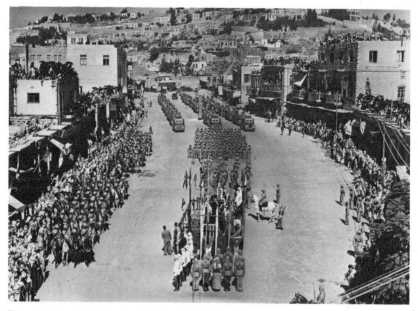

Figure 13. Arab Legion parade through downtown Amman, 1940.

gentsia,[3] while industrial establishments were few and tiny.[4] The formal institutions of political power had not gained any political independence since their creation in 1928; indeed, the British resident exercised even more control over administrative affairs than was explicitly indicated in the Anglo-Transjordan agreement. For example, the new British resident, Alec Kirkbride, noted in November 1939: 'The Prime Minister [Tawfiq Abu'l-Huda] and I have arrived at a satisfactory arrangement for mutual and informal consultation in regard to administrative matters, as distinct from questions specifically provided for in the Trans-Jordan Agreement as referable to His Majesty's Government.'[5] To make absolutely sure that no opportunity for the discussion of Anglo-Transjordanian ties arose, the term of office for the Legislative Council was lengthened from three to five years, postponing elections from 1940 to 1942. When the new council was assembled in November 1942, it exceeded its usual standard of malleability by passing thirty-two new laws in two weeks without recording a single dissenting vote.[6]

The dissidence that did, nevertheless, surface on occasion was scattered, unorganized, and often opportunistic. Against this opposition, or potential opposition, Britain had two weapons: the Emergency Regulations and money. The former suspended due process, allowing detention on suspicion; the latter was not as plentiful as during the First World War, but was none the less welcome. In December 1940, £1,000 was credited to Glubb, who had succeeded

Peake as the commanding officer of the Arab Legion, for 'extraordinary or unforeseen payments.' In the fiscal year 1940–1, £5,000 was given to Abdullah on top of his £18,000 civil list.[7]

Despite the rosy outlook for Britain in Transjordan there was one dark spot on the horizon, or at least Kirkbride believed so: this was the character of Abdullah's eldest son and heir, Talal.

It had been hoped that Talal's marriage in 1934 would help him win some domestic independence from his father and would settle him into a quiet family life in Amman, but this was not to be. There was not enough money for him to set up a separate household and his continued proximity to his father, with whom he had never got on, aggravated by his financial dependence, led to a series of explosions between the two. The birth of Talal's first son, Husayn, in November 1935 reportedly eased the tension temporarily, but within three months Talal was packed off to Cairo for a rest from palace pressures.[8]

The personal enmity between father and son tended to take on political coloring, with Talal being generally identified with the 'opposition.' Britain feared that the division between the two would attract political opportunists. For example, Peake had remarked in 1937:

I believe that the well known quarrel between these two persons may encourage some fanatical persons to make an attempt on the life of H. H. the Amir Abdullah or on the life of Tallal. Both talk most stupidly to all and sundry about the state of the family affairs. While Tallal is well in with the opposition and is I am told egging them on. This young man talks most foolishly he has been known to express very definite anti-English sentiments, and now when he is obsessed with hatred for his father I have little doubt that he gives forth a lot of very dangerous ideas.[9]

Such fears were heightened by the onset of war.

In early 1939 Abdullah wrote Kirkbride, who was not only the new British resident but an old friend, that Talal's conduct compelled him 'to direct my utmost care to my second son.'[10] Kirkbride passed this on to the high commissioner along with his own belief that in the back of Abdullah's mind was the intention that Nayyif, not Talal, should be his successor. In a covering letter to London the high commissioner added, 'There is no doubt that Naif would be the safer and sounder of the two.'[11]

Even before the war broke out Kirkbride had taken preliminary steps towards excluding Talal. He had let Abdullah know indirectly that a different law of succession might be enacted, and he had established that neither the present nor the former chief minister would accept office under Talal. Responding to Kirkbride's prodding, the high commissioner wired the Colonial Office that 'the Amir is showing signs of diabetes' and that a law of succession ought to be drafted. The Colonial Office reacted with some scepticism: 'I thought this had been known for some time' was the comment on the state of Abdullah's health, and 'after a delay of ten years!' was the sarcastic rejoinder to the high commissioner's plea for urgency.[12]

The Colonial Office found the proposition shaky on several grounds. They thought the high commissioner's explanation of Talal's unsuitability 'rather sketchy' and they were not convinced that Nayyif, 'who is reputed to be a very dull and ineffective creature,' would be a suitable replacement.[13] Nevertheless, they decided to leave the decision to the men on the ground, and Kirkbride clinched the matter by describing Talal as 'intemperate in his habits, untrustworthy and at heart, deeply anti-British.'[14] However, by the time the Colonial Office agreed to exclude him from the throne, Abdullah and he had been reconciled. The high commissioner prepared a draft law of succession anyway, and held it ready for the next time the two should fall out, which occurred in November 1940.

The draft law provided for succession to Abdullah's nearest male relative, that is to Talal, then to Nayyif, and then to Talal's son, Husayn. It also made possible the exclusion by royal proclamation (*irade*) of anyone on the grounds of unsuitability. Under this provision Talal was to be passed over.[15]

The substance of the November quarrel between Abdullah and Talal is unclear. It may have been about two of Abdullah's more notorious favorites, whose dismissal Talal demanded,[16] or it may have been over Abdullah's new wife, Nahida, nicknamed by Amman society ʿal-ʿAbdi', meaning both 'slave' and 'black'. Both were topics of dispute between the two at the time.

Nahida was the daughter of a female slave who had served in the sharifian palace in the Hijaz. Mother and daughter came to Amman after the fall of the Hijaz, and Nahida was given to Abdullah's daughter, Maqbula, to be her playmate. She attracted the attention of Abdullah, who gave her her freedom, set her up in her own apartment and eventually her own palace, and finally married her. She gained great influence with Abdullah and used it to amass wealth, mainly through real estate.[17] But she was never given the title, *amira*, held by his other two wives, nor was the marriage ever socially acknowledged. Gossip attributed her power to magic. Abdullah, who had seen signs of the decline of the British monarchy in Edward VIII's abdication since the king could no longer marry whomever he chose, had managed for once to do one better. The family and all of Amman were scandalized by the affair, but only Talal confronted his father.

The quarrel, whatever its specific cause, provided the chance to reopen the question of succession. The new law of succession was duly passed by the Legislative Council, and became effective on 16 January 1941; on that day Abdullah issued a secret *irade* excluding Talal. Three copies were put in sealed envelopes and kept, one in the amir's *diwan* (private office), one in the chief minister's office, and one in the office of the British resident.[18]

With Talal out of the way, Kirkbride felt that Transjordan was securely battened down. And just in time, for by the spring of 1941 the war had come perilously close to Transjordan's borders.

The fall of France in the summer of 1940 and the overnight transformation of the French Army of the Levant into a potentially hostile force brought the war into the heart of the Middle East and on to Abdullah's doorstep. However it was not in Syria that wartime tensions first erupted into fighting – that occurred in Iraq in the spring of 1941, when a coup toppled Abdullah's nephew, the pro-British regent, 'Abd al-Ilah, threatening British interests there and throughout the region.

The coup was a profound shock to Abdullah. It was an unmistakable sign that sentiment in the Arab world was shifting and that new forces, inimical to his style of politics and to his interests, were gathering strength. His brother in anxiety was Nuri al-Sa'id, formerly prime minister and foreign minister of Iraq and inextricably identified with Britain. Nuri had arrived by plane in Amman on 31 March, unannounced, and apparently in 'intelligent anticipation of the coup.' The regent, 'Abd al-Ilah, who escaped from Baghdad with the help of the American legation, and other Iraqis of the pro-British clique, joined Nuri in Amman some two weeks later.[19] While this group waited in the wings, Britain prepared to do something about the new government under Rashid 'Ali al-Gaylani.

The ouster of Britain's closest Iraqi friends marked the end of Britain's diplomatic attempts to bring Iraq actively into the war with the Allies. Fed up with Iraq's refusal to declare war against Germany and to break off relations with the Italians, and alarmed by rumors of Iraqi contacts with Axis powers, Britain decided to ensure Iraq's co-operation by military means before it was too late. A month after the Rashid 'Ali coup, fighting broke out between Britain and Iraq. This was the chance Abdullah had been waiting for, and he dispatched the 350-man Mechanized Brigade of the Arab Legion to guide British troops across the desert. This done, the Arab Legion cut the railway north of Baghdad.[20] With British troops to the west and south, and the Legion to the north, Rashid 'Ali and his supporters fled east to Iran. The regent then re-entered Iraq from the west, having borrowed a fleet of cars from Abdullah and a case of beer from Kirkbride.[21]

The use of the Arab Legion against a 'sister' Arab state had not gone unremarked in Amman. Wary of criticism or worse, the government enacted Emergency Regulations prohibiting meetings and demonstrations, putting a curfew on motor transport, appointing special tribal guards to protect road and railway bridges, censoring radio broadcasts and newspapers, and proscribing rumormongering among government officials. Thanks to such measures, Kirkbride was able to report that the Legion's participation in the Iraq campaign was generally popular. Nevertheless, there were signs of other feelings. Schoolboys demonstrated and were expelled; their teachers were fired.[22] Haditha al-Khuraysha, one of the Bani Sakhr shaykhs, called on his men to resign from the Legion rather than to fight other Arabs at the behest of Britain, and paid a visit to Saudi Arabia to escape the consequences of his deeds.[23] Most ominous was a mutiny in the Transjordan Frontier Force: one squadron refused to cross the border into Iraq and seven non-commissioned officers were implicated in a plot to seize arms and join battle against Britain.[24] The Legion, however, remained loyal to its British officers.

After seizing the initiative in Iraq, Britain went on to carry out its long anticipated campaign against Vichy forces in Syria. The Arab Legion was not included in the initial attack, but it later took part in skirmishes around Palmyra and undertook some patrol work in the Dayr al-Zawr region on the Euphrates. When these tasks were completed, Britain expressed its confidence in the Legion by authorizing its expansion. This had the unintended effect of vitiating the Legion's combat readiness by diverting its attention to recruitment and training. The Legion saw no more combat duty during the war, but by 1946 it had been expanded to four times its pre-war strength.[25]

In this manner, Britain acknowledged the Legion's utility. Yet there remained the thornier problem of how to repay Abdullah. Although his loyalty may have been forged by his dependence, he had always been rewarded before and it was natural that he should entertain similar hopes now. However his idea of just recompense, developed in rhetoric which recalled the Arab revolt, was exorbitant by British standards: he wanted the independence of Transjordan, which was feasible, and the creation of a Greater Syria, which was not.

Abdullah aspired in this war to play a role like his father's in the First World War. He wanted to be the chief Arab ally of Britain, and, by dint of that position, to be recognized as the main Arab leader east of Egypt. But in the twenty years since the first war, Britain had developed too many interests in the Middle East and courted too many allies to have to rely on one alone. Even though there were British statesmen who were also twenty years out of date in thinking of one supreme Arab leader, their thoughts did not turn to Abdullah. Abdullah's 'old friend' Winston Churchill, for example, considered Abdullah's old enemy Ibn Saud to be the 'greatest living Arab', whose power might beneficially be extended to cover Iraq and Transjordan. In terms reminiscent of those once applied to Abdullah's father, Churchill went on to suggest that as the custodian of the Holy Places, Ibn Saud might well be acceptable to the Arabs and, provided he agreed to a settlement in Palestine, to Britain as well.[26]

Abdullah was not the only Arab leader to have his ambitions honed by war. There were other leaders in other Arab countries dreaming of independence and of some sort of wider territorial or moral leadership for themselves in a broader

Arab arena. Syria, Lebanon and Palestine, like Transjordan, hoped to replace their mandates with treaties. Egypt and Iraq, though nominally independent, sought to recast their treaties with Britain in terms of greater equality. Most Arab leaders believed that once the superstructure of conflicting European interests had been washed away, the pieces would fall back together again, magically, into a single entity embodying the shared history, culture, language, and, it was assumed, the shared interests of the Arabs.[27]

For Abdullah, the relationship of unity to independence was reversed. On one hand, he was acutely aware of Transjordan's limitations and of his dependence on Britain – the creation of a larger Arab state with himself at the helm was the only way he could hope to achieve any real independence from Britain. On the other, however, he recognized that Britain was his chief ally in the Middle East, and that if he waited until Britain had ceded its power to independent Arab regimes, his idea of unity would be more difficult to achieve. Therefore he sought unity before independence, and with greater vigor.

For twenty years Abdullah had tried to extend his control over Syria, or the Hijaz, or, most recently, Palestine, but, for the most part, his attention had been riveted on Damascus. He had set his sights on Syria ever since Faysal's expulsion in 1920. Faysal had subsequently been given Iraq, which Abdullah had considered to be his own prize, and from that time on he had aimed to even the score by taking the throne of Syria for himself. His ambition was well-known; Churchill had given it a passing nod in 1921 when he promised Abdullah that if he made good in Transjordan, Britain would do what it could to convince France to accept him in Syria. Both of these incidents – Faysal's taking the throne of Iraq and Churchill's promising to do something for him in Syria – were standard arguments in Abdullah's case for Syria. They were put forward regularly, with numbing effect, along with the evidence of his long and faithful service to Britain or to the Arabs (depending on his audience) as the basis of his claim to Syria.

Syria was thus a constant in Abdullah's political vision; but the level of his activity towards that constant goal rose and fell with the tide of political circumstance. In the three years before the war, for instance, the tide was at low ebb. During that period Syria was dominated by the National Bloc government of Hashim al-Atasi (president) and Jamil Mardam (prime minister), a regime inimical to Abdullah's interests. Fortunately for Abdullah, the Palestine partition plan of 1937 created a new opportunity for expansion in a direction that he had not seriously addressed before. So, with Syria temporarily closed to him, he was able to direct his political energies towards Palestine. By 1939, however, partition had fallen through and the tide of opportunity was flowing again in Syria. The National Bloc government had been discredited by France's refusal to ratify the Franco-Syrian Treaty and by its own failure to prevent

Turkey's annexation of Alexandretta. It resigned and France suspended the constitution, appointing a council to rule by decree instead. A month later war was declared in Europe.

Nineteen thirty-nine, then, was a propitious year for Abdullah to resume seeking his fortune in Syria. He did not forget about Palestine, but cast his ambition for a Syrian throne in a larger and more ambitious context, the unification of Greater Syria, which included Palestine and Lebanon as well as Transjordan and Syria. A month after war was declared, he wrote to the Colonial Secretary about Churchill's 1921 promise and asked him to tell Churchill 'that I am carrying on in conformity with his advice and that I am still waiting the outcome of his promises.'[28] He did not know that in London it had been judged 'inconceivable' that he should acquire the throne of Syria, or that Winston Churchill thought of Ibn Saud, rather than of himself, when he considered questions of Arab unity – for its part, London was not unnecessarily frank with Abdullah lest its cordial relationship with him be disrupted.[29] Nevertheless, he began to see the lay of the land for himself with the Allied occupation of Syria in 1941.

At 6 a.m. on 8 June, Kirkbride informed Abdullah that the Allied invasion of Syria and Lebanon was under way. He received the news with resentment.[30] Two things troubled him in particular: he had not been included in Britain's counsels beforehand, an omission which indicated that Britain did not give any special weight to his claims to the throne of Syria; and Syria and Lebanon had been promised independence on the eve of the invasion, a development which threatened to leave Transjordan and himself behind in an inferior status. Officially he expressed perfunctory gratitude and pleasure, but he warned that 'the absence of any reference whatsoever to Trans-Jordan after its honest co-operation and complete loyalty will appear to be a severe setback to the policy of friendliness which has been followed in this country since its establishment.'[31] Privately he was extremely upset and alarmed. His agitation was compounded by the contradictory nature of the occupation, for at the moment that Britain, by occupying Syria, came into a position to satisfy his claims, it openly spurned them.

The Allied occupation served to introduce British influence directly into Syria. From that point on, Britain worked discreetly (and not so discreetly, as the Lebanese crisis of 1943 and the Syrian crisis of 1945 indicate) to persuade the Free French to give Syria its independence. The underlying idea was that if the Arabs were given satisfaction everywhere else, they would be more willing to compromise on Palestine. But giving the Arabs satisfaction in Syria was not the same as imposing Abdullah as ruler, and in September Sir Oliver Lyttelton, minister of state in Cairo, arrived in Amman to tell Abdullah so.

Abdullah, 'a short man, with a fringe of beard and kindly, rather disenchanted eyes,' dressed in a drab yellow robe, met Lyttelton at the palace. Taking him by the hand, he led him to a drawing room, where imitation French furniture and European bric-à-brac jostled with oriental rugs and Arab artifacts. They sat on a French-looking sofa together, and, with Abdullah still holding his hand, Lyttelton broached his message. He had hardly got through his initial compliments before Abdullah interrupted him and, 'with a rather wan smile,' divined his tidings: 'It is that the British have no intention of making me King of Syria.'[32]

Britain's policy in Syria was guided by its general principle of coming to terms with Arab nationalism. For this purpose Britain approached the National Bloc, Abdullah's republican enemies, and in particular the Bloc's leading member, Shukri al-Quwatli. In early 1943 Shaykh Taj al-Din al-Hasani, France's appointed president of Syria, died. By that time France was anxious to re-establish constitutional government in Syria and to secure its position there by finally promulgating the Franco-Syrian Treaty of 1936, which Syria had ratified but France had not. General Catroux (Free French délégué-général), therefore, announced that elections would be held, and offered a deal to al-Quwatli whereby France would support him for the presidency if he would champion the old treaty once he was in office. Al-Quwatli was tempted by the offer, but both Britain and Iraq urged him to refuse. He would, they argued, damage his reputation by dealing with the French for his own personal gain. The two were also agreed that Syria should avoid any special relationship with France which would bar it from future Arab unity plans in a British-dominated Middle East. British and Iraqi advice won the day and al-Quwatli refrained from making any secret agreements with the French. Thus, in August, when he was chosen as president by the newly elected chamber, Britain already had his ear and he had Britain's tacit support.[33] In reaction, Abdullah tried and failed to forge an alliance with France, the other party to lose out because of the Anglo-Quwatli *entente*.[34]

Abdullah could offer Britain or France no influence in Syria which rivalled al-Quwatli's. The majority of his supporters in Syria were opportunists, since the ease with which he was drawn on the subject of Syria and his value as a bogeyman made him a natural magnet for sporadically disgruntled and dissident Syrians.[35] His stock in Syria rose and fell with internal shifts of policy – even the National Bloc made friendly overtures to him in 1941, when the Free French appointed the overly co-operative Shaykh Taj al-Din al-Hasani as president[36] – but it never remained high enough for long enough to convince anybody but Abdullah himself that he had a future in Syria. Those who turned to him as an expression of opposition to a current regime or policy had no long term interest in him, and their attention stimulated his ambition without providing real support or substance for its achievement.

Abdullah's only supporters who counted in Syrian politics and who had been consistent through the years were a small group of nationalist monarchists exemplified by the Bakri family, long time Hashemite allies, and ʿAbd al-Rahman Shahbandar. For the Bakris, Abdullah embodied Arab culture and tradition, and his ties to them dated to his youth in Istanbul. Shahbandar's support had a different cast.

ʿAbd al-Rahman Shahbandar was a respected nationalist, a monarchist and an Anglophile. He was also implacably opposed to the National Bloc. Abdullah, for him, was the perfect symbol of his sentiments. He had been exiled from Syria, however, after the 1925–7 revolt and was not allowed to return until 1937 (partly owing to the machinations of his National Bloc rivals).

Shahbandar and a delegation of twenty-five Syrians, including Fawzi al-Bakri, visited Transjordan in May 1939 to offer their condolences to Abdullah on the death of his nephew Ghazi, king of Iraq. With the death of Ghazi, Faysal's son and heir, the symbolic position at the head of the Arab movement again fell vacant, and Shahbandar used his visit publicly to champion Abdullah as a candidate for the Syrian throne and as the leader of Arab unity. He also used his own lines of communication with Britain to advocate the unity of Transjordan with Syria under Abdullah and the creation of a loose confederation of Arab states held together by an executive committee with Abdullah at its head.[37]

Shahbandar had a significant following in Syria and it was chiefly through him that Abdullah maintained in any way a credible presence in Syrian politics. So, when Shahbandar was assassinated in July 1940 – an act widely believed to have been perpetrated by his enemies in the National Bloc – Abdullah's cause in Syria suffered irreparable damage.

Without Shahbandar, Abdullah lost ground in Syria. Although monarchical sentiments were not negligible, monarchists were divided in their choice of a candidate. Among Abdullah's more prominent rivals for the post were the regent of Iraq, ʿAbd al-Ilah, the young king of Iraq, Faysal II, and Ibn Saud's son, Faysal. Less serious pretenders to the throne lent an air of buffoonery to the question. For example, after elections were announced in 1943, Amir Saʿid al-Jazaʾiri held meetings of paid stooges in Damascus which concluded with revolver shots and cries of 'Long live King Saʿid of Syria!' But he attracted the attention only of his neighbors, who complained about the noise.[38]

In order to create support for himself, Abdullah distributed largesse and encouraged favorable newspaper coverage. Since his purse was both severely limited and strictly controlled by Britain, money spent in Syria came from windfalls outside of his official budget. It was reported that he made money for disbursement in Syria by sending his cars across the border laden with merchandise which was then sold on the Syrian market where prices were much higher than in Transjordan.[39] His winnings at the Cairo racetrack also funded a brief flutter amongst the Syrian tribes.[40] He had to rely on various agents to disburse money and propaganda on his behalf since he could not visit Syria himself. To his extreme annoyance he was twice forbidden the privilege of passing through on trips to Turkey and Lebanon. The trips were then cancelled, suggesting that the destinations were less important than the route.[41]

Syria was absolutely central to Abdullah's Greater Syrian scheme. It was also, for historical reasons, the most attractive quarry for him. Lebanon figured but briefly in the overall elaboration of his plans: he said only that Maronite separatism was to be accommodated by some sort of autonomous administration. He had no traditional allies in Lebanon and little local appeal. He was approached by the Syrian Social Nationalist Party (better known as the Parti populaire syrien), a predominantly Lebanese party, whose goal like his own was the reunification of geographic Syria.[42] But party ideology, which stressed the idea of a pre-Islamic Syrian entity and ignored any Arab component, was ultimately at odds with the basis of Abdullah's claims to Syrian leadership.

Palestine likewise, despite the interest quickened in Abdullah by the 1937 partition plan, remained of secondary importance. He had less of a problem there than in Syria with an indigenous rival leadership: Hajj Amin and other nationalist leaders had fled or been exiled in the wake of the 1936–9 Palestine rebellion, and Abdullah had simply to keep this leadership from returning to the country in order to promote his own cause.[43] Yet he was unable to capitalize on their absence and he failed to broaden his political appeal beyond Raghib al-Nashashibi's National Defence Party. The attention lavished on Amir Mansur, one of Ibn Saud's sons, during a visit to Palestine in 1943 amply demonstrated Abdullah's lack of appeal in a particularly hurtful way.[44] Towards the end of the war he tried to promote a united front of all Palestinian parties under his aegis, but Hajj Amin's Arab Party, still the largest and most powerful party in Palestine, refused to join.[45]

Abdullah also maintained contacts with the Jewish Agency, hoping to get Zionist backing for Greater Syria in return for autonomy and the possibility of settling in a broader area than that offered by partition,[46] but the agency never seriously considered his offer. Instead, the World Zionist Organization, at its conference in New York in May 1942, adopted the resolutions known collectively as the Biltmore program. These called for the immediate establishment in Palestine of a Jewish commonwealth, the rejection of the 1939 White Paper, unrestricted Jewish immigration and settlement in Palestine supervised by the Jewish Agency, and the formation and recognition of a Jewish military force under its own flag.

Abdullah recognized setbacks and slights, and had anticipated Lyttelton's message, but he did not see, much less accept, the overall hopelessness of his situation. Far from being a political realist, he clung to his dreams of a Syrian throne with such tenacity that the high commissioner, Sir Harold MacMichael, feared for his mental stability.[47] He was, as the succeeding high commissioner,

Sir Alan Cunningham, recognized with more compassion, 'an ageing man, haunted by the fear of missing his last opportunity of realising any of his aims. . .'[48]

What made Abdullah particularly nervous were the activities of other Arab leaders to promote their own ideas of Arab unity. Most energetic in this field were the Iraqis, championed by Nuri al-Saʿid, and the Egyptians, led by the Wafdist prime minister, Nahas Pasha. Ibn Saud was a passive actor whose known antipathy to the Hashemites was enough to cause serious problems for any Hashemite plan of union.

Ideas of Arab unity were in the air throughout the war. Though vague at first, the articulation of such ideas was encouraged by Anthony Eden's 1941 Mansion House speech which promised that His Majesty's Government would 'give their full support to any scheme that commands general approval,' and by the apparent imminence of the independence for Syria and Lebanon promised on the eve of the Allied invasion. With the recession of fighting from the Middle East in 1943, it became possible to talk about its post-war future.

Britain did not consider Abdullah's plans for Greater Syria to have general Arab approval. Rather, Britain looked to the leadership of men like Nuri al-Saʿid of Iraq and Nahas Pasha of Egypt, who were pro-British but at the same time commanded genuine respect in the Arab world. Moreover, Iraq and Egypt were the important centers of power in the Arab world: Cairo's importance in particular had been enhanced for both Arabs and Englishmen by the war. Abdullah, as he himself well realized, was trapped by the inconsequence of Transjordan.

Nuri had been feeling out the general contours of Arab unity since 1939. In particular, he had suggested to Abdullah the federation of the two Hashemite monarchies under the Iraqi branch of the family; but Abdullah had reacted badly. To the suggestion that Ghazi would be the most obvious head of the federation, Abdullah had reportedly replied that he would not be duped by 'a boy and a crook.' The keenness of Abdullah's rivalry with the Iraqi branch of the family carried over into the reign of Faysal II and the regent, ʿAbd al-Ilah. The Iraqi house also challenged Abdullah's claims to Syria. To deflect a clash there, Nuri tried to steer Abdullah's ambitions towards Palestine. Nuri's vision was that Transjordan and Palestine should unite, then that state should form a federation with Iraq (leadership unspecified), and into that federation Syria would drop 'like a ripe date.' Abdullah distrusted Nuri's motives, however, and was as prepared to push his claims in Syria against those of his nephews as against those of anyone else.[49]

Concrete moves towards Arab unity did not really begin until 1943, after Rommel's defeat at al-Alamein. At about that time, two catalysts precipitated a heavy rain of activities out of the mist of vague impulses in that direction. The first was the death of France's chief of state in Syria, Shaykh Taj al-Din al-

Hasani, and the prospect of elections. The second was Eden's reiteration, in the House of Commons, of his support for any unity scheme originating from and generally approved by the Arabs themselves.

Before Eden's speech, Nuri had already submitted a plan in writing to the British government. Afterwards, he dispatched Jamil al-Midfaʿi to the Arab capitals to canvass opinion. It was during Midfaʿi's visit to Damascus that he impressed upon Shukri al-Quwatli the benefits to future Arab unity of not coming to a special agreement with France. Nuri's plan provided for the unification of Greater Syria, whose form of government was to be decided by its citizens. Jews in Palestine would be given semi-autonomy and Maronites in Lebanon might have a privileged regime should they so desire. Then an Arab League of Greater Syria and Iraq would be formed, to which other Arab states might adhere.[50]

The plan was harshly rebuffed in Amman and Riyadh. Abdullah let Midfaʿi know in no uncertain terms that the future of the Syrian states (Transjordan, Palestine, Lebanon and Syria) was no business of Iraq's 'while there were others with better qualifications and claims.'[51] To counter Nuri's ideas, he inspired his *diwan* to issue a rival plan. In fact the two were identical, except that the Transjordan plan provided for Abdullah to be the ruler of the Greater Syrian state on the grounds of his position in Transjordan, 'which is an important part of Larger Syria,' his past and subsequent assistance to the Allies, his being the heir to the rights of his late father, Churchill's 1921 promise, and the Greater Syrians' wish for a constitutional monarchy.[52] On the heels of this memorandum, Abdullah drew up a manifesto to the 'People of Syria, urbanites and nomads, from the Gulf of Aqaba to the Mediterranean Sea to the upper parts of the Euphrates,' calling for a 'Syrian conference' which he hoped to sponsor in Amman.[53] The acting high commissioner blocked its dissemination through the Palestine press and radio, but it was distributed in pamphlet form by Abdullah's agents. When confronted over his attempt to avoid the required consultation with Britain on foreign policy pronouncements (timed when Kirkbride was out of the country), Abdullah admitted he was guilty and that he had done so because he knew that, had he sought permission, it would have been refused. He was sorry but not contrite since he felt he had to remind Britain of his existence 'by sticking a pin into them.'[54]

Ibn Saud's opposition to Nuri's plan was rooted in his chronic distrust of the Hashemites. He saw Nuri's plan as a veil for the extension of Hashemite influence to Syria, and did not appear to realize, or think important, that its loudest and most vehement detractor was Abdullah.[55]

One of the problems with Nuri's plan, aside from the feasibility of its actual proposals, was the general belief that it hid a secret agenda for Iraqi dominance of Greater Syria. For that reason Nuri sought the co-operation of Egypt, which stood aloof from the jealousies that dominated the Fertile Crescent, to create a forum in which Nuri's ideas might be discussed. Nahas Pasha, the prime minister of Egypt, had already established the reputation of an honest broker in 1942, when he had helped Lebanese and Syrian leaders come to an agreement on the future of Lebanon, which, a year later, was incorporated into the Lebanese National Pact.[56] Nuri thought that Egypt wanted only political prestige and that to Nahas in particular a role in regional affairs would be helpful on the domestic front – this, at least, is what he explained to Abdullah.[57] And perhaps that is what Nahas wanted at that moment. But once Egypt became involved in the affairs of the Fertile Crescent, it quickly became Iraq's greatest rival there.

In the summer of 1943, Nahas set about sounding out the Arab governments on the subject of Arab unity. He met with various Arab delegations which were invited to Cairo in turn. In this manner he laid the foundation for the Alexandria Conference and the creation of the Arab League.

The first visitor to Cairo was, appropriately, Nuri. On the way to Cairo, Nuri stopped in Amman to convince Abdullah to co-operate with Nahas. Abdullah at first reacted with hostility. He said that life was short, that he had been in the background for twenty-five years, and that he wanted something done. Nuri, as ever, urged him to concentrate on Palestine and added that if he moved with caution, the Syrians might yet select him as ruler. (To Kirkbride Nuri was more frank. He confessed that Abdullah had few supporters in Syria but that there was no point in telling him so.) Nuri also convinced Abdullah of Egypt's essential lack of interest in Syria, and by the end of their meeting Abdullah had written a friendly letter to Nahas, to be delivered by Nuri, asking him to continue his efforts for the Arab cause on the basis of the foundations laid by his father, King Husayn.[58]

Abdullah seems to have liked Nahas Pasha. He had met him in November 1940 during a ten-day visit to Cairo, and on his return described him to the high commissioner as 'the only really effective force amongst the Egyptians.' However, his appreciation of Nahas may have been in large part a reaction to his extreme dislike of King Faruq. During the same visit, Faruq received him with his hands in his pockets, addressed him as *inta* (the familiar form of 'you'), and offered him tea in a smaller cup than his own. As for Faruq's position in the war, Abdullah declared that Mussolini might as well have been in Abdin Palace.[59] In contrast, Nahas favored taking a clear position on the side of the Allies and was locked in a struggle for power with Faruq. (He had become prime minister in February 1942, after five years out of office, only after Abdin Palace had been surrounded by British tanks.)

Nuri's persuasive arguments coupled with Abdullah's earlier favorable impression of Nahas allayed Abdullah's jealousy for the moment. When he was invited to send a delegate to Cairo in August 1943, he agreed to send his prime minister, Tawfiq Abu'l-Huda. His instructions to Tawfiq Pasha were to make it clear to Nahas that the Syrian countries must be unified or federated before any wider Arab unity was achieved comprising Egypt and Iraq. He was cheerful and optimistic, indeed too optimistic, about the practical results of Tawfiq's representations.[60]

Tawfiq followed his instructions, impressing on Nahas the paramount importance of the reunification of Greater Syria. He added that if there were problems providing for the Maronites and the Jews, Transjordan and Syria could in any case unite and then work out provisions for Lebanon and Palestine. He argued in favor of a monarchical regime, and when Nahas asked him if a king chosen from among the Syrians would be acceptable to Transjordanians, he replied that only descendants of kings could aspire to royalty. Off the record, Nahas said that some favored Faysal II for the position, but Tawfiq pointed out that the body that had proclaimed Faysal I king of Syria in 1920 had also named Abdullah as king of Iraq, and that if one was binding so was the other. Nahas had the last word, however, remarking that if the Syrians wanted a republic, they should have it.[61]

Abdullah was elated by Tawfiq's mission to Egypt – so much so, in fact, that it is not clear whether Tawfiq told him of the tenor of his private conversation with Nahas. In any case his buoyant spirits were soon deflated when he learned that Ibn Saud had been invited to send one of his sons to visit the United States. He misconstrued American intentions to be the promotion of Ibn Saud as its candidate for the leadership of an Arab federation. A week or so later, when 'Abd al-Ilah was invited to London, he thought Britain was likewise lining up its candidate.[62] His dissatisfaction and disappointment increased apace and within six weeks he had plummeted from euphoria to paranoia, claiming that Britain had instigated a conspiracy with his own prime minister and those of Egypt, Iraq, Lebanon and Syria, to prevent him from achieving his ambitions.[63]

On his way to London the Iraqi regent had a stopover in Palestine. He met Abdullah there and tried to mitigate his fears by telling him that his trip was not for political discussions. But in fact, the regent arrived in London just when the War Cabinet's Committee on Palestine was scheduled to meet, and it was inevitable that he should become involved in the discussions, if only peripherally. The Committee on Palestine, dominated by the Colonial Office, was favorable to partition, and, in conjunction with partition, to the idea of Greater Syria. The basic theory was simple: the Arabs would lose something by the partition of Palestine, they would gain something by the unification of Greater Syria, and at the close of this transaction, Britain's position would be unimpaired. But how to go about the unification was as much a problem for Britain as it was for the Arabs.

Abdullah's role was particularly vexing. Britain could not make him king of Greater Syria – the Syrians did not want him and Ibn Saud was sure to make trouble – but it could not let his utility over the past twenty years go

143

unacknowledged, whether out of a true sense of indebtedness or for fear that a policy of friendship with Britain would then appear without benefit to prospective allies. So the committee came to the reluctant conclusion that Greater Syria could not be created in Abdullah's lifetime. To facilitate the partition of Palestine, however, it was proposed that whatever portion of Palestine would be allotted to the Arabs might be united to Transjordan as the first stage in creating Greater Syria. Completion of its unification 'would probably take place on the death of the Amir, whose health is by no means strong.'[64]

Hence, Abdullah's determination not to let London ignore him was perversely successful; he was not ignored, but his goals came no closer to fulfillment. In any case, the Foreign Office opposed Palestine's partition and the creation of Greater Syria. After Lord Moyne's assassination by Jewish terrorists on 5 November 1944, partition was dropped and the idea of Greater Syria along with it.[65]

'Abd al-Ilah learned something of these plans in their early stages while he was in London. He found out at least that Britain was again proposing to partition Palestine, that it would do so by force if necessary, and that it proposed to attach the Arab part of Palestine to Transjordan. This much he passed on to Abdullah.[66] Whether he knew the details of Britain's plans, or dared to tell Abdullah about them if he did, is unknown.

It was perhaps the regent's news about Britain's interest in Greater Syria that stimulated Nuri, in January 1944, to new levels of activity, but the impetus to his renewed activity might also have been his dawning fears about Egypt's intentions. The regent had already expressed doubts about Egypt to Abdullah on his way to London and Abdullah had agreed that a serious effort must be made to assert the leadership of the Hashemites.[67] The idea was that the effort should be made in concert, but Nuri's activities served only to alienate Abdullah. First, he trespassed into Palestine, which Abdullah considered his own sphere of interest, in an attempt to reorganize the Palestinian leadership. He also met with Jewish officials, whom Abdullah considered his own special clients.[68] Worse, he let slip that the Syrian delegation to Cairo had demanded a republic and that copies of the *procès verbal* of the meeting with this demand had been forwarded to London and Washington.

Abdullah was enraged by this news and rebuked Nuri severely for allowing such a development. An impasse between the two was reached when Nuri retorted that the Syrians would not have been so emphatic had not Abdullah's delegate first pushed for a monarchy. Abdullah then accused Nuri of plotting behind Egypt's back to create a republic of Greater Syria so that Iraq might regain the lead in matters of Arab unity, and threatened to expose him to Nahas. Thus the rivalry between Transjordan and Iraq created the prospect of one Hashemite regime running to Nahas in order to check the activities of the other.[69] To bring an end to this unseemly state of affairs, the regent invited

Abdullah to Baghdad, but, judging from Abdullah's remarks about Iraq on his return home, he was not entirely successful. Abdullah's observations of the Iraqi situation were made in bitterness, but nevertheless showed a degree of prescience. He said he would not be surprised if Nuri one day met the same fate as Bakr Sidqi (assassination), and he noted that the officer corps of the Iraqi army was divided into antagonistic cliques.[70]

While the Hashemites were squabbling, Nahas Pasha had got on with his task of meeting delegations from the other Arab states, Saudi Arabia, Syria, Lebanon and the Yemen. He succeeded in coaxing them all to the conference table at Alexandria. In the meantime Abdullah had been able to squeeze out of Britain an announcement of its intention to replace the mandate with a treaty at the end of the war,[71] but this did not add any weight to Transjordan's presence at the Alexandria Conference.

As the time of the conference drew near, Abdullah did what he could to advertise his claims and strengthen his position. He distributed a memorandum to those whom he anticipated would participate in the conference, except for the Saudi representative, recapitulating the role of the Hashemites in the Arab awakening and drawing attention to his own claims as the senior member of the family.[72] He also met with the regent and the Iraqi delegation to plot Hashemite strategy. His idea was that a bloc should be formed to push for a Hashemite monarchy in Greater Syria and to 'liberate' the Hijaz. The Iraqis refused on the grounds that the Alexandria conference was to promote unity, not conflict, and that at most the conference would result in an agreement between Arab states in their present form. Abdullah opposed any agreement which implied recognition of the existing administrative divisions of the Arab world, and the Hashemite meeting ended without issue.

The Alexandria Conference met in the autumn of 1944. The result was a protocol outlining the principles of Arab co-operation and calling for the establishment of a League of Arab states. It was a document that appealed to Arab public opinion, but it did not in fact address Arab unity[73] – rather, it laid the basis for co-operation between Arab governments on their guaranteed sovereignty and merely looked forward to the future integration of the Arab peoples. By the time the Arab League Pact was drafted six months later, the emphasis on individual sovereignty had been strengthened and the expectation that the League would be the first step to greater unity had been diluted. As a consequence, the Arab League, when it was formally constituted in May 1945, symbolized nothing more than 'a network of relationships among states.'[74]

Abdullah later described the Arab League as 'seven heads thrust into a sack,'[75] an apt characterization, since the League was built on the premise of the assured sovereignty of each state. His attitude also reflected his bitterness and frustration that the League did not advance his own idea of Arab unity, which was to

145

begin with the creation of Greater Syria. Indeed, the formation of the League changed the balance of power in the Middle East to the detriment of his position and that of the Hashemites in general by enlisting Egypt and Saudi Arabia in the battle for Syria. And these two states, even before the final constitution of the League, had begun to draw together in an anti-Hashemite bloc.

In January 1945, five months before the Arab League came into existence, King Faruq had visited Ibn Saud. Abdullah was incensed when he heard the news, not least because his two enemies had met in the Hijaz. He feared that Egypt and Saudi Arabia would combine against him and he threatened to pull out of the coming meeting in Cairo which was to finalize the Arab League Pact. He, 'the eldest son of the man who laid the foundations of Arab independence, was not going to submit to the leadership of King Farouk or that of the usurper Ibn Saud . . .'[76] But the regent and Nuri, who had been summoned to Amman to discuss a Hashemite counter-strategy, convinced him that he must send his delegate to Cairo as planned.

Another set of meetings which took place in Cairo at the end of February 1945 was even more disturbing. The 'Big Three,' Churchill, Roosevelt and Stalin, had just met at the Crimean resort of Yalta to discuss the post-war political settlement of Central and Eastern Europe and the Far East. Their prestige was at its height, for victory was at hand and the sordid underside of peacemaking was not yet public knowledge. On the way home, Churchill and Roosevelt stopped in Cairo, where Roosevelt had arranged to meet Ibn Saud. Churchill also saw Ibn Saud, as well as King Faruq and Shukri al-Quwatli who happened to be in town. It was a tremendous blow to Abdullah that neither of these statesmen should have seen a Hashemite. While he had no claims on the president of the United States, he was extremely 'pained that the Prime Minister, an old friend, should have come so near and shown no desire to even see me.' A breach of friendship was bad enough, but the meetings in Cairo also seemed to signal to Abdullah – and, he feared, to the Arab world at large – that the future lay with others than the Hashemites.[77]

So great was his umbrage that the minister resident in the Middle East, Sir Edward Grigg, immediately rushed to Amman from Cairo to smooth his ruffled feathers. Abdullah received Sir Edward politely but coldly and later told Kirkbride that he was not convinced by the minister's explanations that the meetings had been fortuitous and that nothing detrimental to himself had transpired. More feather-smoothing was clearly needed, although Britain was not willing to go to the lengths demanded by Abdullah. It would not, for example, make an official statement to correct the public belief that 'the United Nations were now basing their policy in the Middle East on Ibn Saud, Farouk and their satellites.' Nor would it issue an immediate invitation for him to come to England. Churchill did, however, send him a personal message backing up Grigg's explanations and emphasizing his own regret that he had not been able, during his short visit, to see all his old friends in the Middle East. None the less, for weeks afterwards Abdullah continued to harp on Churchill's unfortunate lapse.[78]

In the meetings of the political sub-committee to draw up the Arab League Pact, these shadowy rivalries became better defined. Egypt and Iraq were clearly two opposite poles competing for leadership. Saudi Arabia aligned with Egypt against its old Hashemite enemies. Lebanon found Cairo, the cultural capital of the Arab world, more cosmopolitan and more understanding of Lebanon's special needs than the Muslim interior – Syria, Iraq and Transjordan – at its back. Memories of Ibrahim Pasha, the son of the viceroy of Egypt who ruled Lebanon from 1830 to 1840, were invoked to stress the historic ties between the two countries. Syria, although not enthusiastically pro-Egyptian, was also drawn into Egypt's orbit by its desire for protection from Hashemite monarchical designs and by its close ties to Saudi Arabia. The Hashemites stood alone, and the League, far from being an instrument of Hashemite ambition, became another stumbling block in the road to Greater Syria, Abdullah, though discouraged, did not accept defeat, and in spite of the forces arrayed against him in the League he continued after the war to strive for a Syrian throne.

By the end of the war, Abdullah had achieved neither the crown of Greater Syria nor the independence of Transjordan. He spent the rest of his life like an alchemist searching for the right combination of elements that, coming together in a single fortuitous instant, would propel him on to the throne of Greater Syria. Independence, however, was a less esoteric goal; it was a matter of simple timing.

Throughout the war London had been sympathetic to Abdullah's pleas for independence in a way that it could not be in regard to his desire for a Syrian throne. After all, the mandate principle had embedded in it the concept of eventual self-government. In particular, Britain's support of Lebanese and Syrian independence in 1941 and after put it in a sensitive position regarding Transjordanian independence. The dilemma was simply this: 'If we are prepared to put an end to the mandate in Syria to buy the support of Arabs who might otherwise be our enemies, are there any good grounds on which we can continue to retain the mandate in Trans-Jordan, where the ruler and his people have for twenty years been our most consistent Arab friends?'[79] The short answer was 'no', but the Colonial Office did not have to be unduly worried about consistency since there was nothing and no one in Transjordan to threaten Britain's position. There was no nationalist movement to speak of, and as one observer later noted, 'the people were less grateful than they would otherwise be for the increase in internal autonomy . . . since every advance in self-government increases the absolute power of the Amir.'[80]

In the absence of popular pressure, independence could wait. The high commissioner sought to make the granting of independence politically useful, and thought a good time to confer it would be when Abdullah finally realized his hopes for a Syrian throne were in vain.[81] The Colonial Office agreed and added other reasons for delay: granting independence might prejudice the post-war settlement in the Middle East; it would lead to agitation in Palestine for independence on the part of Arabs and for matching concessions on the part of Jews; Ibn Saud would be alarmed and would certainly renew his claims to Aqaba and Ma'an; and finally, independence might hamper Britain's unrestricted use of Transjordanian air bases.[82] Nothing of all this was revealed to Abdullah. He was told simply that nothing could be done while the war still raged, hardly a convincing answer since Syria and Lebanon had been promised independence in the midst of fighting.[83]

By the time the fighting stopped Abdullah had not yet given up on Syria, so there was no reason to compensate him for unrealized dreams that he had not yet acknowledged as unrealizable. Britain, however, had decided to seek new terms for its mandate in Palestine. On 13 November 1945 the new foreign minister, Ernest Bevin, announced that an Anglo-American Committee would proceed to Palestine in an attempt to discover an acceptable and workable arrangement. Abdullah's favorable reaction to this announcement was secured by inviting him to London for treaty talks.[84] The high commissioner's original decision to wait for a politically opportune moment had finally paid off.

Abdullah arrived in London at the end of February 1946. The negotiations proceeded smoothly and within a month a very unexceptional treaty had been written providing for Transjordan's independence, Abdullah's sovereignty, and perpetual peace and friendship between Transjordan and Britain. One question had particularly worried Abdullah beforehand: he feared that, with independence, Whitehall might stop or greatly reduce its support of the Arab Legion. Therefore, before leaving Amman he had met with the regent and Nuri to arrange that Iraq should pick up the tab if Britain refused to do so. The Iraqis were happy to agree, for they were anxious to supersede Britain in Transjordan. But Abdullah had only wanted a bargaining chip in case of problems in London, and he was relieved that in a special military annex to the treaty, Britain agreed to continue supporting the Legion in return for military facilities in Transjordan.[85] Later, however, the annex proved troublesome – it gave Britain virtually free run of Transjordan's military installations and provided the United States and the Soviet Union, which for different reasons wanted to withhold recognition, with an excuse to do so.

The treaty did not instantaneously call forth the infrastructure of real independence: Transjordan remained financially and militarily dependent on Britain. Moreover the habits of twenty-five years could not be broken in a day. The prime minister and the members of the ministerial council, after a brief period of 'standing on their dignity,' resumed their old practice of consulting Kirkbride informally on all sorts of matters. He was, he reported, frequently 'asked by the Prime Minister to use my personal influence over the King in matters of purely local and internal concern.'[86] Equally, Abdullah maintained his habit of informing Kirkbride 'what he has in his mind in both official and private matters with a frankness which is sometimes startling – and, naturally,' Kirkbride assured the Foreign Office, 'I report anything which is of interest.'[87]

Despite the limited nature of his achievement Abdullah made a triumphal return to Transjordan. He arrived at Lydda airport, where a crowd of notables had come to meet him, and drove in procession from there to Amman. On the Transjordanian side of the frontier, large crowds assembled along the route, which was decorated with triumphal arches, flags and carpets. Camels were slaughtered in the road in celebratory sacrifice.[88]

In the region, Transjordan's new status was officially welcomed but privately denigrated. King Faruq said he was in favor of the principle of independence for Transjordan, but felt Britain had acted precipitately. Ibn Saud scoffed at Britain's concern that he might oppose Transjordan's independence, saying that Abdullah was 'not . . . a serious person of whom he could be afraid.' He nevertheless 'let off a lot of steam against the Sheriffs who . . . always wanted to destroy him,' and called attention to his right of transit through Transjordan to Syria and his claims to Aqaba and Ma'an. The Syrian press considered the military annex of the treaty to be inconsistent with independence, but the Syrian government was secretly pleased since the annex and Abdullah's continued dependence on Britain were a fatal blow to Abdullah's case for the Syrian throne. Zionist leaders in Palestine, Britain and the United States opposed Transjordan's independence, which contradicted Zionist dogma that Transjordan was part of Palestine. This pressure contributed to the American delay in recognizing Transjordan.[89]

The consummation of Abdullah's independence occurred on 25 May, when he crowned himself king. Present for the coronation were ranking British, Transjordanian and Iraqi officials, a Lebanese delegation, a number of Syrian and Iraqi tribal chiefs, and a gate-crasher, 'Abd al-Rahman 'Azzam, the secretary-general of the Arab League. The Yemeni delegation arrived a day late and missed the ceremonies.[90] Syria had not been invited to send a delegation, and it tried to prevent private citizens from attending and refused to allow a truckload of fruit for the official luncheon to cross the border.[91] Talal, Abdullah's eldest son, was conspicuously present, for he had managed to win his way back into his father's – and Kirkbride's – good graces in the latter years of the war.

Talal's five-year exclusion from the succession to the throne was said to have been one of the few secrets Abdullah ever managed to keep. The *irade* excluding him from the throne had been torn up just before Abdullah went to London to negotiate the treaty, and he became crown prince when Abdullah became king.[92] There were two reasons for Talal's reinstatement, put forth by Kirkbride during the trying year of 1948 when Britain became especially concerned about Transjordan's future. Firstly, he had 'mended his ways,' establishing good relations with Kirkbride himself and doing his best to further British policy in Transjordan. Secondly, Nayyif, the next in line to the throne, had got involved in a series of black market and smuggling scandals, proving himself to be a 'bonehead . . . [who] did not appear to possess sufficient intelligence to play any political role whether it be good or bad.' Talal was therefore judged capable of succeeding his father, and Kirkbride declared himself 'not pessimistic' about Transjordan's ability to survive Abdullah's death.[93]

Although Talal mended his fences with Britain, his relations with his father continued to be characterized by a cycle of fights and reconciliations. Abdullah gave Talal few responsibilities, ceremonial or otherwise; this, it was said, was due to his jealousy and his natural disinclination to be confronted by his own mortality in the shape of his successor. Abdullah's jealousy also made it difficult for Talal to maintain friendships or build political alliances with those likely to serve him in the future. Comings and goings at his home were reported to the palace, and regular contact with him was known to cause 'august displeasure.'[94]

By 1946, Abdullah had achieved the formal independence of Transjordan. Yet he was aware, as were his detractors, of the limited nature of this independence. For him, it was not Britain that stood in the way of full independence – Britain had given him what he already had of independence – but the other Arab states. By Abdullah's lights, it was his neighbors that prevented his expansion and the creation of an economically viable and politically weighty kingdom. Therefore he spent the closing years of his reign in increasingly deadly conflict within the region.

Chapter 9

Abdullah, Britain and the Arab world, 1945–8

Abdullah was quite content with the degree of independence accorded by the Anglo-Transjordanian treaty in spite of Arab, American and Soviet objections that the annex, granting Britain extensive military facilities, compromised Transjordan's true independence. When the United States postponed recognition 'until we have the opportunity to observe how the new arrangement between Great Britain and Trans-Jordan works out,'[1] and the Soviet Union blocked Transjordan's admission to the United Nations,[2] Abdullah's anger was directed at those two countries, rather than at Britain or at the treaty. When he initiated talks aimed at revising the treaty less than two years after its original passage, his purpose was less to alter its substance than to disguise it in more abstract and diplomatic language.[3] At that time, what could not be well enough disguised for public consumption was hidden in secret letters. One of these allowed Kirkbride to oversee the expenditure of the subsidy, much as he had under the mandate.[4]

Transjordan's continued close relations with Britain set Abdullah at odds with the general post-war trend of Arab affairs away from Britain's grasp. Unlike Transjordan, both Egypt and Iraq failed to ratify new treaties with Britain which would have secured British policy in the Middle East in the changed circumstances of the post-war era. Other of Abdullah's policies and inclinations further distanced him from his fellow Arabs. His insistent meddling in Syrian affairs, aimed at the creation of Greater Syria, aroused anger and suspicion in virtually every Arab capital, and he was believed to favor the partition of Palestine, contrary to the wishes of the Palestinians and to Arab sentiments in general. Both policies were seen in the Arab world as being motivated by selfish ambition, a view conveyed by 'a somewhat pitying smile and deprecating shrug of the shoulders,' when Abdullah was discussed outside of Amman.[5]

In addition to the discordance of Abdullah's policies, described by one onlooker as 'the greatest irritant in inter-Arab relations,'[6] he cultivated an abrasive personal style with his peers. His famous charm, to which many Britons were susceptible, was not in evidence in his dealings with Arabs. He had uniformly poor personal relations with most Arab statesmen, including his Iraqi relatives, and he seemed even to relish the prospect of annoying them. He

Figure 14. Amir Abdullah playing chess with Shaykh Muhammad Amin al-Shanqiti, Amman, 1945.

published his memoirs in 1945, stirring up considerable ill-feeling in the Arab world with his waspish comments about Arabs in general and Ibn Saud in particular.[7] His visit to Turkey in 1947, like his visit ten years earlier, also caused unnecessary friction. Embarking for home from Alexandretta, which Turkey had annexed in 1939, he expressed his regret at leaving 'Turkish territory' and saluted the Turkish flag, acts which were meant to recall the failure of the Syrian government to hold on to the territory and to cause the present government, consisting of the same men, maximum irritation.[8]

Abdullah's only Arab allies, his kinsmen in Iraq, were as embarrassed by his abrasiveness as his enemies were vexed. His extravagant claims to Syria queered their own pitch for a union of the Fertile Crescent, and his antagonism to the Arab League added to Iraq's difficulties within it. One outcome of the fear of being too closely identified with Abdullah on the part of his nephews in Iraq was that the long-rumored Iraqi-Transjordan federation culminated in June 1947 in nothing more profound than a treaty of friendship between the two states. The treaty, which 'produced nothing that did not already exist in practice,' was kept secret for days, causing, perhaps intentionally, grave consternation in Damascus and Riyadh.[9]

The agitation which Abdullah stirred up around virtually everything his hand touched outside of purely Transjordanian concerns even threatened to embroil

British diplomats in the Middle East with one another and with the governments to which they were accredited. Because of the Anglo-Transjordanian treaty and Abdullah's historical closeness to Britain, his activities were popularly believed to be emanations of British policy. When he made particularly provocative pronouncements – usually in regard to Syria where he was especially vociferous – Damascus, Cairo, Riyadh and Beirut habitually called on London to muzzle him. Here Britain was caught on the horns of a dilemma. Attempting to stick to the legalities of Transjordanian independence, it publicly could do no more than reiterate its neutrality and deny its ability to control the acts of an independent monarch. The fact that it had the situation well in hand between Kirkbride, the British resident turned minister to Amman, and Glubb, the British commander of the Arab Legion, could not be divulged, since to do so would have been to admit that Abdullah was indeed less than independent.

This posture made life very difficult at times for the British diplomatic corps in the Middle East, to the point of putting continued close relations with Abdullah at the expense of maintaining good relations with other Arab regimes. But Kirkbride was against any public reprimands, on the grounds that these would simply annoy Abdullah and make him more obdurate, although he regularly lectured him quietly about his machinations. Glubb, too, was quietly but none the less fully aware of the necessity of preventing Abdullah from using the Legion in connection with Greater Syria.[10] This veiled control, however, did little to mitigate the discomfort of British diplomats in Arab capitals whenever Abdullah's activities annoyed the governments to which they were accredited. Sir Iltyd Clayton, who, in his capacity as adviser on Arab affairs to the head of the British Middle East Office, met many Arab statesmen and all manner of opinion, complained:

There are few people in the Arab States who do not believe that we are instigating Abdullah's activities and when assured that we are not they come back with the assertion that we could stop them if we liked. I am faced with this again and again, and my questioners are not in the least satisfied by being told that King Abdullah being a reigning and independent monarch we cannot correctly interfere with his actions.[11]

While Kirkbride in Amman could excuse Abdullah's peccadilloes as a species of impishness and ascribe his major offenses to advancing age,[12] other British officials regarded him with far less indulgence. Clayton thought that Abdullah, 'a great fraud and liar,' ought to be told to keep quiet.[13] Laurence Grafftey-Smith, British Minister in Jidda, agreed:

. . . I have gathered an impression during the past twenty-five years that King Abdullah is almost universally considered to be no more than a puppet of British policy and a rather bad joke. Even in the Hejaz, when I served here with his father, . . . the Emir Abdullah appeared to enjoy the respect of none. (Whenever he played chess at the British Agency, he cheated.) In Egypt, in Saudi Arabia and even in Iraq, I have never heard his name mentioned except with some contempt.[14]

Into these dangerous currents of opinion eddying around the figure of Abdullah, the commander-in-chief of the British fleet in the Mediterranean unwittingly ventured. Between himself and Kirkbride the thought had taken shape that Abdullah might be taken for a cruise on the Gulf of Aqaba,[15] and Kirkbride broached the idea with Abdullah, who readily agreed. Unfortunately, Foreign Office approval had not been solicited beforehand, and when the British legations in the other Arab capitals heard of the plan there was a unanimous chorus of disapproval: embarking from Aqaba would draw attention to territory which was disputed between Transjordan and Saudi Arabia; unusual attention to Abdullah would confirm the belief that he was Britain's 'particular pet,' and would be taken as a mark of British support for him in the ongoing Greater Syrian controversy; both Faruq and Ibn Saud would be irritated by the cruise in their territorial waters.[16] In the light of this overwhelmingly negative reaction, the Foreign Office decided the cruise would not be a good idea and the commander-in-chief agreed to withdraw the invitation on the grounds that the ship could not be spared after all, an excuse rendered palatable to Abdullah by the additional information that it was needed to patrol the coast of Palestine against illegal immigration.[17]

Kirkbride was embarrassed by the withdrawn invitation and embittered by his colleague's reactions. He wrote angrily to the Foreign Office that the telegrams exchanged seemed to indicate that Abdullah was a 'wicked provocative person who should not be permitted to be associated with His Majesty's ship.' (A note in pencil, added in the Foreign Office, commented, 'but he is rather!') Hoping to set the record straight, he recalled Abdullah's previous and happy associations with the British navy, emphasized that Aqaba was considered Transjordanian territory by Britain, called Cairo's linking of a cruise with the problem of Greater Syria a 'magnificent flight of imagination' and dourly dismissed Jidda's 'all-embracing disapproval' as 'only what would be expected from that quarter.' He concluded on a note of superior wisdom: 'No one knows better than myself the King's lack of discretion and his tendency to take precipitate action, both characteristics become more marked as his age increases, but they are not going to be cured or even counteracted by a sort of collective diplomatic suppression exercised by His Britannic Majesty's representatives in the Middle East.' Although Kirkbride did not know it, his missive did not help Abdullah's standing in London. The Foreign Office received it coolly and neither circulated it nor responded to it. Rather than inspiring forbearance, it moved Sir Peter Garran to observe, 'It is a terrifying thought that King Abdullah's shortcomings of indiscretion and provocativeness will get worse as he grows older!'[18]

Abdullah, however, got in the last word. He asked Kirkbride to forward his 'sincere thanks' and a silver cup bearing the name of the ship to the commander-in-chief, because 'I consider the mere invitation to be a noble sentiment on the part of the Royal Navy . . . [which] I appreciate . . . as if the cruise had been carried out in fact . . .' Kirkbride, a trifle self-righteously, did as he was bidden without further comment.[19]

Abdullah could and did embarrass Britain in the Middle East, but he was unable to mold British policy to his own ends. Rather, it was British interest which defined the success or failure of Abdullah's policies. His most tenaciously pursued goals in the post-war period were the addition of Palestine, or of whatever part of Palestine the Arabs should keep, to Transjordan and, as ever, the crown of Greater Syria. For Abdullah the former was merely the first step toward achieving the latter, but history separated the two by allotting success in Abdullah's lifetime to the one and failure to the other. And certainly, one of the most important forces which shaped that history was the force of British interest.

Viewed from the present day, the unresolved status of Palestine stands out as the single most important problem confronting British and Arab statesmen after the war. Indeed it was. But it symbolized far more general problems facing Britain and the Arabs at the time. The over-riding post-war dilemma for Britain was how to reconstitute Anglo-Arab relations in a period when Britain had little of material value to offer the Arabs but wished to retain its influence in the region, its military and communications facilities and its privileged access to oil.[20] The Arabs were concerned not only with their relationship to Britain in the era of independence, but with their relations to one another at a time when, theoretically at least, Arab unity was finally achievable after the lengthy mandate interlude.

Questions of future relations with Britain and indeed with the world at large were tackled by the Arab countries individually, each separately pursuing treaty negotiations with Britain or economic arrangements with the United States. They were also addressed collectively in the effort to keep Palestine Arab. The struggle for Arab unity, or more accurately for leadership of the Arab world, also manifested itself in Palestine. But the key to the future of the Arab world – geographically, strategically and emotionally – was still, perhaps from habit, Syria; and the rivalry of Arab states for regional leadership was largely played out in what has been called the 'struggle for Syria.'[21] Abdullah, satisfied with his relationship with Britain but dissatisfied with his position in the Arab world, turned his attention first to Syria immediately following the war, rather than concentrating on the more pressing issue of the future of Palestine.

Abdullah's ambition to sit on a throne in Damascus was an old one. Neither the substance nor the impetus of his ambition changed after the war, although the framework of his rhetoric shifted to accommodate post-war realities. With Britain he adopted the language of the emerging Cold War, presenting himself as an ally whose interests, like Britain's, lay in holding the line against Soviet expansionism. The 'reunification' of Syria, in Abdullah's view, would help that cause. As he explained to Attlee:

Russia is following a forward policy in Iran and Kurdistan, a policy which may well aim at expansion to the Persian Gulf and the Mediterranean. Against this, it is desirable that a defensive front should be built up covering Turkey, Iran and Afghanistan backed by the 'fertile crescent' of the Arab countries . . . Syria is now ruled by a number of native politicians but, if we follow its history from the days of the Amir Faisal . . . we realise that Syria needs other rulers who will base their policy on friendship with Great Britain. If France leaves Syria, it might be possible for that country to be reunited and I believe that such an event would be in the interests of His Majesty's Government.[22]

As had become Abdullah's habit during the war, he kept up a steady stream of notes and memoranda informing Whitehall of his opinions on Middle Eastern affairs. All of them emphasized the Russian menace and included some criticism of the current Syrian regime, making the case that Syrian 'weakness' would be overcome by unification with Transjordan and the application of his own steadying hand at the tiller. London, however, was unresponsive. The letters, in Foreign Office opinion, added nothing to their understanding of Middle Eastern problems, nor did they improve Abdullah's chances of getting British support for his Greater Syrian ambitions. However the one-sided correspondence was allowed to continue, because Kirkbride felt that it provided Abdullah's 'active brain and ambitions [with] a harmless safety valve.'[23] It certainly meant something to Abdullah, who wrote in one letter, 'My letters and the contents are so important that their continuation is in the interest of both our countries.'[24]

To make his point in the Arab world, where all the lands of Greater Syria except Palestine were now independent, Abdullah adopted a new holiday commemorating 8 March 1920, the day when the General Syrian Congress had elected Faysal king of Syria. This holiday allowed him to stress his belief that Faysal's kingdom of Syria had represented the true will of the Syrian people (i.e., desiring a Hashemite monarchy), and the natural state of that country, which at the time had included Transjordan. From that premise he built his case, arguing that since Syria was now free of foreign control the monarchy should be restored, and that he, as Faysal's brother and the eldest living Hashemite, who was moreover presently ruling a part of the original Kingdom of Syria, was the logical heir to the throne of the reconstituted whole. He was careful in making his case to outflank both 'Abd al-Ilah, the regent of Iraq, who could claim the throne as the eldest son of Abdullah's older brother, and Faysal II, the only direct male descendant of Faysal I.

Despite the altered regional and global conditions after the war, Abdullah's chances of achieving a throne in Syria had not changed significantly. Nor had his methods, which continued to rest on propaganda efforts, the disbursal of money, and contact with Syrian monarchists and malcontents. However, he did have more latitude for these activities than he had had under the mandate, even though Kirkbride continued to provide a damping effect and the Arab Legion was held firmly *hors-concours* by Glubb.

Money, for one thing, was more accessible than it had been when the budget was strictly under British scrutiny. No Transjordanian prime minister could refuse Abdullah's demands for funds point blank and hope to remain in office for long. Money was slightly more plentiful as well: public funds had been boosted by the 1946 agreements with the Iraq Petroleum Company and the Trans-Arabian Pipeline Company, by which each paid £60,000 per year for the right to pump oil through Transjordan irrespective of the actual flow.[25] The royal family's private resources were also growing through their involvement in drug smuggling, using the special privileges accorded royal automobiles at the frontiers. Rumours of royal connections with the drug trade had been around for years, and in April 1947 the queen's car was stopped near Gaza and found to be carrying some 200 lbs of hashish. In the car along with the regular chauffeur was Nayyif al-Atrash, the son of the Druze chieftain Sultan al-Atrash, which perhaps links at least some of the proceeds of royal trafficking with Syrian politics, although Kirkbride declared himself satisfied that Abdullah personally had had no knowledge of it.[26]

With independence, Abdullah was also able to mix more freely with Syrian malcontents who encouraged Abdullah's claims for their own ends. Generally they represented factional and minority interests alienated from the urban politics of Damascus, and from their marginal position they hardly afforded the sort of support necessary to put Abdullah on a Syrian throne. Among these elements in the post-war period were Alawite rebels led by Sulayman Murshid, certain tribal shaykhs of the Jazira, and the Druze al-Atrash clan.[27] In addition there were rumors of new dissident groups – army officers, ambitious and dissatisfied – seeking the support of the Arab Legion through Abdullah's worn out dreams.[28] And, as always, there was the core of sincere monarchists who had been loyal to Faysal and who had transferred their allegiance to Abdullah after Faysal's death. The most prominent of these was Hasan al-Hakim, a former prime minister of Syria who had served Abdullah briefly in 1921 as financial adviser. He urged Abdullah to invest his money in the Syrian elections scheduled for the summer of 1947, and leave the realization of the Greater Syrian monarchy to 'democratic' processes. Abdullah did give several thousand pounds to monarchist candidates, but his campaign contributions paled in comparison with the sums disbursed by the Syrian political parties and by the Saudi government to secure the continuity of the republic.[29]

Abdullah's penchant for making and publishing pronouncements on Greater Syria could be exercised more openly with the relaxation of his accountability to Britain. His annual speech at the opening of Parliament in 1946, his first such speech since becoming king, was not vetted as usual by Kirkbride and contained an appeal for the unity of Transjordan and Syria.[30] After that, given the chance of any public occasion, however slight (he made one of his most contentious statements on the subject of Greater Syria at the opening of an agricultural school), he would deliver himself of thoughts on the topic. He also readily met reporters, resisting Kirkbride's advice not to give interviews.[31]

The creation of Transjordan legations in neighboring countries provided a natural conduit for his propaganda. Syrian forces raided the Transjordan consulate in Damascus and confiscated thousands of leaflets bearing a royal appeal for the unity of Syria and Transjordan, after which the consulate was closed and its staff expelled.[32] The most famous of his propaganda efforts, however, was the so-called *Transjordan White Paper*, a 294-page collection of documents dating from the First World War. Published in May 1947, with elections impending in both Syria and Lebanon, it marshalled evidence in support of his idea of a Greater Syrian monarchy. But its cumulative effect is of a sad catalogue of wishful thinking and of failure, rather than the documentation of a just claim maliciously sabotaged.[33]

In retrospect, the sheer repetitiveness of Abdullah's efforts and their seemingly inevitable failure has lent an air of unreality to the question of Greater Syria, and even given it the exaggerated quality of farce. Yet Greater Syria was a sensitive subject in Syria, and in the Arab world generally. The National Bloc government in Damascus was especially vulnerable to Abdullah's point that the Arab lands had been divided according to imperialist interests and should now, in the era of independence, be reunited. To do less would be to acknowledge benefit from imperialism and to imply, after the fact, a certain complicity with it. In rebutting that implication the most potent and persistently used charge against Abdullah, and one to which he was particularly vulnerable, was that he was a British stooge and that his version of Greater Syria was simply a device to introduce British hegemony in the place of French. (Various British officials did periodically raise the possibility that a Greater Syria under Abdullah might be useful to Britain, but these suggestions were always defeated by the majority opinion that sponsoring Abdullah in Greater Syria would make Britain less, rather than more, secure in the Middle East.)[34]

Damascus and to a lesser extent Beirut were directly affected by Abdullah's active pursuit of his ambitions. Cairo, Baghdad and Riyadh were no less opposed to seeing an extension of his authority. The cacophony of recriminations emanating from these five capitals at once was at times deafening, and in August 1947 this din increased to an unbelievable pitch when Abdullah issued a call for an all-Syria conference. The idea was not new; he had tried to make a similar appeal during the war, but had been prevented by the high commissioner. With independence, Britain no longer exercised such control over his foreign policy statements, and, judging the results of the Syrian elections that summer to be propitious, he renewed his efforts.

The elections were not a victory for the government of President Shukri al-Quwatli and Prime Minister Jamil Mardam, but neither were they a defeat. Al-Quwatli's National Party won only twenty-four seats in the new Chamber of Deputies to fifty-three won by a rival nationalist coalition,[35] but both he and Mardam managed to remain in office. Abdullah took heart from al-Quwatli's setback,[36] although it was not in fact a gain for himself since the rival coalition was as solidly republican as the National Party. What was significant was the election of some fifty 'independents' (landowners, businessmen, tribal and minority leaders, and heads of large and powerful families) with no party or ideological affiliation who held the balance between the rival nationalist coalitions, forming a stalking ground for political fortune hunters in Syria like Abdullah.[37]

Taking advantage of the erosion of support for al-Quwatli's government, Abdullah called for an all-Syria conference to create first a Greater Syrian government and then an Arab union of Greater Syria and Iraq. Attacking both the Syrian government and the Arab League, he declared:

The supporters of disunity, separation, and surrender, are still continuing their seditious propaganda against the call for a united Covenant. They are also still creating by means of that form of Government [republican] established in the northern part of our dear home [Syria], considerable obstacles in the way of the achievement of union or federation of the country . . . A mere regional republican system, founded as a result of frontiers devised for the convenience of Mandatory powers and maintained by force of arms, can never overrule the validity of a solemn national Covenant [the Syrian Congress of 1920 which elected Faysal King] . . . The National intelligence is insulted by those who claim that the Covenant of the Arab League involves the retention of the Arab World in its present form which retards Arab progress by maintaining frontiers imposed by colonisation. . .[38]

Reaction to this pronouncement was immediate and sharp. Al-Quwatli and his ally Ibn Saud issued sharply worded protests and privately excoriated Abdullah to British diplomats.[39] Then, to rally a united response to what was an attack on the Arab state system as a whole, al-Quwatli proceeded to Beirut, Jamil Mardam went to Baghdad, and a third Syrian emissary was sent to Cairo and Riyadh. Iraq, Abdullah's closest friend, issued no public statement, but distanced itself from his declaration.[40] Lebanon published a joint communiqué with Syria calling attention to Abdullah's violation of the Arab League Covenant.[41] Cairo supported the Saudi protest. The newspapers of all the Arab capitals hummed with denunciations – one in Damascus even reported a civil war in Transjordan featuring riots in Amman, the flight of Abdullah, a mutiny of the Arab Legion followed by the flight of Glubb in disguise and the incarceration of his second in command, 'Abd al-Qadir al-Jundi, and the arrest of most of the Transjordan notables.[42] On a more down-to-earth level, there was talk of censuring Abdullah in the Arab League, or even expelling him from it.[43]

The brouhaha was cut short, however, by the publication of the report of the United Nations Special Committee on Palestine (UNSCOP) at the end of August 1947. Its majority recommendation of partition immediately redirected Arab attention to Palestine. (A minority report proposed federalization.) In an effort to create a united front against partition, the furor over Abdullah's Greater Syria pronouncements was allowed to die down. 'Abd al-Rahman 'Azzam, the secretary general of the Arab League, visited Amman in early October to smooth things over. He remarked that the union of all Arab countries was the ultimate goal of the Arab League, Abdullah replied that his recent actions had been entirely unselfish and in the interests of the Arab nation as a whole, and the matter was temporarily laid to rest.[44] At Arab League meetings at Sofar and Aley, Lebanon, called to formulate a response to UNSCOP, Transjordan's representative, Samir al-Rifa'i, kept a low profile and voted in line with the rest.

UNSCOP was the last of a series of post-war bodies created to explore 'the problem of Palestine.' The series included the Anglo-American Committee of Inquiry, a London Conference of Jews and Arabs convened by Britain (like the 1939 conference, Britain met with each separately), and finally, the referral of the problem to the United Nations and the creation of UNSCOP. Through these bodies, Britain had been occupied with the task of reconstructing the terms for its continued administration of Palestine. UNSCOP's proposal to partition Palestine, however, was unwelcome, and its later adoption by the United Nations caused Britain to withdraw from Palestine, rather than to be responsible for implementing a policy which was judged to be detrimental to Britain's position in the region.[45]

Partition had first been proposed in 1937 by the Royal Commission under Lord Peel. Abdullah had jumped at the proposal, which included the proviso that the Arab portion of Palestine might be attached to Transjordan, incurring, thereby, the wrath of the Arab world at large. Later, Britain decided partition was impossible to carry out, but the idea, once raised, cropped up with regularity. Since 1937, however, Abdullah had been more discreet. Unlike his approach to Greater Syria, he was surprisingly cautious when it came to Palestine.

During the war the idea of partition had been revived by the Colonial Office under Oliver Stanley, and for a time it was considered very seriously in Whitehall. Abdullah, more prudent by then, had declared that if partition were proposed again, he would be the last Arab to make a pronouncement on the subject.[46] In spite of his public reticence, partition was not rejected by him or by his then prime minister, Tawfiq Abu'l-Huda, in confidential discussions.[47]

The divergence between Abdullah's public stance and private beliefs continued after the war. As Britain searched for a new policy in Palestine and attempted to associate the United States with this new policy, Abdullah quietly advocated partition to both. He did not meet the Anglo-American Committee; when it was in the Middle East he was in London negotiating the Anglo-Transjordan treaty. But he put his ideas about Palestine forcefully before both the foreign minister, Ernest Bevin, and the prime minister, Clement Attlee. Many people, he claimed, favored partition but would not dare say so. He advised Britain, therefore, to make a decision and enforce it, and to dispense with consultation.[48]

Back home, Abdullah had joined the unanimous Arab opposition to the Anglo-American report, which envisioned the continuation of the mandate until a United Nations trusteeship could be arranged. He attended the Arab summit convened by King Faruq at Inshass, Egypt, at the end of May 1946, and joined in the unanimous condemnation of the report. He undoubtedly shared the general dismay over the committee's plan, and especially its recommendation to give out up to 100,000 more immigration certificates, but he also opposed the report because, as he later confided to Kirkbride, he was against any solution which envisioned the maintenance of a unitary state in Palestine.[49] A week later Transjordan's prime minister, Ibrahim Hashim, chaired an extraordinary session of the Arab League Council at Bludan, Syria, where secret resolutions were taken against Britain and the United States, to be put into effect should the Anglo-American report be implemented. While an effort was made to associate Transjordan with general Arab policy towards Palestine, no special relationship between Transjordan and Palestine was ever implied. Indeed, at the Bludan Conference a new Arab Higher Committee was formed to represent the Palestinians, chaired *in absentia* by Hajj Amin al-Husayni.

Later that summer when a specific plan of federalization was put forward to implement the Anglo-American report, Abdullah, as before, added his voice to the general Arab rejection of the idea. However, whereas Arab opposition to federalization grew out of a vision of Palestine as a unitary constitutional state, Abdullah let both the British and the Zionists know that he opposed federalization in favor of partition.[50] The Zionist movement was also in favor of partition.

The London Conference in the fall of 1946 gave Abdullah another chance to put forward his ideas on partition. Samir al-Rifaʿi, Transjordan's prime minister and delegate at the conference, was instructed not to break ranks with his Arab colleagues, but he had been armed with a letter from Abdullah to Bevin asking the foreign minister to arrange a private meeting with him. Abdullah had also sent a telegram to the secretary of state for the colonies, Arthur Creech-Jones, asking him to see al-Rifaʿi privately as well. Neither apparently did so, but had they seen him there is little doubt that he would have put before them a partition plan which he and Abdullah had discussed with Kirkbride just prior to the conference.[51]

Washington too understood Abdullah's position on partition: he 'would feign opposition and squawk,' but he would be in favour of it, seeing in partition a good chance to expand his domain.[52] His conversation with George Wadsworth, American ambassador to Iraq, a week before UNSCOP was to arrive in the Middle East, confirmed American perceptions. He told Wadsworth what he had told Bevin and Attlee more than a year before: The majority of Palestinian Arabs would accept partition, but only if they were not consulted beforehand. He cautioned that UNSCOP should pose the question of partition only to himself and a few others, 'who in their patriotism would have the courage to reply.' To the rest, the 'pretended patriotic leaders who would testify to the contrary,' the question should be put indirectly. He also warned Wadsworth that if the other Arab rulers unanimously refused any form of partition, he would have to reorient his policy accordingly. A report of this conversation found its way to the Jewish Agency, confirming that Abdullah shared its interest in partition.[53]

When UNSCOP did arrive in the Middle East, Abdullah was helped in his desire to limit its access to various shades of opinion by the Palestinian boycott of the committee. The Arab states, however, agreed to send representatives to meet the committee in Beirut. There, they once again expressed unanimous opposition to the idea of partition. Abdullah had assured himself a more or less private audience by refusing to send a delegate to Beirut on the specious grounds that since Transjordan was not a member of the United Nations, he could not send a representative to meet a United Nations committee outside of Transjordan. Instead, he invited the committee to Amman. However, on the heels of the united Arab rejection of partition in Beirut, he did not dare to come out in favor of partition himself (just as he had warned Wadsworth a month before). Consequently he disappointed committee members by his 'extreme discretion' and 'failed to give them any lead as to his real views,' even though the chairman, hoping perhaps to draw Abdullah out, did ask some British officers of the Arab Legion if it could be relied on to occupy the Arab parts of Palestine if partition were decided on.[54]

After the committee left, Abdullah sent a message to Bevin saying that for political and tactical reasons he had been obliged officially to dismiss partition and to advocate the establishment of an independent unitary state. He explained that as Transjordan was the one Arab state which stood to gain substantially from partition, it could not be the only state to advocate that course contrary to the official view of the whole Arab world. He assured Bevin that he did in fact consider partition to be the only solution possible and he felt he would be able to accept it publicly should the United Nations recommend that he do so. His prime minister, Samir al-Rifaʻi, acknowledged his agreement with Abdullah on the subject of partition and reiterated the tactical nature of his own statement to the committee.[55]

Thus, despite ʿAzzam Pasha's attempt to bring Abdullah back into the Arab fold, Abdullah did not drop his interest in partition. Indeed, as far as he was concerned, the UNSCOP report was a step in the right direction. Yet it was not all he might have wished for, since there was no mention of attaching to Transjordan the part of Palestine allotted to the Arabs – to achieve that end he still had some distance to go. In his ambition for Palestine, just as in his ambition to rule Greater Syria, he was swimming against the tide of Arab opinion, yet in Palestine the circumstances of history were with him, chief among these being that – once the United Nations had passed the partition proposal – his interests in Palestine were in harmony with those of Britain.

Presented with partition by UNSCOP, Britain did what it could to see that any resulting damage to Britain's position in the region was kept to a minimum. Despite Colonial Office support for partition as the easiest solution, the Foreign Office, conscious of Britain's relations with the Middle East as a whole, resisted being a party to the creation of a Jewish state.[56] Foreign Office aversion to partition won out in the end. When the UNSCOP report was published, Britain gave notice of its intention to withdraw from Palestine rather than to oversee its partition. Three months later, on 29 November 1947, the United Nations General Assembly passed, by a narrow margin and after the use of tremendous American pressure, a resolution to partition Palestine on the basis of the UNSCOP report. Britain abstained from the voting. After the partition resolution passed, it announced its final decision to evacuate Palestine and terminate its civil administration as of 15 May 1948.

By abstaining from the vote on partition and by refusing to oversee its implementation, Britain retained a surprisingly strong position in the Arab world, particularly in contrast to the Americans, who, by their last minute lobbying in favor of the resolution, were seen as the architects of partition.[57] Even in Amman, a town where strong political emotions were not usually given vent, the Trans-Arabian Pipeline Company (TAPCO) office, an American concern, was looted and burned by an enraged crowd.[58] Nevertheless, Britain still had much to do to salvage its position in the Middle East: for one thing, it still had to get out of Palestine safely without leaving its former mandate in total chaos on 15 May. To this end, Abdullah's ambition to occupy the allotted Arab portion of Palestine came to be regarded as the best chance to reduce fighting to a minimum, the quickest way to re-establish order, and even, given the Anglo-Transjordan treaty, a possible conduit for the reintroduction of British forces into the area.[59] And so Abdullah, who in the midst of the Greater Syrian imbroglio had been regarded by London as 'completely obsessed . . . to the extent almost of monomania,'[60] was suddenly rehabilitated in the context of Palestine, where his opinions were heralded, somewhat confusedly, as a 'welcome breath of common sense.'[61]

Britain felt its way in Palestine carefully and quietly. Having washed its hands of partition, Britain none the less hoped to guide it along channels least damaging to its regional position, and to do so London came to the conclusion that the Arab Legion, 'if used prudently by King Abdullah in that part of Palestine allotted to the Arab States by the United Nations . . . can do much to prevent the spread of disorder and contribute to the re-establishment of security; indeed it is the only force in sight which is capable of performing these functions.'[62] However, fearing Abdullah's 'notorious inability to keep a secret,'[63] it shrouded the degree to which its interests now marched with Abdullah's.

There were other significant difficulties in using the Legion in this manner. On one hand, it exposed Britain to the charge of collusion in the very partition it had refused to support in the United Nations; on the other, it gave substance to the accusation that Abdullah was a British stooge. Britain was acutely aware that if the Legion went beyond the United Nations borders of Arab Palestine, Britain could be censured by the United Nations and might be forced, by international opinion, to withdraw its officers and its subsidy, depriving Britain ultimately of a valuable ally in the Middle East. Yet if the Legion stopped at those borders, Abdullah would be viewed as a traitor to the Arab cause, his usefulness as an ally would deteriorate, and his throne might even be in peril.[64]

To escape this dilemma Kirkbride suggested dissembling: clashes between the Arab Legion and Jewish forces might be avoided, but 'For purposes of publicity [justification for] Transjordan's intervention in Palestine should be to save the Arabs . . .'[65] The Foreign Office had an even better idea: Abdullah might avoid either consequence of intervening if the Legion joined the Arab front in Palestine, collaborating with Arab forces operating in the Jewish areas, but without itself transgressing the Jewish frontiers.[66] (This is indeed what happened, although the unfortunate Abdullah none the less suffered the withdrawal both of British officers and of the subsidy for a brief period and the obloquy of the Arab world.)

The Legion, on which the success of the idea hung, had been transformed during the war from a gendarmerie to an effective fighting force. By 1947 its military wing, as distinct from its much smaller police force, numbered 191 officers and 7,200 other ranks, divided into three mechanized regiments and sixteen infantry companies.[67] Although it was not the largest Arab army – Egypt's and Iraq's were larger – it was far better trained and equipped. Moreover, Britain, through the forty-one British officers with the Legion, could hope to guide it.[68] In this, Glubb, the commander of the Legion, was instrumental. He agreed to pass information to London by the 'backstairs,'[69] and even after his formal attachment to the Palestine Civil Service was automatically severed on 15 May, he continued, he felt, to serve Britain.

In theory, I am an adventurer who has taken service as a mercenary with a foreign government . . . In practice . . . the Arab Legion plays a part in British strategy and the British Government spends many millions a year upon it. I, therefore, consider that I am serving the British Government in my present post. If I did not believe that, I should [not] remain here.[70]

Equally important to the successful use of the Legion in Palestine was the overall tranquillity of Transjordan. While Egypt, Iraq and Syria were preoccupied at this time with internal upset and could ill afford to send their best troops, or even very many troops at all, to Palestine, Transjordan was firmly controlled, allowing the bulk of the Legion to be stationed in Palestine without fear of internal problems at home. After independence, as before, Transjordan was ruled by the trinity of king, prime minister and British minister. In 1947 the legislature was reorganized, without increasing its political autonomy, into a twenty-member elected Council of Representatives and a ten-member appointed Council of Notables. The number of electoral districts was increased from four to nine, giving the impression of a more precise system of representation, but in fact shifting electoral weight away from the towns, rapidly growing in population and in political sophistication, to the countryside where Abdullah had his most loyal and least politicized constituency. The first Council of Representatives elected after redistricting was overwhelmingly composed of landowners and merchants. There were only two members of the liberal professions, one lawyer and one journalist.[71]

Such alterations had not been made entirely without reason. Middle Eastern supply patterns during the Second World War had created in Transjordan a group of wealthy merchant-landowners, markedly distinct for the first time from the rest of the population. War profits and inflation introduced a class of merchant-moneylenders into Transjordan villages, where settlement of title had concurrently made it possible to mortgage land. Land also became more valuable and cultivation was extended owing to high wartime prices for cereals.[72] The gap between a small group of wealthy citizens and the majority of those of modest means or worse, however, was nothing like that in Syria or Iraq.

Also during the war a new generation of politically active young men had matured in the towns of Transjordan. Afterwards, they began to challenge Abdullah's patriarchal ways and his continued reliance on Great Britain. The politicization of this younger generation was marked by the development of two rival trends. One, articulated by the Faysali or Young Men's party led by Sulayman Nabulsi, was secularist and pan-Arab nationalist. These young men considered Abdullah's administration to be a 'not very benevolent autocracy.' They chafed against the narrow confines of political expression and social and cultural discourse imposed in Amman, where, for example, one could be fined one hundred pounds for listening to Syrian radio broadcasts.[73] The other trend was the growth of the Transjordan branch of the Muslim Brotherhood. Abdullah looked with benevolence on this movement because 'it recalled the younger generation to their religious duties and obligations and was, therefore, of value in checking the spread of Communism in Transjordan.'[74] Communism was a term loosely applied by Abdullah to any opposition movement of a secular progressive bent, and he tolerated and even encouraged the Muslim Brotherhood as a counter-weight to such movements as that led by Sulayman al-Nabulsi. Yet where Palestine was concerned, the Muslim Brotherhood was as strongly opposed to Abdullah's policy as were Nabulsi and his ilk, and Abdullah did not, in the end, benefit by his encouragement of the former against the latter. In spite of the growing politicization of Transjordan's youth, Kirkbride could still describe the country on the eve of Britain's evacuation of Palestine as politically 'healthy' and free of the 'problem' of nationalism.[75]

The structure of Transjordan allowed Abdullah to pursue his objectives in Palestine with less regard for popular opinion than any other Arab leader. This included keeping in touch with the Jewish Agency. Just before the United Nations vote on partition in November 1947, he met with Golda Meir.[76] Mutual interest put them both on the side of partition.

Arab popular opinion was not quite so easy to manage as that of Transjordan. It was axiomatic in the Arab world that, concerning Palestine, no Arab government could take a stand which might be interpreted as betraying the Arab cause without being swept away. Abdullah knew this; it was the reason for the gulf between his public and private utterances on Palestine since 1937. He also knew that he was under special scrutiny, for he had never been able to eradicate the belief, held by most Arabs since 1937, that he favored partition because he would gain by it.

For the Arab world, therefore, he had to rest his case for Palestine on the exigencies of desperation and his unique ability, because of the Arab Legion, to relieve that desperation. He had to wait until the Palestinians asked him to intervene, and he had to wait until the Arab regimes, fearful of the repercussions of the loss of Palestine on their own positions, deferred to the superior strength of his army and his ability to use it.[77] Careful to avoid the strident measures that had signally failed him in Syria, Abdullah and his representatives remained in the background during the numerous Arab meetings which were held in the fall and winter of 1947–8 with the intention of producing a concerted strategy to meet the emergency in Palestine.[78]

Waiting was one of the most difficult things for Abdullah to do. Nicknamed ʿAjlan, 'the hurried one', in his youth, he had not mellowed with age.[79] But his strategy paid off. By January the British and the Americans agreed that he was in a very good position: there was a chance the Arabs of Palestine would invite him to come in and that the Arab League would encourage him to do so.[80]

At about the same time, Transjordan's prime minister, Tawfiq Abu'l-Huda, and Glubb went to London to discuss Transjordan's intentions in Palestine behind the screen of treaty revisions. Tawfiq Pasha told Bevin that Abdullah proposed to send the Arab Legion across the Jordan river as soon as the mandate had ended to occupy the part of Palestine allotted to the Arabs. Since the Foreign Office had already decided to support a greater Transjordan instead of an independent Palestinian state, Bevin responded favorably, though he warned against crossing the United Nations frontiers into territory allotted to the Jews.[81]

Chapter 10

1948

Abdullah's envoys returned from London quietly triumphant. The Anglo-Transjordanian treaty had been revised in such a way as to look less encumbering to Transjordan's external detractors and to Abdullah's internal critics, but it retained Britain's intimate connection to the state, an involvement which, if it traduced the aims of post-war Arab nationalism, none the less stood to protect Abdullah's Transjordan in the uncertain tides bound to flow on Britain's withdrawal from Palestine. Even more important, Tawfiq Abu'l-Huda had clearly been given to understand that Britain agreed to the Arab Legion's occupation of the portion of Palestine allotted to the Arabs by the United Nations partition plan after Britain's withdrawal.

Between February and May the balance of power between Arab and Jewish forces in Palestine changed dramatically, in favor of Jewish forces. This shift jeopardized Abdullah's ability to keep to his understanding with Britain about the limits of his involvement. Since March, Jewish forces had taken the offensive, consolidating their hold within the United Nations boundaries of Jewish Palestine and taking strategic points outside.[1] In April the Jewish underground Irgun massacred 254 unarmed villagers – men, women and children – at Deir Yasin on the road west of Jerusalem. During the following days morale among the Arabs in Palestine plummeted. Terrified civilians began streaming towards Amman, seeking refuge and help to save their homes and their country. The Arab Liberation Army, an irregular force sponsored by the Arab League, acknowledged its critical position and demanded more men and arms from the Arab states. Popular feeling demanded immediate and direct intervention.

Abdullah was appalled by the massacre at Deir Yasin. Although the Jewish Agency immediately sent him a telegram disclaiming responsibility, he rejected the disclaimer.[2] The effect of the massacre on his intention to occupy Arab Palestine was twofold: on one hand it precipitated a rush of Palestinians to Amman seeking his help and protection and hence legitimizing his intentions, while on the other it raised feelings of such hostility and bitterness throughout the Arab world that the Arab states, unable any longer to shield their inactivity behind the ineffectual Arab Liberation Army, began to move towards direct involvement. Such involvement threatened to throw Abdullah off course.

In order not to lose the initiative in Palestine, Abdullah moved decisively to take charge of Arab plans for intervention. By so doing, however, he stood a chance of being pushed beyond the limits of his understanding with Britain. He sent a message to the Arab League offering to rescue Palestine, and this message was accepted over the objections of Hajj Amin al-Husayni and the Syrian prime minister, Jamil Mardam, on condition that Transjordan reject partition and take over Palestine as a whole.[3] The Arab states urged that the Legion be deployed immediately to protect Palestinian villages from attacks like the one at Deir Yasin. Although units of the Legion were in Palestine at the time – under British command and guarding British supply lines as Britain withdrew – the British forbade their use for any other purpose. Indeed, by 14 May all Legion forces had been pulled back across the river except for one infantry company, which was isolated in Hebron when Jewish forces cut the road to Jerusalem.[4]

As 15 May approached, the Arab League grappled with the conditions of Abdullah's intervention. The struggle was over the question of whether the Legion would come under League command or whether Abdullah would command League forces in addition to the Legion. During this period Amman became a Mecca for Arab prime ministers, foreign ministers, and chiefs of staff. When Jewish forces attacked the southern portions of Jerusalem at the end of April, even the Syrian prime minister was forced to make the pilgrimage. As the Arab towns of Tiberius, Haifa, Safad and Jaffa fell, Palestinians in growing numbers came to Amman to beg him to save their towns.[5] Kirkbride reported that Amman had become a 'bedlam.'[6]

Tension rose. According to Kirkbride Abdullah spent 'most of his days, and some of his nights, in alternate moods of lucidity and something approaching a complete nervous breakdown.'[7] The Arab states were pushing for a greater commitment than his continued dependence on Britain would allow. He was no longer certain of Jewish intentions, since Jewish aggression within the portions of Palestine allotted to the Arabs by the United Nations belied his November understanding with Golda Meir. Rumor had it that he was losing his nerve, that he feared the Arab Legion would be destroyed in the coming conflict.[8] A final meeting with Golda Meir on the night of 11 May was unsatisfactory. Looking 'worried' and 'harassed', anxious to cancel the joint Arab action which he might lose control of, he urged her to put off the proclamation of an independent Jewish state.[9] No agreement was reached, and he faced the prospect of getting caught between the onrush of Arab sentiment and Jewish military capabilities. Negotiations between Glubb's assistant, Colonel Goldie, and the Haganah to co-ordinate plans 'to avoid clashes without appearing to betray the Arab Cause'[10] were equally unsuccessful.

Official American and British efforts to stave off the fighting failed as well. American officials, who had been trying since March to arrange a truce and United Nations trusteeship for Palestine, disapproved of Abdullah's efforts:

they believed that the prospect of a 'behind the barn' deal with Abdullah had stiffened the attitude of the Jewish Agency and convinced Jewish leaders that they could establish their state without coming to terms with the Arabs of Palestine.[11] Last-minute British efforts to arrange a cease-fire for Jerusalem to neutralize the area where Jewish forces and the Legion would most likely join battle foundered in light of the movement forward by Jewish troops into positions abandoned by the British army on 14 May.

Two days before the end of the mandate, the Arab League political committee convened in Amman, where it confirmed that Lebanon, Syria, Iraq and Egypt would send troops to Palestine in addition to the Arab Legion. The secretary-general of the League, 'Azzam Pasha, promised the Legion three million pounds and gave Glubb £250,000 cash on the spot. Abdullah won a pyrrhic victory by being named supreme commander of the Arab forces, but it was a title without function as all Arab armies obeyed their own commanders and there was no co-ordination among them.[12]

The Jewish offensive in Palestine since March had caused an escalation of Arab feelings of outrage and hence of Arab commitment to war. Initially, the prospect of direct involvement by other Arab armies in Palestine had dismayed Abdullah, as it seemed to call into question his own claims and to jeopardize his strategy of staying within the Arab areas of the United Nations partition plan. Latterly, however, Jewish victories, especially those within the Arab areas, made him fear both Jewish military strength and Jewish intentions. He became alarmed that the Legion, going in alone, might be defeated.[13] He was therefore ultimately relieved that in the changed circumstances of April–May 1948, the Legion would not be the sole protector of Palestine. On the eve of Britain's final withdrawal from Palestine, the relative strength of Arab and Jewish forces mobilized for action was estimated at 19,200 and 74,000 respectively.[14]

When the last high commissioner of Palestine set sail from Haifa on the night of 14 May 1948, he did so with little fanfare. A brief display of fireworks, the stately strains of 'God Save the King' and a silent salute marked the end of the mandate. There was no real or ceremonial handing over of power, for Britain had failed in its mandatory duties. It had failed to create institutions of self-government representing all of Palestine and there was no one to hand power to.

The two communities left behind, Arab and Jewish, entered a new phase in their thirty-year-old struggle. The Jews, who had prepared carefully for this day, proclaimed a Jewish state. The Arabs of Palestine, although they outnumbered Jews by two to one, made no rival proclamation. Rendered impotent by years of political factionalism in the face of British policy, they had consigned their future to the uncertain care of the neighboring Arab states.

Of all Arab heads of state, Abdullah had the clearest idea of what he wanted in Palestine and of the political considerations that bound his aims. His desire, constant since his early days in Amman, was to expand his domain and increase his stature in the region. That his desire by 1948 had fixed on Palestine was a product of the peculiar history of that troubled land. The political bounds on his actions uppermost in his mind on the morning of the 15th were those imposed by his military and economic dependence on Britain. Lest he should have forgotten them Kirkbride reminded Tawfiq Abu'l-Huda that 'if Transjordan went beyond the plan regarding the Arab areas of Palestine, His Majesty's Government would doubtless have to reconsider their position regarding the subsidy and the loan of British Officers.'[15] In fact, British officers on secondment were under standing orders to withdraw from the fighting should the Arab Legion enter United Nations-defined Jewish areas of Palestine.[16]

There were other bounds on Abdullah's actions in Palestine, however, that were less plain and less clearly understood by him. For example, in this struggle, which touched all Arabs in some measure, he was accountable to Arab public opinion in a way that he had never been before in his life. He conceived of the other Arab countries in personal terms. Egypt, for example, was to him Faruq, much as Germany was Willie to Queen Victoria. Hence he tended to view differences of policy over Palestine as projections of personal conflicts between himself and other Arab leaders, rather than anything more profound.[17]

In particular, Abdullah was accountable to the Palestinians as he gradually assumed, by default as much as by intention, responsibility for their future. The bounds of his accountability were not clearly laid out because they could not be: the public opinion that shaped them was itself amorphous and shifting, its message too easily mistaken. Sheltered in Transjordan, Abdullah was wont to ignore public opinion and do as he pleased in any case. He lacked sensitivity to popular feeling, especially when it contradicted his own ambitions, as his lifelong and fruitless campaign for Syria showed. The effects of his Syrian misperceptions were not serious – at worst he wasted his money and squandered his reputation in an unrealisable enterprise. But in Palestine his cumulative violations of public sentiment and public aspirations led in the end to his demise.

As Abdullah gave a last exhortation to his troops at dusk on 14 May, his immediate task lay plainly before him: it was to establish a military presence in Palestine which would legitimize his personal ambitions there. By design, the Legion was the only Arab army to enter Palestine solely via territory allotted to the Arabs. It crossed the Allenby bridge at dawn, and from the Jordan valley marched unopposed up into the hills of Nablus and Ramallah in the heart of Arab territory. A dirt track, recently widened on Glubb's orders, allowed the troops to avoid the main road through embattled Jerusalem. Two infantry companies were separated from the main body of Arab Legion troops and deployed on the Mount of Olives on the 16th, but they did not enter Jerusalem. Fighting had begun there the day before as the last British troops withdrew, and

Jewish forces, privy to the withdrawal, moved forward through Arab quarters in an attempt to take the Old City.[18]

Glubb hoped to avoid fighting in Jerusalem. The Legion had a lot of territory to cover elsewhere, its ammunition supplies were limited, and it was not trained in urban warfare. Even more to the point, both he and Abdullah were unsure of the consequences of involvement, since, by the United Nations partition plan, Jerusalem was to have been an international zone.

Abdullah, for political as well as military reasons, could hardly ignore the battle for Jerusalem. Messages had begun to pour into Amman before the 15th, begging him to save the city. As the fighting escalated afterwards, he grew increasingly impatient and distraught. On the 17th he ordered Glubb to intervene with Legion troops from Ramallah, but Glubb continued to hang back in hopes that a cease-fire would be imposed. On the 18th Glubb sent one of the infantry companies from the Mount of Olives, about one hundred men, to man the walls of the Old City. On the 19th, unable any longer to ignore Abdullah's repeated orders and aware of growing public criticism and mounting restlessness within the Legion itself, he intervened in force.[19] As Kirkbride explained to London:

Glubb had the choices of turning outwards on operations which might ultimately lead him into a Jewish area or inwards to relieve the Arab areas of Jerusalem. He chose the latter, I think wisely. To have saved the Holy Places of Jerusalem would give Transjordan great merit in the Arab world and the troops can be given the battle for which they are clamouring without the risk of being involved in what might be described as an act of aggression against the Jewish state.[20]

The first phase of the war lasted a month. During that time the Arab Legion fought chiefly in Jerusalem and at Latrun, astride the main road to Jerusalem from Tel Aviv. Indeed, a close look at the pattern of engagement between the Arab Legion and Jewish forces shows that the Legion was singularly engaged with the defense of Jerusalem, whether this meant fighting within the city or protecting its strategic approaches. And this pattern suggests not only that a battle plan by which the Legion would stay in Arab Palestine did emerge from Bevin's meeting with Abu'l-Huda in February, but that Abdullah stuck to the plan as far as the then unforeseen circumstances in Jerusalem permitted. Early in May, Kirkbride had warned that the failure to establish a truce in Jerusalem would upset the 'original and reasonable plan of a campaign with which Transjordan started.'[21] Later, in the midst of the fighting, the American ambassador in London confirmed Kirkbride's analysis:

We understand that the Jews knew the Arab Legion would enter Arab areas and that this was not unwelcome to them. The Arab Legion have not entered UN defined Jewish state. Attack on parts of Jerusalem was consequence of breaking of cease-fire by Jews. We are confident the attack would not have taken place if the Jews had accepted the truce for Jerusalem.[22]

While Transjordan followed its plan, complicated by the engagement in Jerusalem, each of the Arab states followed its own strategy, with little that demonstrated a spirit of common cause among them. Except for Iraq, which co-operated with Transjordan by sending troops into the Nablus area in order to free Legion forces for battle in Jerusalem, the other Arab states crossed their borders directly into the nearest parts of Palestine. Their aim was to hold on to whatever territory they could, irrespective of the United Nations partition. Syria and Lebanon made little headway in the north and no co-ordinated plan emerged out of a rare meeting between Abdullah and the President of Syria, Shukri al-Quwatli, at Dir'a on 20 May. Egypt advanced up the coast as far as Isdud, and sent another column inland to Hebron and Bethlehem where, to Abdullah's consternation, it challenged his authority to name a military governor. Rumor had it that Abdullah and Faruq were competing to see which one would be the first to perform the Friday prayer in liberated Jerusalem.[23] Certainly Abdullah wasted no time in making the trip. On 27 May, when a stalemate had been reached between Arab and Jewish forces dividing the city in two, he rushed to visit its eastern sections, including the Old City and its religious sites, which were under Legion control.

By the end of May a serious effort to arrange a cease-fire was under way. A United Nations mediator, Count Folke Bernadotte, had been appointed and sent to the Middle East. Britain, to facilitate the passage of its cease-fire resolution in the Security Council, unilaterally banned the delivery of small arms (contracted in its treaties with Transjordan, Egypt and Iraq and which did not fall under the United Nations embargo) and announced its intention to withdraw seconded officers from active duty with the Legion in Palestine and to review the quarterly payment of Transjordan's subsidy, due on 12 July.[24] Britain's resolution for a four-week truce passed, but the ten days before it went into effect were anxious ones in Amman, where Kirkbride and Glubb feared that without supplies the Legion might be forced to abandon Latrun, setting in motion a series of Arab withdrawals which 'might well end in their countries of origin,'[25] and in the destruction of Britain's position in the Middle East as well.

Abdullah was infuriated by Britain's restrictive measures. He considered them a violation of the prior understanding between himself and Britain, and remarked caustically to Kirkbride that 'allies who let one become involved in a war and then cut off our essential supplies are not very desirable friends.'[26] For some time thereafter Kirkbride was excluded from his complete confidence. Nevertheless, when the cease-fire finally took hold on 11 June the Legion was still in place; moreover, it had achieved just what Kirkbride had earlier predicted: without crossing the partition borders into Jewish territory, it had none the less justified its course of action by saving the Holy Places.

Owing to the Legion's defense of Jerusalem, Abdullah emerged from the first month of the war in a surprisingly good position. To be sure, his aims in Palestine still aroused suspicion and distrust, feelings that were fueled by Weizmann's revelation, at a Paris press conference at the beginning of the cease-fire, of Abdullah's pre-war meetings with Golda Meir. But his immediate goal of establishing a credible presence in Palestine had been more than achieved by the Arab Legion's defense of Jerusalem.[27]

During the ensuing four-week truce, Abdullah was active on another front, a political front far from Palestine where he hoped to allay Arab fears about his aims. He chose his ground with care and not a little courage, travelling to Egypt, Saudi Arabia and Iraq.

Egypt was the leading power in the Arab League and the only other Arab country besides Transjordan whose army held significant portions of Palestine. Abdullah was entertained lavishly in Cairo by King Faruq, who, emulating Hollywood, threw a party for him attended by Egyptian stars of stage and screen including one of the greatest singers of the era, Umm Kulthum. During his stay he met privately with Hajj Amin al-Husayni, although exactly what passed between them is not known. He left official talks with the Egyptian government to Fawzi al-Mulqi, his foreign minister, and 'Abd al-Qadir al-Jundi, the highest-ranking Arab in the Legion. They discussed the prolongation of the cease-fire, and tried without success to get Egypt to give up a boatload of British ammunition and arms bound for Transjordan, which had been stolen just before the war.[28]

From Cairo, Abdullah travelled on to Riyadh, where he swallowed his dynastic pride and finally faced his lifelong enemy, Ibn Saud. He took with him a very large retinue composed mainly of tribal leaders, the intention being to establish better relations in a general sense rather than to discuss the technicalities and politics of the war. On his way he was heard to grumble that buying presents for the huge Saudi royal family would cost him a 'pretty penny,' but in return he was showered with costly gifts, including a 100,000 gold sovereign riposte to his overheard comment that it was a pity Saudi Arabia was nothing but sand.[29] Although the trip was a milestone in Transjordanian–Saudi relations, Abdullah could not later resist criticizing the extent of American installations at Dhahran, implying that Ibn Saud was well on his way to becoming an American puppet.[30]

Abdullah's last stop was Baghdad, where he stood the greatest chance of getting a sympathetic hearing. However, quarrels within families being more virulent than the guarded maneuverings of rivals, it was, in some ways, the most difficult stop. The Iraqi regime faced an internal crisis that put its interests at odds with Abdullah's. His nephews needed a resumption of hostilities to protect themselves from accusations of a lack of Arab nationalist feeling; he himself needed a continuation of the cease-fire because the Arab Legion did not have the ammunition to fight on. He exchanged sharp words with the Iraqi prime minister, and later, at the Arab League meeting in Cairo to discuss the extension of the cease-fire, the prime minister argued for the resumption of hostilities. Abdullah did enjoy one brief triumph, however. When the American *chargé d'affaires* in Baghdad offered to relay any messages he might have to Washington, he vented his disapproval of American policy by replying that all he wanted from the United States was true neutrality.[31]

Abdullah failed to gain from the Arab rulers what he had hoped for in the way of tacit support for his objectives in Palestine. One of the things that hurt his efforts was Bernadotte's recommendation that two entities be carved out of Palestine and Transjordan, one Arab and the other Jewish. Although Bernadotte left the borders open to discussion, the Arab entity would comprise all of Transjordan and some parts of Palestine which were purely, or in large majority, Arab, while the Jewish entity would be the rest of Palestine where the Jewish population was more concentrated and the Arab majority, consequently, less overwhelming. The two entities would then co-operate in specified areas of common interest, especially in economic endeavor. This idea appealed to Abdullah, who saw in it a chance to extend his domain under a United Nations umbrella, but was received with hostility everywhere else. It put the Arab states on their guard against his ambitions just when he was trying to disarm them.[32] Shortly after he returned to Amman, the Arab League created a Palestine Administrative Council to act as a civil authority in Palestine, directly challenging his aspirations.[33]

Even more harmful to Abdullah's aspirations than the League's creation of a Palestine Administrative Council was its refusal to prolong the month-long truce. Meeting in Cairo in early July, the League voted to resume fighting when the cease-fire ended on 9 July. The states least engaged in combat – Lebanon, Syria and Iraq – were the most bellicose. Egypt and Transjordan, more deeply engaged and with more to lose, wanted a truce. But Egypt, fearful of internal reverberations, was wary of taking a strong stand for what looked like acceptance of Israel, and Transjordan alone could do nothing. In the League discussions Transjordan took a back seat, afraid of appearing too eager for a truce and settlement proposal that uniquely benefited Transjordan. Once sentiment was clearly set in favor of war, Transjordan voted with the majority in accordance with Prime Minister Tawfiq Abu'l-Huda's policy to avoid a break with the League at all costs.

Thirty-six hours before the cease-fire was to end, Abdullah learned that he faced the prospect of renewed hostilities. He suspected that the decision to resume fighting had been made in the knowledge of the Legion's lack of ammunition and for the purpose of thwarting his ambitions, and he feared committing the Legion to a potentially disastrous battle since it was the backbone of his regime and the source of his regional importance. In a panic he summoned Bernadotte to Amman to tell him he would accept his proposal with modifications and to ask him to force the Arab states to back down by all the powers vested in the United Nations including armed intervention. He also told Kirkbride he would declare a truce unilaterally.[34] Yet, when the four weeks' cease-fire was up, the Legion joined the battle, unable to remain neutral as the other Arab states resumed fighting.

During the cease-fire both sides had broken the stipulation that the *status quo* be maintained. Egypt, Iraq and Transjordan mobilized more soldiers, but the addition of more men had little effect in the absence of arms and ammunition from Britain, these states' sole supplier, which scrupulously honored the United Nations arms embargo. Israel also increased its mobilized manpower. More importantly, through its diverse contacts in Europe and especially in Czechoslovakia, it was able to replenish and increase its armaments, dramatically tilting the military balance of power in its favor. Hence, the second round was short but not sweet for the Arabs, who lost ground on all fronts. The Legion, with little ammunition and no reserves of soldiers, was ordered to fire defensively only. It abandoned its forward positions in Lydda and Ramla, the better to defend Latrun and the road to Jerusalem. Within a matter of days Lydda and Ramla fell.

The loss of the two towns, and the expulsion of all but 1,000 of their 50,000 to 70,000 inhabitants, caused Abdullah's standing to plummet from the high point it had reached after the Legion's defense of Jerusalem in May. Israel's decision to expel the inhabitants had been made, in part, to hamper the movement of troops and to weaken Transjordan's war effort. The roads clogged with refugees would prevent a Legion counter-attack (the Israelis did not know of Glubb's decision to abandon the towns), and a Transjordan burdened with the care of destitute refugees would have fewer resources for its military.[35] However, the significant repercussions were internal: strikes and demonstrations broke out in the towns of Transjordan and eastern Palestine, and Glubb's car was stoned and two British men were manhandled in the streets of Amman. The anger in Transjordan was projected mainly against Britain and especially against Glubb, whose decision not to defend the two towns was interpreted as a deliberate act of sabotage to force a new truce. Britain's apparent guilt seemed to be confirmed by the announcement that it would withhold the scheduled payment of Transjordan's subsidy on 12 July. Britain's tarnished reputation also affected Abdullah's position for the worse. From Beirut came whispers of plots against his life.[36]

A detachment of Arab Legion and Iraqi troops sent through Amman toward the front helped to quell some of the outward signs of discontent. And Abdullah proved to be adept at protecting his own reputation. He broke up a demonstration in front of the palace by slapping one of its leaders across the face. In the shocked silence that followed he upbraided the demonstrators, telling them that if they wanted Palestine to be saved they should enlist in the Legion, and began to take down names.[37] He also allowed Glubb to bear the brunt of the blame, calling him to account for the loss of Lydda and Ramla in front of his ministers.

Glubb was deeply wounded by Abdullah's accusations that he had purposely withheld ammunition from the Legion and allowed Lydda and Ramla to fall. But the semi-public nature of the showdown suggests that it was a piece of theater on Abdullah's part. Rumors of Glubb's dressing-down, reported by those present, helped to deflect criticism from Abdullah himself. A month later a related drama was staged. In mid-August Glubb was sent to London. Officially it was given out that he was on leave, but the impression was that he was in disgrace and might not return to Amman. The reality behind both the official story and the general belief was that he had been sent to London by Abdullah, carrying a personal letter to Bevin and with instructions to put the financial plight of the Legion before the War Office.[38] By the time Glubb returned to Amman in September the crisis had blown over in government circles; his reputation, however, was never restored on the popular level, especially among Palestinians.

The second round of fighting proved catastrophic for Arab forces. In ten days they lost ground on all fronts, and most especially they lost all of Galilee. Consequently the mood of the Arab public also changed for the worse; having been promised victory, they were handed a crushing and humiliating defeat.[39]

When the Arab League met in Aley to consider the new United Nations cease-fire proposal, it was plagued by hourly calls from Abdullah who was anxious lest this truce, like the first one, slip through his fingers. But this time the League accepted, and on 18 July a new cease-fire came into effect. For Abdullah it came just in time. Not only was the Legion hard-pressed in Latrun, but it was needed in Amman to control rising discontent.[40]

In spite of Arab losses, once the fighting stopped Abdullah was reported to be in 'very good spirits . . . prospect of large kingdom agree[s] with him.'[41] Indeed, the war had brought him closer to his goal – it had destroyed the territorial integrity of Palestine and allowed the Arab Legion to occupy part of it. But he had achieved all he could hope to achieve on the battlefield. Jewish forces had seized the initiative, and the loss of Lydda and Ramla had caused his stock to drop precipitately from its earlier high point. Henceforth his battle to add Arab Palestine to Transjordan would be fought in the political arena. There he faced a variety of foes: the hostile Arab states, an aggressively defensive Israel, and the confused and disaffected Palestinians. For his support he could count on Britain, and, more distantly, the United States.

The Arab states, for reasons of principle or pride, of historical enmity to Abdullah or concern for public opinion and domestic tranquillity, could not openly acquiesce to the partition of Palestine or to Abdullah's gain thereby. Egypt, which had invested heavily in the coin of Arab nationalism in order to dominate the Arab League, feared the devaluation of that coin and was itself the only rival to Transjordan in possession of Palestinian territory. The Syrian and Iraqi regimes, facing internal upheaval, had to keep up a pretense of continued struggle in hopes of catching and taming the runaway discontent in their countries. Syria also, as well as Lebanon, disliked Abdullah's Greater Syrian dreams, of which the dismemberment of Palestine was but the first step. Ibn Saud, in spite of the apparent reconciliation between himself and Abdullah, still distrusted Abdullah's ambitions of territorial expansion and viewed his takeover of Arab Palestine as potentially threatening to the Hijaz.

Thus, all of the Arab states were, to varying degrees and for various motives, opposed to Abdullah's gaining territory in Palestine. They were especially concerned about the implications of his policy which pointed to an early agreement with Israel. These attitudes were expressed rhetorically but none the less forcefully, although little of a concrete nature could be done either about the existence of Israel or to offer the Palestinians an alternative to Hashemite rule.

Israel seemed slightly to favor an independent state in Arab Palestine, because it judged that such a state would be an economically and politically weak creation easily dominated by itself,[42] but an Arab Palestine absorbed by Transjordan was not strongly opposed and had the advantage, for Israel, of wiping Palestine off the map of international law. Some favored Transjordan's rule over Arab Palestine because they judged the economic burden to be so great that Transjordan would eventually become economically and politically dependent on Israel.[43] Israeli policy did not ease Abdullah's position, however. Rather, it gradually became apparent that Israel did not intend to trade territory for a settlement; hence a territorial compromise which might have helped Abdullah to justify his policy to the Palestinians or to the Arab states was not possible.

The Palestinians, divided and disorganized before the war, were even more hopelessly divided afterwards by their varied fates. Some remained a threatened minority in Israel. Others, the most numerous group, became refugees, pushed into the parts of Palestine that had not been conquered and occupied by Israel or into the neighboring Arab states of Transjordan, Egypt, Syria and Lebanon. Yet others remained in their homes in unoccupied Palestine, but were not untouched, since refugees poured into their areas and the erection of a hostile border nearby cut them off from the fields and markets and the ports and urban centers that had formed the fabric of their economy and society.

The first group, the some 160,000 Palestinians who remained in Israel,[44] was by its very existence a threat to the idea of the Jewish state. The lives and livelihoods of Arabs who suddenly found themselves under Israeli rule were restricted and precarious, as measures, both subtle and bold, were taken to encourage them to leave.[45] In addition, Israeli policy from the very beginning singled out two groups for favor – the beduin and the Druze – to divide and more easily to rule the Palestinians in Israel.

The second group, those who fled their homes in numbers around 700,000,[46] was divided by wealth and by geography according to where they ended up after the war. Those with little or nothing ended up in camps; those with some capital or with family connections outside of Palestine were better able to integrate into their places of exile. All were torn between the desire to return to their homes and property and the need to begin new lives. The property owners among them were further divided on the issue of compensation. A minority, in the hope of cutting their losses, urged a speedy settlement with Israel that would include the right to liquidate their own property. The majority refused to concede their rights in return for paltry compensation. All were insecure – unsure of their welcome in neighboring Arab states, fearful of further Israeli aggression, lacking secure livelihoods.

The third group, the roughly 460,000 residents of unoccupied Palestine, was swamped by refugees. The population of what became known as the West Bank, for example, doubled virtually overnight. In the Gaza strip some 250,000 refugees crowded in amongst the local population of 60,000.[47] Although the refugees were generally treated with compassion, tensions naturally arose as competition for scarce space and even scarcer resources grew. An even greater source of tension was the fear that refugee attempts to regain lost homes and property would invite further Israeli aggression. The original inhabitants of the West Bank and the Gaza strip were torn between the desire to regain the rest of Palestine in order to restore the social and economic fabric of the country and the need to settle with Israel to forestall further loss of territory and their own possible eviction from their homeland.

Disoriented and divided, fearful of continued Israeli aggression, lacking in many cases the basics of life, the Palestinians were unable to project a unified voice into the international arena where their future was being decided. In that arena, of course, there was no question of all their lands being restored to them, although both Britain and the United States wanted to see some territorial concessions on the part of Israel to make possible a lasting peace. At issue was the question of what to do with the territory that remained Palestinian. The Palestinians themselves seemed to prefer an independent government, but this desire was tempered by fear of Israeli expansionism and the need, therefore, to put themselves under the protection of a neighboring country with an army and a defensive alliance with Britain – namely Transjordan or Egypt. The disarray in Palestinian ranks, coupled with the Palestinians' fear of Israel, allowed Britain to ignore Palestinian voices that ran counter to the British wish that the Arab portions of Palestine be added to Transjordan.

Britain opposed an independent Palestinian government, because, in its view, it would necessarily be 'a hotbed of ineffectual Arab fanaticism and after causing maximum disturbance to our relations with the Arabs would . . . be finally absorbed in the Jewish state, thereby increasing the area of possible Russian influence and excluding the possibility of our obtaining strategic requirements in any part of Palestine.'[48] Along with the United States, Britain may have influenced Bernadotte to include such a recommendation in the interim report. His report, submitted on 16 September, the day before he was murdered in Jerusalem by Jewish extremists, recommended that

The disposition of the territory of Palestine not included within the boundaries of the Jewish State should be left to the Governments of the Arab States in full consultation with the Arab inhabitants of Palestine, with the recommendation, however, that in view of the historical connexion and common interest of Transjordan and Palestine, there would be compelling reasons for merging the Arab territory of Palestine with the territory of Transjordan . . .'[49]

Abdullah, therefore, despite his numerous antagonists, might expect to get Arab Palestine with British help and in default of any other energetically pursued alternative.

Abdullah's prospects were checked, however, by the creation of an all-Palestine government under the aegis of the Arab League, and, with its seat at Gaza, apparently beholden to Egypt. The Palestinians who created this government acted 'so that Palestine Arabs would have a legal position . . . and as evidence [of their] determination to continue [to] fight . . .' Other Arab leaders supported it, Hamid Franjiyya the Lebanese foreign minister explained, 'as opposition to Abdullah . . . to thwart Abdullah's ambitions for federation of Arab regions with Transjordan [and] concomitant recognition of Israel.'[50]

In Amman, the all-Palestine government was viewed as the product of machinations in Cairo by Hajj Amin al-Husayni, that 'devil straight from hell' in Abdullah's opinion.[51] For obvious reasons he refused to recognize it. But he could not safely ignore it, for Egypt began to arm and organize irregulars in Transjordanian-occupied Palestine. In villages around Ramallah these irregulars began to set up courts and levy taxes in a manner reminiscent of what had taken place during the 1936–9 Palestine revolt.[52] He talked wildly of fighting Egypt, and in a scarcely more sensible vein (at least as far as achieving Abdullah's ambitions was concerned), his prime minister, Tawfiq Abu'l-Huda, toyed with the idea of withdrawing the Arab Legion altogether and writing off the 'Palestine adventure.'[53] On a more down-to-earth level Abdullah organized a Palestine conference in Amman which duly denounced the Gaza government and called for the unification of Arab Palestine and Transjordan. But the Amman Conference was small, attended only by known Hashemite loyalists, and was not a very convincing projection of Abdullah's desirability among Palestinians.

Abdullah's efforts were further undercut by the poor record of his administration in Palestine so far. Transjordanian-occupied Palestine was reported by British observers to be less well managed than either the Egyptian or the Iraqi sectors. There were widespread complaints, for example, that Transjordan was holding up relief efforts and obstructing commercial and professional activities in Palestine in hopes of attracting capital and business to Amman. Abdullah aggravated such grievances by his high-handed treatment of Palestinians who sought reconciliation with him. Rather than welcoming them, he meted out insults for their dilatory and entirely utilitarian (but no less useful to himself) recognition of his new importance in Palestinian affairs.[54]

Britain did what it could to bolster his claims and to influence Arab governments against recognizing the Gaza government. Britain's only point of leverage, that an independent Arab Palestine would not be covered by any defence treaty, made little impact on the Arab states. There was little else Abdullah or Britain could do but hope the all-Palestine government would founder on the rocks of Arab rivalry and sink under the weight of its own impotence.

Deliverance came from an unexpected quarter. On 15 October Jewish forces attacked Egyptian positions in the Negeb, and during a week's fighting they pushed the Egyptians out of the northern Negeb and back along the coast almost to Gaza. No Arab army went to the aid of the Egyptians, and by the time a cease-fire was imposed on 22 October they had lost significant territory. Part of the Egyptian army was cut off in Hebron and Bethlehem. Taking advantage of the situation, Glubb sent 350 Legionnaires to that district ostensibly to save it, but more importantly to establish a political presence there.[55] The all-Palestine government in Gaza withdrew to the safety of Cairo. Owing to the failure of the Arab states to give it sustained support and to Britain's policy of excluding it from international forums, it began to decline thereafter and gradually ceased to be a serious challenge to Abdullah's claims or Britain's interests.

Although Abdullah feared he would be the next target of Israeli aggression, he had at the same time reaped great advantage in the inter-Arab struggle over Palestine from Egypt's setback. His advantage increased when Israel turned on the Arab Liberation Army in the northern Galilee, pushing it and Lebanese and Syrian troops back across the northern borders by the end of October 1948. As the prospect of an independent Palestinian state receded and the likelihood of annexation by Transjordan increased, there was a perceptible shift of opinion in his favor. However he again proved to be his own worst enemy. Rather than wooing the Palestinians, he broadcast a message saying that he could offer no further economic aid to them. He also continued to insult Palestinian visitors by telling them he was inclined to discount their present protestations of loyalty in view of their past 'fickleness'.[56]

*   *   *

By prior agreement within the Arab League, the individual Arab armies in Palestine were responsible for the territories which they succeeded in protecting from Israeli occupation so long as hostilities continued. Since 15 May, therefore, as the Arab Legion moved into Ramallah and Nablus, East Jerusalem, Bethlehem, and southward to Hebron, Abdullah had made *ad hoc* decisions about the administration of the lands and people coming under his sway. He was anxious to transform this administration from one of military occupation to one of popular acclamation as a prelude to formal annexation. At his instigation a Palestinian conference was held on 1 December in Jericho, and in the changed circumstances of December, the Jericho Conference – with an estimated 3,000 in attendance – was a far more impressive affair than the Amman conference two months earlier.

The choice of Jericho was meant to give the impression of a grass roots movement for unification with Transjordan among the Palestinians themselves, but the impetus for the conference came from Abdullah. It was his idea to hold it, he contributed a small sum toward expenses, the Ramallah radio station under Legion control advertised it, and 'Umar Pasha Mattar, the military governor of Transjordanian-occupied Palestine, was instructed to secure the attendance of as many notables as possible, using force if necessary. Abdullah's men – friends and allies without formal position, government officials, and army officers – went around to villages and refugee concentrations to persuade local leaders of opinion and men of affairs that it was in their best interests to attend. On the day before the conference, Transjordan and Israel concluded a truce designed to reinforce the one imposed by the United Nations, so that Abdullah enjoyed at least a temporary respite from his worries about Israel's intentions in the West Bank.[57] On the eve of the conference, Shaykh Muhammad 'Ali al-Ja'bari, mayor of Hebron and a long-time supporter of Abdullah, met with him at Shuna to compose a list of resolutions.[58]

The next day in Jericho the conference proceeded as planned: al-Ja'bari was elected chairman and his slate of resolutions calling for unification was adopted. As it turned out, however, the resolutions were not only cooked beforehand, they were reheated afterwards as well. Several different versions were publicized, all elaborating on the theme of unification. One inserted an additional clause recalling that Palestine was part of natural Syria, a particularly unhappy allusion for Kirkbride who had hoped that Palestine would divert Abdullah from his Syrian hobby-horse for ever. Another welcomed Abdullah as the ruler of all Palestine and exhorted him to continue his efforts to liberate the rest of the country.[59] Picking up on the latter, Britain reminded him that he would lose British support unless he clearly limited his aspirations to Arab Palestine as defined by the 1947 United Nations partition resolution.

By creating an image of popular support, the conference was intended to legitimize Abdullah's ambitions in Palestine. He certainly anticipated that formal unification would shortly follow – but this was not to be, owing to Arab opposition and British and American prudence.

Predictably, the Jericho Conference set off a new round of vituperation in the Arab world, led by Egypt. King Faruq delivered a stinging public rebuke to Abdullah, who proposed to retaliate by broadcasting a slur on the sexual morality of the Egyptian royal family, whose not-so-private life was the talk of the Arab world.[60] He was stopped then, but he did get in a sly dig at Egypt when he sent a telegram of congratulations to ʿAbd al-Rahman al-Mahdi, the standard bearer of the Sudanese Umma party which stood for complete independence from Egypt, on his victory in the Sudanese elections. Relations reached their nadir when an unidentified plane dropped six bombs near Shuna. Fragments from the bombs bore the Arabic inscription, 'From King Faruq to M. Shertok,' referring to Moshe Shertok, former head of the Jewish Agency's political department and the first foreign minister of Israel. Abdullah, assuming they were dropped by Egypt, was highly insulted by the effort to intimidate him. British and American observers thought the incident might have been the work of Israeli skullduggery, aimed at deepening the fissures in the Arab world that served Israel so well, but no conclusive proof was found either way.[61]

But it was not the vociferous Arab opposition to the merger, or that alone, that stymied Abdullah's plans. Rather, his plans were put off because both Britain and the United States, for a variety of reasons, thought he ought to proceed more cautiously. London, with an eye to its relations with the rest of the Arab world, and especially with Egypt, drew back in the face of the controversy in the Arab world over the Conference. Owing to this controversy British support of Abdullah became a topic of concern and intense debate among the British legations in the Middle East. This debate mirrored the one in the Arab world and was nearly as nasty. Kirkbride in Amman and Sir Hugh Dow in Jerusalem defended Abdullah by castigating other Arab leaders. Diplomats in Cairo took strong exception to Kirkbride's denigration of the Arab League and Dow's exaggeration of Transjordan as Britain's 'only consistent and militarily valuable ally in the Middle East.' Sir John Troutbeck, head of the British Middle East Office in Cairo, explained Arab feeling for Abdullah as hatred for a 'land-grabber' who ignored the principles of the conflict. He was particularly eloquent in defense of the Arab League:

. . . I feel strongly that the way they have been pushed out of one morally impregnable position after another is a very grave reflection on our western civilisation. I think it is because Azzam for all his wildness has the same kind of feeling about it and because, so far as I can make out, Abdulla has not, that my sympathies tend to go out to the childish and imbecile [paraphrasing Kirkbride] Arab League.[62]

The main axis of the argument was that Kirkbride felt Britain should give more support to Abdullah, while British diplomats in Egypt and elsewhere felt that a more careful balance ought to be maintained: Britain should support him, but not to the extent that he grew arrogant and careless about his relations with other Arab states. As during Abdullah's Syrian adventures, the bedrock of the problem was that whatever he did was considered by other Arabs to be British policy, and British interests and credibility in the region suffered accordingly. The problem, being inherent to his relationship with Britain, was not resolved. Britain encouraged him to seek a *rapprochement* with Egypt before taking any steps in the West Bank, but without success; instead, Egyptian–Transjordanian rivalry in Palestine helped Israel finally to gain control of the Negeb.

Beyond the controversy attached to everything Abdullah touched outside his own country, there were other important considerations governing Britain's preference for restraint. These considerations had to do with Britain's assessment of the likelihood of an Israeli attack on the Arab Legion in the West Bank should Abdullah annex it, the ability of the Legion to defend itself, and Britain's ability to go to Transjordan's aid if the Anglo-Transjordanian treaty were then invoked. At the time of the Jericho Conference and for several months thereafter, Britain felt the chances of an Israeli attack were high, the Legion's ability to protect itself low (due to lack of ammunition, which was still embargoed), and, surprisingly, its own ability to aid the Legion in Arab Palestine also low, even though British land forces were sent to Aqaba in early January to protect that town from a threatened Israeli attack as Jewish forces moved southward to claim the Negeb.[63] In view of imminent Israeli elections, Britain was also worried that the addition of the West Bank to Transjordan at that moment might swing Israeli voters behind Menachem Begin, whose dogmatic belief in Israel's manifest destiny in all of Palestine and Transjordan would scotch any hope of a negotiated settlement in the region.[64] Finally, both Britain and the United States preferred that Abdullah should get most or all of what the Arabs retained of Palestine as part of an overall settlement which would include compensation, territorial and otherwise, for the Palestinians. They feared that if he made his move independently of such a settlement no such compensation would be forthcoming.[65]

It was for these reasons, not all of which were made clear to Abdullah, that he was encouraged to put off formal annexation. Luckily for Kirkbride, not much pressure was needed, since Tawfiq Abu'l-Huda, clinging steadfastly to his guiding principle of avoiding a complete break with the Arab League, refused to introduce the necessary legislation immediately anyway; but to avoid a complete break with Abdullah, the cabinet did pass a general resolution welcoming the Jericho decisions.

Abdullah was not allowed to stew for long over the failure of the Jericho Conference to achieve immediate unity, for there were other important matters pressing on him. By December 1948 the United Nations, Britain and the United

States were pushing the Arab states and Israel strongly toward the armistice table. If the Jericho Conference had failed him, there were other ways to make his hold over the West Bank more secure – one of these ways was to seek an understanding with Israel. Transjordan was therefore quite prepared to lead the way in the armistice talks. Britain, however, feared that such a move would put Transjordan in an impossibly vulnerable position, and that instead of this, either the Arab states should seek an armistice together or Egypt, the largest and most influential among them, should go first.

In spite of Britain's disapproval, informal talks between Transjordan and Israel took place throughout December 1948. At the same time Egypt was also secretly meeting with Israelis.[66] But fighting erupted between Egypt and Israel again on 22 December. The Egyptian army was surrounded and cut off from Egypt by Israeli action on and across the Egyptian frontier, and on 7 January Egypt agreed to enter into armistice negotiations.

The Israeli strikes into Egypt had alarmed Britain, which threatened to come to Egypt's defense under the terms of the Anglo-Egyptian treaty of 1936. A similarly dangerous situation developed at the same time between Israel and Transjordan. Israeli forces moved into the southern Negeb, skirmishing with the Legion across the Transjordanian frontier in Wadi ʿAraba and advancing towards Aqaba. Simultaneously Israel adopted a menacing tone in the ongoing talks with Transjordan. Although Britain had not mobilized on Egypt's behalf, owing to American intercession which got the Israelis to withdraw from Egyptian territory, Britain now took steps to 'carry out [its] obligations under the Anglo-Transjordan Treaty of March 15th, 1948 in the event of further Jewish aggression threatening the integrity of Transjordan.' These steps included moving additional equipment to Amman for use by British forces there and for the Arab Legion, though delivery was not made to the latter in conformity with the United Nations arms embargo, and putting a unit of British land forces at readiness should the Transjordanian government ask for protection under the treaty.[67] On 2 January Transjordan invoked the treaty and one British battalion was sent to Aqaba.[68]

The year 1948 had begun on a high note for Abdullah, with Britain's acquiescence in Transjordan's plan to send the Legion into Arab Palestine in accordance with the United Nations partition plan, and in the hope that this could be carried out with a minimum of fighting. It ended with Transjordan's army the only effective Arab force in what was left of Arab Palestine. Transjordan's position, however, had been achieved at a high cost after months of intermittent fighting. The war left Israel in possession of all territory inside, and some outside of the United Nations partition boundaries. Transjordan, for its part, had been weakened by lack of arms, by its political isolation in the Arab world, and by the sense of failure and defeat which it none the less shared with the Arab world, despite the relative success of the Arab Legion. This disparity of weight between Israel and Transjordan extended well beyond the imbalance of their military strength. Israel had been recognized by both the United States and the Soviet Union; Transjordan had been recognized by neither, ostensibly because Transjordan was still lodged too deeply in Britain's embrace. (The United States recognized Transjordan a month later, but the Soviet Union did not do so until 1955, which enabled Transjordan finally to enter the United Nations.) Affirming that perception of continued dependence on Britain, Transjordan had been thrown back on British protection with the arrival of British forces at Aqaba, in a way that was reminiscent of the early twenties. The scale of Israel's potential military threat was vastly greater than the Wahhabi raids of that era, however.

Transjordan badly needed an agreement with Israel, to safeguard its position in Palestine and even, it was feared, its own territorial integrity, but it had little leverage to gain the sort of agreement that could safeguard its long-term position in the region. In particular the fate of Jerusalem, always the outstanding point of territorial disagreement, remained at issue. From Abdullah's vantage point the future was exceedingly perilous.

Chapter 11

The end of ambition

Following in Egypt's foosteps, Transjordan proceeded to the armistice table in March 1949. The meetings were for form's sake, however: most of the negotiations were carried out secretly at Shuna, directly between Abdullah and the Israelis.[1] Outside of the framework of semi-public scrutiny and international control, these meetings proved costly. Transjordanian–Egyptian rivalry also took its toll of Palestinian land.

One of the chief issues of the armistice negotiations was the disposition of the Negeb. It had been designated as part of the Jewish portion of Palestine by the 1947 United Nations partition. After Jewish forces had occupied the western Galilee in defiance of the partition, however, British strategists advocated a trade which would form the basis of a negotiated settlement: Israel would be allowed to retain the western Galilee in return for giving up a part or all of the Negeb. Until October 1948, Israeli forces had not established a presence south of Beersheba, which made such a trade feasible.

This sort of settlement had the virtue of untangling Jewish and Arab Palestine, 'entwined in an inimical embrace like two fighting serpents,'[2] by making both more compact. For Britain's strategic purposes it would allow British forces and installations in the canal zone to be connected by land with Transjordan. But Israeli military actions against Egypt in October and December and the march to Aqaba in December 1948 had introduced Israeli troops into the area. Neither Egypt, owing to military weakness, nor Transjordan, owing to its policy of not fighting within Jewish portions of the United Nations partition, was able to defend the Negeb, nor could Britain intervene militarily beyond protecting Transjordanian territory at Aqaba.

Unable to act directly, Britain encouraged its allies, Egypt and Transjordan, to adopt a single negotiating position at Rhodes regarding the Negeb, but the bad relations between the two countries stood in the way of concerted action. Egypt's animosity toward Abdullah had been fed by allegations that he had connived at Israel's attacks on Egyptian forces in the Negeb in October and December.[3] Egypt did not want to see the aggrandizement of Abdullah's position and felt that he was too 'versatile' to be a trustworthy negotiating partner. As for Abdullah, he refused to deal with the Egyptians, who he believed supported Hajj Amin al-Husayni. While Egypt was negotiating its armistice with Israel he reportedly urged the Israelis to deny Egypt Gaza and give it to himself instead.[4]

By the time Transjordan reached Rhodes in March, Israel had already secured the western Negeb from Egypt and was therefore in a stronger position *vis à vis* Transjordan. Indeed, Israel delayed signing a cease-fire which would govern the positions of the two states during the armistice talks, while it completed its occupation of the Negeb. In response Britain sent reinforcements to Aqaba to protect Transjordan's only water outlet.[5] By establishing its presence in the Negeb, Israel effectively took that territory out of the realm of the armistice negotiations, which were concerned only with securing the frontiers as they stood when the fighting ended. Hence, Abdullah's wish for access across the Negeb to the Mediterranean coast was put off for a future peace settlement. His keen desire for such an adjustment helped to propel him beyond armistice talks toward peace negotiations based on territorial exchange.

The Negeb was not the only place where Abdullah was outflanked in the armistice negotiations. In the north, Israel massed troops on the Iraqi front between Jenin and Tulkarm, where 2,000 Arab Legionnaires were about to replace 20,000 Iraqi troops. (For reasons of its own internal stability, the Iraqi regime refused to sign an armistice with Israel. It preferred to withdraw from Palestine, maintaining an official but meaningless state of belligerency, rather than to acknowledge defeat.) In secret talks at Shuna the Israelis told Abdullah that they considered the replacement of Iraqi by Transjordanian troops to be a violation of the cease-fire, to which they would respond with force unless Abdullah agreed to cede a ten-mile deep strip along the length of the front. Glubb urged Abdullah to 'call Israel's bluff,' and Kirkbride drew parallels between Israel's action and Hitler's in Czechoslovakia, but Britain could not, and the United States would not, intervene. Indeed, the American representative in Amman who had written the State Department in strong terms condemning Israel's strategem had, in reply, been sharply reminded of his junior rank. Abdullah, who feared for the Legion, which still lacked vital ammunition, finally agreed to give up a strip of land three miles deep and forty long at 3 a.m. on 24 March, just as the time of Israel's ultimatum ran out. The results, drawn on a map at Shuna, were carried to Rhodes where they were incorporated in the armistice agreement signed on 3 April. As a sort of *quid pro quo* it was agreed to smooth out the frontier in the Hebron area, which would result in a small gain of territory for Transjordan, but this in no way balanced the loss of the Tulkarm–Jenin area where sixteen villages and 35,000 inhabitants were adversely affected.[6]

When the terms of the armistice were announced riots broke out in the West Bank. The villagers whose lands were suddenly on the Israeli side of the border were especially bitter. They denied Abdullah's right to negotiate over land that was not his, land that they had protected during the war, and they attempted without success to revise the armistice. They concluded that Abdullah cared more for an agreement with Israel than he did for their welfare, and accused the Transjordanian armistice delegation of incompetence in the technicalities of map-reading. British and American observers concurred. John Pruen, writing for Britain's consul-general in Jerusalem, Sir Hugh Dow, remarked on the 'universal impression of stupidity and carelessness' conveyed by the Transjordanians, and Mark Etheridge, the American member of the Palestine Conciliation Commission, said that his already difficult task had been made much the more so by 'Abdullah selling everything all down the garden.'[7]

The net effect of the armistice was the loss of more land and the creation of more refugees. It also committed Transjordan to policing the border between Israel and the West Bank, some of whose new inhabitants sought to cross the border to retrieve their abandoned property and cultivate their land and others of whom hoped to continue the struggle against Israel. Thus, Abdullah and the government of Transjordan appeared to be pitted against the interests of the Palestinians under its care.

The armistice was a severe setback to the consolidation of Abdullah's position in Palestine. Attention was somewhat diverted from him, however, by the coup d'état in Syria on 31 March 1949, which unseated his long-time foe in Damascus, Shukri al-Quwatli, in favor of a military regime under Colonel Husni Za'im. Although his interest in Syria was reawakened by this evidence of its internal instability,[8] the coup made all too real the dangers ahead. For one thing it helped to popularize the idea that military men might make better rulers than the civilians who had presided over the loss of Palestine. Such talk was said to have spread to the Legion from Iraqi troops and disaffected Palestinians. Within a month of Za'im's successful coup, rumors were rampant about an impending coup against Abdullah being organized among the Arabs of the West Bank with the complicity of some elements of the Arab Legion. These rumors were weighed carefully in Amman and London, and protective troop dispositions were made by the British-commanded beduin regiments of the Legion which were judged to be loyal.[9]

Because Abdullah had been prevented from annexing Arab Palestine outright at the time of the Jericho Conference, he embarked on what has since been called a policy of 'creeping annexation.'[10] This was a policy of gradual political and economic transformation by which he extended his administration and influence throughout Transjordanian-occupied Palestine, naming his supporters to key positions and stifling independent political voices and organizations. He used the offices at his disposal in Palestine to reward old friends, rather than to make new ones. Since his supporters in Palestine had always been a minority faction, his administrative apparatus was inherently narrow, created to impose his will on Palestine rather than to develop new bases of support in the changed circumstances of Palestinian politics.

189

Owing to these measures, to the lack of alternatives, and to the disarray inherent in war and consequent uprooting, Palestinians increasingly came to recognize the inevitability of rule by Abdullah. Inevitability, however, did not make the idea more appealing. Generally better educated and more sophisticated than most Transjordanians, Palestinians regarded Abdullah and his 'goatherd' ministers with disdain. Like some Transjordanians, they commonly considered him to be despotic and his government autocratic in the extreme. The systematic exclusion from office of former supporters of Hajj Amin al-Husayni substantiated their fears and perpetuated the deep divisions among them. Allowed little choice in the matter of their own future, they bowed to the inevitable with barely concealed resentment.

Abdullah hoped to hurry along the inevitable, in a symbolic sense, by legislating a linguistic uniformity of identity. The use of Jordan instead of Transjordan, which had first appeared in the constitution of 1947, passed into British usage after the armistice. The designations Palestinian and Transjordanian were discouraged, and finally outlawed in official usage just before the 1950 elections, in an effort to weld a single Jordanian identity. The two parts of the kingdom were henceforth to be referred to as the East Bank and the West Bank.[11] It was a change of name that did not entirely work. Jordan easily replaced the cumbersome Transjordan, but Palestinians continued to be identified and to identify themselves as Palestinians. West Bank became a term of differentiation, while East Bank, despite its use in official circles, never really entered the popular vocabulary. Indeed, popular usage spoke simply of 'the bank' (*al-diffa*), meaning the West Bank, directional reference being superfluous. (Hereafter Transjordan is used to refer exclusively to the area of Jordan east of the Jordan river.)

Rule by Jordan may have been inevitable, but identity was not easily disposed of. Palestinians continued to identify themselves as such, and, ironically, to be so identified by Abdullah's discriminatory economic policies and by the necessity of organizing relief for the majority who were now destitute.

Palestinians continued to be expelled from Israel during 1949,[12] but by the time of the armistice the mass movement of refugees had slowed and their numbers and needs could be more accurately assessed. In May 1949, the United Nations International Children's Emergency Fund gave the total number of refugees on relief in Transjordan and Arab Palestine as 518,488. Of these about 100,000 were in Transjordan proper and the rest were in the West Bank.[13] (Numbers varied in the following months by as much as 20,000 owing to continued shifts of population and to the success of some in finding means of support which enabled them to come off the relief rolls.)[14] The refugees settled in amongst 433,000 native West Bank inhabitants and 476,000 Transjordanians. They were spread throughout the West Bank with the greatest concentrations in and near the towns of Hebron, Ramallah, and

Nablus, while in Transjordan the greatest numbers were at Irbid in the north, at Amman, whose population had burgeoned from 50,000 at the beginning of 1948 to 120,000 by October 1950, and in the Jordan valley near Abdullah's winter residence at Shuna.[15]

From the beginning, Transjordan had provided bread for the destitute at a cost of something like £P8,000 a day.[16] This sum, already burdensome to the small Transjordanian budget, rose as Transjordan expanded its presence in Palestine, taking over areas previously administered by Iraq and Egypt, and as refugee numbers mounted. By the fall of 1948, Kirkbride estimated that Transjordan was spending £P40,000 a month.[17] But although the Transjordanian budget was over-strained with the effort, the sum was small relative to the needs of the refugees, whose 'enforced idleness and gloomy employment prospects coupled with uncertainty over the future and the duration of local assistance, made for increasing uneasiness and growing resentment.'[18] The situation was ameliorated somewhat when the United Nations Disaster Relief Fund took over in November 1948, providing simple relief until the newly created United Nations Relief and Works Agency was able to take on the task of relief and settlement in May 1950.

Despite United Nations aid, the economic prognostication for Transjordan and the West Bank was not encouraging, owing to the high density of population on the West Bank and the limited arable land and scarce water everywhere. The loss of coastal Palestine as a market for agricultural products and as the nearest outlet to the Mediterranean gave further cause for pessimism. The United Nations Economic Survey Mission (Clapp Mission) of late 1949 felt that despite the bleak situation at present, the long-term prospects for the economic development of Transjordan and the West Bank were not so bad, provided that joint Jordanian and Israeli development and usage of the Jordan river could be worked out,[19] but in the absence of such a project, which in fact was never realized, there did not appear to be much ground for optimism. (None the less, Kirkbride was hopeful, owing to his belief that although Jordan's 'economic position and particularly the balance of payments did not make sense by ordinary Western standards . . . this did not mean that they were impossible for an Oriental country . . .')[20]

Some Transjordanians prospered in the crisis. Land prices rose precipitously, especially in urban real estate. Abdullah's third wife, Nahida, who owned shares in the Transjordan–Iraq Carrier Company, was reportedly willing, for a price, to help facilitate the passage of Iraqi Jews bound for Israel through Transjordan.[21] In contrast the majority of Palestinians, regardless of their previous status, were now destitute.

No general survey of the means or former occupations of Palestinians who now found themselves under Jordanian care exists. Some had means, and did not have their names inscribed on the relief rolls that formed the basis of tallying the number of refugees; capital transfers from banks in Palestine to Jordan approximated £P10 million by 1952. Others had their bank balances frozen in what was now Israel until 1956 or later. But two-thirds of Palestinian refugee assets were in land and other immovable property and this was irrevocably lost, although for a while some Palestinians entertained hopes of compensation.[22]

A survey of Zarqa' refugee camps, kept by the camp organizer, Miss Coates, reports the occupations of the breadwinners of the refugee families as follows.[23] (The reporting was done mainly by women since most of the men had either been killed in the fighting, were still prisoners, or were seeking work elsewhere.)

occupation	number	percentage
agriculture	259	28.5
government service and trade	115	12.6
building	100	11.0
public services	90	9.9
food salesmen	84	9.2
street vendors	82	9.0
motor trade	72	7.9
craftsmen	66	7.3
others	41	4.6

The tabulation reveals that even among a group of refugees from a relatively densely settled area – the families at Zarqa' camp came from Jaffa, Ramla, Lydda and surrounding villages – the single largest occupation was that of farmer. That sort of work and that of the second largest group, government service and trade, were probably the two most difficult areas in which to start again: agriculture because of the land and water shortage, and government service and trade because the Amman government in the years immediately after 1948 favored Transjordanians in those areas.

The economic frustration of the Palestinians in Transjordan and the West Bank reinforced their political dissatisfaction and similarly tended to focus on the figure of Abdullah. Although he was not responsible for, and could do little about, the limited economic resources of Transjordan and the West Bank, his economic policies exacerbated feelings of loss, displacement and alienation among the Palestinians. Development plans and the availability of loans favored Transjordan and its inhabitants: small sparsely populated Transjordanian towns received municipal budgets equal to those of the larger densely populated West Bank towns.[24] Palestinian merchants were generally refused import licenses in spite of the £P10 million brought in by Palestinians which doubled Transjordan's money supply.

To improve the economic situation, Britain, in anticipation of the eventual merger of Transjordan and Arab Palestine and keenly aware that 'the pill of Transjordan will need some gilding,'[25] decided to loan Jordan £1 million for development aimed at settling refugees on a more permanent basis than the relief programs to date. It was hoped that if the loan were used as seed money, economic development might bring concomitant political benefits in its train. Yet the loan had an effect contrary to British intentions, for its expenditure was directed almost entirely to Transjordan, drawing attention to Jordan's neglect of the West Bank. Two years after plans for its expenditure had been approved, a report admitted that 'the British loan . . . originally granted for the resettlement of refugees has not yet directly settled any in housing or employment.'[26] Instead, the money had been spent primarily on road-building in Transjordan, which at best had provided temporary work for some 3,000 men. Worse, the roads that had been built had wasted money that might have been better spent elsewhere; George Walpole, Director of Lands and Surveys, described them as tens of thousands of pounds too extravagant.[27] On the dearth of plans and funding for the development of the West Bank, one Palestinian commented bitterly that 'since they could not transfer Jerusalem the only thing they allowed was the development of the tourist industry.'[28]

Similarly, Jordanian commercial policies did not begin to soften the hard facts of political geography that now placed Jerusalem and the West Bank at the end of a circuitous supply route, starting in Beirut and circling around via Amman. Commercial policies emanating from Amman favored a clique of Amman merchants and worked against merchants and consumers in West Bank towns. Transjordan, with a significantly smaller economy than pre-war Palestine, had limited resources of hard currency; consequently imports were restricted by means of licensing procedures which favored Amman. This compelled merchants in the West Bank to deal through importers in Amman, driving up import prices in the West Bank twenty-five per cent over Amman prices. At the same time prices of Palestinian commodities, mainly perishable agricultural products, olive oil and soap, dropped. Cut off from the usual markets, now in Israel, and from long-distance trade through nearby Mediterranean ports, trade in these commodities ranged from sluggish to non-existent. Merchants in Amman prospered both ways, serving as middlemen for West Bank importers and between Palestinian producers and Arab markets.

Palestinian merchants, however, were able to organize themselves in a League of Palestinian Arab Chambers of Commerce, and in 1950 they won half of the total currency allocation available. Yet the proliferation of import licenses did not in the end mean the expansion or diversification of trade in the West Bank; rather, import licences themselves became commodities, sold at a ten per cent premium by small merchants to larger ones.[29] West Bank towns, the victims of the insuperable political differences with Israel which caused both a hardening of boundaries and a fear of Israeli expansionism, became economic backwaters compared with booming Amman. For financial reasons, if not for political ones, Palestinians invested their capital in businesses and construction across the river in Transjordan, rather than in the West Bank.

Economic hardship affected political life in two contradictory ways. On one hand, it undoubtedly reinforced political opposition and dissatisfaction with Abdullah; on the other, however, it imposed a certain political quiescence on those whose daily lives and means of support had been so suddenly and so completely disrupted, and who were, in consequence, dependent on government handouts. Abdullah's government did mete out certain rewards to Palestinians who supported him: for example, an agricultural mortgage program begun in 1950 had, by 1954, lent more than JD 3 million, chiefly to pro-Hashemite West Bank landowners.[30] This and similar measures helped him to solidify the group of West Bank landowners and notables which formed the core of Hashemite support.

Although Abdullah's linguistic and economic policies had mixed success, and, at times, worked at cross purposes, legislatively, 'creeping annexation' continued apace. The major milestones along this route were the offering of Jordanian citizenship to all Arab Palestinians in February 1949, the replacement in March of military government by civilian government responsible to the appropriate ministries in Amman, the naming of three Palestinian ministers to the Cabinet in May, the removal of customs and travel controls across the Jordan river in November, and finally in December 1949, one year after the Jericho Conference, the issuing of a law by which Abdullah assumed all powers that had previously been vested in the mandatory power in Palestine. This law meant, in effect, that Abdullah had assumed all the duties of a ruler in the West Bank. However, it had been decided not to make any formal announcement until elections for Parliament could be held in both East and West Banks. The idea was that elections would give annexation a popular mandate and that the Palestinians, having participated in forming the new governing arrangements, would be less inclined to want to see them fail. The elections were set for March 1950. In preparation for them, all Palestinians under Jordanian rule were declared Jordanian citizens automatically, since the earlier offering of Jordanian nationality had not received, for the most part, a positive response.

Palestinians on both banks had in the meantime begun to get used to the idea of rule by Abdullah, for the simple reason that they had no other viable option. Amongst the ruling elite of urban notables and landowners, many had switched their allegiance to him after the Jericho Conference and Egypt's defeat. Those among the elite who continued to support an independent Palestinian state or Hajj Amin al-Husayni were, for the most part, barred from areas under Jordanian control.

Despite the changeover to civilian government, the Arab Legion continued to occupy the West Bank, and was therefore able to muzzle opposition before and during the elections. By the time of the elections the only legal political party there was the pro-Abdullah Liberal party (*hizb al-ahrar*), which united with the Transjordanian Renaissance party (*hizb al-nahda*) in conformity with Abdullah's general policy of merging the two populations and discouraging political organization around specifically Palestinian (or Transjordanian) issues.

Most Palestinians regarded Abdullah with an ominous ambivalence. Kirkbride remarked that most would answer no whether they were asked if they wanted to be independent, if they wanted to become King Abdullah's subjects, or if they wanted to be ruled by Israel.[31] Allowed no choice in the matter, they acquiesced in Abdullah's rule, but they did not do so with good grace or necessarily in good faith. While they appeared to respond favorably to Abdullah's increasingly frequent visits, lurking just beneath the surface was an abiding animosity. As one Palestinian explained to the American consul in Jerusalem: 'The officials, the notables, and the people rush forward to kiss His Majesty's hand, when actually many of them would rather break it.'[32] A British observer, from the heights of moral rectitude and racial superiority, described with revulsion how Palestinians of all classes made an 'ugly greasy rush to meet him, see him, applaud him, and pay him flowery compliments only to return to their houses to talk hate of him. These people certainly know which side their bread is buttered.'[33]

British calculations were for the most part untouched by these undercurrents of hostility. Kirkbride, though aware of Palestinian opposition to Abdullah, habitually trivialized it, attributing it to the work of outside agitators or to the character of the Palestinian Arab, 'notorious for his habit of querulous complaint.'[34] By his reckoning, what was needed to remedy Palestinian discontent was more discipline; the more recalcitrant the Palestinians appeared the more he advocated union with Transjordan to settle, once and for all, the internal debate over the future of Palestine.

In London the chief concerns were Abdullah's relations with other Arab leaders and Jordan's position in the Arab world. These concerns were the natural outgrowth of Britain's desire to maintain its own position in the area – the aspirations of Palestinians were of secondary importance. When Abdullah visited London in August 1949, the Foreign Office reassured him that Britain supported the amalgamation of Arab Palestine and Transjordan. Since the Jericho Conference of the previous December, British calculations had changed radically in Abdullah's favor. Britain now felt that unification would make the possibility of an Israeli attack less, rather than more, likely, that it would put a stop to current tendencies toward independence among the Palestinians, and that it might provide a firm starting point for the final settlement of the Palestine conflict, rather than itself being dependent on an overall settlement. The lifting of the United Nations arms embargo and the resumption of arms delivery in

Figure 15. King Abdullah and Amir Talal visiting Jerusalem, 1949.

August 1949 also made it possible to put more confidence in the Legion's ability to protect itself and the territory under its control. The Americans, however, still attached importance to the principle of territorial compensation and continued to believe that Israel might give way on this point. Abdullah was therefore advised to hold off a while longer.[35]

American hopes for territorial adjustments faded during the fall of 1949, in view of persistent Israeli intransigence. By December both the United States and Britain were ready for the merger, and preparations for elections that would clear the way for the final and formal declaration of unification were set in motion. Voter registration took place in January among a male franchise of eighteen years and older. Almost equal numbers registered in the West Bank and the East Bank, although the population of the West Bank was twice as large as that of the East Bank.[36]

In Amman there was a persistent fear that Palestinians would boycott the elections. To encourage their participation, Abdullah took the unprecedented step of announcing that after the new parliament was assembled, the constitution would be amended to make the cabinet responsible to parliament rather than to himself as at present. This was a measure that Transjordanians had been pressing for since the first elections in Transjordan in 1928. That he appeared willing to cede this step now was a harbinger of changes to come. The unpleasant by-product, for Abdullah, of his enlarged constituency was a more fluid internal balance of power which was not so consistently in his favor as before and which therefore needed more attention.

The elections took place in April. They were vigorously contested in the West Bank between supporters of Abdullah and opponents, who had decided that since union with Transjordan was inevitable, they ought to use the political institutions at hand to make their voices heard. Although there were charges that election practices had favored Abdullah's candidates, dissident candidates were elected in some instances, making the new parliament less of a rubber stamp than the old Transjordan Chamber of Deputies. Twenty deputies were elected from each side of the river. The difference between the two groups of deputies was marked. From Transjordan the landowning contingent was largest: twelve landowners, five professionals (two civil servants, two lawyers and one dentist), and two merchants were elected. From the West Bank only seven deputies were identified as being landowners first and foremost, while two others were merchant-landowners. The majority of those elected from the West Bank were highly educated professionals – lawyers, civil servants, school teachers, journalists and doctors. Among these, two were members of the proscribed Ba'th Party and at least three others were nationalist activists whose sympathies had formerly been with the Husaynis.[37]

Parliament opened on 24 April 1950. On the next day, as planned,[38] a group of Palestinian deputies introduced the motion to unite 'both banks of the Jordan,' which was passed unanimously. Britain recognized the unification three days later. The Arab League pressured Abdullah to issue a statement that his administration of the West Bank was only temporary (to keep intact the principle that there was a state called Palestine whose inhabitants had certain rights), but stopped short of expelling Jordan when he refused to do so.[39]

At the core of Arab opposition to Abdullah's desire to add the West Bank to Transjordan, lay the very real and prescient fear that he could only do so in agreement with Israel. Such an easy and prompt acceptance of the disappearance of Palestine and the massive dispossession of an Arab people had serious ramifications for all Arab states. It would call into question the already strained ties between ruler and ruled in the Arab world, and transgress the tenets of Arab nationalism on which all Arab regimes, to some degree, based their legitimacy. This did not mean that there were no meetings at all between Arabs and Israelis – there were, with astonishing frequency – but the other Arab states, which had invested so heavily in the currency of Arab nationalism, could not and did not concede the principle of the national rights of the Palestinians. They talked with Israel to ensure their own borders without explicitly trading on the identity or rights of the Palestinians. Even Egypt, which by its armistice

197

with Israel retained the Gaza strip, did so without explicit prejudice to Palestine's future. The majority Arab position thus left Palestinian rights intact, at least in theory, implying a continuing struggle with Israel, diplomatically and economically if not militarily, until Israel should in some way also recognize those rights. It was just those rights, however, that Abdullah was apt to concede, for his ambitions required the disappearance of Palestine as surely as did Zionist aims.

The addition of the West Bank to Transjordan and of nearly one million Palestinians to Transjordan's population of 476,000 did queer things with regard to the internal configuration of Abdullah's power. The motion for unification was the first and virtually the last piece of legislation passed by the new parliament. During the year of its existence not a single new law, beyond the act of union and certain measures to unify existing legislation, was passed. In taking on the West Bank, Abdullah had got something of what he wanted, namely more territory, but more than he had bargained for in other directions. The sudden tripling of population underlined the shortcomings of his patriarchal style of rule. With such a large population he could no longer make up for the lack of institutionalized democracy through personal contact, for example at his Friday *majlis*. The Palestinians, a more diverse population with varied needs and interests, inevitably widened the spectrum of political dialogue in the country. They had a grievance and they were not predisposed to trust either Abdullah or the framework of his rule. They were, on average, better educated and politically more sophisticated than most Transjordanians, and, joining forces with the growing Transjordanian opposition, they demanded a greater voice in political processes than Transjordanians had enjoyed up to that time. They also had ties, independent of Amman, with other Arab countries and a cause which, however briefly, had marched across the world stage. What happened to them would henceforth, for good or ill, reverberate beyond Jordan's borders.

Abdullah had given a nod of recognition towards Palestinian political sensitivities when he announced that after the new enlarged parliament convened, the constitution would be rewritten to make the cabinet responsible to parliament rather than to himself as at present. He did not live up to his pre-election promise, however, and the questions of whom the cabinet should be responsible to and how and when cabinets should be changed became a focus of struggle in parliament between Abdullah and the broadened spectrum of opposition. Kirkbride wrote dramatically, 'we are in the throes of a revolution here,' and predicted 'a major battle for power between the Legislature, stuffed with politically-minded Palestinians, and the Executive, which consists of King Abdullah and his Ministers.' The challenge to Abdullah's power also affected Kirkbride's, for, as he readily acknowledged, 'my famous influence was exercised over a number of "Transjordanians", including the King himself, but when those whom I can influence lose their own power to guide events, I also lose potency.'[40]

A related area of dispute was the degree of British control over Jordanian affairs. The parliament which had made unification possible was dissolved by Abdullah a year after its election for questioning foreign control of the Legion and the high salaries paid to foreign experts, as well as for opposing some of Abdullah's favorite projects such as the Royal Hashemite Regiment, which served as his personal bodyguard, and the creation of a council of religious experts. Kirkbride summed up the 1950 parliament as 'a thoroughly irresponsible body of men in which the more reasonable east bank elements were led astray by west bank trouble makers,' and together with Abdullah he counted on new elections to produce a 'better type of deputy.'[41] But the addition of the West Bank had forever changed the old Transjordan. The aggrieved and highly vocal Palestinians added weight and a sense of urgency to the rudimentary Transjordanian opposition, making it more difficult for the old triumvirate of king, British minister and prime minister to share out power amongst themselves, with at best a paternalistic regard for the interests and aspirations of the people they ruled.

With the events of 1948 and their aftermath, Abdullah's familiar world began to pass away. New forces were bubbling upwards throughout the region, given impetus by the castastrophe in Palestine. These forces overthrew Abdullah's enemies in Syria in 1949, but they were no more friendly to himself or those like him. The Iraqi regime had barely survived the civil disturbances in that country in 1948.

Nationalism was becoming a dangerous ideology. Arab leaders who had used it for the past twenty-five years to rally the Arab people against British and French interference and to bolster their own positions of social and political privilege became the prey of a new sort of nationalist message, one that contained elements of social and economic reform and that pinned the loss of Palestine to the robes and frock coats of the old nationalist elites. Abdullah, given his equivocal role in the Palestine crisis, his long identification with Britain, and his old-fashioned ideas about monarchical rule, stood exposed to this new current of nationalist orthodoxy. To replace what was becoming a double-edged ideology he fell back on the rhetoric of Islam, counselling his subjects to avoid 'the imitation of false habits,' by which he meant both communism and democracy, and 'keep your old traditions and customs and . . . keep your Islam.'[42]

Using the calling card of Islam, Abdullah also attempted to reach out beyond the circle of hostile Arab states and tottering Arab regimes to create an anti-Communist bloc and attract Western attention and support. In 1949 he visited

Spain, where he acted the part of a Muslim leader and interceded with Franco on his treatment of the Muslims of Spanish Morocco, and Iran. In 1951 he finally succeeded in visiting an unenthusiastic Turkey as a private citizen. But he achieved no concrete success. Iran and Turkey were lukewarm toward his idea of a pro-West defensive alliance based on common religion. In Spain he embarrassed Britain by being the first head of state to visit Franco and by his obvious enthusiasm for the fascist regime. Although he described Franco as 'a man of principle [with whom] a working agreement is always possible,' little changed in Spanish Morocco following Abdullah's intercession. He did, however, manage to convince the governor-general of Spanish Morocco that a sum of £10,000 collected there for Palestinian refugees should not be given to Hajj Amin.[43] In a related bid to enter the comity of Western nations, and in particular to win American and United Nations attention, he offered to send troops to Korea (perhaps in emulation of Israel). But his offer was refused.[44] There appeared to be no ready source of recognition and support to relieve his isolation or to shore up his crumbling world.

What remained for Abdullah was the possibility of coming to terms with Israel. The two states between themselves could decide and secure the fate of the West Bank, taking it out of the realm of international concern altogether. Already publicly castigated by the Arab states, he may have felt that he had little to lose and something to gain in the way of direct access to the Mediterranean and Western approbation. He may also have calculated that some Palestinians would be attracted by compensation or by the chance to liquidate their property themselves – attracted enough to divide Palestinian ranks and vitiate opposition to his policies.

Since the 1947 partition act, Abdullah had maintained sporadic contact with Zionist, later Israeli, officials. If Israeli actions had often been threatening, Israeli words suggested that he could secure himself through negotiation and an eventual peace agreement. Even in the midst of the 1948 war, he had managed to let Israel know that he was ready to reach an understanding.[45] He considered the 1949 armistice the first step towards a final settlement with Israel and had been anxious to forge ahead with a separate peace. However neither Britain nor the United States had supported his efforts at that time. They wanted a comprehensive settlement in the region and felt that Abdullah's individual efforts might jeopardize that end; they also felt that by going it alone, Abdullah risked losing considerable territory as he had during the armistice talks – more than he could afford to give up and still retain his throne. Both therefore had encouraged him to work only through the Palestine Conciliation Commission, created by the United Nations to explore the possibilities of a comprehensive settlement. The Conciliation Commission moved too slowly for Abdullah's taste, however, and so he maintained direct contacts with the Israelis, hoping to control the content and the pace of negotiations much as he had controlled the armistice talks in Rhodes from his winter residence in Shuna.

Another body, the Mixed Armistice Commission, had also been created under United Nations auspices. Written into the armistice agreement, its purpose was to mediate any problems on the ground in implementing the armistice and demarcating armistice lines. It was composed of five members: two Israelis and two Jordanians, whose votes always cancelled each other out, and a chairman appointed by the United Nations, who by default made all decisions. In the absence of mutual agreement, not only was the United Nations representative responsible for all Mixed Armistice Commission decisions, but it was left to the United Nations to see that its decisions were carried out. The result was that every incident brought before the Mixed Armistice Commission became a diplomatic dispute to be judged not on the merits of the individual case, but as a part of a potential overall settlement.[46]

Thus the functions of both commissions, the Palestine Conciliation Commission and the Mixed Armistice Commission, became hopelessly entangled. In the midst of the tangle stood Abdullah, the central figure in all talks with Israel and the one person Israeli representatives could appeal to when Jordanian delegates were unbending. Hoping to smooth the way toward a larger settlement (and, he believed, larger gains for himself), he gave way on the relatively small points raised in the Mixed Armistice Commission; the Israelis, hinting at concessions in a future peace agreement, won small territorial victories in the present. For the Arabs, such losses at Abdullah's hands constantly reinforced the suspicion and mistrust surrounding his motives and activities in Palestine. His continuing alienation from the Arab world in turn diminished his usefulness to Israel as a negotiating partner and added fuel to the arguments of those in Israel against compromise with him. As Abdullah's standing declined so, inevitably, did the price Israel might be willing to pay for a settlement.

Hence Abdullah found himself caught in an ugly cycle. Shortly after the March 1949 armistice, Moshe Sharett visited him at Shuna to present Israel's case in some outstanding matters before the Mixed Armistice Commission. He conceded everything Sharett wanted and, having bought (he hoped) a sympathetic ear, he set forth his own wants in the coming peace – an outlet to the Mediterranean, a corridor to that outlet, the return of Ramla and Lydda. Sharett agreed to the possibility, in principle, that a free port for Jordan's use might be established, but to nothing more.[47] Nothing came from his concessions, and, stung by the experience, Abdullah began to avoid Israeli representatives. However, if there was neither movement in the Mixed Armistice Commission nor any larger talks in the offing, Israel appeared ready to use force to get what it wanted, at least from the Jordanian point of view.[48] Jordan was particularly susceptible to threats of force in the West Bank: the balance of

201

military force was clearly in Israel's favor, with 85,000 armed men to the Arab Legion's 13,500;[49] Britain had not yet affirmed that its treaty with Jordan would pertain to Jordanian-held territory in Palestine; and the United Nations arms embargo was not lifted until August 1949, and even then arms deliveries were firmly controlled by Britain.

After several months of few if any contacts, during which time Abdullah tried to strengthen his hand through international contacts, direct meetings between Abdullah and Israeli representatives were resumed at the end of November 1949. At that time M. A. Novomeysky, the founder and director of the Palestine Potash Company and an old acquaintance of Abdullah's, approached him hoping to get him to agree to supply the works with fresh water from Transjordan. He offered in return some Arab quarters in Jerusalem now held by Israel, a trade he said Israeli authorities had sanctioned. Abdullah, having learnt a lesson from his previous meeting with Sharett, did not want to engage in piecemeal restitutions of this sort – rather, he suggested embarking on discussions toward a general settlement which would allow him to recover a sufficient amount of Arab territory so that he could sell a separate peace to his subjects, to the Palestinians, and to the Arab world at large. He outlined his requirements to Novomeysky: restoration of the Arab quarters of Jerusalem, an amendment of the frontier in the south which would put Bayt Jibrin and Beersheba on the Arab side of the border, and access to the Gaza strip. He offered Israel a free port at Aqaba in return for similar facilities at Haifa. He appointed Samir al-Rifa'i, minister of the palace and his translator during this meeting, to be his personal representative in getting the talks off the ground.[50] Al-Rifa'i, anxious to be the next prime minister, obliged. Britain and the United States, which had begun to lose hope in the usefulness of the Palestine Conciliation Commission and had abandoned their insistence on a comprehensive peace settlement, cautiously supported these talks as better than none at all.

The talks began at the end of November 1949 and lasted until March 1950,[51] when, on the eve of the elections which were to bring unification in their train, they were leaked in the Tel Aviv press. First there were preliminary talks between Samir al-Rifa'i and Eliahu Sasson, the Damascus-born director of the Middle East division of the foreign ministry, and Reuven Shiloah (formerly Zaslani), one of Ben Gurion's closest advisers, which were to set the agenda and the parameters of discussion. The official negotiations which followed included the Jordanian foreign minister, Fawzi al-Mulqi, and two Palestinians, Khulusi Khayri and Jamal Tuqan. Abdullah took part in many of the meetings, most of which were held at Shuna, intervening to break stalemates, but giving away more than he ought in the opinion of al-Rifa'i.

The preliminary meetings culminated on 13 December, when both parties agreed on the following points which would form the substance of the negotiated territorial settlement between the two. Israel agreed that an outlet on the Mediterranean was of vital interest to Jordan and offered to cede a corridor from Hebron to a point on the Gaza coast, provided that Israel be allowed fixed points of transit across the corridor, that it be demilitarized, and that the provisions of the Anglo-Jordanian treaty not apply to it. In return Jordan agreed to grant Israel a road along the west coast of the Dead Sea to link the Palestine Potash Company works at the north end with Israeli territory at the south end. The chief sticking points concerned the width of the corridor leading to the coast and the term 'Gaza coast', by which Israel meant the area that was held by Egypt, leaving it to the Egyptians to arrange port facilities for Jordan, but by which Jordan meant a coastal strip north of Egyptian-held territory. On the question of Jerusalem, both preferred partition to internationalization. Jordan agreed to hand over the Jewish quarter of the Old City and the Wailing Wall to Israel and to arrange Israeli access to Mt. Scopus, while Israel agreed to link the Bethlehem road with the Arab part of Jerusalem. Final partition boundaries and questions relating to compensation were left open to agreement on 'practical' grounds.

Official talks began on the basis of these points at the end of January. Almost immediately they reached deadlock on the question of Jerusalem. Jordan suggested that some exchange of territory in Jerusalem might be desirable to smooth out the partition boundaries; Israel objected that all Arab quarters in Israeli possession had been filled with Jewish occupants who could not be moved. Israel insisted on gaining possession of the Jewish quarter in the Old City; Jordan had in the meantime grown fearful of giving Israel access to the Old City. No settlement was reached, but a breakdown was avoided by agreeing to disagree for the moment and to reflect further on the problem for the future.

Failing to make any progress on the thorny problems in Jerusalem, the negotiators turned to wider territorial issues, but here too there was no headway. A map, presented by the Jordanians, was 'laughed out of court' by the Israelis, who now offered to pay for territory in preference to territorial exchange. But Jordan and Abdullah needed territory, not cash, to justify a separate peace. To break the deadlock Abdullah intervened and proposed a new 'basis for negotiation'. It included a five-year non-aggression pact, freedom of access to the holy places, Israeli access to Mt. Scopus, Jordanian access to Bethlehem, the resumption of trade, and a free zone for Jordan at Haifa. Committees were to be created to examine the provision of a harbor and access to it for Jordan, the payment of compensation to property owners in Jerusalem whose property remained under the control of the other party, and the means to liquidate Arab property in Israel and Jewish property in Jordan (the electric works at Jisr Majamiʿ and the potash works at the north end of the Dead Sea). The Israeli representatives initialled Abdullah's memorandum, and with difficulty the Jordanian prime minister, Tawfiq Abu'l-Huda, was persuaded to accept it as a starting point for further talks.

However, two days later on 1 March 1950, accurate reports of the talks were published in the Tel Aviv papers.[52] News of the negotiations threatened to upset plans for the upcoming elections in Transjordan and the West Bank and their subsequent unification. At the same time Abdullah al-Tall, former military governor of Jerusalem, revealed in the Egyptian press what he knew of Abdullah's contacts with Israel through the end of 1949.[53] The three Palestinian ministers on the council of ministers resigned in protest, citing in particular their opposition to the resumption of trade clause, and Tawfiq Abu'l-Huda resigned in his turn. But Abu'l-Huda was persuaded to stay on when his rival for the office, Samir al-Rifa'i, failed to form a Cabinet which would support negotiations with Israel on the present terms. Abu'l-Huda remained in office on condition that no further negotiations be attempted before the elections.[54] None were, and the elections and the declaration of unity came off to Abdullah's satisfaction. Government-level contacts with Israel were not resumed until almost a year later in January 1951, although Abdullah secretly kept in touch in the interval.

The Arab League responded to the news of the negotiations by passing a resolution which provided for the automatic expulsion from the League of any Arab state which entered into negotiations with Israel for a separate peace or for any sort of separate political, economic, or military arrangement. A state so expelled would also face economic sanctions and diplomatic isolation.[55] While Abdullah personally had suggested withdrawing from the Arab League on more than one occasion, most of his government regarded such a break with trepidation. To those in Israel who were reluctant to negotiate with Abdullah in any case, the Arab League threat confirmed that peace with Jordan would not be an *entrée* into the Arab world which would mitigate Israel's regional economic and political isolation.

After the leakage, the negotiations were pushed back into the realm of privacy and secrecy. A new Cabinet was formed in the wake of unification with Sa'id al-Mufti, a leader of the Circassian community and a close ally of Tawfiq Abu'l'Huda, as prime minister. Like Abu'l-Huda he was extremely wary of negotiations with Israel and his government fought shy of official involvement.

With the onset of the hot season the secret meetings were no longer held at Shuna, but in Jerusalem at the home of a young palace official, 'Abd al-Ghani al-Karmi,[56] or in Amman. No progress toward mutual understanding was achieved in the intermittent secret meetings and their purpose, as far as Abdullah was concerned, appeared to be to keep the Israelis in play until he could get a government that would participate. In an effort to convince his cabinet that the Palestinians of the West Bank favored a separate peace he sent the prime minister and the minister of foreign affairs on a fact-finding mission there in the summer of 1950. Far from convincing them, however, the trip was an abysmal failure. Abdullah was furious and Kirkbride grudgingly admitted that 'even after making allowances for weak-mindedness and double-dealing, there seems to be no doubt that there is a concensus [sic] of opinion on the west bank against direct peace negotiations between Jordan and Israel.'[57]

Few in Jordan were willing to become involved unless they were convinced in advance that Israel would make concessions significant enough to enable them to meet the criticism of the Arab world,[58] and no such concessions were in the offing. Indeed, after the breaking off of official talks in March 1950, tension along the armistice lines increased, more Arabs were expelled from Israel, and the Israeli army occupied a stretch of road in Jordanian territory in Wadi 'Araba and the Palestine Electric Company works at Jisr Majami' (Naharim) on the east side of the Jordan river in the north.[59] Such incidents perpetuated a climate of discontent, born of injustice, frustration and impotence, that militated against any eventual reconciliation to the idea of Israel on the popular level. Although the incidents had a similar effect on Abdullah, they elicited a different response. They manifested daily his weakness, his inability either to protect his subjects or to obtain redress, but he drew the conclusion that there was only one way out of his impossible situation – to negotiate. Hence the distance between Abdullah and the majority of his subjects grew, as did the gap between him and his government.

Unable to push Sa'id al-Mufti toward participation in peace talks, Abdullah finally managed to engineer a change in government in December 1950 and Samir al-Rifa'i became prime minister. Al-Rifa'i's willingness to engage in negotiations was well-known and he was immediately attacked in parliament on the subject. Others, however, welcomed his appointment. General Riley, the American chairman of the Mixed Armistice Commission, told al-Rifa'i that the Israelis were pleased with his accession to office. Riley then met with Abdullah to tell him that he should resume meeting with Israel to forestall the danger of further clashes on the armistice line. Israel followed up by sending Abdullah a conciliatory letter. He and Reuven Shiloah then met twice, and in January 1951 al-Rifa'i agreed to participate in talks with the limited goal of settling the outstanding disputes pending in the Mixed Armistice Commission.[60]

Meetings between al-Rifa'i and Shiloah and between Abdullah and Shiloah took place throughout the spring of 1951. The tension along the armistice line eased, but little progress was made in settling outstanding disputes. These meetings culminated in an exchange of notes in which it became apparent that, far from moving toward an eventual peace agreement, the two disagreed fundamentally on the meaning of the original terms of the armistice. Al-Rifa'i suggested that a binding interpretation be adjudicated by the international court of justice,[61] but although Shiloah met with Abdullah several more times in May,[62] it is not clear whether he saw al-Rifa'i again.

Abdullah's contacts with Israel led nowhere. Several months after his assassination the assessment of British officials in the region was that Jordan and

Israel had come close to an agreement in early 1950, just prior to unification. Kirkbride, surveying the talks from Amman, felt that a small concession by Israel at that time would have precipitated an agreement.[63] Knox-Helm in Tel Aviv faulted Jordan for having to break off the discussions (though for understandable reasons).[64] However, although the two sides were then perhaps as close as they might ever come to agreement, there were still insurmountable obstacles on both sides.

While Abdullah personally appeared to be willing to concede much to gain an agreement with Israel, it was not at all certain that he would have been able to carry his constituents with him. The time when 'the King could act as a benevolent autocrat without giving rise to serious opposition by his subjects [was] drawing to an end.'[65] Abdullah had not simply met his match in men who were willing and able to stand up to him – he now presided over a complex polity of clashing interests and of diverse class and political identities. The politicians who refused to be driven by him were symbolic of this large and varied population which no longer fit into Abdullah's patriarchal world view and which shared no particular identity with the Hashemites. Beyond Jordan, Abdullah's *rapprochement* with Israel stood to cost him his regional identity. Israel's assurance of his hold on the West Bank and even an outlet on the Mediterranean could not offset the loss of access to the vast Arab lands economically, or to his cultural and political identity rooted in Arabism.

As for Israel, it was unwilling to make the sort of territorial concessions that would have allowed Abdullah to sell his peace to his own subjects, to the Palestinians, or to the Arab world at large. At stake for Israel was the question not only of territory, but of the nature of the state itself. The possibility of territorial compromise, like the question of a constitution, raised the spectre of internal dissension about the relationship of religion to the state. Religion held the land of Israel to be inviolable and to include all of Palestine and, for some, Transjordan as well. By broaching this issue Ben Gurion stood to lose more than his parliamentary coalition – he stood to ignite an identity crisis that would jeopardize Israel's fragile internal solidarity, its appeal to immigrants, and its external sources of support. In order to avoid such a crisis, boundaries could not be definitively laid down, just as a constitution could not be written.[66]

Ben Gurion never had any faith in the talks with 'King' (as he snidely wrote) Abdullah. He had wanted to take Jerusalem, Hebron and Bethlehem by force, but had been defeated in Cabinet discussions. Others – Sharett, Sasson and Shiloah – saw some value in a peace treaty with Jordan. But after the armistice, which secured Israel without raising awkward issues of identity, government enthusiasm for peace-seeking gradually ebbed. By 1950, Shiloah, who had staked his political career on achieving a treaty with Abdullah, was virtually alone in the field.[67] Israel seemed to prefer a certain tension along the armistice lines which could be exploited to round out its borders, either through outright aggression or by taking advantage of Abdullah's anxiety to avoid aggression, rather than the final demarcation of absolute boundaries.

Israel, in spite of its appearance of economic weakness and geographic vulnerability, could afford to act cavalierly toward Abdullah. Israeli thinking seemed to be that since the addition of any part of Palestine to Transjordan was a bonus to Abdullah, therefore Israel, far from having to make concessions, could expect concessions; the net gain to Abdullah would always be more than he would have gotten otherwise.[68] Abdullah wanted confirmation of his position in the West Bank very badly, but had little to offer in return, either in the way of territory or in the way of a diplomatic or economic *entrée* to the region. Politically he was isolated in the Arab world; militarily he was vulnerable to the threat of Israeli force. Thus, although his accommodating attitude toward Israel passed for political realism outside of the Arab world, even his strongest supporter, Kirkbride, acknowledged at the time that his determination to negotiate was 'basically selfish and not really due to far-sighted statesmanship'.[69]

Despite, or perhaps because of, the failure of Abdullah's negotiations with Israel, he did not remain forever isolated. In the spring of 1951, Arab attitudes toward him began to soften. The Iraqi regime, which had avoided consorting too closely with him since 1948 owing to its tenuous internal position, had weathered the storm and could again address the perennial topic of a Hashemite federation. Abdullah, who had recently had to rush home from Turkey when Talal had a nervous breakdown,[70] introduced the topic, worried about the succession to his throne. His idea, itself not new but made urgent by the circumstances, was that Jordan and Iraq should unite, under himself, with the throne passing to the Iraqi branch of the family after his death. The Iraqi regent, Abdullah's nephew 'Abd al-Ilah, and prime minister, Nuri al-Sa'id, visited Amman at the beginning of June to discuss the matter.[71] In July, Riyad al-Sulh, former prime minister of Lebanon and a severe critic of Abdullah, also visited Amman, another sign of a shift in Arab political currents. But Sulh's visit ended in disaster. He was assassinated on his way to the airport outside of Amman by members of the Syrian Social Nationalist Party in retaliation for the execution of Antun Sa'adih, the founder of the party, who had been found guilty of treason in 1949 during Sulh's ministry.

Sulh's assassination, wrote Abdullah's grandson, King Husayn, ten years later, 'had a profound effect on the country, . . . at every street corner, one could see the sullen faces, and the stony silences were broken by sharp cries of argument or sudden violence that signalled a moment of crisis . . .' He noticed the same 'sullen, suspicious faces' in Jerusalem the following Friday, 20 July, when he accompanied his grandfather on his usual visit to al-Aqsa for the Friday prayers.[72] They had spent the previous night in Jerusalem, at a house formerly

Figure 16. King Abdullah with his sons Talal (on his right) and Nayyif (on his left), late 1940s.

belonging to Fakhri al-Nashashibi,[73] getting up at dawn on Friday to visit Ramallah, where a villa was being built for Abdullah, and Nablus, where he met informally with local leaders and friends at the home of the mayor, Ma'zuz al-Masri. They got back to Jerusalem around 11 a.m., and Abdullah performed his ablutions and changed from the Arab Legion uniform he had been wearing to his more customary robe and turban. At about 11.45 a.m., accompanied by his grandson, the military commander of Jerusalem, Radi 'Inab, and his entourage, he entered the *haram*, the vast courtyard surrounding the Muslim holy places in Jerusalem, which had been cleared of people. He first visited the tomb of his father and then headed toward the entrance of al-Aqsa. Inside the mosque, the Quran was being recited to over a thousand worshippers. Microphones were on and the service was being broadcast live. As he approached the entrance, a shaykh came forward to pay homage to him. Abdullah's guards dropped back slightly to let him pass through the doorway of the mosque first. As they did so, a young man, dressed in trousers and a shirt, stepped out from behind the huge door opened outward on Abdullah's right. He raised his arm and shot Abdullah behind his right ear from the distance of a few paces, killing him instantly.[74] On radio, the shots were heard throughout the region.

Chapter 12

Epilogue

When the shots were fired inside the *haram*, the Arab Legion troops on guard outside rushed in with bayonets fixed and started firing indiscriminately. Some twenty people were killed and as many as one hundred wounded in the panic. The Hashemite Regiment, which provided the king's guard, then ran amok in the streets of the Old City, shooting at anything that moved, smashing store windows, looting, and beating people in the streets with their rifle butts and fists.[1] Known followers of Hajj Amin were rounded up for interrogation. Seventy were arrested that Friday, and many hundreds detained for questioning.[2] The worshippers in al-Aqsa at the time of the assassination were locked inside, to be released, one by one, after individual interrogation. Two days later some had still not been allowed to go home.[3]

The atmosphere in Jordan was tense and, especially among Palestinians, filled with fear and dread. Feelings between Palestinians and Transjordanians ran high. Rumors in the Old City had it that the Legion would withdraw from Jerusalem and allow the Israelis to capture it as punishment.[4] Cars with Palestinian license plates were stoned in Salt, where, in earlier years, Abdullah himself had suffered the same indignity. Many Palestinians were not unhappy at what had happened, though they displayed the requisite signs of mourning to protect their lives and property. At some of the refugee camps, however, there was public rejoicing. Three refugees were killed and more wounded, in attacks by enraged Transjordanians, at a camp near the Philadelphia Hotel in Amman.[5]

Abdullah's body was flown back to Amman immediately. Kirkbride was in England on leave at the time and he flew into Amman on the 21st. Talal was also out of the country, at a hospital in Switzerland where he had been undergoing treatment for an unspecified mental disorder since the previous May when he had attacked his wife and newborn daughter.[6] In his stead, Nayyif was appointed regent.

Nayyif's immediate problems were with his family. Umm Talal, afraid that her own son was about to be passed over in the succession to the throne, announced that she would not permit the funeral to take place till Talal had returned. One of Nayyif's sisters was convinced that the current prime minister, Samir al-Rifaʿi, was to blame and publicly demanded immediate vengeance. The division of Abdullah's property was put off for the time being, but promised to be a sticky problem since most things of value had ended up in the hands of his third wife, Nahida, who was ostracized by the rest of the family.[7]

Over Umm Talal's objections, the funeral was held on the 23rd. The ceremony began at 9 a.m., when special envoys were admitted to the throne room at Raghdan to pay their last respects to the flag-draped coffin in the presence of Nayyif, Abdullah's eldest grandson Husayn, 'Abd al-Ilah, the regent of Iraq, and members of the Jordanian government and court. From there a procession formed to accompany the coffin to its final resting place within the palace grounds where, two days before his death, Abdullah had suggested building a mosque. To the piercing screams of the women of the family, the coffin was carried out of the palace and put on a gun carrier drawn by a jeep. Followed first by Nayyif, Husayn and 'Abd al-Ilah, then by the Jordanian cabinet and the prime minister of Iraq, and finally by the diplomatic corps and special envoys representing Britain, Saudi Arabia, Lebanon, Syria, Turkey, Indonesia, Afghanistan, India and Argentina (the Egyptian delegation arrived late, appearing just in time for the burial), the coffin slowly wound its way past the British residency and a recently constructed guest palace to the grave site on the edge of the royal hill in front of Abdullah's *diwan*.

The procession was confined to the hill, which had been cordoned off by barbed wire. No spectators were allowed closer than the hill opposite, and only a small number of Abdullah's subjects gathered there to pay their final respects. The ceremony at the graveside was short. Two eulogies were delivered, one by the minister of court, Abdullah's confidant, Muhammad al-Shurayqi, and the other by Prime Minister al-Rifa'i. Afterwards, Nayyif, 'Abd al-Ilah, and Husayn received condolences in the *diwan*, and tents were set up over the grave, where the imams would chant the Quran for the repose of Abdullah's soul.[8] Later, it was intended to build a mosque on the site, as Abdullah had wished.

At about the same time, Churchill spoke in Abdullah's memory to the House of Commons. His words, no doubt meant respectfully, but tinged with Britain's habitual condescension towards Abdullah, inadvertently summed up the controversy that surrounded his political role in life and that would continue long after his death.

I was myself responsible for . . . his appointment or creation as Emir of Transjordan in 1922 . . . [He was] a man of the greatest fidelity and a vehement Arab patriot if ever there was one, who left Mecca to endeavour to expel the French from Syria by force of arms. When I was on the spot, having the great advantage of Colonel Lawrence's advice, we persuaded him not to take this disruptive step . . . He ran every risk to keep good faith with those with whom he worked . . . the Arabs have lost a great champion . . . the Jews have lost a friend and one who might have reconciled difficulties, and . . . we have lost a faithful comrade and ally.[9]

Abdullah's assassin, Mustafa 'Ashu, was a twenty-one-year-old tailor's apprentice who lived in the Old City and who was, according to Kirkbride, a 'former terrorist'.[10] He did not live to tell his own story, but a story of sorts, drummed out of his family and friends, tied him to a neighborhood *qabaday* (boss), 'Abid 'Ukah, and a group of 'assassins,' who, again according to Kirkbride, had worked for Hajj Amin al-Husayni during the 1937–9 rebellion. One of these, Mahmud Antabli, turned king's evidence. Through his testimony and the confession of 'Abid 'Ukah, ten men were brought to trial in front of a specially constituted military tribunal of three officers of the Arab Legion. These three men, Lt. Gen. 'Abd al-Qadir al-Jundi, Col. Habis al-Majali (who had been present at the assassination and who might more properly have been a witness), and Col. 'Ali Bey Hayari, listened with 'commendable patience (and probably very little understanding)' to the arguments of the prosecuting lawyer, Walid Salah, who was also the judicial adviser to the court, and the nine defense lawyers. The trial lasted a brief nine days. At its end, in an unusual expression of amity, both the prosecution and the defense publicly praised each other and the court for the spirit of co-operation exhibited throughout the proceedings.[11]

Four of the ten were acquitted. They were Father Ibrahim Iyad, Dawud al-Husayni and Tawfiq al-Husayni, both relatives of Hajj Amin al-Husayni, and Kamil Abdullah Kaluti. The rest were found guilty and sentenced to death. Two of the six were Transjordanians, at present safe in Cairo. Abdullah al-Tall, formerly Abdullah's military governor of Jerusalem, who had since fled to Cairo and revealed everything he knew about Abdullah's negotiations with Israel, was said to have been behind the plot. Musa Ahmad Ayyubi, originally from Salt, was found guilty of aiding and abetting him. Extradition from Egypt was not asked, in anticipation, Kirkbride wrote, of certain refusal.[12] Their death sentences were passed *in absentia*.

'Abid 'Ukah, his younger brother Zakariyya 'Ukah, 'Abd al-Qadir Farhat and Musa Abdullah al-Husayni were found guilty and sentenced to death by hanging. The first, a cattle broker, and the second, a butcher, were accused of finding the assassin to do the job. The third owned the café where the final plans were laid and was accused of supplying the gun. The three were 'notorious gangsters,' responsible for a number of killings of Arab and British officials in 1937, according to Kirkbride and his assistant, although they were unable to find records of their activities in police files.[13] The fourth, Musa al-Husayni, was a distant relative of Hajj Amin who, in recent years, had gone out of his way to display his allegiance to Abdullah. He had spent some of the war years in Berlin where he met and married a German woman. Back in Jerusalem in 1945, he was interned briefly by the British for having been in Germany during the war. After his release he came into some local prominence in the absence of the Palestinian national leadership, and in 1949 he befriended Abdullah al-Tall, then military governor of Jerusalem, and acted as his personal representative with the consular corps in Jerusalem and the Conciliation Commission. In 1951 he was the owner of a travel agency in Jerusalem and the Jerusalem correspondent of the Sharq al-Adna broadcasting network. He travelled regularly between Cairo and Jerusalem and was accused of carrying money and promises to the assassins.[14] One week after these four were found guilty and sentenced, they were hanged.

The quickness of the trial and the rapidity with which the sentences were carried out was said to have been Kirkbride's work. He wanted the trial over swiftly for the sake of Jordan's political stability, and, it was rumored, he feared the accused would be pardoned unless they were executed immediately. But the very quickness of the trial and the executions, the three-man military court inexperienced in judicial matters, the dual role of Walid Salah as prosecuting attorney and legal adviser to the court, all gave rise to doubts – not so much that the wrong men had been punished, but that the plot had been so small and so neat. The belief at the time, and today, was that the plot was wider and the motives deeper and more complex.

The assassin and those who plotted with him in Jerusalem were depicted as hired guns, men doing a job for the basest of motives – monetary gain. The trial spun threads between the plotters in Jerusalem and paymasters in Cairo, but once the skein had been followed to Cairo, away from the site of immediate tensions dangerous to Jordan's future, it came unravelled. Abdullah al-Tall was in Cairo, but who was behind him? In Cairo, in 1951, one could meet almost anybody.

The shadow of Hajj Amin loomed behind the plot, not because he was connected by concrete evidence, but because he personified the hatred many Palestinians felt for Abdullah. Personified, it was a hatred made personal and petty, robbed of its political meaning and of its threatening aspect. Others saw Egyptians, Saudis or Syrians behind the plot. Some saw in Kirkbride's haste a British cover-up. Britain, it was claimed, feared that Abdullah was about to engineer the union of Jordan and Iraq, which, so this line of reasoning went, Britain did not want because it would then lose its influence in Jordan and because the new state would be more threatening to Israel. The figure of Father Eugene Hood figured largely in tales of British perfidy. He was an Irish priest, who, reputedly, had taken to the cloth to flee the Black and Tans in Ireland in the early 1920s. Although some credited him with teaching the Palestinians about the use of incendiaries during the revolt, others claimed he had agreed to work for British intelligence in exchange for being allowed to leave Ireland. Other theories fixed on the United States, which failed to warn Abdullah of the plot against him.[15] Like Britain, America was supposedly against the union of Iraq and Jordan.

These theories, held to the present day,[16] are as revealing for what they say as for what they skip. The motives for the supposed British or American involvement are contrived: Iraq and Jordan were not on the verge of unification, nor did the United States or Britain believe they were. Assigning blame to either expressed resentment of the influence those powers wielded in the Middle East, but not the true state of their relationship with Abdullah. Both, indeed, supported him. Assigning blame to Syria, Egypt or Saudi Arabia accurately reflected the bad relations of those states with Abdullah at the time, but begged the question. If mere hatred of him were the motive, there were the Palestinians nearer at hand. But no official wanted to acknowledge publicly that a violent act might have comprehensible motives, and ones that were close at hand. Understanding was confused with condoning, and finding reasons too close to home was threatening.

There was an element of cover-up in the conduct of the trial. The grievances and frustrations of the accused were not broached. The deliberate gloss on that topic was necessary for political reasons, stemming from the structure of Jordan at that moment. Although there was immense tension between Transjordanians and Palestinians because many Palestinians felt Abdullah had got his just deserts, Palestinians had no political alternative to continued life within the Jordanian framework. Their communal life in 1951 was too tentative to explore past injustices and future possibilities of redress. The idea of an independent Palestine was, for the moment, dead. Abdullah's assassination was a terrible revenge wreaked for the death of that idea, but it signified retribution for events that were already history, not the beginning of a new order. It was thus an act that was an end, rather than a beginning. Though not without parallels in the future, it was without echoes. It struck a responsive chord in the hearts of many Palestinians who felt that Abdullah had betrayed them, but it did not signal a rebellion against their fate. In the clashes that followed the assassination, it was Transjordanians who were the aggressors, venting their rage and anger on the Palestinian population.[17]

Abdullah's assassination did not mark the failure of his life's work. On the contrary, the lack of repercussions afterwards measured the extent of his success. He had spent his life searching for a balance of forces which would assure him regional importance. Transjordan was an artificial creation with little meaning beyond its importance to British strategy and imperial communications. This meaning was ephemeral; it would pass away when British interests changed or when British power itself receded. For these reasons, Abdullah had always looked outside of Transjordan for a role which would be greater than Britain's interests alone and which would allow him an existence independent of Britain's fortunes. As the British tide ebbed in the Middle East after the Second World War, he not only had his chance to find a new regional role, but he found it imperative to do so.

With the destruction of Palestine, Abdullah finally found what he was looking for. It was not the simple addition of territory, or the prestige of having the Old City of Jerusalem within his domain, that spelled Abdullah's success. The West Bank was after all quite small and Jerusalem was divided. Rather, with the destruction of Palestine Abdullah had discovered a new balance of forces which finally gave Jordan and himself greater weight in the region and a broader historical meaning. This balance was struck first between British, American and Israeli interests. Britain and the United States had decided not to support an independent Palestine, but at the same time they wanted to limit the damage that the creation of Israel – which, it could not be denied, had been brought about largely through British and American support – would do to their relations with Arab countries. Abdullah's death also heightened a self-awareness in the West that was valuable for Jordan's continued existence. For his death removed the veil of 'tradition' and 'prestige' which Britain had grown accustomed to invoking to account for his position and reminded Britain, and its successor the United States, of their role in the support and maintenance of Jordan and its Hashemite dynasty.[18]

For its part Israel wanted first the disappearance of Palestine as a country, and then the extinction of Palestine as an idea, for the very mention of what had existed between the time of the Kingdom of David and 1948 threatened to undermine the foundations of the Jewish state and the face of courage, humanity, and success in the face of adversity that the post-war West found so compelling. That Jordan should soak up the identity of Palestine suited Israel's real and ideological needs perfectly. Gradually the Arab states too came to appreciate the utility of Jordan's new role, for Jordan saved them either from having to champion the Palestinian cause directly or from having absolutely to admit their inability to do so.

By the time of Abdullah's assassination the framework for this emerging balance had been built. Indeed, it had been built so well that, despite the circumstances of Abdullah's assassination and the difficult succession owing to Talal's mental instability, there were no serious internal or external threats to the regime during this otherwise troubled time. Iraq attempted, not very seriously, to draw Jordan under its wing, claiming Abdullah had been about to legislate his succession to the Iraqi branch of the family owing to his own heirs' shortcomings,[19] but there was no proof and few were convinced by the claim.

After two months of rampant rumormongering along the lines that Britain would not allow Talal to ascend the throne because he was disliked and distrusted as a nationalist, that Britain favored union with Iraq since it 'controlled the Regent down to his socks,' or that it favored a regency with the pro-British Nayyif standing in till Talal's eldest son, Husayn, came of age, Talal arrived back home.[20] He came the day after the sentences of execution were carried out and was crowned king the day after that on 6 September 1951.

Within a year, however, the Jordanian parliament declared him mentally incapable of ruling. He abdicated in favor of his eldest son Husayn, the present king of Jordan.

British high commissioners of Palestine

Sir Herbert Samuel	1920–5
Field Marshal Viscount Plumer	1925–8
Sir John Chancellor	1928–31
Lt. General Sir Arthur Wauchope	1931–8
Sir Harold MacMichael	1938–44
Field Marshal Viscount Gort	1944–5
Sir Alan Cunningham	1945–8

British residents* in Transjordan

Albert Abramson	April 1921–November 1921
H. St John Bridger Philby	November 1921–April 1924
Sir Henry Fortnam Cox	April 1924–March 1939
Sir Alec Seath Kirkbride†	March 1939–December 1951

*The title was changed from chief British representative to British resident in 1927.
†He became minister to Transjordan after its independence in 1946 and later ambassador to Jordan.

Prime ministers* of Transjordan

Rashid Tali'a	April 1921–August 1921
Mazhar Raslan	August 1921–March 1922
'Ali Rida' al-Rikabi	March 1922–February 1923
Mazhar Raslan	February 1923–September 1923
Hasan Khalid Abu'l-Huda	September 1923–April 1924
'Ali Rida' al-Rikabi	April 1924–June 1926
Hasan Khalid Abu'l-Huda	June 1926–February 1931
Abdullah Sirraj	February 1931–November 1933
Ibrahim Hashim	November 1933–September 1938
Tawfiq Abu'l-Huda	September 1938–October 1944
Samir al-Rifa'i	October 1944–May 1945
Ibrahim Hashim	May 1945–February 1947
Samir al-Rifa'i	February 1947–December 1947
Tawfiq Abu'l-Huda	December 1947–April 1950
Sa'id al-Mufti	April 1950–December 1950
Samir al-Rifa'i	December 1950–July 1951
Tawfiq Abu'l-Huda	July 1951

*Until 1939 the title was chief minister.

Notes

1 Prologue

1 Transjordan became the Hashemite Kingdom of Jordan in the constitution of 1947.
2 John Bagot Glubb, *A Soldier with the Arabs* (London, 1957), pp. 63 and 66. Glubb Pasha, the British commander of the Arab Legion, was the translator at this meeting between the two men. That the meeting took place is confirmed by British documents, which, although they do not quote Bevin directly, certainly confirm the substance of this message. See the brief for conversation with Transjordan Prime Minister on Palestine, 6 February 1948, FO 371/68367.
3 See for example, Samuel to Churchill, 12 August 1922, CO 733/23, and Milner to Churchill, 3 September 1922, CO 733/38.
4 Julian Huxley, *From an Antique Land* (London, 1954), pp. 111–13. For evidence that Abdullah knew his position all too well see Mendel Cohen, *be-Hatser ha-Melekh Abdullah* (Tel Aviv, 1980), p. 59. Compare with Lawrence's description:

> His brain often betrayed its intricate pattern, disclosing idea twisted tightly over idea into a strong cord of design; and thus his indolence marred his scheming, too. The webs were constantly unravelling through his carelessness in leaving them unfinished. Yet they never separated into straight desires, or grew into effective desires. Always he watched out of the corner of his bland and open eye our returns to his innocent-sounding questions, reading an insect-subtlety of significant meaning into every hesitation or uncertainty or honest mistake. T. E. Lawrence, *Seven Pillars of Wisdom* (London, 1983), p. 220.

5 See the table on p. 56.
6 'A Note on the Possible Political Results of Disbanding the Arab Legion Infantry Companies,' J. B. Glubb, 1946, FO 371/52930.
7 See Chapter 4 below.
8 See for example, Abdullah to Bevin, 30 August 1947, and Pirie-Gordon to FO, 10 September 1947, FO 371/62226.
9 See Elizabeth Monroe's book of the same name, *Britain's Moment in the Middle East* (London, 1963).

2 Mecca and Istanbul

1 King Abdullah ibn al-Husayn, *al-Mudhakkirat*, in 'Umar al-Madani (ed.), *al-Athar al-Kamila li'l-Malik 'Abd Allah* (Amman, 1977), p. 39. This edition of Abdullah's memoirs, *Mudhakkirati*, first published in Amman in 1945, is used throughout.

2 C. Van Arendonk, 'Sharif,' *Encyclopaedia of Islam*, Vol. 4 (London, 1934), pp. 328–9.

3 The official title was 'sharif of Mecca and its amir.' British usage popularized 'sharif' or 'grand sharif' in the West.

4 King Abdullah, *al-Mudhakkirat*, p. 40.

5 Note by Hubert Young, 18 June 1919, FO 371/4194. The 'Abadila were also known as the Dhawi 'Awn.

6 Saleh al-Amr, 'The Hijaz under Ottoman Rule 1869–1914: The Ottoman Vali, the Sharif of Mecca, and the Growth of British Influence' (unpublished Ph.D. dissertation, University of Leeds, 1974), pp. 1–3.

7 C. Snouck Hurgronje, *Mekka in the Latter Part of the Nineteenth Century* (London, 1931), pp. 185–95.

8 Al-Amr, *The Hijaz under Ottoman Rule*, p. 210.

9 *Ibid.*, pp. 205–6 and 209.

10 Charles M. Doughty, *Travels in Arabia Deserta*, Vol. 2 (Cambridge, 1888), pp. 661–2; William Ochsenwald, *Religion, Society and the State in Arabia* (Columbus, 1984), pp. 201–2.

11 Ochsenwald, *Religion, Society*, pp. 6–8 and 164.

12 *Ibid.*, pp. 29–36. Although it was somewhat risky, the sharif could stir up the tribes in order to win concessions from Istanbul. For example, in 1902 the sharif was suspected of encouraging the tribes to attack the *hajj* so that he could accuse the *vali* of incompetence and have him removed. René Tresse, *Le Pèlerinage Syrien aux villes saintes de l'Islam* (Paris, 1937), p. 57.

13 Karl K. Barbir, *Ottoman Rule in Damascus, 1708–1758* (Princeton, 1980), p. 109.

14 *Ibid.*, pp. 108 ff; Ochsenwald, *Religion, Society*, pp. 32–3.

15 The description of Mecca is based on the following sources: al-Amr, *The Hijaz under Ottoman Rule; Arab Bulletin*, no. 29 (3 November 1916); John Lewis Burckhardt, *Travels in Arabia* (London, 1824); David George Hogarth, *Hejaz Before World War I* (Cambridge, 1978); H. Kazem-Zadeh, 'Relation d'un pèlerinage à la Mecque en 1910–1911,' *Revue du Monde Musulman* 19 (1912), 169–82; John F. Keane, *Six Months in the Hijaz* (London, 1887); Ochsenwald, *Religion, Society*; Snouck Hurgronje, *Mekka*; René Tresse, *Le Pèlerinage Syrien*; A. J. B. Wavell, *A Modern Pilgrim in Mecca* (London, 1918); R. Bayly Winder, 'Makka, the Modern City,' typescript of article for the *Encyclopaedia of Islam*, new edition.

16 For information on sources of income and expenditure see: Burckhardt, *Travels*, pp. 220–36; Snouck Hurgronje, *Mekka*, pp. 22 and 28; Ochsenwald, *Society, Religion*, pp. 101–6.

17 King Abdullah, *al-Mudhakkirat*, pp. 40–3; Snouck Hurgronje, *Mekka*, p. 41.

18 King Abdullah, *al-Mudhakkirat*, p. 43; *al-Hilal* (special issue, April 1939), entire.

19 Ochsenwald, *Religion, Society*, p. 7.

20 King Abdullah, *al-Mudhakkirat*, p. 43.

21 *Ibid.*, pp. 45 and 50.

22 Niyazi Berkes, *The Development of Secularism in Turkey* (Montreal, 1964), pp. 255–9.

23 For more information on Abu'l-Huda al-Sayyadi, see Butrus Abu-Manneh, 'Sultan

Abdulhamid II and Shaikh Abdulhuda Al-Sayyadi,' *Middle Eastern Studies* 15:2 (May 1979), 131–54.
24 H. St John Philby, *Stepping Stones Across the Jordan* (unpublished manuscript), p. 34, Philby Papers.
25 King Abdullah, *al-Mudhakkirat*, p. 52.
26 *Ibid.*, p. 52. The following studied in Istanbul during Abdullah's residence there: Rashid Tali'a, a Druze from the Shuf district of Lebanon, Mazhar Raslan from Homs, and 'Ali Rida' al-Rikabi from Damascus, all future chief ministers of Transjordan; Muhammad 'Ali al-'Abid and Shukri al-Quwatli, future presidents of Syria; Riyad al-Sulh, a future prime minister of Lebanon; 'Awni 'Abd al-Hadi from Nablus, a future leader of the Istiqlal party in Palestine; and Nuri al-Sa'id, Ja'far al-'Askari, and Yasin al-Hashimi, all future prime ministers of Iraq.
27 Conversation with Princess Fawzi, Hasan Khalid's daughter, London, 23 October 1978; HRH Princess Musbah Haidar, *Arabesque* (London, 1944), p. 80. Abdullah and his brothers particularly liked to visit Chamlujah, 'Ali Haidar's estate on the Asian side of the Bosporus, where he kept Arabian horses. According to Princess Musbah, 'Their own father was too miserly to allow them to keep any [Arabian horses] – their household was not run on the same lavish and lordly way things were done at Chamlujah.'
28 George Stitt, *A Prince of Arabia the Emeer Shereef Ali Haidar* (London, 1944), pp. 93–4.
29 Muhammad Labib al-Batanuni, *al-Rihla al-Hijaziyya* (Cairo, 1911), pp. 80–1. Regarding the disturbances in Mecca see also PRO, FO 371/561, Monahan (British Consul in Jidda) to Sir Gerard Lowther (British Ambassador in Istanbul), 2 December 1908.
30 King Abdullah, *al-Mudhakkirat*, pp. 46–8. The *irade* appointing Husayn sharif of Mecca is in Başbakanlik Arşivi, Dahliye 1326/Şevval No. 45, 'Mekke-i Mükerreme Emaretine Şerif Hüseyin Paşa'nin tayinine dair. It is a *re'ser irade*, meaning one that was not initiated by the government.
31 Husayn Nasif, *Madi al-Hijaz wa Hadiruhu* (Cairo, 1930), Vol. 2, p. 6; al-Amr, *The Hijaz under Ottoman Rule*, p. 158; C. Ernest Dawn, *From Ottomanism to Arabism* (Urbana, 1973), p. 5; King Abdullah, *al-Mudhakkirat*, pp. 47–8; Stitt, *Prince of Arabia*, p. 103.
32 Lowther to FO, 24 November 1908, FO 371/561.
33 King Abdullah, *al-Mudhakkirat*, pp. 54–5.
34 Conversation with Princess Fawzi, London, 23 October 1978; conversation with Sir John Bagot Glubb, former Commander of the Arab Legion, Mayfield, Sussex, 14 June 1978; King Abdullah, *al-Mudhakkirat*, pp. 50–3.
35 King Abdullah, *al-Mudhakkirat*, p. 60.
36 Monahan to Lowther, 5 December 1908, FO 195/2286.
37 Wavell, *Modern Pilgrim*, pp. 75, 78, and 200; Tresse, *Pèlerinage*, pp. 88 and 335; Dawn, *Ottomanism*, p. 6; King Abdullah, *al-Mudhakkirat*, pp. 65–6; Philip S. Khoury, *Urban Notables and Arab Nationalism: The Politics of Damascus, 1860–1920* (Cambridge, 1983), p. 87.
38 Report from Akaba, 20 June 1918, MD, Service Historique de l'Armée, Série 7N–2141.

39 Khoury, *Urban Notables*, p. 57.
40 King Abdullah, *al-Mudhakkirat*, p. 68.
41 Khayr al-Din Zirikli, *Ma Ra'aytu wa Ma Sama'tu* (Cairo, 1923), p. 109; Alec Seath Kirkbride, *A Crackle of Thorns* (London, 1956), pp. 169–70.
42 C. E. Vickery, 'Arabia and the Hedjaz,' *Journal of the Royal Central Asian Society* 10:1 (1923), 58–9.
43 Monahan to Lowther, 7 March 1912, FO 371/1487.
44 Monahan to Lowther, 12 March 1909, FO 371/767.
45 Monahan to Lowther, 23 March 1909, FO 195/2350.
46 See al-Batanuni, *Rihla Hijaziyya*, for an account of the khedive's pilgrimage.
47 See George Antonius, *The Arab Awakening* (New York, 1965), pp. 101 ff; Zeine Zeine, *The Emergence of Arab Nationalism* (Beirut, 1966), pp. 83 ff.
48 King Abdullah, *al-Mudhakkirat*, p. 89.
49 Monahan to Lowther, 7 March 1912, FO 371/1487. See also G. P. Gooch and Harold Temperly (eds.), *British Documents on the Origins of the War, 1898–1914* (London, 1938), Vol. 10, part 2, p. 829. Antonius claims otherwise: see *Arab Awakening*, p. 126.
50 Again, Antonius claims otherwise: *Arab Awakening*, p. 129.
51 Feroz Ahmad, *The Young Turks* (Oxford, 1969), p. 67.
52 Neville Mandel, *The Arabs and Zionism Before World War I* (Berkeley, 1976), pp. 104–5.
53 Lowther to Grey, 4 December 1911, FO 371/1259.
54 King Abdullah, *al-Mudhakkirat*, pp. 78–9.
55 'Fi Mudhakkirat Sulayman Shafiq Kamali Pasha,' *al-'Arab* no. 10, year 5 (June 1971), p. 913, and no. 2, year 6 (October 1971), p. 92.
56 Monahan to Lowther, 18 September 1911, FO 371/1231; Abd al-Rahman (acting British consul) to Lowther, 24 August 1911, FO 195/2376; and report on the Turkish Campaigns in Yemen and Asir, January 1912, FO 882/10; King Abdullah, *al-Mudhakkirat*, pp. 81, 84–5; 'Fi Mudhakkirat Sulayman Pasha' *al-'Arab*, no. 5, year 6 (January 1972), pp. 357–8. The quote is from 'Fi Mudhakkirat Sulayman Pasha,' p. 358.
57 Monahan to Lowther, 18 September 1911, FO 371/1231.
58 King Abdullah, *al-Mudhakkirat*, p. 71; Dawn, *Ottomanism*, p. 9. The trip from Damascus to Medina by rail took three days and nights and cost two gold pounds for a third-class ticket. Tresse, *Pèlerinage*, p. 337.
59 Memorandum on the position on the Grand Sherif, enclosure in a letter from Mallet to Grey, 18 March 1914, FO 371/2128.
60 King Abdullah, *al-Mudhakkirat*, p. 94.
61 Abdullah may have met Kitchener before this, in 1912 or 1913. For a complete discussion and evaluation of the conflicting evidence see Dawn, *Ottomanism*, pp. 58–63.
62 Kitchener to Grey, 6 February 1914, FO 371/2130.
63 King Abdullah, *al-Mudhakkirat*, pp. 90–1.
64 Memorandum on Hijaz affairs by Devey (British consul in Damascus), 30 March 1914, FO 371/2130.
65 King Abdullah, *al-Mudhakkirat*, p. 96.
66 *Ibid.*, pp. 102–3.

67 Note by Storrs, 19 April 1914, FO 141/460.
68 King Abdullah, *al-Mudhakkirat*, pp. 103–4.
69 *Ibid.*, pp. 111–12; Ameen Rihani, *Around the Coasts of Arabia* (London, 1930), p. 110.
70 Abdullah to Storrs, 20 October 1914, FO 371/6237.
71 Sulayman Musa (ed.), *al-Murasalat al-Tarikhiyya 1914–1918* (Amman, 1973), pp. 27–8.
72 Abdullah to Storrs, 30 November 1914, FO 371/6237.
73 Wingate to Clayton, 28 November 1914, Clayton Papers, Box 469/7.

3 The Arab Revolt

1 'The Sherifs,' by T. E. Lawrence, 27 October 1916, FO 882/5, p. 41.
2 Notes by T. E. Lawrence, 24 April 1917, FO 686/6.
3 Dawn, *Ottomanism*, pp. 45–9.
4 See for example *Arab Bulletin*, no. 36 (26 April 1916), p. 558, which contains Faysal's account of the genesis of the revolt as told to Lawrence; King Abdullah, *al-Mudhakkirat*, p. 113; Antonius, *Arab Awakening*, pp. 130–1; and Dawn, *Ottomanism*, pp. 54–68.
5 Note on the sums paid to the King of the Hedjaz, n.d., FO 371/3048.
6 Amin Sa'id, *al-Thawra al-'Arabiyya al-Kubra*, Vol. 1 (Cairo, n.d.), p. 128.
7 For texts of the letters, see Antonius, *Arab Awakening*, Appendix A.
8 Ahmad Djemal, *Memories of a Turkish Statesman, 1913–1919* (New York, 1922), p. 222; King Abdullah, *al-Mudhakkirat*, pp. 114–16; 'Note on the sums . . .,' FO 371/3048.
9 'Note sur le mouvement Arabe,' Paris, 13 February 1917, MD, Service Historique de l'Armée, Série 7N-2140.
10 *Arab Bulletin*, no. 23 (26 September 1916), p. 303.
11 Information on the siege of Ta'if was found in *Arab Bulletin*, no. 23 (26 September 1916), p. 303; *ibid.*, no. 30 (15 November 1916), p. 439; and King Abdullah, *al-Mudhakkirat*, pp. 124–7.
12 Extract from Ronald Storrs' diary, 16, 17 and 18 October 1916, in McMahon to FO, 28 October 1916, FO 371/2782.
13 'The Sherifs,' by T. E. Lawrence, 27 October 1916, FO 882/5, pp. 40–1.
14 C. E. Wilson (British consul, Jidda) to McMahon, 5 November 1916, FO 371/2792; E. Brémond, *Le Hedjaz dans la Guerre Mondiale* (Paris, 1931), pp. 74–5.
15 'Attitude of Great Britain and France to the Sherif's proclamation of the assumption of the title, "Malik el Bilad el Arbia [sic]",' n.d., FO 882/5.
16 Telephone message from Abdullah, 1 November 1916, FO 882/5.
17 'The Sherifs,' by T. E. Lawrence, 27 October 1916, FO 882/5; C. E. Wilson to General [?], 5 October 1916, Arab Affairs File, Box 141/1; Wingate to Clayton, 30 November 1916, Clayton Papers, Box 470/4.
18 Summary of the Hejaz Revolt, 30 September 1919, FO 882/7.
19 'The Sherifs,' by T. E. Lawrence, 27 October 1916, FO 882/5.
20 Note on the Arab Forces, 26 June 1917, FO 882/6.

21 Notes by T. E. Lawrence, 24 April 1917, FO 686/6, part 2; Maurice Larès, *T. E. Lawrence, la France et les Français* (Paris, 1980), pp. 151–3.
22 Brémond, *Hedjaz*, p. 72. The reference is to the famous meeting of Henry VIII and François I in 1520, known to English historians as 'the Field of the Cloth of Gold.'
23 Report by T. E. Lawrence, 16 April 1917, FO 686/6, part 2.
24 Interview with Fakhr al-Din Pasha, 15 April 1919, FO 686/57.
25 T. E. Lawrence, *Seven Pillars of Wisdom* (New York, 1935), p. 216. Lawrence constantly compared Abdullah with Faysal, to Abdullah's detriment. John Mack, author of *A Prince of our Disorder* (London, 1976), speculated that it was Faysal's relative tallness, like that of Lawrence's brother Will, which drew Lawrence to Faysal rather than to Abdullah, who was even shorter than himself. Conversation with John Mack, Boston, July 1978.
26 Report by T. E. Lawrence, 16 April 1917, FO 686/6, part 2.
27 King Abdullah, *al-Mudhakkirat*, p. 71.
28 'The Politics of Mecca,' 1916, FO 371/2771.
29 For text of treaty see Gary Troeller, *The Birth of Saudi Arabia* (London, 1976), pp. 254–6.
30 Cornwallis to Clayton, 9 December 1917, FO 882/8.
31 King Abdullah, *al-Mudhakkirat*, p. 139.
32 Lawrence, *Seven Pillars*, p. 213.
33 Note on conversation with the Amirs Abdulla and Faisal, 1 May 1917, FO 882/16.
34 Britain gave Husayn a monthly stipend of £125,000 which he was to divide among his sons according to their needs. On occasion Abdullah got a douceur directly from Britain over and above this sum. Note on the sums . . ., FO 371/3048; Treasury to FO, 20 November 1916, FO 371/2782; Wilson to Husayn, 29 March 1917, FO 686/34; Wingate to FO, 25 March 1918, FO 371/3393.
35 Davenport to Bassett, 16 March 1918, FO 882/7; Davenport to Bassett, 13 April 1918, FO 686/49; Bassett to Arab Bureau, 22 August 1918, FO 686/5; 'Hejaz Post-War Finance,' Garland, n.d., FO 882/23; St Quentin (Cairo) to Ministère de la Guerre, 6 March 1918, MD, Service Historique de l'Armée, Série 16N-3201, 'Egypte,' no. 13.
36 *Arab Bulletin*, no. 74 (24 December 1917), pp. 511–13.
37 Jidda to Cairo, 20 March 1918, FO 686/38.
38 *Arab Bulletin*, no. 96 (9 July 1918).
39 Conversation with Crown Prince Hasan, Amman, December 1978; Khayr al-Din Zirikli, *al-'Alam; Qamus Tarajim li-Ashhar al-Rijal wa al-Nisa' min al-'Arab wa al-Musta'ribin wa al-Mustashriqin* (Cairo, 1954–7, 10 vols) 3rd edition, Vol. 2, pp. 340–1.
40 C. E. Wilson to Abdullah, September 1918, FO 686/15.
41 Conversation with Sulayim ibn Jabir (who, as a slave of Sharif Shakir, fought at Khurma), Amman, 21 November 1978; Davenport to Arab Bureau, 19 September 1918, FO 882/9.
42 Sulayman Musa, *al-Thawra al-'Arabiyya al-Kubra. al-Harb fi'l-Urdun 1917–1918. Mudhakkirat al-Amir Zayd* (Amman, 1976), p. 110; Cairo to Jidda, 28 October 1918, conveys message from Faysal to Husayn, FO 141/438.

43 Cornwallis to General Headquarters, 25 October 1918, FO 141/438; interview with King Husayn, 16 November 1918, FO 686/40.
44 Elie Kedourie, 'The Surrender of Medina, January 1919,' *Middle Eastern Studies* 13:1 (January 1977), p. 132; C. E. Wilson to Husayn, 30 December 1918, FO 686/40; minute by G. K. [George Kidston], 6 January 1919, FO 371/4166.
45 Wingate to FO, 7 December 1918, FO 371/3416; *Arab Bulletin*, no. 108 (11 January 1919), pp. 6–7.
46 Kedourie, 'Surrender,' p. 134; *Arab Bulletin*, no. 108 (11 January 1919), pp. 6–7.
47 *Arab Bulletin*, no. 109 (6 February 1919).
48 Beirut to Ministère de la Guerre, 24 January 1919, MD, Service Historique de l'Armée, Série 16N–3201, 'Egypte,' dossier 1.
49 Conversations with Juabir (a member of the 'Utayba tribe), Amman, 13 December 1978 and Sulayim ibn Jabir, Amman, 21 November 1978. Both men were at the battle. See also Husayn to Faysal, 2 June 1919, FO 686/17, and Intelligence and Political Report, 27 October to 21 November 1919, FO 686/26.
50 Telegram from Catroux, 25 May 1919, MD, Service Historique de l'Armée, Série 7N–2143, Mission du Hedjaz, dossier Raho. Abdullah praised Raho as a 'soldier to the last minute.' See also Larès, *T. E. Lawrence*, p. 87.
51 Abdullah to C. E. Wilson, 3 June 1919, FO 686/17.

4 The creation of Transjordan

1 For the struggle in each country between imperial and anti-imperial forces see Monroe, *Britain's Moment*, pp. 137 ff.; Christopher M. Andrew and A. S. Kanya-Forstner, *France Overseas* (London, 1981), pp. 164 ff.
2 Col. Georges Catroux (Jidda), 11 October 1919, MD, Service Historique de l'Armée, Série 7N–4184, dossier 4.
3 The twenty-nine included Ja'far al-'Askari, Naji al-Suwaydi, and 'Ali Jawdat, all future prime ministers of Iraq. Ernest Scott (Ramleh) to FO, 24 September 1920, FO 371/5040.
4 Ernest Scott (for Samuel) to Curzon, 16 May 1920, FO 141/510; Catroux, 1 June 1920, MD, Service Historique de l'Armée, Série 16N–3203, dossier 7.
5 Minutes of a meeting of the Eastern Committee held on 27 November 1918, FO 371/4148. Neither Cecil nor Montagu was speaking from first-hand knowledge, but both were presumably relying on reports from British political officers in the Middle East. Abdullah's connection with Iraq had grown out of the so-called 'Sharifian solution', whereby the sons of Husayn were to rule parts of the promised Arab Kingdom under British or French tutelage. By involving Husayn's sons it was hoped to get Husayn's agreement to the division of Arab territory and its mandated status.
6 Bell wrote on 14 June 1920: 'What really would simplify matters would be if they would ask for Abdullah, Faisal's brother, for Amir. Abdullah is a gentleman who likes a copy of the Figaro every morning at breakfast time. I haven't any doubt that we should get along with him famously.' Elizabeth Burgoyne, *Gertrude Bell from her Personal Papers 1914–1926* (London, 1961), p. 140.

7 Minutes of a meeting of the Eastern Committee held on 27 November 1918, FO 371/4148.
8 See the exchange, Arab Bureau to C. E. Wilson (Jidda), 27 January 1919, C. E. Wilson to Arab Bureau, 28 January 1919, and Arab Bureau to FO, 30 January 1919, FO 882/23.
9 Brinton Cooper Busch, *Britain, India, and the Arabs, 1914–1921* (Berkeley, 1971), pp. 412–14.
10 See Sati' al-Husri, *Yawm Maysalun* (Beirut, n.d.).
11 King Abdullah, *al-Mudhakkirat*, p. 156; Sulayman Musa, *Ta'sis al-Imara al-Urduniyya 1921–1925* (Amman, 1971), pp. 46 and 181; Zirikli, *Ma Ra'aytu*, p. 25.
12 A. T. Wilson to FO, 31 July 1920, FO 371/5038. Until that point Wilson had advocated direct British administration. Just two days previously he expressed the opinion that Britain must either 'govern or go.' Busch, *Britain, India, and the Arabs*, pp. 412–14. Some Arab historians also acknowledge that Faysal learned a lesson at Maysalun that he was never able to forget. See for example, Zirikli, *Ma Ra'aytu*, p. 125.
13 A. T. Wilson to FO, 31 July 1920, FO 371/5038; Arnold Talbot Wilson, *Loyalties Mesopotamia. Vol. II. 1917–1920* (Oxford, 1931), p. 244.
14 Samuel to FO, 30 July 1920, and FO to Samuel, 5 August 1920, FO 371/5038.
15 Husri, *Yawm Maysalun*, p. 201.
16 Nasir al-Din Ahmad (Mecca), report for period ending 31 August 1920, FO 686/12.
17 Report by Major Batten (Jidda), 10–20 September 1920, FO 371/5243.
18 Report by Vickery (Jidda), 6 March 1920, FO 371/5061.
19 Jidda reports for period ending 19 August 1920 and for period 1–10 September 1920, FO 371/5243; Batten to FO, 5 September 1920, FO 371/5064.
20 Nasir al-Din to Batten, 26 September 1920, FO 686/12; Jidda Report, 20–30 September 1920, FO 686/26; Jidda Report, 10–20 October 1920, FO 371/5243.
21 Allenby to FO, 13 November 1920, FO 371/5066.
22 Khayr al-Din Zirikli, *'Aman fi 'Amman* (Cairo, 1925), p. 24.
23 Hubert Young to Lord Hardinge (British Ambassador in Paris), 27 July 1920, FO 371/5254.
24 Curzon to Samuel, 6 August 1920, ISA 2/50a.
25 During Faysal's reign, France had tried to win support in Transjordan by distributing gifts to tribal shaykhs. Huge sums and gifts inscribed 'From Paris to Great Sheikhs of Transjordania' were reportedly distributed which helped to cause discord between the tribal leaders and Arab nationalists in Damascus. Mithqal Ibn Fayiz, the paramount shaykh of the Bani Sakhr, came back from a trip to Haifa in a French car, and, it was said, £1,000 richer. After the French occupation, a governor was appointed to Salt and all shaykhs as far south as Karak were summoned to a meeting in Damascus. Officially, however, the French government disclaimed any intention of extending French influence to Transjordan. Report by I. N. Camp (Political Liaison Officer), 19 February 1920, ISA 2/1; Samuel to FO, 6 August 1920, FO 371/5038; FO to Samuel, 11 August 1920, FO 371/5121.
26 FO to Samuel, 6 August 1920, FO 371/5121.
27 Chaim Weizmann wrote Samuel a letter on the eve of Faysal's expulsion from Syria stressing the importance to the Jewish national home of the plateaux across the

Jordan river. Meyer W. Weisgal (ed.), *The Letters and Papers of Chaim Weizmann*, Vol. 10, series A (Jerusalem, 1977), pp. 4–5.

28 The quote is from Monckton to C. P. Cook, 16 August 1974, Monckton Papers. Monckton was one of the British political officers in Transjordan. For the duties of the political officers sent to Jordan, see: Note of a conversation between R. F. C. Monckton and P. A. Alsberg (ISA archivist), Monckton Papers; FO to Samuel, 11 August 1920, FO 371/5121; Deedes to Tilley, 27 September 1920, FO 371/5123. See also Kirkbride, *Crackle of Thorns*, pp. 18–28.

29 FO to Samuel, 11 August 1920, FO 371/5121.

30 Samuel to his wife, 13 August 1920, Samuel Papers/41.

31 Samuel to Faysal and Faysal to Samuel, 16 August 1920, FO 371/5039.

32 Diary, Samuel Papers/41, 20 August 1920.

33 Diary, Samuel Papers/41, 22 August 1920. Among those present were Rufayfan Pasha al-Majali from Karak, Hamid Ibn Jazi of the Huwaytat tribe, and Shaykh Sultan of the 'Adwan tribe. The pardon was requested by Rufayfan Pasha and Sultan al-'Adwan. Note of a conversation between R. F. C. Monckton and P. A. Alsberg, Monckton Papers. See also Elie Kedourie, *The Chatham House Version and Other Middle Eastern Studies* (London, 1970), p. 61.

34 Samuel to FO, 28 November 1920, FO 371/5290; Philip S. Khoury, *Syria and the French Mandate: The Politics of Arab Nationalism* (Princeton, 1987), Chapter 4.

35 GHQ Egypt to WO, 20 December 1920, FO 371/5290.

36 Zirikli, *'Aman*, pp. 4–5; Samuel to FO, 30 November, 7 December and 12 December 1920, and 'Summary of events' by Deedes, 20 December 1920, FO 371/5290.

37 The distinction was noted at the time by Fu'ad Salim, who classified those who met with Abdullah as 'leaders of the country' (*zu'ama al-balad*) and 'men of the awakening' (*rijal al-nahda*). See Musa, *Ta'sis*, p. 53.

38 The traditional leaders were, 'Auda Abu Tayih (Huwaytat), Ghalib Sha'lan (Rwala), Hamid Ibn Jazi (Huwaytat), Mithqal Ibn Fayiz (Bani Sakhr), Haditha al-Khuraysha (Bani Sakhr), Shaykh al-'Isa (unknown), Husayn al-Tarawna (Karak), 'Atawi al-Majali (Karak), Sa'id Khayr (Mayor of Amman), Sa'id al-Mufti (Amman, leader of the Circassian community). Two important leaders of whom no mention has been found among those who visited Abdullah are Sultan al-'Adwan of the 'Adwan tribe and Rufayfan al-Majali of Karak, though both had been at Samuel's meeting at Salt.

39 The nationalists were 'Abd al-Qadir al-Jundi, Muhammad 'Ali al-'Ajluni, Khalaf al-Tall (Irbid), Ahmad al-Tall (Irbid), Fu'ad Salim (Lebanese Druze), Muhammad Muraywid, Mahmud al-Hindi (Damascus), Kamil Budayri (Jerusalem), Bahjat Tabbara (Beirut), Shaykh Kamil al-Qassab (Damascus), Amin al-Tamimi (Nablus), 'Awni al-Qudamani (Damascus), 'Awni 'Abd al-Hadi ('Araba), Mazhar Raslan (Homs), Subhi al-Khadra (Safad).

40 See for example: Samuel to FO, 19 October 1920, FO 371/5123; Wyndham Deedes (civil secretary to the British administration in Palestine) to Tilley, 25 October 1920, FO 371/5124; GHQ Egypt to WO, 4 November 1920, FO 371/5289.

41 Minute by Hubert Young on papers submitted on 6 November 1920, FO 371/5289.

42 WO to General Officer Commanding (Egypt), 22 October 1920, FO 371/5124; WO to FO, 22 November 1920, FO 371/5289.

43 Résumé of a conversation between Comte Robert de Caix and the British vice-consul in Damascus, Gilbert MacKereth, 2 December 1920, FO 371/5293.

44 Memorandum on possible negotiations with the Hijaz by Hubert Young, 29 November 1920, CO 732/3.

45 Minute of Cornwallis's interview with Faysal, 8 January 1921, FO 371/6349.

46 Minute by Curzon on negotiations with Faysal, n.d. [January 1921], FO 371/6371; minute after discussion with Young and Lawrence by John Shuckburgh for Churchill, 25 February 1921, CO 732/3.

> HMG are responsible under the terms of the Mandate for establishing in Palestine a national home for the Jewish people. They are also pledged by the assurances given to the Sherif of Mecca in 1915 to recognise and support the independence of the Arabs in those portions of the Turkish vilayet of Damascus in which they are free to act without detriment to French interests. The western boundary of the vilayet of Damascus before the war was the River Jordan. Palestine and Transjordania do not therefore stand upon quite the same footing. At the same time the two areas are economically interdependent and their development must be considered as a single problem. Further, HMG have been entrusted with the Mandate for 'Palestine'. If they wish to assert their claim to Transjordania and to avoid raising with other Powers the legal status of that area, they can only do so by proceeding upon the assumption that Transjordania forms part of the area covered by the Palestine Mandate. Draft agenda for the Cairo Conference, 26 February 1921, CO 732/3.

47 Zirikli, ʿAman, pp. 5 and 8.

48 ʿAwni ʿAbd al-Hadi, *Awraq Khassa*, ed. Khayriyya Qasimiyya (Beirut, 1974), p. 42.

49 Monckton to his mother, 1 February 1921, Monckton Papers.

50 Kirkbride, *Crackle of Thorns*, pp. 26–7.

51 ʿAbd al-Hadi, *Awraq Khassa*, pp. 42–3; Samuel to CO, 10 March 1921, FO 686/78.

52 Until that time responsibility for the Middle East had been divided between the Foreign, India and War Offices. The scope of the new department encompassed Iraq, Aden, Palestine and Transjordan. The Hijaz, as an independent kingdom, remained under the Foreign Office. The date of the transfer of responsibilities was 1 March 1921.

53 The minutes of the Cairo Conference are found in the Report on the Middle East Conference held in Cairo and Jerusalem from March 12th to 30th, 1921, FO 371/6343. See also Aaron S. Klieman, *Foundations of British Policy in the Arab World: The Cairo Conference of 1921* (Baltimore, 1970).

54 Deedes to Young, 15 April 1921, CO 733/17A.

55 Churchill to prime minister, 18 March 1921, FO 371/6342.

56 Prime minister to Churchill, 22 March 1921, FO 371/6342.

57 ʿAbd al-Hadi, *Awraq Khassa*, p. 44; Sulayman Musa, *al-Murasalat al-Tarikhiyya 1920–1923* (Amman, 1978), vol. 3, pp. 203–6.

58 Larès, *T. E. Lawrence*, pp. 260–1.

59 Zirikli, ʿAman, pp. 47–8.

60 King Abdullah, *al-Mudhakkirat*, pp. 162–3.

61 Churchill to Samuel, 2 April 1921, CO 733/13.

62 Report on the Middle East Conference held in Cairo and Jerusalem from March 12th to 30th, 1921, FO 371/6343. The idea that France might be induced to invite Abdullah to rule in Damascus was entertained in London, but seems to have developed out of wishful thinking rather than a realistic appraisal of French intentions. See minute by John Shuckburgh (assistant under-secretary of state, CO) for Churchill, 18 February 1921.

63 George Antonius to Thomas Hodgkin, 24 June 1936, Thomas Hodgkin Papers.

64 For descriptions of the territory of Transjordan under Ottoman administration see: Barbir, *Ottoman Rule in Damascus*, pp. 134–5 and 145; Gertrude Bell, 'Turkish Rule East of the Jordan,' *The Nineteenth Century and After* 52 (1902), pp. 227 and 234; Claude Regnier Conder, *Heth and Moab. Explorations in Syria in 1881 and 1882* (London, 1883), p. 189; Archibald Forder, *With the Arabs in Tent and Town* (London, 1902), p. 76; Le Père Antonin Jaussen, *Coutumes des Arabes au Pays de Moab* (Paris, 1948), p. 119; Walid Kazziha, *The Social History of Southern Syria (Trans-Jordan) in the 19th and Early 20th Century* (Beirut, 1972), p. 8; A. Konikoff, *Trans-Jordan, an Economic Survey* (Jerusalem, 1943), pp. 13–14; Selah Merrill, *East of the Jordan. A Record of Travel in the Countries of Moab, Gilead, and Bashan During the Years 1875–1877* (London, 1881), pp. 102 and 200; Henry Baker Tristram, *The Land of Israel: A Journal of Travels in Palestine Undertaken with Special Reference to its Physical Character* (London, 1886), pp. 473–4 and 560, and *The Land of Moab. Travels and Discoveries on the East Side of the Dead Sea and Jordan* (London, 1873), p. 94.

65 The Circassians had been preceded by a small group of Chechens following the Russian conquest of Daghestan in 1864. On Circassian settlement see: Bell, 'Turkish Rule,' p. 229; G. Lankester Harding, "Amman,' *Encyclopaedia of Islam*, new edition, Vol. 1, p. 447; Konikoff, *Economic Survey*, p. 18; Laurence Oliphant, *The Land of Gilead with Excursions in the Lebanon* (New York, 1881), p. 218; Frederick G. Peake, *A History of Jordan and its Tribes* (Coral Gables, Florida, 1958), p. 222. Peake lists Circassian settlements at Amman (1878), Wadi Sir (1880), Jarash (1885), Na'ur (1900), Suwaylih (1905) and Rusayfah (1909). Konikoff lists Chechen settlements at Suwaylih, Zarqa, Rusayfa and Sukhna, and Circassian settlements at Amman, Wadi Sir, Jarash and Na'ur.

66 Henry Baker Tristram, *Pathways of Palestine* (London, 1881), p. 124; Oliphant, *Land of Gilead*, p. 232.

67 The information on the Hijaz railway is from Jane M. Hacker, *Modern Amman* (Durham, 1960), p. 19; PP Jaussen et Savignac, *Mission Archéologique en Arabie (Mars–Mai 1907) de Jérusalem au Hedjaz Medain-Saleh* (Paris, 1909), pp. 20 and 33; Konikoff, *Trans-Jordan*, p. 95; Sulayman Musa and Munib al-Madi, *Tarikh al-Urdun fi'l-Qarn al-'Ashrin* (Amman, 1959), p. 13; Conversation with Sa'id al-Mufti, Amman, 12 December 1978.

68 Eliahu Epstein, 'The Bedouins of Transjordan: Their Social and Economic Problems,' *Journal of the Royal Central Asian Society* 25 (April 1938), 232–4. The small tribes of the 'Ajlun and Balqa' districts were engaged in agriculture by the turn of the century. The 'Adwan, one of the largest tribes of the Balqa', began to settle before the First World War and even the Bani Sakhr owned land on which were installed

tenants from client tribes. Epstein further contends that the Huwaytat had farmed
until the turn of the century, when two war-like shaykhs, Abtan Ibn Jazi and 'Awda
Abu Tayih, revolutionized the tribe's way of life by transforming it into one of the
most predatory in northern Arabia and Syria. This transformation was completed by
the war and the huge amounts of gold to be won by fighting on the side of Britain.
'Awda Abu Tayih was one of Faysal's chief tribal allies and was instrumental in the
capture of Aqaba in 1917. The pre-war trend towards tribal settlement is borne out
by numerous contemporary travellers.
69 Cited in A. Ruppin, *Syrien als Wirtschaftsgebiet* (Berlin, 1917), p. 8.

Qada'	Population
'Ajlun	61,500
Salt	37,235
Karak	19,551
Tafila	7,750
Ma'an	5,752
Total Population	131,788

These figures do not include nomads, and are otherwise low since in general people
were loath to be counted, fearing taxation and conscription.
70 'Observations on Dr. Weizmann's letter to the Secretary of State for the Colonies
with Reference to Transjordania,' by Major Somerset and Captain Peake, 14 March
1921, CO 733/15. This was written to refute a letter from Weizmann to Churchill (1
March 1921, in Weisgal (ed.), *Letters and Papers*, Vo. 10, series A, p. 161) in which
Weizmann argues for Transjordan's inclusion in Palestine and within the bounds of
the national home policy. One of the bases of Weizmann's argument was population:
'The beautiful Trans-Jordanian plateaux . . . lie neglected and uninhabited, save for
a few scattered settlements and a few roaming Bedouin tribes.' Peake and Somerset's
general figures are as follows:

Area	Population
'Ajlun, comprising Irbid, Jarash and the Bani Hasan country	100,000
Balqa', comprising Salt, 'Amman and Ma'daba	80,000
Karak, including Tafila	40,000
Ma'an, 'Aqaba, and Tabuk	10,000
Total Population	230,000

71 Musa, *Ta'sis*, pp. 177–8. The author cites a report, dated 23 August 1922, from the
assistant secretary for tribal affairs to Sharif Shakir Ibn Zayd. The district of Ma'an
and Aqaba is not included since it did not become officially a part of Transjordan
until 1925.
72 'Observation . . .' by Peake and Somerset, 14 March 1921, CO 733/15.
73 Epstein, 'The Bedouins of Transjordan,' pp. 232–4; Peake, *History and Tribes*,

pp. 155–7, 168–72, 210–14, 215–19; 'Personalities of South Syria II Trans-Jordan,' Arab Affairs File 206/5/2.

5 Settling in

1 Churchill to Samuel, 2 April 1921, CO 733/13. Abdullah, who was supporting his Hizaji troops and some of Faysal's former administrators and who had to entertain and make gifts to build local support, estimated his monthly expenditure at £10,000. Samuel to CO, received 12 April 1921, FO 371/6372.

2 Churchill to Samuel, 2 April 1921, CO 733/13; 'Transjordania,' Memo by Churchill, 2 April 1921, CAB 24/122.

3 Hacker, *Modern Amman*, p. 59; Musa, *Ta'sis*, p. 178. Hacker estimates the population as between 3,000 and 5,000 and Musa puts it at 2,400.

4 On arrival in Amman, Abdullah stayed at the home of Sa'id Khayr. After his long journey, however, he wanted a bath and so was invited to the Mufti home which was right next to the spring. He was ill with hepatitis at the time and Sa'id al-Mufti's wife contracted it. He liked the home and asked for it, and so the Mufti family moved elsewhere. Conversation with Sa'id al-Mufti, Amman, 12 December 1978.

5 Confidential report by Abramson, 20 September 1921, FO 371/6373.

6 The house in which Abdullah stayed, belonging to the Abu Jabir family, happened to overlook the town well where women went to collect water. Abdullah's guard watched them and annoyed them with comments, thereby inciting the wrath of the men of Salt. This story was first told to me by Sa'id al-Mufti (Amman, 12 December 1978) and was confirmed in subsequent interviews with Ra'uf Abu Jabir (Amman, 15 December 1978) and 'Abd al-Rahman Khalifa (Amman, 26 December 1978), both originally from Salt.

7 Tali'a had served Faysal as *mutasarrif* and military governor of Hama, acting minister of the interior, and military governor of Aleppo. Amin al-Tamimi had been one of Faysal's advisers. Mazhar Raslan was the former *mutasarrif* of Salt. Hasan al-Hakim had served Faysal as inspector of finance. Philby, *Stepping Stones*, pp. 235–6, Philby Papers. See also short biographies in Zirikli, *al-'Alam*.

8 One evening when Mr. Churchill, H. E. [Samuel], Abdullah, you, Lawrence and I were discussing names, that of [Iltyd] Clayton was put forward . . . H. E. asked me what I thought. I said I know him but do not feel very enthusiastic about him. I said that I had thought of Abramson. We settled nothing further that night but promised Abdullah to give him the best and to consult him before deciding. Deedes to Young, 15 April 1921, CO 733/17A.

Of the two candidates, Clayton and Abramson, the former is rather junior for so important a post. Nothing is known here about Abramson, but the recommendations of Sir H. Samuel and Colonel Lawrence of course carry great weight. Sir H. Samuel says that he is not a Jew by religion; not that he is not a Jew by extraction, which to judge from his name he probably is. This seems to me to be something of an objection for the particular post in question but I do not think it is sufficient to justify us, on the information before us, in overruling the local recommendation. Minute by Shuckburgh for Churchill, 8 April 1921, CO 732/1.

9 Admiralty to FO, 18 July 1921, FO 371/6372.

10 Deedes to Young, 27 May 1921, CO 733/17A; Deedes to CO, 28 May 1921, FO 371/6372.

11 Zirikli, *'Aman*, p. 118.

12 Report no. 4 from Amman, 5 June 1921, CO 733/3. See also Report no. 5 from Amman, 1 July 1921, CO 733/4. Previously minister of the interior, al-Tamimi had been appointed *mutasarrif* in May.

13 Report no. 2 from Amman, 3 May 1921, CO 733/3. Abdullah was extremely annoyed over Rufayfan's long stay in Jerusalem. When Samuel visited Transjordan in April Abdullah requested him not to make a fuss over Rufayfan whenever he might next come to Jerusalem. Later, while visiting Rufayfan in Karak, Abdullah told him that he need not think the British really thought so much of him and that Rufayfan would have proof of that next time he visited Jerusalem. Report no. 7 from Amman, 1 September 1921, FO 371/6373.

14 Report by Abramson, 9 June 1921, FO 371/6372.

15 Samuel to CO, 25 July 1921, FO 371/6372.

16 Major C. S. Jarvis, *Arab Command. The Biography of Lieutenant Colonel F. W.* [sic] *Peake Pasha* (London, 1942), pp. 75–7. Peake subsequently had to rebuild the force from scratch.

17 Samuel to CO, 13 June 1921, FO 371/6372.

18 Congreve to Young, 16 June 1921, CO 733/17A.

19 Minute by Lawrence on Congreve's letter to Young, CO 733/17A. A month later Lawrence made the comment that 'Had Abdulla's regime been efficient and popular Palestine would now be clamouring to join Trans Jordan. This is the danger to avoid. We have by giving Abdulla rope enough to hang his reputation, eliminated a disturbing political factor.' Samuel to CO, 25 July 1921, FO 371/6372.

20 On the Gouraud incident see: French Ambassador in London to Curzon, 2 August 1921, FO 371/6373; Abramson to Deedes, 29 September 1921, FO 371/6462; and report on the political situation in Palestine and Transjordan, October 1922, CO 733/27. France demanded the extradition of eighteen people, despite British findings that nine of them either did not exist or were not known to the Transjordan authorities, three could prove valid alibis, two were still in Syria, and one was shot dead while evading arrest in Dir'a. Philby to Samuel, 15 February 1923, CO 733/44.

21 For more complete information on Hananu's nationalist activities in Syria and on his arrest and trial, see Philip S. Khoury, *Syria and the French Mandate*, pp. 319 ff.

22 Samuel to CO, 5 September 1921 and confidential report from Abramson, 20 September 1921, FO 371/6373; Jarvis, *Peake Pasha*, pp. 90–2.

23 Young to Congreve, 6 July 1921, CO 733/17A.

24 Deedes to Samuel, 2 July 1921 and Samuel to CO, 23 July and 3 August 1921, FO 371/6372. Curzon's summation of the six months was terse and crass: 'Abdulla was

much too big a cock for so small a dunghill and the experiment was foredoomed to failure.' Minute by Curzon on 18 September 1921, FO 371/6243.

25 According to British sources, Rashid Bey fell due to a disagreement with Abdullah over the appointment of Shaykh Shanqiti as adviser on religious affairs, Tali'a holding the opinion that a religious shaykh was unsuitable for such a post (Report no. 10 from Amman, 1 September 1921, FO 371/6373). Zirikli ('*Aman*, pp. 139–42), however, said that Tali'a opposed Britain's control of the reserve force to which Abdullah had acquiesced. Peake later wrote that Samuel had demanded Tali'a's resignation over the Gouraud incident in his article, 'Trans-Jordan,' *Journal of the Royal Central Asian Society* 23:3 (July 1939), p. 385.

26 Zirikli, '*Aman*, pp. 3–4.

27 'Feisal arrived in Baghdad and got quite a good reception, Abdulla, of course, is sick . . . from jealousy.' Peake to Somerset, Amman, 10 April 1921, Somerset Papers. 'He [Abdullah] did not appear to be at all pleased when he heard that Feisal had had a good reception in Basra and in Baghdad.' Report no. 5 from Amman, 1 July 1921, CO 733/4.

28 Report no. 5 from Amman, 1 July 1921, CO 733/4.

29 Abramson to Deedes, 29 August 1921, FO 371/6462.

30 Had Husayn signed the treaty it would have meant he accepted the division of Arab lands, the imposition of mandatory control, and Britain's Jewish national home policy. See Suleiman Mousa (Sulayman Musa), 'A Matter of Principle: King Husain of the Hijaz and the Arabs of Palestine,' *International Journal of Middle East Studies* 9:2 (May 1978), pp. 188–9.

31 Young to Shuckburgh, 30 September 1921, CO 733/17B.

32 Young to Shuckburgh, 7 October 1921, CO 733/17B.

33 Abramson and Alan Kirkbride (the younger brother of the later British Resident, Sir Alec Kirkbride) were the only two British political officers still at their posts. Regarding military support, Britain had not fulfilled its March agreement with Abdullah: the reserve force had no rifles, little or no ammunition and no machine guns, and there were only two armored cars, which were useless because they had neither spare parts nor crews to man them. Young to Shuckburgh, 15 October 1921, CO 733/7. On Lawrence's stay in Amman see Uriel Dann, *Studies in the History of Transjordan, 1920–1949* (Boulder, 1984), pp. 37–46.

34 Philby's peers summed up his character with the joke about the soldier's proud mother who exclaimed, while watching her son on parade, 'They're all out of step but our Jack.' Sir Reader Bullard, *The Camels Must Go* (London, 1961), p. 198.

35 Elizabeth Monroe, *Philby of Arabia* (London, 1973), p. 113. For a full account of Philby's career in Iraq and the steps by which he came to be appointed in Amman see *ibid.*, pp. 95–113.

36 Philby Diary, 29 November 1921.

37 Minute by Shuckburgh, 31 January 1922, CO 733/8.

38 Samuel to Churchill, 7 October 1921, CO 733/6.

39 Philby, *Stepping Stones*, p. 4.

40 Philby Diary, 3 December 1921.

41 Philby Diary, 10 and 12 January 1922.

42 Philby to Gertrude Bell, 17 February 1922, Philby Papers.

43 Philby Diary, 12–27 December 1921.
44 Churchill to Samuel, 7 February 1922, CO 733/8.
45 Report on the situation in Transjordan, 1 April–30 June 1922, CO 733/23.
46 Minute by H. Young on Milner's letter to Churchill of 3 September 1922, CO 733/38.
47 Report on the political situation in Palestine, August 1922, and Lieutenant Colonel W. F. Stirling to Jerusalem, 11 September 1922, CO 733/25; Report on the political situation in Palestine, September 1922, CO 733/26; Deedes to Shuckburgh, 15 September 1922, CO 733/38.
48 For example Abdullah gave extensive tracts of land to Mithqal Ibn Fayiz, the paramount shaykh of the Bani Sakhr, and assessed the tax on one of Mithqal's villages at the nominal sum of £10 per year. Philby, *Stepping Stones*, p. 116.
49 FO to CO, 22 December 1924, FO 371/10121; Additional Notes to 1919 'Who's Who in Damascus,' 27 April 1921, FO 371/6454; Palmer (British consul in Damascus) to FO, 18 October 1921, FO 371/6373.
50 Philby Diary, 22 March 1922.
51 Samuel to Churchill, 4 April 1922, CO 733/20.
52 Philby Diary, 4 April 1922. Catroux told Philby that he had rescued al-Rikabi from a court trial for the murder of 'Abd al-Qadir al-Jaza'iri. Catroux believed al-Rikabi would almost certainly have been condemned. Catroux knew al-Rikabi well and admired him as a man of unusual intelligence and energy even though he had made himself unpopular by amassing considerable wealth while at Damascus.
53 Minute by H. Young regarding Abdullah's proposed visit to London, 31 July 1922, CO 733/23.
54 Philby Diary, 24 September 1922.
55 'Record furnished by Riza Pasha Rikabi of a conversation between His Highness the Emir Abdullah and Sir Gilbert Clayton at the Carlton Hotel on Monday October 16th 1922,' and memorandum for the Middle East Department by Sir G. Clayton, 18 October 1922, Clayton Papers 471/3.
56 Memorandum by G. Clayton, 25 October 1922, CO 733/37.
57 Minute by Shuckburgh, 5 December 1922, CO 733/35; Clayton to Rikabi, 18 December 1922, CO 733/28; Philby, *Stepping Stones*, pp. 54–5.
58 FO to CO, 15 November 1922, FO 406/50; FO to CO, 4 December 1922, FO 371/7792; FO to CO, 17 March 1923, CO 733/55. For details of the Druze uprising see Khoury, *Syria and the French Mandate*, Chapters 6 and 7.
59 Philby, *Stepping Stones*, p. 87.
60 Political report for Palestine and Transjordan, May 1923, FO 371/8998.
61 Musa, *Ta'sis*, p. 163; Uriel Dann, *Studies*, pp. 47–80.
62 Philby to G. Bell, 20 June 1923, CO 733/59.
63 Monroe, *Philby*, p. 129.
64 Clayton to Shuckburgh, 13 July 1923, Clayton Papers 513/5.
65 Philby to Clayton, 1 July 1923, CO 733/47.
66 According to Philby, Abdullah gave cars with chauffeurs to Mithqal Ibn Fayiz, Haditha al-Khuraysha, and Rufayfan al-Majali, a wedding present of £1,000 to Mazhar Raslan, a wedding present of £500 to Muhammad al-Unsi, and was build-

ing a house for Muhammad al-Asbali at a cost of £3,000–£4,000. Regarding land, Abdullah gave *miri* lands in Ziza village and its surroundings to Mithqal Ibn Fayiz; 'Abd al-Mahdi al-Shamayli received 2,000 dunums of *miri* land in a village near Karak (Philby reckoned that Abdullah owed al-Shamayli money); Nakhl village, 20,000 dunums of miri land, was given to Rufayfan al-Majali and Husayn al-Tarawna; and five villages, 70,000 dunums, was given to 'Atawi al-Majali. Philby to Samuel, 1 July 1923, CO 733/47.

67 Clayton to Shuckburgh, 13 July 1923, Clayton Papers 513/3.

68 Philby, *Stepping Stones*, pp. 116–17; Philby to Clayton, 1 July 1923, CO 733/47; Philby to Samuel, December 1923, CO 733/52.

69 For information on the 'Adwan rebellion see: B. S. Thomas to Samuel, n.d., CO 733/64; Monthly report on Transjordan, September 1923, CO 733/50; Philby to Samuel, 17 September 1923, CO 733/49; Musa, *Ta'sis*, pp. 165–6; Philby, 'Trans-Jordan,' *Journal of the Central Asian Society* 11:4 (1924), p. 306; Draft of an address for the Royal Central Asian Society anniversary meeting, 12 June 1924, and *Stepping Stones*, p. 149, Philby Papers. Those arrested and later deported were 'Awda al-Qasus, from a Christian family of Karak and judge on the Court of Appeal; Salih al-Najdawi, Assistant Commander of the Arab Legion in the Karak district; Shams al-Din Sami, Circassian lawyer from Amman; Mustafa Wahbi al-Tall, from an Irbid family and *mudir* of Wadi Sir.

70 The Jordanian historians Sulayman Musa and Munib Madi, for example, believe the British were behind the rebellion and that they later removed Fu'ad Salim from the Legion because the rebellion was suppressed. (Musa and Madi *Tarikh al-Urdun*, p. 233). The evidence now available does not altogether clear Philby (Monroe, *Philby*, p. 130), but Philby was not 'the British' and the reasons for Salim's removal were clearly quite otherwise.

71 Monroe, *Philby*, pp. 130–1.

72 Philby to Samuel, 17 September 1923, CO 733/50. The officers included Fu'ad Salim, who a year before had saved Peake from an Amman crowd during the Hananu crisis.

73 Philby to Samuel, 13 December 1923, and Clayton to CO, 28 December 1923, CO 733/52.

74 Monthly reports on Transjordan, January and February, 1924, CO 733/66; Samuel to CO, 16 February 1924, FO 371/10101.

75 Colonel Kisch, Chief Rabbi Jacob Meyer, and Dr David Yellin. Philby Diary, 27 January 1924.

76 Philby Diary, 6 March 1924; Dawn, *Ottomanism*, p. 41.

77 Jidda report for 1–29 March 1924, FO 371/10006.

78 'Hussein the New Khalif,' *Manchester Guardian*, 13 March 1924.

79 W. A. Smart (British consul in Damascus) to FO, 10 March 1924, FO 371/10217; Smart to FO, 22 March 1924, FO 371/10218.

80 Sir R. Storrs (district governor, Jerusalem–Jaffa) to Clayton, 14 March 1924, FO 684/2.

81 Albert Hourani, *Arabic Thought in the Liberal Age, 1798–1939* (London, 1962), p. 305.

82 Lord Allenby (Cairo) to FO, 11 March 1924, FO 371/10217. For Egypt's interest in the Caliphate see Kedourie, *Chatham House Version*, pp. 177–207.
83 Philby Diary, 10, 14 and 15 January 1925.
84 Anecdote related to the author by Edward R. F. Sheehan, Cambridge, Mass., 21 April 1985.
85 Uriel Dann, *Studies*, p. 86.
86 Memorandum by Shuckburgh for the Secretary of State for Colonial Affairs, 26 April 1924, CO 733/78.
87 Minute by Shuckburgh, 24 April 1924, CO 733/67. The 1923–4 grant-in-aid was £150,000, the loss of which was only partially covered by the £60,000 balance of the Ottoman Public Debt funds collected from Transjordan and held in Palestine.
88 Samuel to CO, 20 April 1924, CO 733/67.
89 Reports by F. G. Peake, n.d., Somerset Papers.
90 Cox to Clayton, 5 May 1924, CO 733/68.
91 Cox to Clayton, 28 May 1924, CO 733/68.
92 Peake to Cox, 11 May 1924, CO 733/68.
93 Samuel to CO, 30 May 1924, CO 733/68.
94 Cox to Clayton, 1 July 1924, CO 733/71.
95 Clayton to Abdullah, 14 August 1924, FO 371/10102.
96 Clayton to CO, 14 August 1924, and General Officer Commanding (Palestine) to Air Ministry, 14 August 1924, FO 371/10102. Uriel Dann in his article, 'The Political Confrontation of Summer 1924 in Transjordan' (*Studies*, pp. 81–92), is incorrect in writing that the 9th Lancers were sent to Amman because of the Wahhabi raid and only appeared to be there in connection with the political crisis. The opposite was the case: the Wahhabi raid was the published reason, but the political crisis was the real reason. See Clayton to CO, 14 August 1924 (two separate dispatches), FO 371/10102.
97 Cox to Clayton, 20 August 1924, CO 733/72.

6 Discovering the limits

1 The figures do not include extraordinary sums or the grant-in-aid for the TJFF. Summary of revenue for the period 1 April 1924–31 March 1929, CO 831/8; Annual reports to the Council of the League of Nations on the administration of Palestine and Transjordan, 1928–35.
2 See: Budget estimates for 1923–24 and CO 733/76, Cox to Clayton, 20 November 1924, CO 733/48; Peake to Clayton, 5 August 1926, CO 733/116; 'Arif al-'Arif, *Amman Diary* (unpublished manuscript in Arabic), al-'Arif Papers (September 10, 1926), p. 54. Al-'Arif mentions that Kirkbride even complained about the use of paper and envelopes between departments when word of mouth would do.
3 Cox to Shuckburgh, 4 November 1928, CO 831/3.
4 Cox to Plumer, 27 August 1928, CO 831/3.
5 Treasury to CO, 23 October 1928, CO 831/3; Cox to Shuckburgh, 4 November 1928, CO 831/3; Pirie-Gordon (*Times* special correspondent in Jerusalem) to Shuckburgh, 11 December 1929, CO 831/6.

6 Peake to Cox, 11 May, CO 733/68.
7 Annual report to the Council of the League of Nations on the administration of Palestine and Transjordan, 1925, p. 61.
8 Annual report to the Council of the League of Nations on the administration of Palestine and Transjordan, 1926, p. 71.
9 Treasury to CO, 17 February 1927, CO 733/133.
10 On his objections see: Plumer to CO, 3 February 1927 and Ormsby-Gore to Churchill, 16 November 1927, CO 733/133; Plumer to Amery, 1 May 1928, CO 733/151.
11 A popular contemporary theory among Arabs was that the Wahhabi attack against Transjordan was engineered by Britain as a means of getting rid of Abdullah. Salisbury-Jones (British liaison officer to HQ French Army of the Levant) to Palestine Command, 4 September 1924, PRO, FO 371/10118.
12 On the last days of Husayn's kingdom of the Hijaz see: Bullard, *Camels*, p. 126; Burgoyne, *Gertrude Bell*, Vol. 2, p. 352; Arnold Toynbee, 'Arabia: Rise of the Wahhabi Power,' in *Survey of International Affairs 1925* (Royal Institute of International Affairs), Vol. 1, p. 292; Rihani, *Around the Coasts of Arabia*, p. 109.
13 For a complete account of Britain's attempts to get a treaty and Husayn's resistance see Mousa, 'A Matter of Principle,' pp. 183–94.
14 Samuel to CO, 16 November 1923, FO 686/75. In the end, it was considered fortunate that Husayn had never ratified the Anglo-Hijazi treaty since it might have committed Britain to supporting him in a losing venture. George Rendel, *The Sword and the Olive* (London, 1957), p. 58.
15 Sir Laurence Grafftey-Smith, *Bright Levant* (London, 1970), pp. 171–2.
16 Burgoyne, *Gertrude Bell*, Vol. 2, p. 356.
17 Conversation with Sulayim ibn Jabir (Amman, 21 November 1978), who attended Husayn in his final illness. Colonel F. H. Kisch, head of the political department of the Jewish Agency and chairman of the Zionist Executive in Palestine, visited Husayn in Amman in February. He reported that during their conversation Husayn held up his hand, extending two fingers side by side, to indicate the close relationship of Arabs and Jews, and instructed Abdullah to act accordingly for ever. Notes by Colonel Kisch on his interviews in Amman, 20 February 1931, CZA S25/3506.
18 Chancellor to CO, 11 June 1931, FO 371/15289.
19 On the Syrian revolt, see Khoury, *Syria and the French Mandate*, Chapters 6–8.
20 Information on Transjordan during the Syrian revolt can be found in the draft report on the administration of Palestine and Transjordan for the year 1926, CO 733/131; 'Activities in Transjordan undertaken on behalf of the French authorities in Syria during 1926,' by E. R. Stafford, Robert Parr (Damascus) to FO, 8 July 1927, Stuart Symes (Jerusalem) to CO, 8 July 1927, L Rees (RAF) to Symes, 26 July 1927, and Cox to Symes, 5 August 1927, CO 733/132; Report on Transjordan by Cox, 1 July to 31 July 1925, CO 733/96.
21 Al-'Arif, *Amman Diary*, pp. 57, 63 and 64 (17 September, 28 September and 7 November 1926), al-'Arif Papers.
22 Alec Seath Kirkbride, *From the Wings* (London, 1976), pp. 152–3.
23 Conversation with Yasser Tabbaa, Boston, June 1984.

24 Sulayim ibn Jabir, a family retainer, remembers being sent to the Hijaz to escort the families of Abdullah, 'Ali and Faysal to Transjordan. After a short stay in Amman, the families of 'Ali and Faysal moved on to Baghdad. Conversation with Sulayim ibn Jabir, Amman, 21 November 1978.

25 Her family in Çatalca were farmers and were not well off. The children worked for their keep in wealthier homes. Conversation with the Amir 'Ali ibn Nayyif, Abdullah's and her grandson, Amman, 21 November 1978.

26 For the arrangements that were made for Talal and information on this three-year period of his life see: F. Ezechial (Crown Agent for the Colonies, who agreed to act as Talal's director and supervisor in England) to Clauson, 18 February 1926, and Ezechial to Lord Plumer's Private Secretary, 16 February 1926, CO 733/119; Cox to Plumer, 22 December 1926, and Ezechial to Shuckburgh, 4 February 1927, CO 733/136; Ezechial to Cox, 27 April 1927, Shuckburgh to Symes, 28 July 1927, Stickland to Ezechial, 12 December 1927, and Ezechial to Cox, 22 December 1927, CO 733/140; Bowman to Mayhew, 17 April 1929, CO 831/6; Minute by Shuckburgh, 19 December 1939, CO 831/54.

27 Ezechial to Shuckburgh, 4 February 1927, CO 733/136, and Ezechial to Cox, 22 December 1927, CO 733/140. Ezechial elaborated in another letter, 'Of his personal character I have formed a very favourable opinion. He is steady and appears to have grit and I think he should develop well. He is also well liked by people with whom he has overcome his first shyness and reserve.' Ezechial to Cox, 27 April 1927, CO 733/140.

28 Transjordan register of correspondence, 1930, CO 870/2.

29 Minute by Shuckburgh, 19 December 1939, in which he quotes a letter to him from Chancellor dated 14 March 1931, CO 831/54. See also Minute by [?] Howard, 14 July 1931, CO 831/15.

30 Wauchope to CO, 15 July 1932, CO 831/19.

31 Report on the political situation for the month of August 1934, FO 371/17880. The engagement of Talal and Sfyneh had been arranged on condition that Sfyneh, whose mother was English, would not always be confined to the house, that she and Talal would have a house of their own, and that Talal would not take a second wife. Talal's mother did not, apparently, object to the conditions of the marriage; rather, she preferred to have her son marry someone more closely related to herself to strengthen her position in the family.

32 'Arif al-'Arif, civil secretary for the Transjordan government, related that Abdullah and Cox argued over Nayyif's education. Abdullah wanted to place him in a national school and Cox wanted to place him in a missionary establishment (St George's in Jerusalem). See his *Amman Diary*, pp. 87 and 99 (3 December 1926 and 22 January 1927), al-'Arif Papers.

33 Conversation with Walid Khalidi, Cambridge, Mass., 27 July 1978; Bowman to Mayhew, 17 April 1929, CO 831/6.

34 On Nayyif's education see: H. E. Bowman to F. Ezechial, 28 May 1929, and Pirie-Gordon to Shuckburgh, 11 December 1929, CO 831/6; Report on the political situation for the month of March 1934, FO 371/17880.

35 Thomas Hodgkin, 'Antonius, Palestine and the 1930s,' *Gazelle Review of Literature on the Middle East* 10 (1982), p. 24.

36 Conversation with Hashim Dabbas, Aide-de-Camp to Abdullah, Amman, 8 November 1978. Mr Dabbas related that if Abdullah ever saw a window open, he would shout for it to be closed.

37 Conversation with Lady Cox, Chipstead, Surrey, May 1978.

38 Philip Hayne to Philby, 5 July 1927, Philby Papers.

39 Annual reports to the Council of the League of Nations, 1925–7.

40 Conversation with Eliahu Elath (formerly Epstein), Jerusalem, 8 January 1979.

41 Conversation with Mr and Mrs Graham Cox (son of the British Resident) Chipstead, Surrey, February 1978. The entrance hall of Abdülhamid's palace, Yildiz, was also filled with mirrors, for the purpose not of humor, but of misleading and confusing possible assassins. See also 'Emir Abdullah the Smart Little Arab Ruler of Transjordan is No. 1 British Pawn in the Middle East,' *Life* (1 December 1941), p. 67.

42 Cohen, *be-Hatser ha-Melekh Abdullah*, pp. 77–9.

43 Plumer to Shuckburgh, 21 December 1927, CO 831/1, and Plumer to Shuckburgh, 6 January 1928, CO 733/134.

44 Agreement between the United Kingdom and Transjordan, signed at Jerusalem, February 20, 1928 (Cmd. 3029), FO 371/13021.

45 Text is in Helen Miller Davis, *Constitutions, Electoral Laws, Treaties of the States in the Near and Middle East* (Durham, NC, 1947), 303–13.

46 See Legislative Council Electoral Law, in Davis, *Constitutions*, pp. 315–20. The number of beduin in the northern and southern districts is not known. In 1938 Eliahu Epstein estimated the Bani Sakhr at 1,140 tents, the Huwaytat at 1,000 tents, and the Bani Hasan at 860 tents. Glubb in 1938 classified the Bani Sakhr, the Huwaytat and the Sirhan as nomadic and the Bani Hasan and the Hajaya as semi-nomadic, although all by that time owned some land for agricultural use. See Epstein, 'The Bedouins of Transjordan,' pp. 232–5, and John Bagot Glubb, 'The Economic Situation of the Trans-Jordan Tribes,' *Journal of the Royal Central Asian Society* 25 (July 1938), p. 449.

47 In Salt, schoolboys threw onions at Abdullah. In Amman a student demonstration caused Abdullah to give the final oral exams for the year himself, passing and failing students according to their political loyalty. Saʿid al-Mufti, mayor of Amman, took no action against the demonstrators there and so was transferred to Maʾdaba as a punishment. Conversations with Raʾuf Abu Jabir, Amman, 15 December 1978; Farhan Shubaylat, Amman, 15 December 1978; and Saʿid al-Mufti, Amman, 12 December 1978.

48 Some members of the so-called opposition were, Husayn al-Tarawna (Karak), Rufayfan Pasha al-Majali (Karak), Mithqal Ibn Fayiz (Bani Sakhr), Haditha al-Khuraysha (Bani Sakhr), Muhammad al-Hamud and Nimr al-Hamud (Salt), the leaders of Irbid and ʿAjlun, and Saʿid al-Mufti (Circassian from Amman). The make-up of the group suggests a certain opportunism in its creation. Mithqal and Rufayfan generally followed Abdullah in most matters: Saʿid al-Mufti's opposition won the Circassians another seat on the Legislative Council. Some mildly repressive action on the part of the government helped to discourage the boycott – for example, confinement to home village, summons to Amman, police surveillance, and one case of forced residence at Aqaba. Conversation with Saʿid al-Mufti,

Amman, 12 December 1978; 'Yadhkuru Saʿid al-Mufti,' part 3, *al-Dustur* (Amman daily), 25 February 1976; and *Oriente Moderno*, September 1928, pp. 404–6.

49 Report on the political situation for May 1931, pp. 24–6, CO 831/12.

50 Report on the political situation for the month of November 1931, p. 21, CO 831/12.

51 Emanuel Neumann, *In the Arena* (New York, 1976), p. 127.

52 Between 1931 and 1946 the members of the Legislative Council came from thirty-six families, generally reinforcing the pre-existing social structure. See Kamel S. Abu Jaber, 'The Legislature of the Hashemite Kingdom of Jordan: A Study in Political Development,' *Muslim World* 59 (July–October 1969), pp. 226–7.

53 G. F. Walpole, 'Land Problems in Transjordan,' *Journal of the Royal Central Asian Society* 35 (January 1948), pp. 52–65.

54 Hedley V. Cooke, *Challenge and Response in the Middle East. The Quest for Prosperity 1919–1951* (New York, 1952), pp. 112–16.

55 Annual report to the Council of the League of Nations on the administration of Palestine and Transjordan, 1924, p. 67.

56 Peake instructed Glubb, 'if you consider it necessary to punish on the spot, do so, and I will put it right here; but if you have a case you can send here occasionally, send it along for Shakir to play with; this for diplomatic reasons.' Peake to Glubb, 10 February 1931, Peake Papers.

57 In the early 1940s, Ibn Saud assessed Abdullah's tribal policy to a visiting American, H. B. Hoskins. 'Abdullah, he feels, is wrong in having broken the power of the tribal chiefs and has, as a result, become dependent on British force rather than on his own friendly relations with the sheikhs and people of Transjordan.' 'King Ibn Saud – Man not Myth,' 18 October 1943, FO 371/34976.

58 FO to British Agent (Jidda), 18 November 1923, FO 686/69.

59 Samuel to CO, 3 April 1924, and Minute by Young, 7 April 1924, CO 733/67; monthly report on Transjordan by Philby, 1 March–15 April 1924, CO 733/58.

60 Storrs to Cox, 18 November 1924, FO 371/10815; Monthly report on Transjordan, 1 March to 1 May 1925, CO 733/92.

61 Ibn Saud to Bullard (British consul, Jidda) 14 May 1925, Clayton Papers, 471/5.

62 Randall Baker, *King Hussein and the Kingdom of the Hijaz* (Cambridge, 1979), p. 221.

63 Clayton was sent before the end of hostilities because it was feared that afterwards Ibn Saud might feel strong enough to eschew diplomacy for force in delimiting his borders with Iraq and Transjordan. Notes on the Hijaz–Najd frontier, June 1930, FO 371/14465. For details of the negotiations see Sir Gilbert F. Clayton, *An Arabian Diary* (Berkeley, 1969).

64 Lloyd (Egypt) to CO, 31 December 1926, and Plumer to Shuckburgh, 20 January 1927, CO 733/134.

65 Rees to ?, 27 February 1928, and Plumer to CO, 10 April 1928, CO 831/1.

66 Memorandum on the Syria–Iraq and Syria–Transjordan frontier, 12 November 1931, CO 732/50.

67 Clayton to Amery, 10 December 1925, Clayton Papers 471/7.

68 For example, preceding the elections of 1928 and 1931–2. See Khoury, *Syria and the French Mandate*, Chapters 12 and 13.

69 The list came to include Husayn's four sons, ʿAli, Abdullah, Faysal and Zayd; Husayn's 1908 rival for the post of Sharif, ʿAli Haydar and his son ʿAbd al-Majid; the ex-Khedive of Egypt, ʿAbbas Hilmi and Prince Yusuf Kamal, another member of Egypt's royal family; Ibn Saud's son, Faysal; Amir Saʿid al-Jazaʾiri, a notable of Damascus and the grandson of ʿAbd al-Qadir al-Jazaʾiri who was exiled to Damascus from Algeria by the French; and the Damad Ahmad Nami, a son-in-law (divorced) of Sultan Abdülhamid.

70 Memorandum on secret reports regarding Hashemite intrigues against Ibn Saud, 10 June 1932, FO 371/16014; HC Palestine to CO, 1 July 1932 and CO to HC, 7 July 1932, FO 371/16015; 'The Rebellion in the Northern Hijaz and Ibn Rifada's Incursion' by G. W. Rendel, 25 July 1932, FO 371/16016; Ryan (Jidda) to FO, 8 August 1932, FO 371/16024; Cox to British Consul (Damascus) 25 August 1932, FO 686/6; Ryan to Sir John Simon, 31 July 1932, and HC Palestine to CO, 27 August 1932, FO 406/70; CO to HC Palestine, 29 September 1932, HC to CO, 7 October 1932, and Hope-Gill (Chargé d'Affaires, Jidda) to FO, 25 November 1932, FO 371/16017.

71 H. W. Glidden, 'The Hashemite Question as a Source of Near East Tensions,' in William Sands (ed.), *Tensions in the Middle East* (Washington DC, 1956), p. 9. Ryan described the negotiations as follows: 'we went at the negotiations hammer and tongs for nearly a fortnight, Cox and I being the protagonists on the Anglo-Trans-Jordan side, while Fuad Hamza and Yusuf Yasin fought hard on the other.' Sir Andrew Ryan, *The Last of the Dragomans* (London, 1951), pp. 286–7.

72 On Abdullah's ambitions and their place in the general impulse towards Arab unity of the 1930s and 1940s see Yehoshua Porath, *In Search of Arab Unity 1930–1945* (London, 1986).

73 Chancellor to CO, 4 November 1929, FO 371/13748.

7 Abdullah and Palestine, 1921–39

1 The London *Times* of 4 April 1921 reported Abdullah's statements as follows:

While it is perhaps natural that many Palestine Arabs should fear an eventual Jewish domination with unpleasant religious, political and economic consequences as a result of Zionism, yet the Arabs must remember the question of Zionism is one which interests not them and the Jews only, but Christendom as well. I think myself that if representative Arabs of Palestine would agree to meet representative Jews in conference they might find that Zionism is not so menacing a thing as they supposed.

To an Arab delegation requesting support in getting the Balfour Declaration revoked, Abdullah was reported to have replied: 'It is not for Arabs to urge the English to break their pledged word,' a rather clever side-step considering that one of the cornerstones of the Arab case against the Palestine mandate was exactly that – that the mandate violated Britain's pledged word.

2 Report by Lt. Col. Easton, Damascus, 25 April 1921, FO 371/6455.

3 Major Somerset to his father, Lord Raglan, 20 June 1921, Somerset Papers.

4 Philby Diary, 3 and 11 September 1922; Deedes to Shuckburgh, 15 September 1922, CO 733/38.

5 Deedes to Shuckburgh, 15 September 1922, CO 733/38. Deedes wrote that Abdullah's attendance at the ceremony was

> the culminating point of a consistently correct and politically courageous attitude. Its value to us is very great morally and materially. Materially because if he encouraged or permitted the activities of extremists in Trans-Jordan we could certainly not recommend a reduction in the garrison of Palestine and should have to keep a constant watch on our eastern frontier. Morally because his loyalty heartens the wobblers of this country. It is not surprising then that we urge you to do what you can to meet his wishes. £25,000 a year to Abdulla as pocket money is cheaper than £150,000 a year in Palestine for an Indian battalion.

6 Meyer Weisgal (ed.), *Letters and Papers of Chaim Weizmann*, pp. 160–1.
7 Colonel Meinertzhagen was a gentile Zionist, at that time Military Adviser to the Middle East Department. Colonel R. Meinertzhagen, *Middle East Diary 1917–1956* (London, 1959), p. 100.
8 Note of an interview given by the HC to Sokoloff, Arlosoroff and Neumann, 2 February 1933, CO 831/21.
9 Meyer Weisgal (ed.), *Chaim Weizmann, Scientist and Builder of the Jewish Commonwealth* (New York, 1944), p. 57.
10 Colonel F. H. Kisch, *Palestine Diary* (London, 1938), pp. 63–4; Conversation with Eliahu Elath, Jerusalem, 8 January 1979. Elath and a group of fifteen to eighteen Jewish workers remained in Amman and Salt for eight months. Among their clients were Hashim Khayr, ex-mayor of Amman and the brother-in-law of Mithqal Ibn Fayiz, and Sa'id al-Mufti, a Circassian leader and later prime minister. Later Elath lived amongst the tribes in Transjordan and Syria. In Transjordan his host was Mithqal Ibn Fayiz.
11 See for example Abdul Qadir ('Abd al-Qadir al-Jundi) to Officer Commanding, Arab Legion, 29 May 1932, FO 816/103; GAD's Information (Taysir Duwaji), 29 July 1932, CZA S25/4143; and 'A Report on a visit to Amman on 4–5 August 1932 by AHC' [Aharon Haim Cohen], CZA S25/6313.
12 A. M. Novomeysky, *Given to Salt* (London, 1958), pp. 28–30.
13 Aharon Cohen, *Israel and the Arab World* (New York, 1970), p. 190.
14 Cox to Plumer, 27 July 1928, CO 733/165; Neil Caplan, *Futile Diplomacy Vol. II: Arab–Zionist Negotiations and the End of the Mandate* (London, 1986), pp. 216–17.
15 Note of an interview given by the high commissioner, supported by the chief secretary, to Dr Sokoloff, Dr Arlosoroff and Mr Neumann on Thursday, 2 February 1933, CO 831/21. The Jewish Agency also regarded good relations with the Transjordan shaykhs, and especially with Mithqal Ibn Fayiz, head of the Bani Sakhr, as insurance against tribal participation in future trouble in Palestine. See also memorandum on Transjordan [by Arlosoroff ?], n.d. [c. May 1932], CZA S25/3490. Four reasons are here outlined for Zionist interest in Transjordan:

> Firstly: the land problem west of the Jordan has become more and more urgent, especially in consequence of the publicity which it has received through the Shaw and Hope-Simpson Reports, and which it is almost sure to receive from the French Report.

Secondly: the development of land prices in certain districts of Western Palestine, particularly under the influence of speculative competition, is such that even a mere reference to a land reserve for Jewish colonization available elsewhere outside these districts would have a noticeable effect upon the relief of the tension.

Thirdly: the economic distress and stagnation in Transjordan has assumed such proportions that its inhabitants are forced, also much sooner than they expected, to look to Jewish energy and capital for overcoming it.

Fourthly: (partly arising out of the third point) the menace which an impoverished, discontented and rapacious Transjordan may mean at any moment to Jewish settlements in Palestine makes the establishment of friendly contacts, as a measure of precaution, a matter of immediate importance.

16 G. F. Walpole, 'Land Problems . . .,' p. 59. On the growing volume of contacts across the Jordan at this time, see Caplan, *Futile Diplomacy II*, pp. 11–14.

17 Arlosoroff to Brandeis, 8 May 1932, CZA S25/3489. On Jewish Agency strategy in Transjordan, see Kenneth W. Stein, *The Land Question in Palestine 1917–1939* (Chapel Hill, NC, 1984), pp. 175 and 192–9.

18 See 'Law for the distribution of taxes in Kerak Qadha and the Beni Hassan Tribe, 1932,' Cox to HC, 18 June 1932, FO 816/36; Memorandum by Mr Mitchell (Director of Lands), 3 February 1932, Cox to HC, 23 February 1933, and Cox to Officer Commanding, Arab Legion, 25 March 1933, FO 816/37; Annual report to the Council of the League of Nations on the administration of Palestine and Transjordan, 1933, pp. 246–8.

19 Monthly report on the administration of the deserts of Transjordan, January 1933, CO 831/23.

20 In 1922 Mithqal was allowed to buy (by special decree) 10,000 dunams at Jiza for £E 1,000 (10 piastres a dunam), payable over ten years. In 1924 Abdullah took one-half of that land and it was arranged that each, Mithqal and Abdullah, should pay £E 500 over five years for their respective halves. Abdullah paid his £E 500 in full and then sold his 5,000 dunams to Sa'd al-Din Shatilla for a threefold profit of £E 1,500. Abdullah was not paid in cash; rather the sum was subtracted from what Abdullah already owed Shatilla who was the contractor for Abdullah's palace. In 1926–7 the Transjordan government reviewed the whole deal and discovered that the area of land originally sold to Mithqal was not 10,000 dunams, but 33,968 dunams, and thus that the government had been deprived of £E 2,396 (at the original price). The matter was referred to the courts and it was decided that the transfer of one-half of the land to Abdullah in 1924 had been illegal, which then voided Shatilla's purchase and put Abdullah in his debt £E 1,500. Mithqal was given the choice of buying the whole area at the original price and paying the balance of what was owed the government, or dropping the deal altogether. He decided to buy the land. Chancellor to CO, 27 June 1930, CO 831/10.

21 Nahum Papper to Kisch, 16 March 1931, CZA S245/3490. Papper was the proposed buyer; Hanna Farah (as written, but the name was most probably Farha) of Ma'daba served as the go-between.

22 To members of the Zionist Executive from Chaim Arlosoroff, 6 December 1932, CZA S25/3492. No sale was finalized, although to maintain relations the Jewish Agency dribbled small amounts of cash to Mithqal from time to time. By January 1933 he had received £P 145. A conversation with Mithqal Ibn Fayiz on 12 January 1933 by M[oshe] S[hertok], 23 January 1933, CZA S25/3491.

23 Report by Nathan D. Kaplan, 29 September 1932, CZA A264/18. At least part of Kaplan's report is confirmed in the report on the political situation for the month of July 1932, FO 371/16017.

24 These included 'Atawi Pasha al-Majali, Shaykh 'Atallah al-Majali and Za'al al-Majali of the Karak District; Sultan al-'Adwan, shaykh of the 'Adwan tribe; Rashid al-Khuza'i of 'Ajlun; and Sa'id Pasha Abu Jabir of Salt. It is not always clear whether the Transjordan landowners mentioned in the Jewish Agency's correspondence were in fact interested in selling or leasing land, or whether the Jewish Agency had simply made contact in the hope that they were. To members of the Executive from Arlosoroff, 6 December 1932, CZA S25/3492.

25 Emanuel Neumann, *In the Arena* (New York, 1976), p. 134; Arlosoroff to Brandeis, 8 May 1932, CZA S25/3489.

26 On British reactions to Zionist initiatives at this time see: Comments on Jewish Agency memo, January 1931 and Minute by Shuckburgh, 2 February 1931, CO 733/197; Note of an interview given to Dr. Weizmann by the high commissioner, 20 March 1931, and Note of an interview with Baron Edmund de Rothschild, Paris, 5 May 1931, FO 371/15324; Wauchope to Cunliffe-Lister (secretary of state for the colonies), 5 March 1932, CO 733/215; Wauchope to Cunliffe-Lister, 23 April 1932, CO 831/18.

27 Précis of events, 24 August–14 September 1929, and Peake to Cox, 18 September 1929, CO 733/175 (box 3); Transjordan situation report, 1 July–30 September 1929, CO 831/5. See also 'Yadhkuru Sa'id al-Mufti,' part 3, *al-Dustur* (Amman daily), 25 February 1976.

28 The high commissioner wrote London that Abdullah, 'by his loyal and resolute conduct both during and after the disturbances in August 1929 . . . has well earned a favour at the hands of HMG.' Chancellor to Lord Passfield, secretary of state for the colonies, 1 March 1930, CO 831/9. Discussion and arrangements regarding the gift of state lands to Abdullah and exemption from taxation can be found in Cox to Chancellor, 17 December 1929; CO 831/5, Pirie-Gordon (*Times* special correspondent to Jerusalem) to Shuckburgh, 11 December 1929, CO 831/6; and Shuckburgh to Chancellor, 13 April 1931, CO 831/14. The gift was made by law and published in the *Official Gazettes*, dated 25 August 1931 and 1 August 1933. The land was also declared to be inalienable.

29 Cox to Chancellor, 10 June 1930, CO 831/9; Acting HC to CO, 31 May 1933 and HC to CO, 2 September 1933, CO 831/21. Britain was considering exempting Abdullah from the taxes due on his land and so assessed the land to see how much revenue the government would forfeit.

30 Wauchope to Cunliffe-Lister, 2 January 1932, CO 831/18; 'A Visit to the Amir Abdullah by M[oshe] S[hertok],' 28 March 1932, CZA S25/6313.

31 Text of the option and attached lease between Abdullah and Emanuel Neumann

and Joshua Farbstein, 3 January 1933, CO 831/21. On the negotiations leading to the option, see Neumann to members of the Executive of the Jewish Agency, 9 December 1932, CZA S25/3492, and Neumann, *In the Arena*, pp. 121–8.

32 'Abbas Hilmi Papers, reel 10, file 63/276 and 278. It is not certain whether the Compagnie was in fact interested in the land or whether it was used as a way to transfer money from Hilmi to Abdullah for political purposes of mutual interest. Shortly thereafter they were both implicated in a tribal uprising in the Hijaz.

33 Two letters from Abdullah to Neumann and Farbstein, both dated 17 March 1933, CZA S25/3514. See also Wauchope to Parkinson, 12 April 1933, CO 831/21.

34 In refutation to the false rumours about leasing Ghor al-Kibd to a foreign company or to foreign persons, the High Diwan of His Highness declares that those rumours have no foundation whatever and the Amir's Khassa [private office] after publishing a previous Notice offering to lease the land has now withdrawn the same and the lands of the Ghor al-Kibd are no longer offered for lease after to-day.
Official communiqué from His Highness's Diwan, 24 January 1933, CO 831/21.

35 Abdullah to [Jewish Agency], 15 February 1933, CZA S25/4143.

36 Rendel, *The Sword and the Olive*, pp. 76–7.

37 They were Rashid Pasha al-Khuza'i (Jabal 'Ajlun), Mitri Pasha Zurayqat (Karak Christian leader), Shams al-Din Sami (Amman, Circassian leader), Salim Pasha Abu al-'Ajam (Balqa'), Mithqal Ibn Fayiz (paramount shaykh of the Bani Sakhr), and his secretary Muhammad Abu Khalid. Minutes of the Banquet held between Dr Weizmann, members of the Executive Committee of the Jewish Agency and leaders of the Arab movement in Transjordan at the King David Hotel on 8 April 1933, by A. H. Cohen, CZA S25/3510. See also Neumann, *In the Arena*, p. 129. Other Transjordanian landowners who began or resumed financial dealings with the Jewish Agency at this time were Dalwan and Za'al al-Majali and Khalil Madinat, all from Karak. Rufayfan al-Majali to Moshe Shertok, two letters dated 22 May and 24 May 1933, and Za'al al-Majali to Shertok, 25 May 1933, CZA S25/3515.

38 He was the only Transjordan landowner actually to complete a mortgage with the Jewish Agency, as far as can be determined from available documents. Original mortgage certificate, dated 13 April 1933, CZA S25/3491. The document has been reproduced in Sulayman Bashir, *Judhur al-Wisaya al-Urduniyya* (Jerusalem, 1980), Appendix.

39 On the new Istiqlal see 'Awni 'Abd al-Hadi, *Awraq Khassa*, pp. 66–7, and Darwaza, *al-Qadiyya*, Vol. 1, pp. 86–9 and 309–10.

40 Report on the political situation for the month of July 1933, FO 371/16932; Monthly reports on the administration of the Transjordan deserts, July and August 1933, CO 831/23. When Faysal came to Amman, one reason why Palestinian leaders used to meet him was simply to tease Abdullah. Conversation with Farhan Shubaylat, Amman, 15 December 1978.

41 Report on the political situation for the month of August 1933 and monthly report on the administration of the Transjordan deserts, August 1933, CO 831/23.

42 Kirkbride to HC, 26 September 1933, CO 732/57; Report on the political situation for the month of September 1933, CO 831/23.

43 A contemporary assessment divided the population into three groups: (1) big merchants and big landowners (numbering about 100 and owning 10 million dunams) who rely on Abdullah and support the option; (2) peasants, small merchants and low ranks in the government bureaucracy who are against the option; (3) bedouin, who do not care one way or the other. Report by A[haron] H[aim] C[ohen], CZA S25/4143.

44 Philby Diary, 17 December 1921, Philby Papers.

45 Wauchope to Cunliffe-Lister, 17 May 1934, CO 831/27.

46 Report on the political situation for the month of June 1934, FO 371/17880.

47 Program of events for the visit of HH the Amir of Transjordan, 9 June–7 July 1934, CO 831/28. Abdullah was so fond of horses that he wrote a book about them: *Jawab al-Sa'il 'an al-Khayl al-Asa'il* (Amman, n.d.), reprinted in Madani (ed.), *al-Athar.*

48 Hodgkin, 'Antonius,' p. 24.

49 The high commissioner further explained to Moshe Shertok 'that if the Bill had so far been shelved . . . This was the result of his [the high commissioner's] own influence, exerted in the face of great difficulties . . .' Note of a conversation with the high commissioner on 19 December 1933 by M[oshe] S[hertok], CZA, S25/3493.

50 Report on the political situation for the month of March 1933, CO 831/21.

51 The conditions were that the land was to be managed by a corporation distinct from the Jewish Agency, that this corporation would pay for the necessary increase in the Transjordan Frontier Force (1 brigade = £30,000), that the high commissioner would designate the areas open to settlement, and that Arab cultivators were to be retained on the land on adequate holdings. Talk between Wauchope and Cunliffe-Lister, 22 April 1933, CO 732/62. See also extract from a record of a conversation between Sir Philip Cunliffe-Lister, Sir S. Wilson and Mr. C. Parkinson, 1 May 1933, CO 831/21.

52 Regarding Britain's changing attitude towards land sales and settlement and Jewish Agency payments to Abdullah and his go-between, Muhammad al-Unsi, see: Wauchope to Cunliffe-Lister, 22 July 1933, CO 831/21; Note of a conversation with the high commissioner on 19 December 1933 by Shertok, CZA S25/3493; Agreement between Abdullah and the Palestine Land Development Company, 3 January 1934, CZA S25/10122; 'A report on my visit to the Amir Abdullah on the occasion of renewing the option on Ghawr-al-Kibd for the year of 1934,' by A. H. Cohen, 12 January 1934, S25/3487; Notes of subjects mentioned by Dr Brodetsky or Mr Lourie at a luncheon given by Dr Brodetsky to Sir C. Parkinson and Mr Williams, 10 January 1935, CO 733/271.

53 Conversation with T[aysir] D[uwaji] by M[oshe] S[hertok], 28 February 1932, CZA S25/3051; Shertok to Brodetsky, 7 June 1934, CZA S25/3515; Addendum to agreement between Abdullah and the Palestine Land Development Company, 3 January 1935, CZA, S25/3864. An additional £P 1,800 was paid to Muhammad al-Unsi for his services as a go-between.

54 Muhammad 'Izzat Darwaza, *al-Qadiyya al-Filastiniyya* (Sidon and Beirut, n.d.), Vol. 1, p. 124, and Subhi Yasin, *al-Thawra al-'Arabiyya al-Kubra fi Filastin 1936–1939* (Beirut, 1961), p. 132.

55 Report on the political situation for the month of April 1936, CO 831/37; RAF intelligence summary, May 1936, FO 371/20030.

56 A. H. Cohen to M. Shertok and Y. Ben Zvi, 18 May 1936, CZA S25/3253. The Jews in Palestine were in fact very worried that the strike would cause Britain to reassess and change its policy, and the voluntary suspension of immigration was considered seriously by some factions as a means of bringing the strike to a rapid end. See Michael J. Cohen, 'Secret Diplomacy and the Rebellion in Palestine, 1936–1939,' *International Journal of Middle East Studies* (July 1977), pp. 385–7. See also Caplan, *Futile Diplomacy II*, pp. 40–2.

57 He said:

> His Majesty's Government can contemplate no change of policy whatsoever with regard to Palestine until they have received and considered the report of the Royal Commission. As regards, however, the suggestion that there should be a temporary suspension of immigration while the Commission is carrying out its inquiry, I am not at present in a position to make any statement as to the intention of His Majesty's Government beyond saying that there is no question of it being influenced by violence or attempts at intimidation. Answer to a question posed by David Adams in the House of Commons on 22 July 1936.

58 'Between the Political Department and the palace in Amman,' by A. H. Cohen, 28 July 1936, CZA S25/3243. The suggestion was made in a letter from Cohen to Muhammad al-Unsi, dated 28 June 1936.

59 'Between the Political Department and the palace in Amman,' by A. H. Cohen, 28 July 1936, CZA S25/3243.

60 Muhammad al-Unsi was Abdullah's chief go-between with the Jewish Agency. He came from Beirut and first appeared in Transjordan in 1921. Philby described him as an insignificant person with a genius for intrigue who occupied the nominal position of second secretary and the actual position of treasurer. To Philby he appeared to be the chief beneficiary of the then existing financial arrangements of the court. Report on the situation in Transjordan, 1 April–30 June 1922. Peake mentioned him in 1924 in the context of financial corruption as having had to borrow a suit of clothes to visit Abdullah in 1921. Peake to Cox, 11 May 1924, CO 733/68. In 1931 Abdullah was said to have schemed to get him re-elected to the Legislative Council. At that time Cox wrote that as Abdullah's secretary he had robbed him left and right but that Abdullah was 'unable to discount the flattery and protestations of loyalty of any scoundrel who approaches him.' Report on the political situation for April 1931, CO 831/12.

61 Minute of an interview with the high commissioner on Tuesday July 28, 1936, by M. Shertok, CZA S25/3243.

62 Periodical appreciation summary, Police Intelligence, no. 14/36, 18 August 1936, FO 371/20018.

63 Those present at the Arab Higher Committee meeting which framed the letter were Hajj Amin al-Husayni, Raghib al-Nashashibi, Husayn al-Khalidi, 'Abd al-

Latif Salah, Ya'qub Farraj, Alfred Rok, Ya'qub Ghusayn and Fu'ad Saba. It is not clear that they all agreed to send the letter, and Raghib al-Nashashibi in particular continued to support Abdullah's intervention. Minutes of the Arab Higher Committee session of 15 August 1936, ISA 65/2520.

64 Abdullah expressed his anger to Ahmad Hilmi. Registered telephone conversations, Abdullah to Ahmad Hilmi, 10.40 p.m., 21 August 1936, CZA S25/3769. On Nuri's intervention, see the report on the political situation for the month of August 1936, CO 831/37, and RAF intelligence summary for week ending 4 September 1936, FO 371/20030.

65 On Abdullah's last-minute efforts to regain control of mediation himself see: Abdullah to Hajj Amin, 6 September 1936, CZA S25/3243; Report on the political situation for the month of September 1936, CO 831/37. On Raghib al-Nashashibi's intervention on Abdullah's behalf, see David Ben Gurion, *My Talks with Arab Leaders* (Jerusalem, 1972), p. 117.

66 Robert John and Sami Hadawi, *The Palestine Diary* (Beirut, 1970), Vol. 1, p. 266.

67 Monthly report on the administration of the deserts, June 1936, and monthly reports on the political situation for the months April through September 1936, CO 831/37; RAF intelligence summary for May 1936 and for the week ending 9 July 1936, FO 371/20030; Yasin, *al-Thawra*, pp. 218–19.

68 RAF intelligence summary for May 1936, FO 371/20030; Report on the political situation for the months of April, June and September 1936, CO 831/37; HC to CO, 31 August 1936, CO 831/39.

69 'Between the Political Department and the palace in Amman,' by A. H. Cohen, 28 July 1936, CZA, S25/3243; Peake to Cox, 21 August 1936, Peake Papers.

70 Muhammad 'Izzat Darwaza, *Hawla al-Haraka*, Vol. 3, p. 145; Report of the Royal Commission, Cmd. 5479, July 1937, pp. 102–3.

71 RAF intelligence summary, week ending 29 November 1936, CO 371/20031; Note of a call on HH the Amir Abdullah, 24 November 1936 by M. Shertok, CZA S25/6313; Information of the Arab Bureau, A.S., 4 December 1936, CZA S25/3252.

72 Report of the Royal Commission, Cmd. 5479, July 1937, p. 103. See also Muhammad al-Unsi to A. H. Cohen, 8 February 1937, CZA S25/9783. Al-Unsi wrote that Abdullah was purposely ignored in the decision to co-operate with the Royal Commission.

73 Report on the political situation for the month of January 1937, CO 831/41; Report of what took place between Abdullah and the Royal Commission on 9 January 1937, CZA S25/9783; HC to CO, 12 January 1937, CO 733/320.

74 Extract from a note of an interview between Sir C. Parkinson and the Amir Abdullah, May 1937, CO 831/41.

75 A conversation between David Hacohen, David Huz and the Amir Abdullah in London on 15 May 1937, CZA S25/3486.

76 Statement made orally by Atatürk to Northfield in the presence of Amir Abdullah and suite on 31 May 1937, James Morgan (British Embassy) to FO, 5 June 1937, CO 831/44.

77 HC to CO, 12 June 1937, CO 831/44.

78 HH's speech to the people of Transjordan on his return from the coronation, 13 June 1937, CO 831/44.

79 Palestine, Report of the Royal Commission, Cmd. 5479, July 1937, pp. 376–81. Simha Flapan presents convincing evidence that the idea of partition became policy owing to the intense efforts of the Zionist leadership. Flapan, *Zionism and the Palestinians*, pp. 241–51.

80 The Palestine report, preliminary departmental comments, G. W. Rendel, 23 June 1937, FO 371/20807.

81 Shuckburgh to Rendel, 1 July 1937, Ormsby-Gore to Eden, 2 July 1937, Note by Rendel, 3 July 1937, FO 371/20808.

82 Note on the position in Transjordan regarding the Report of the Royal Commission, by A. S. Kirkbride, 17 July 1937, CO 733/351.

83 Note on the position in Transjordan regarding the Report of the Royal Commission, by A. S. Kirkbride, 17 July 1937, CO 733/351; Note of a conversation with Mr Merton, 5 August 1937, CZA S25/10122; Information of the Arab Bureau, 10 August 1937, CZA S25/10097.

84 Extract from a personal letter to Dr Weizmann from a friend in Jerusalem, 18 August 1937, CO 733/351; Yehoshua Porath, *The Palestinian Arab National Movement 1929–1939* (London, 1977), pp. 229 and 234.

85 Ormsby-Gore to Eden, 15 July 1937, FO 371/20809.

86 Sir A. Clark Kerr, Baghdad, to FO, 2 January 1937, FO 406/75; 'Between the political department and the Amir's palace, 16 February 1937,' by A. H. Cohen, CZA S25/3584.

87 Sir A. Clark Kerr to FO, 21 February 1937, Kerr to Rendel, 23 March 1937, Kerr to FO, 14 April 1937, Wauchope to CO, 11 May 1937, FO 371/20787.

88 Report on the political situation for the month of September 1937, CO 831/41; Glubb to Cox, 17 September 1937, FO 371/20818; Jackson Fleming, 'A Visit to Amir Abdullah,' *Asia* 38 (January 1938), p. 65.

89 The Agency reserved the right to talk to any Arab interested in reaching an amicable settlement, but promised not to do anything behind Abdullah's back. Later it gave him between £P 700 and £P 800 for propaganda purposes. Record of a conversation with M[uhammad] U[nsi] by B[ernard] J[oseph], 11 August 1937, and A. H. C[ohen] to M. S[hertok], 1 November 1937, CZA S25/3486; A. H. C[ohen] and M. S[hertok], 1 March 1938, S25/3491; List of amounts paid to Abdullah and al-Unsi since the beginning of 1936, prepared by Mr Zagagi, 8 May 1938, S25/3515.

90 Note of a conversation with Lady Reading and Hafiz Bey Taji, 15 May 1936, CO 733/289; Cox to Moody, 11 February 1937, CO 733/326; Record of a conversation with M[uhammad] U[nsi] by B[ernard] J[oseph], 11 August 1937, CZA S25/3486.

91 Tom Bowden, 'Arab Rebellion in Palestine 1936–1939,' *Middle Eastern Studies* 11 (1975), p. 148.

92 Darwaza, *al-Qadiyya*, Vol. 1, p. 137; Emil Ghuri, *Filastin 'Abra Sittin 'am* (Beirut, 1973), Vol. 2, p. 131. When a British member of the forestry department was kidnapped near Irbid in 1939, no amount of force served to wrest the names of his kidnappers from the villagers even though it was known exactly which villages had harbored them. Report on the political situation for the month of February 1939, CO 831/51.

93 Report on the political situation for the month of November 1938, CO 831/46; Yasin, *al-Thawra*, p. 219.
94 On developments in Transjordan by A. H. C[ohen], 5 January 1938, CZA S25/3501; Periodical appreciation summary, Police Intelligence, no. 73/38, 18 October 1938, CO 733/359; Report on the political situation for the month of November 1938, CO 831/46.
95 Palestine Partition Commission Report, Cmd. 5854, October 1938, p. 243; Palestine Statement of Policy, Cmd. 5893, 9 November 1938.
96 Memorandum submitted by Amir Abdullah to the Palestine Partition Commission and to the secretary of state for the colonies, 11 June 1938, FO 371/21885. See also Caplan, *Futile Diplomacy II*, pp. 92–5 and 238–9.
97 *Palestine and Transjordan*, 4 June 1938, p. 3; Report on the political situation for the month of June 1938, CO 831/46.
98 HC to CO, 17 November 1938, CO 831/50.
99 Abdullah to HC, 11 December 1938, CO 831/50; HC to CO, 13 December 1938, CO 831/46.
100 Note of a CO–FO meeting, 23 September 1938, FO 371/21864.
101 Palestine, Statement of Policy, Cmd. 6019, 17 May 1939. The gulf between Arab and Jewish positions was revealed in the informal meetings held with both delegations attending. See Caplan, *Futile Diplomacy II*, pp. 240–59.
102 On the discussions and their results see: Conversations between Abu'l-Huda and MacDonald, 16, 19 and 25 January 1939, MacDonald to Abu'l-Huda, 6 April 1939, and CO to HC, 12 May 1939, FO 371/23247.
103 Kirkbride to HC, 3 June 1939, CO 733/406; Report on the political situation for the month of June 1939, CO 831/51.

8 War and politics

1 Report on the political situation in Transjordan for the month of September 1939, CO 831/51; J. B. Glubb, 'Transjordan and the War,' *Journal of the Royal Central Asian Society* 33:1 (January 1945), pp. 25–6.
2 Annual report to the Council of the League of Nations on the administration of Palestine and Transjordan, 1938, p. 370; Konikoff, *Trans-Jordan*, p. 127.
3 The pupils of all schools – elementary and secondary, government and private, male and female – numbered 13,854 in 1938–9. There was only one government secondary school for boys which offered the complete four-year curriculum. Three others offered a two-year program. There were 243 boys enrolled in these four schools, which were located in Salt, Amman, Irbid and Karak. There were no government secondary schools for girls. Two private schools started giving secondary courses in 1937 – the Anglican boy's school and the girl's school of the Church Missionary Society. A very limited number of Transjordan students went to Jerusalem or Beirut for secondary and higher education. Annual report to the Council of the League of Nations on the administration of Palestine and Transjordan, 1938, pp. 361–8. Although the number of students was small,

secondary school pupils were the most frequently mentioned demonstrators against Britain and Abdullah in the British political reports.

4 In 1939, industrial activities in the broadest sense of the term included: two cigarette factories in Amman employing a total of 180 workers, the 'All-Zement Works' at Amman which made cement and terrazzo tiles, two small ice factories, three distilleries (two at Salt and one at Fuhays) employing a total of twenty-two workers, one press at Amman which acted as the government printing press and took on private orders, weaving and similar crafts operated by hand at home or in small workshops, flour milling and olive pressing (mills were run by water or by hand and both modern and old-fashioned olive presses were used). Konikoff, *Trans-Jordan*, pp. 71–3.

5 Kirkbride to HC, 7 November 1939, CO 831/54.

6 Report on the political situation in Transjordan for the month of March 1940, CO 831/55; and report on the political situation in Transjordan for the month of November 1942, CO 831/58.

7 HC to CO, 7 December 1940, and Treasury to CO, 25 January 1941, CO 831/55. In a draft report entitled 'Measures to Influence Minor Powers and Arab States' it was recommended that £10,000 be put at the disposal of the British resident when it became clear that war was about to begin. This sum could be used to assist Abdullah and to subsidize tribal shaykhs and the one newspaper published in Transjordan. Committee of Imperial Defence, standing official sub-committee for questions concerning the Middle East, 24 January 1939, CO 732/84.

8 See: Extracts from secret reports on the political situation in Transjordan for the months of January and March 1935, CO 831/31; RAF intelligence summary, November 1935, FO 371/18960; Report on the political situation for the month of February 1936, CO 831/37.

9 Peake to Kirkbride, 5 July 1937, Peake Papers.

10 Abdullah to Kirkbride, 23 March 1939, CO 831/54.

11 HC to Shuckburgh, 28 March 1939, CO 831/54.

12 Kirkbride to HC, 20 October 1939, and HC to CO, 30 October 1939, CO 831/54. The two chief ministers were Ibrahim Hashim and Tawfiq Abu'l-Huda. The latter served Talal when he succeeded Abdullah in 1951.

13 Minute by J. S. Bennett, 7 December 1939, CO 831/54.

14 Kirkbride to HC, 20 October 1939, and minute by Shuckburgh, 19 December 1939, CO 831/54.

15 HC to CO, 12 April 1940, CO 831/57.

16 Answers to Questions of A. Sasson by M. Shibli, 16 December 1940, CZA S25/3504. They were Muhammad al-Unsi and Muhammad al-Dubati.

17 Cohen, *be-Hatser ha-Melekh Abdullah*, pp. 75–81; Conversation with Mrs Every, Jerusalem, 5 January 1979; 'Emir Abdullah the Smart Little Ruler of Transjordan,' p. 69.

18 HC to Shuckburgh, 5 November 1940, and HC to CO, 13 December 1940 and 19 January 1941, CO 831/57.

19 Reports on the political situation in Transjordan for the months of March and April 1941, CO 831/58. These included Jamil Midfa'i, 'Ali Jawdat, Da'ud al-

Haydari, Sharif Husayn ibn Nasir (Abdullah's first cousin and his wife's brother) and Sharif Fawaz (a distant relation).

20 For an account of the Arab Legion in Iraq and Syria during the war see John Bagot Glubb, *The Story of the Arab Legion* (London, 1946), pp. 279–94 and 309–45.

21 Kirkbride, *A Crackle of Thorns*, p. 134.

22 Report on the political situation in Transjordan for the month of May 1941, CO 831/58.

23 Kirkbride to HC, 9 September 1941, CO 831/58.

24 HC to CO, 21 May 1941, CO 831/59.

25 The Legion, all ranks, numbered 1,624 in 1938. Annual report to the Council of the League of Nations on the administration of Palestine and Transjordan, 1938, p. 348. By 1946 Kirkbride reported the Legion at 6,624. 'The Military Units of the Arab Legion,' by A. S. Kirkbride, 4 June 1946, FO 371/52605.

26 Note by the prime minister and minister of defence, 19 May 1941, FO 371/27043.

27 Fayez Sayegh, *Arab Unity* (New York, 1958), pp. 81–94.

28 HC to CO, 11 October 1939, FO 371/23281.

29 CO to FO, 3 October 1939, and CO to HC, 7 October 1939, FO 371/23281.

30 Kirkbride to HC, 8 June 1941, CO 831/59.

31 Abdullah to HC, 8 June 1941, CO 831/59.

32 Oliver Lyttelton, Viscount Chandos, *The Memoirs of Lord Chandos* (London, 1962), p. 256. For a summary of Abdullah's attempts to create Greater Syria to 1943, see Porath, *In Search of Arab Unity*, pp. 22–39.

33 *Elections Syriennes*, Mars–Décembre 1943, MAE, Guerre 1939–1945, Alger (CFLN), Vol. 1,004; Gardener to Spears, 13 March 1943, Spears to Catroux, 16 March 1943, Furlonge to Spears, 18 March 1943, and Altounyan to Lascelles, 16 June 1943, FO 226/240.

34 Beirut, 3 January 1944, and Chatigneau (Beirut) to Massigli (Paris), 25 January 1944, MAE, Guerre 1939–1945, Alger (CFLN), Vol. 1,030, pp. 242–3.

35 For example, when the National Bloc government was formed in August 1943 under Shukri al-Quwatli, some Druze threatened to secede from Syria and join a union with Transjordan because no Druze was appointed to the cabinet. Report on the political situation in Transjordan for the month of August 1943, FO 371/35045. Another instance of Druze opportunism occurred when Ha'il Bey al-Atrash threatened to declare the unification of Jebel Druze with Transjordan because his candidate for *qadi* of the Druze community was about to be passed over in favor of another. His threat led to the swift appointment of his man. Ha'il Bey al-Atrash to Glubb Pasha, 20 March 1944, FO 684/15. Amir Fa'ur al-Fa'ur of the Fadl tribe, who was antagonistic to the National Bloc, called on Abdullah shortly after Shukri al-Quwatli was elected president. Report on the political situation in Transjordan for the month of October 1943, CO 831/60. Diverse urban politicians also on occasion got in touch with Abdullah, for various reasons. See, for example, reports on the political situation for the months of December 1943, January 1944, June 1944 and July 1945, CO 831/60.

36 Kirkbride to HC, 19 September 1941, CO 831/59.

37 HC Beirut to Paris, 10 June 1939, MAE, Puaux Papers, Carton 33, Dossier

'Relations avec la Palestine'; A. L. Kirkbride (Acting British Resident for his brother) to HC, 10 June 1939, FO 371/23280; Conversation with Dr Shahbandar, 22 January 1940, FO 371/24548. The National Bloc solicited Saudi support against the Shahbandar–Abdullah alliance.

38 Diary of the political officer, Damascus, week ending 13 March 1943, FO 686/14. In 1939 the Damascus paper *La Chronique* listed nine candidates for the throne: Sa'id al-Jaza'iri, Damad Ahmad Nami Bey (Circassian son-in-law of Sultan Abdülhamid), Amir 'Abd al-Ilah, King Ibn Saud, Amir Abdullah, Prince Muhammad 'Ali (cousin of King Faruq), Amir Zayd, Faysal II, and ex-King Zog of Albania. *La Chronique*, 20 May 1919.

39 British Legation, Damascus, to Jerusalem, 16 November 1945, FO 371/45415.

40 Story told by Sir Harold MacMichael to Elizabeth Monroe, who passed it on to me.

41 Kirkbride to HC, 8 May 1940 and HC to CO, 17 May 1940, CO 831/56; HC to CO, 14 July 1944, Spears (Beirut) to HC, 17 July 1944, Abdullah to HC, 8 August 1944, and HC to CO, 15 August 1944, FO 371/40120; Beynet (Beirut) to Massigli (Paris), 8 August 1944, MAE, Guerre 1939–1945, Alger (CFLN), Vol. 1,324, pp. 188–9.

42 Kirkbride to HC, 7 July 1942, CO 831/59; enclosure no. II in HC to CO, 28 July 1942, FO 816/42. Abdullah had first been approached by the party, without apparent result, in 1936. Report on the political situation in Transjordan for the month of March 1936, CO 831/37.

43 Abdullah turned a deaf ear to requests that he intercede on their behalf. See for example: Report on the political situation in Transjordan for the month of December 1939, CO 831/51; HC to CO, 16 November 1943, FO 371/35047; Report on the political situation in Transjordan for the month of December 1944, CO 831/60.

44 Report on the political situation in Transjordan for the month of November 1943, CO 831/60.

45 Report on the political situation in Transjordan for the months of December 1944 and July 1945, CO 831/60.

46 A conversation with M[uhammad] U[nsi] at the house of D. Joseph on 3 April 1940, and E. Sasson to M. Shertok, 30 April 1940, CZA S25/3051; a conversation with M[uhammad] U[nsi], n.d., CZA S25/3054.

47 HC to Lord Cranborne, 23 November 1942, CO 831/59.

48 HC to CO, 20 April 1945, FO 141/1011.

49 MacMichael to Parkinson, 6 April 1939, FO 371/23276; British Ambassador, Baghdad, to FO, 20 October 1939, FO 371/23281; Kirkbride to HC, 9 April 1940, FO 371/24569; HC to CO, 14 August 1940, FO 371/24548.

50 Nuri al-Sa'id, *Arab Independence and Unity* (Baghdad, 1943).

51 HC to CO, 22 March 1943, FO 816/42.

52 Political memorandum on the solution of the Syrian problem in particular and the Arab problem in general, forwarded to Kirkbride by Abdullah, April 1943, FO 816/42.

53 Abdullah's manifesto, 8 April 1943, FO 371/34960. See also *al-Kitab al-Urduni al-Abyad* (Amman, 1946), pp. 75–7.

54 Diary of the political officer, Damascus, week ending 24 April 1943, FO 684/14; acting HC to CO, 24 April 1943, CO 732/87.

55 Jidda to FO, 2 March 1943, FO 371/34956.

56 Ahmed M. Gomaa, *The Foundation of the League of Arab States* (London, 1977), pp. 153–4.

57 HC to CO, 24 July 1943, FO 371/34960.

58 HC to CO, 24 July 1943, FO 371/34960.

59 HC to CO, 30 November 1940, CO 831/57.

60 Special instructions on the matter of Arab unity, August 1943, CO 732/87; Report on the political situation in Transjordan for the month of August 1943, FO 371/35045.

61 HC to CO, 16 September 1943, and Cairo to FO, 6 October 1943, CO 732/87.

62 Report on the political situation in Transjordan for the month of September 1943, CO 831/60.

63 Report on the political situation in Transjordan for the month of October 1943, CO 831/60.

64 'The Nature and Constitution of the Succession States,' HC to Col. Stanley (Colonial Secretary), 4 February 1944, CO 733/461. The development of Britain's Greater Syria policy which stretched over two years can be traced in the following documents: Note of a meeting held in the secretary of state's room on Friday 24 April 1942, CO 732/87; Committee on Palestine, memo by the secretary of state for the colonies, 1 November 1943, FO 371/35040.

65 Michael J. Cohen, *Palestine: Retreat from the Mandate* (New York, 1978), pp. 175–9.

66 E. Sasson to B. Joseph, 17 December 1943, CZA S25/3504.

67 HC to CO 3 November 1943, CO 732/87.

68 E. Sasson to B. Joseph, 30 January 1944, CZA S25/5633.

69 HC to CO, 31 January 1944, CO 732/88.

70 HC to CO, 10 April 1944, and HC to CO, 6 May 1944, CO 732/88.

71 Statement to the Transjordan government, June 1944, CO 732/8.

72 Report on the political situation in Transjordan for the month of August 1944, CO 831/60.

73 Gomaa, *Foundation*, p. 226.

74 Sayegh, *Arab Unity*, p. 121.

75 King Abdullah of Jordan, *My Memoirs Completed* (London, 1978), p. 7.

76 Kirkbride to HC, 31 January 1945, FO 816/44.

77 HC to CO, 25 February 1945, FO 371/45415; Report on the political situation in Transjordan for the month of February 1945, CO 831/60.

78 Record of a conversation between Amir Abdullah and Sir Edward Grigg (by Kirkbride), on 26 February 1945, CO 733/462; Lord Killearn (Cairo) to FO, 28 February 1945, CO 732/88; Kirkbride to Abdullah, 3 March 1945, FO 816/44; HC to CO, 18 March 1945, FO 371/45415.

79 Minute by J. S. Bennett, 13 June 1941, CO 831/59.

80 'Great Britain and Arab Nationalism' by A. H. Hourani, August 1943, CO 732/87.

81 HC to CO, 12 July 1941, CO 831/59.

82 CO to HC, 26 August 1941, CO 831/59.
83 See for example: HC to CO, 26 February and 15 November 1943, CO 732/87; Record of a conversation with Amir Abdullah by R. H. Casey (minister of state in the Middle East) on 30 November 1942, CO 831/59.
84 CO to Acting HC, 9 November 1945, FO 371/45415; HC to CO, 1 December 1945, CO 733/456.
85 'A note on the possible political results of disbanding the Arab Legion Infantry Companies,' J. B. Glubb, 1946, FO 371/52930.
86 Kirkbride to FO, 24 September 1946, FO 371/52936.
87 Kirkbride to FO, 16 February 1948, FO 371/68819.
88 Conversation with Mrs Every (Jerusalem, 5 January 1979), who at the time ran a clinic at Fuhays, near Amman. See also report on the political situation in Transjordan for the month of March 1946, FO 371/52930.
89 On the different reactions to Transjordan's independence see: Cairo to FO, 5 April 1946, FO 371/52426; Lord Killearn to FO, 17 January 1946, FO 141/1098; Beirut to FO, 2 April 1946, CO 537/1845; Jewish Agency to FO, 22 January 1946, FO 371/52572; Daily News Bulletin issued by the Jewish Telegraphic Agency, 28 January 1946; Dominion Office to Canada etc., 6 March 1946, FO 371/57136; 'Current US Policy Towards Transjordan,' 26 February 1946, USNA 890i.01/2-2646; Uriel Dann, *Studies*, pp. 93–116.
90 HC to CO, 18 June 1946, FO 371/52935.
91 Report on the political situation in Transjordan for the month of May 1946, FO 371/52935; Mattison (Damascus) to secretary of state, 25 May 1946, USNA 890i.001/5-2546; Mattison to secretary of state, 1 July 1946, USNA 890i.001/7-146.
92 Kirkbride to Baxter, 25 March 1947, FO 371/62220.
93 Kirkbride to Burrows, 21 October 1948, FO 371/68864.
94 Pirie-Gordon to Burrows, 12 July 1949, FO 371/75316.

9 Abdullah, Britain and the Arab World, 1945–8

1 Memorandum from Loy Henderson to the secretary of state, 3 June 1936, USNA, 890i.01/5-2846.
2 FO to Amman, 10 September 1946, FO 816/110.
3 Eric Beckett (Legal Adviser to the FO) to Attorney-General, 20 February 1950, FO 371/82714.
4 Kirkbride to Furlonge, 31 March 1950, FO 371/82751.
5 US Embassy (Cairo) to Washington, 6 February 1947, USNA 890i.001/2-647.
6 Minute by Geoffrey Furlonge on a letter from Clayton (BMEO) to Baxter dated 14 December 1946, FO 371/52355.
7 King Abdullah, *Mudhakkirati* (Amman, 1945). For Arab reactions to his memoirs see: Grafftey-Smith (Jidda) to Jerusalem, 14 February 1946, FO 371/52597; Beirut to FO, 14 February 1946, FO 371/52879.
8 Weekly political summary for Syria and Lebanon, 13 February 1947, FO 371/62119; annual political review of Syria, 1947, FO 371/68810.
9 Baghdad to FO, 14 June 1947, FO 371/61526.

10 See for example, Kirkbride to FO, 14 August 1946, and Furlonge to Jidda, 9 October 1946, FO 371/52906; Kirkbride to FO, 7 October 1947, FO 371/62193.
11 Clayton to FO, 4 September 1947, FO 371/61496.
12 Minute by Kirkbride, 9 September 1947, FO 371/61497.
13 US Embassy (London) to Washington, 30 June 1947, USNA 741.90/6-3047.
14 Grafftey-Smith to FO, 7 September 1946, FO 371/52355.
15 Kirkbride originally reported that the idea of a cruise was the commander-in-chief's brainchild which he then encouraged, feeling that 'anything which would keep the King amused and away from Middle Eastern politics would be beneficial . . .' The commander-in-chief later said that the idea had originated with Kirkbride and that he had agreed because 'it seemed important to be nice to the King who has recently got his independence and is being very friendly and cooperative.' Kirkbride to FO, 24 February 1947, and commander-in-chief to Admiralty, 9 March 1947, FO 371/62189.
16 See Cairo to FO, 3 February 1947, Jidda to FO, 5 March 1947, Baghdad to FO, 7 March 1947, and Damascus to FO, 8 March 1947, FO 371/62189.
17 Commander-in-chief to Admiralty, 9 March 1947, and Cairo to FO, 11 March 1947, FO 371/62189.
18 Kirkbride to FO, 15 March 1947, FO 371/62189.
19 Abdullah to Kirkbride, 30 March 1947, forwarded by Kirkbride to the commander-in-chief on 1 April 1947, FO 371/62189.
20 Monroe, *Britain's Moment*, p. 155.
21 For example see Patrick Seale, *The Struggle for Syria, 1945–1958* (London, 1965).
22 Note of views expressed to the prime minister by King Abdullah, by Kirkbride, 13 March 1946, FO 371/52574.
23 Minute by Kirkbride, 8 September 1947, FO 371/62226.
24 Abdullah to Bevin, 30 August 1947, FO 371/62226.
25 Kirkbride to FO, 12 August 1946, FO 371/52599; Monthly situation report on Transjordan, December 1946, FO 371/62206.
26 Kirkbride to FO, 10 May 1947, FO 371/62229. Nayyif al-Atrash was pro-Hashemite and had received money previously from Amman for political purposes. See below n. 27.
27 Shortly before the Second World War, Murshid had founded a politico-religious cult near Latakia. In 1946 the movement revived and there was armed fighting with Syrian forces. Murshid was captured and hanged, as a lesson to other potential rebels. See Seale, *Struggle*, p. 144 n.; Beirut to Amman, 17 September 1946, FO 371/52867. Part of the Rwala tribe moved to the H4 area where the Transjordan government allocated lands for them to settle on and gave them food and guns. Information from Transjordan by P.S., 20 June 1946, CZA S25/9036. The Druze shaykh, Saud al-Fawaz, and the Amir Nayyif al-Atrash received £500 each. Amir Nayyif received an additional £2,000 to distribute among his clansmen. Information from Transjordan, 1–6 November 1946, CZA S25/9036; Kirkbride to FO, 27 September 1946, FO 371/52867.
28 Kirkbride to FO, 14 August 1946, FO 371/52906.
29 Kirkbride to FO, 27 September 1946 and 28 September 1946 (two letters), FO 371/52867; Annual report for Transjordan, 1946, FO 371/62202.

30 Speech from the throne, 11 November 1946, FO 371/52936.
31 Kirkbride to FO, 2 April 1947, FO 371/61492.
32 Information from Transjordan by P.S., 14 March 1947, CZA S25/9037.
33 *Al-Kitab al-Urduni al-Abyad.*
34 See for example, Talbot (British legation in Beirut) to FO, 22 August 1946, FO 371/52355.
35 Seale, *Struggle*, p. 31. This rival nationalist coalition adopted the name 'People's party' in 1948.
36 Monthly situation report for Transjordan, July 1947, FO 371/62206.
37 Seale, *Struggle*, p. 31.
38 Royal statement, 4 August 1947, FO 371/61494. This statement was actually delivered on August 12th.
39 Damascus to FO, 17 August 1947, and Jidda to FO, 25 August 1947, FO 371/61494; Damascus to FO, 25 August 1947, FO 371/61495; Monthly situation report for Transjordan, August 1947, FO 371/62206; Clayton, BMEO, to FO, 4 September 1947, FO 371/61496. On Syrian and Saudi reactions see also Walid Khalidi's essay, 'The Arab Perspective,' in William Roger Louis and Robert Stookey (eds.), *The End of the Palestine Mandate* (Austin, 1986), pp. 115–16.
40 Baghdad to Amman, 27 August 1947, FO 371/61495.
41 Beirut to FO, 30 August 1947, FO 371/61495.
42 Amman to FO, 18 September 1947, FO 371/61497.
43 See for example, Beirut to FO, 30 August 1947, FO 371/61495, and FO to Beirut, 15 September 1947, FO 371/61529.
44 Kirkbride to FO, 14 October 1947, FO 371/61882.
45 On the evolution of Britain's policy in the post-war period see William Roger Louis's essay, 'British Imperialism and the End of the Palestine Mandate,' in Louis and Stookey (eds.) *The End of the Palestine Mandate*, pp. 1–31, and his recent book, *The British Empire in the Middle East 1945–1951: Arab Nationalism, the United States and Postwar Imperialism* (London, 1984).
46 Kirkbride to HC, November 1944, FO 371/39991.
47 See for example HC to CO, 16 January 1944, CO 733/461.
48 Note of views expressed to prime minister, 13 March 1946, FO 371/52574; FO to CO, 22 March 1946, CO 537/1845.
49 Kirkbride to FO, 2 July 1946, FO 371/52551.
50 Jerusalem to Zionist Office, London, 13 August 1946; CZA S25/9036; Kirkbride to FO, 16 August 1946, FO 371/52553; Caplan, *Futile Diplomacy II*, pp. 146–8, and 268–71.
51 Abdullah to Bevin, 24 August 1946, and Abdullah to Creech-Jones, 4 September 1946, FO 371/52643. Abdullah and al-Rifaʿi told Kirkbride that partition followed by an exchange of populations was the only practical solution. Both appealed to Kirkbride to avoid any hint of union between Transjordan and Arab Palestine at the London discussions, since that would automatically turn Saudi Arabia and Syria against partition, if only to prevent Hashemite expansion. FO 371/52555, Kirkbride to FO, 27 August 1946.
52 Washington to FO, 26 November 1946, CAB 127/281.
53 George Wadsworth to Washington, 23 June 1947, CZA S25/3885.

54 Amman to FO, 28 July 1947, FO 371/61876.
55 Amman to FO, 30 July 1947, FO 371/61876.
56 For a full account of inter-departmental relations, see Michael J. Cohen, *Palestine and the Great Powers* (Princeton, 1982), pp. 203–28.
57 *Ibid.*, pp. 299–300.
58 Jerusalem to Washington, 1 December 1947, USNA 890i.00/12-147.
59 HC to CO, 17 November 1947, FO 371/62194; Beeley to Bromley, 20 January 1948, FO 371/68403.
60 Clayton to FO, 27 September 1947, FO 371/61497.
61 Note by Burrows on letter from Kirkbride to FO dated 22 October 1947, FO 371/61885.
62 FO to Treasury, 22 January 1948, DEFE 7/388.
63 Amman to FO, 21 January 1948, FO 371/68817.
64 FO to Amman, 12 November 1947, FO 371/62194; Minute by Harold Beeley, 6 January 1948, FO 371/68364.
65 Kirkbride to FO, 17 November 1947, FO 371/62194.
66 Note for the secretary of state's conversation with the prime minister of Transjordan, B. A. B. Burrows, 24 January 1948, FO 371/68817.
67 The conventional figure for the Arab Legion as of May 1948 is 6,000, 4,500 of which were sent to Palestine. Contemporary documents show larger figures. See for example: 'The military units of the Arab Legion,' by Kirkbride, 4 June 1946, FO 371/52605; 'Arab Legion Quarterly Historical Report,' no. 2, 31 December 1946, WO 261/535; 'The Arab Legion,' memorandum by Garran, 15 October 1947, FO 371/62193; Note on the Arab Legion financial situation by Glubb, 1950, FO 371/82751.
68 Thirty of these officers were on attachment from the British army and served the Legion as advisers and teachers. It was decided that they would maintain their connection with the Legion but, if necessary, they could be extracted from combat and restricted to training schools or garrison duty in Transjordan. Six more were mercenaries with no current connection to British forces; they were employed on contract directly by the Transjordan government and presented no problems of accountability to Britain. The status of five more officers, which included Glubb, Brigadier R. J. C. Broadhurst and Brigadier N. O. Lash, was more problematic. They had been seconded from the Palestine Police Force and had retained their rank in the hierarchy of the Palestine Service; moreover, they were integral to the Legion command structure. With the demise of the Palestine Service, they could either retire and take their pensions or seek transfer within the Colonial Service. They decided on a third course, to stay in Transjordan, which meant the automatic cutting of their ties to the Colonial Service. In effect they became mercenaries, on contract to Transjordan. Glubb and those who served under him on contract were warned during the war that they might be liable to prosecution under the terms of the Foreign Enlistment Act for being in the service of a foreign state engaged in war without the cognizance of the British government. The Arab Legion, 'Officers serving with the Legion who are on Palestine pensionable establishment,' April 1948, FO 371/68853; FO to Amman, 12 August 1948, FO 371/68830. See also Kirkbride, *From the Wings*, pp. 35–6, and Glubb, *Soldier*, p. 134.

69 Record of a conversation with Brigadier Glubb, 30 January 1948, FO 371/68369.
70 Glubb to Kirkbride, 7 August 1951, FO 371/91821. To Glubb's mind, what was good for Jordan was good for Great Britain and *vice versa*.
71 Monthly situation report, November 1946, FO 371/52936; Annual report 1946, FO 371/62202; Kirkbride to FO, 4 March 1947, and 30 October 1947, FO 371/62219; Kirkbride to FO, 30 April 1947, FO 371/62221.
72 Doreen Warriner, *Land and Poverty in the Middle East* (London, 1948), p. 80; Marcus Mackenzie, 'Transjordan,' *Journal of the Royal Central Asian Society* 33 (July–October 1946), p. 263; James Baster, 'The Economic Problems of Jordan', *International Affairs* 31 (January 1955), p. 27.
73 Information from Transjordan, 29 May 1946, CZA S25/9036; 'The History of the Arab nationalist movement and the origins of the Arab League,' by Gerald DeGaury, Research Department, 28 March 1947, FO 371/45241; George E. Kirk, 'Cross-currents within the Arab League: The Greater Syria Plan,' *World Today* (January 1948), p. 24.
74 Kirkbride to FO, 20 May 1947, FO 371/62231.
75 Kirkbride to FO, 26 April 1948, FO 371/68386. What Kirkbride considered political health was due in part to political repression through the use of Emergency Regulations which had not been rescinded after the war. For example, when demonstrations erupted in March 1948 against the new terms of the military annex to the Anglo-Transjordan treaty, which were nearly the same as the old, opposition figures, including Sulayman al-Nabulsi, were arrested and jailed without trial. 'Abd Allah al-Tall, *Karitha Filastin* (Cairo, 1959), p. 48.
76 Letter from Abraham Daskal, general manager of the electrical works, who helped to arrange the meeting, to me, 20 September 1983. Daskal was also known as Abu Yusuf. He was a member of the Haganah and was one of the go-betweens for the Jewish Agency and Amman. Golda Meir, *My Life* (New York, 1975), p. 207; Caplan, *Futile Diplomacy II*, pp. 159–61 and 277–9.
77 The Lebanese minister of foreign affairs predicted that if the Arabs lost Palestine, the governments of Egypt, Syria and Iraq would tumble like a house of cards. Beirut to FO, 2 May 1948, FO 371/68371.
78 So Samir al-Rifaʻi reported about his attendance at the meetings of the Political Committee of the Arab League. Beirut to FO, 11 October 1947, FO 371/61530; British Middle East Office to FO, 10 December 1947, FO 371/62226.
79 Kirkbride, *Crackle of Thorns*, p. 33. Kirkbride described him as one of the least patient people he had ever met. Kirkbride to FO, 8 December 1947, FO 371/62226.
80 US Embassy (London) to Washington, 6 January 1948, USNA 867N.01/1-647.
81 Glubb, *Soldier*, pp. 65–6. Kirkbride, *From the Wings*, pp. 11–12. The conversation is mentioned in FO memorandum, 9 February 1948, FO 371/68366, but Bevin's remarks were not recorded.

10 1948

1 Netanel Lorch, *The Edge of the Sword: Israel's War of Independence 1947–1949* (New York, 1961), pp. 87–9.

2 *Al-Ahram*, 17 April 1948.
3 Amman to FO, 16 and 19 April 1948 (two dispatches), FO 816/117.
4 Glubb, *Soldier*, p. 89.
5 Yusuf Haykal, *Jalsat fi Raghadan* (unpublished manuscript), p. 17, Institute for Palestine Studies.
6 Kirkbride to FO, 1 May 1948, FO 816/118.
7 Kirkbride to FO, 29 April 1948, FO 371/68372.
8 Amman to FO, 25 April 1948, FO 816/118.
9 Louis, *British Empire*, p. 374; Joseph Nevo, 'Abdallah and the Arabs of Palestine,' *The Wiener Library Bulletin* 31 (1978), p. 57; Meir, *My Life*, pp. 208–12; al-Tall, *Karitha Filastin*, pp. 66–9; conversation with Abraham Daskal, Jerusalem, 12 February 1979. Daskal and his wife dressed Golda Meir in Arab clothes at Naharim for the journey to Amman. Caplan, *Futile Diplomacy II*, pp. 163–4.
10 FO to Amman, 9 and 10 May 1948 (two dispatches), FO 816/119; Bevin to Minister of Defence, 13 May 1948, FO 371/68853.
11 *The Foreign Relations of the United States* [*FRUS*], 1948, Vol. 5, part 2, pp. 973 and 1043–4.
12 Glubb, *Soldier*, p. 85.
13 Amman to FO, 25 April and 1 May 1948 (two dispatches), FO 816/118.
14 Quarterly Historical Report, GHQ MELF, 21 March–20 June 1948, WO 261/549.
15 Kirkbride, to FO, 15 May 1948, FO 816/120.
16 *FRUS*, 1948, Vol. 5, part 2, pp. 1049–50.
17 *The Observer*, London, 2 May 1948.
18 Glubb, *Soldier*, pp. 83–4; Edgar O'Ballance, *The Arab Israeli–War 1948* (London, 1956), pp. 95–7.
19 Glubb, *Soldier*, pp. 108–13.
20 Kirkbride to FO, 19 May 1948, FO 816/120.
21 Kirkbride to FO, 1 May 1948, FO 816/118.
22 *FRUS*, 1948, Vol. 5, part 2, p. 1049. Glubb wrote in August that there had been a Transjordanian plan, of which Britain was aware, that after the proclamation of the Jewish state, the Legion would occupy the Arab parts of Palestine without conflict with Jewish forces. According to him this plan had been partially derailed in April, before the end of the mandate, when Jewish forces attacked the Arab inhabitants within and outside of the future Jewish state, making the intervention of the Arab armies inevitable. Nevertheless, the Legion still hoped to occupy Hebron, Ramallah, and Nablus without fighting. But this presumed that Jerusalem was to be an international zone under the United Nations, and not a battlefield. When the Jews moved into British positions and proceeded to attack Arab quarters, there was no way strategically or politically that the Legion could avoid a fight. See Glubb 'Transjordan Situation', 12 August 1948, FO 371/6882.
23 Muhammad Husayn Haykal, *Mudhakkirat fi'l-Siyasa al-Misriyya* (Cairo, n.d.), Vol. 2, p. 338.
24 *FRUS*, 1948, Vol. 5, part 2, p. 1064; Kirkbride to Tawfiq Abu'l-Huda, 28 May 1948, FO 816/121. The withdrawal of the officers was an especially hard blow since these men included all operational staff officers, both brigade commanders, the commanding officers of three out of four infantry regiments and all the trained

artillery officers. Glubb, *Soldier*, pp. 133–4. The harm to the Legion, however, was mitigated, for as Kirkbride later wrote, 'I took steps which enabled me to report that all personnel concerned were back in Transjordan before the deadline set by the Foreign Office, but I was not sure that they stayed there for long.' Kirkbride, *From the Wings*, p. 35.

25 Chiefs of Staff Committee, Joint Planning Staff, 12 June 1948 (citing a telegram from Kirkbride to the FO of 6 June 1948), DEFE 6/6; Cairo to FO, 8 June 1948 (reporting Glubb's assessment), FO 371/68413.

26 Kirkbride, *From the Wings*, pp. 34 and 37.

27 For a Jordanian account of the Legion's achievements in the first month of the war, see Sulayman Musa, *Ayyam la Tunsa* (Amman, 1982), pp. 119–304.

28 On Abdullah's visit to Cairo see: Haza' al-Majali, *Mudhakkirati* (Amman, 1960), pp. 74–5; Kirkbride to Burrows, 26 June 1948, and Sir R. Campbell (Cairo) to Bevin, 1 July 1948, FO 371/68857; minute by Ravensdale (Cairo), 26 June 1948, FO 141/1291.

29 Kirkbride to FO, 17 June 1948, FO 371/68770. Other presents which Abdullah reportedly received were four automobiles loaded with slaves, twelve Arab horses, one jewelled sword, one gold dagger, two gold swords for his sons, and pearl necklaces for the women of the family. See Trott (Jidda) to Burrows, 4 July 1948 and Jidda to FO, 11 July 1948, FO 371/68770, and Childs (Jidda) to Secretary of State, 6 July 1948, USNA 890i.001/7-648. On Abdullah's visit to Riyadh, see also Majali, *Mudhakkirati*, pp. 75–6.

30 H. B. Mack (Baghdad) to M. R. Wright, 6 July 1948, FO 371/68770.

31 On Abdullah's visit to Baghdad see Majali, *Mudhakkirati*, pp. 76–7, and Baghdad to FO, 1 July 1948, FO 371/68839.

32 The Council consisted of Ahmad Hilmi, Jamal al-Husayni, 'Awni 'Abd al-Hadi, Husayn Fakhri al-Khalidi, Sulayman Tuqan, Michel Abcarius, 'Ali Husni, Raja'i al-Husayni, Yusuf Sahiyun and Amin 'Aqil.

33 Count Folke Bernadotte, *To Jerusalem* (London, 1951), pp. 74–5. Amman to FO, 7 July 1948, and Cairo to FO, 8 July 1948, FO 371/68375.

34 Bernadotte, *To Jerusalem*, p. 164. See also Amman to FO, 25 July 1948, FO 371/68822; Amman to FO, 7 and 8 July 1948 (two telegrams), FO 371/68375; and *FRUS*, 1948, Vol. 5, part 2, pp. 1202–5.

35 Benny Morris, 'Operation Dani and the Palestinian Exodus from Lydda and Ramle in 1948,' *Middle East Journal* 40:1 (Winter 1986), pp. 100–1.

36 Glubb, *Soldier*, pp. 157–62; Musa, *Ayyam*, pp. 345–72; Amman to FO, 14 and 19 July 1948 (two telegrams), FO 371/68854; Monthly situation report on Transjordan, July 1948, FO 371/68845; Stabler to secretary of state, 14 July 1948, USNA 890i.00/7-1448.

37 Kirkbride, *From the Wings*, pp. 47–8.

38 Glubb, *Soldier*, pp. 165–6; Amman to FO, 11 August 1948, and minute by Burrows, 13 August 1948, FO 371/68830; Abdullah to Bevin, 12 August 1948, FO 371/68822.

39 *FRUS*, 1948, Vol. 5, part 2, p. 1242.

40 Amman to FO, 25 July 1948, FO 371/68822.

41 *FRUS*, 1948, Vol. 5, part 2, pp. 1237–8.
42 Bernadotte, *To Jerusalem*, p. 211; Amman to FO, 11 August 1948, FO 371/68645.
43 Tom Segev, *1949. The First Israelis* (New York, 1986), pp. 38–9.
44 Ian Lustick, *Arabs in the Jewish State* (Austin, 1980), pp. 48–9.
45 See for example, Segev, *1949*, pp. 43–67.
46 Louis, *The British Empire*, p. 394.
47 Population estimates vary. Kirkbride reckoned that the population of Arab Palestine (excluding refugees) including the West Bank, Gaza and Beersheba, was 550,000. Kirkbride to FO, 28 September 1948, FO 371/68862. For Gaza strip figures see Troutbeck to Bevin, 16 June 1948, FO 371/75343.
48 Notes by B. A. B. Burrows, 17 August 1948, FO 371/68822.
49 *Yearbook of the United Nations 1947–1948*, pp. 304–12.
50 *FRUS*, 1948, Vol. 5, part 2, p. 1447. 'Arif al-'Arif, *al-Nakba* (Beirut, n.d.), pp. 703–5.
51 Stabler to secretary of state, 3 September 1948, USNA 890i.00/9–348.
52 Kirkbride to FO, 25 September 1948, FO 816/129.
53 Kirkbride to FO, 4 October 1948, FO 371/68822.
54 Jerusalem to FO, 30 September 1948, FO 371/68642.
55 Glubb, *Soldier*, pp. 199–200.
56 Jeusalem to FO, 29 October 1948, and Amman to FO, 2 November 1948, FO 371/68643.
57 Text of a talk by Glubb Pasha, 6 May 1949, FO 371/68643.
58 Background to the Jericho Congress, 6 December 1948, FO 816/142; Avi Plascov, *The Palestinian Refugees in Jordan, 1948–57* (London, 1981), pp. 13–14; conversations with 'Abd Allah Rimawi, Amman, 16 December 1978 and 19 February 1979, and 'Aziz Shihadi, Ramallah, 14 February 1979.
59 Endorsing Abdullah as ruler of all-Palestine was a deliberate attempt on the part of those who opposed Abdullah to make their support conditional. Conversation with 'Abd Allah Rimawi, Amman, 19 February 1979.
60 Faruq's rebuke was published in *al-Ahram*, 17 December 1948. Abdullah was dissuaded by those in his retinue. Conversations with Hashim Dabbas, Amman, 8 November 1978, and Yusuf Haykal, Washington, 28 May 1979.
61 Amman to FO, 25 and 28 December 1948, and Cairo to FO, 27 December 1948, FO 371/68377; *FRUS*, 1948, Vol. 5, part 2, pp. 1699–700.
62 Troutbeck to Michael Wright, 3 March 1949, FO 371/75064.
63 WO to FO, 26 November 1948, FO 371/68822; Monthly situation report for Transjordan, December 1948, FO 371/75273; Amman to FO, 2 January 1949, FO 371/75293; Jerusalem to FO, 23 February 1949, FO 371/75331.
64 FO to Amman, 16 December 1948, FO 371/68644; Minute by Hector McNeil, 15 December 1948, FO 371/68862. Begin was also anathema to Britain, owing to his leadership of the Irgun which had killed so many British soldiers and civilians during the 1944–7 period.
65 FO to Washington, 13 September 1949, FO 371/75287.
66 FO to Amman, 6 December 1948, FO 816/314; *FRUS*, 1948, Vol. 5, part 2, pp. 1687–8.

67 FO to Amman, 30 December 1948, FO 371/68644.
68 Kirkbride to FO, 2 January 1948 and FO to Kirkbride, 3 January 1948, FO 371/75293.

11 The end of ambition

1 Al-Tall, *Karitha Filastin*, pp. 467 ff; *FRUS*, 1949, Vol. 6, pp. 716 and 773; conversation with Yehoshafat Harkabi, Jerusalem, 9 January 1979; Walter Eytan, *The First Ten Years: A Diplomatic History of Israel* (New York, 1958), pp. 28–42.
2 George Kirk, *The Middle East 1945–1950* (London, 1954), p. 246.
3 Several months later Abdullah al-Tall revealed that talks had been going on between Abdullah and Israel at the time. Al-Tall, *Karitha Filastin*, pp. 344–5.
4 *FRUS*, 1949, Vol. 6, p. 684; Stabler to State Department, 24 January 1949, USNA 867N.01/1-2449.
5 MEDME to Air Ministry, 11 March 1949, FO 371/75294; Glubb, *Soldier*, pp. 229–33.
6 Amman to FO, 18 March 1949, FO 371/75381; FO to Amman, 19 March 1949, FO 371/75382; Amman to FO, 19 March, 21 March, 22 March, 23 March 1949 (two dispatches), FO to Washington, 23 March 1949, Washington to FO, 23 March 1949, and Amman to FO, 24 March 1949, FO 371/75386; Amman to FO, 27 March 1949, Jerusalem to FO, 28 March 1949, and Amman to FO, 31 March 1949, FO 371/75387; *FRUS*, 1949, Vol. 6, pp. 859–62, and pp. 900–2; Majali, *Mudhakkirati*, pp. 90–2; Plascov, *Palestine Refugees*, pp. 14–15. Some Israeli authors have suggested that Israel's tactics were not as forceful as American and British reports indicated, that Abdullah was prepared to give up the territory, and that Kirkbride and Stabler, who judged such a step to be dangerous for Abdullah, exaggerated the situation in an attempt to get their governments to intervene. See Ilan Pappé, *British Foreign Policy towards the Middle East 1948–1951: Britain and the Arab-Israeli Conflict* (unpublished D.Phil. dissertation, Oxford, 1984), pp. 306–12.
7 Minute by John B. Pruen, 11 May 1949, FO 816/146; Beirut to FO, 29 March 1949, FO 371/75454.
8 Three days later in a meeting with Israelis, the suggestion was made that the Israeli Air Force help Abdullah conquer Damascus. Segev, *1949*, p. 12.
9 Damascus to FO, 27 April 1949, FO to Amman, 27 April 1949, Jerusalem to FO, 11 May 1949, Paris to FO, 12 May 1949, and Amman to FO, 17 May 1949, FO 371/75275; Paris to FO, 21 May 1949, FO 371/75376.
10 See Avi Plascov's chapter 'Creeping Annexation', in his *Palestinian Refugees*, pp. 10–40.
11 Monthly situation report, May 1949, FO 371/75253; *Official Gazette*, 1 March 1950.
12 Segev, *1949*, pp. 43–67.
13 These numbers excluded those not on relief. Amman to FO, 4 May 1949, FO 371/ 75426; Jerusalem to FO, 7 October 1949, FO 371/75442.
14 Summary of events in Arab Palestine, September 1949, FO 371/75329; Monthly situation report, November 1949, FO 371/75273; Monthly situation report, March 1950, FO 371/82703.

15 Jerusalem to FO, 7 October 1949, FO 371/75442; FO research department report on the union of Transjordan and Arab Palestine, October 1949, FO 371/75287; Monthly situation report, March 1950, FO 371/82703; Amman to FO, 5 October 1950, FO 371/82705.

16 Amman to FO, 18 August 1948, FO 371/68677.

17 Kirkbride to FO, 11 October 1949, FO 371/68679.

18 Plascov, *Palestinian Refugees*, p. 41.

19 Hedley V. Cooke, *Challenge and Response in the Middle East*, (New York, 1952), pp. 105–6.

20 Notes of a meeting, 28 March 1949, FO 371/75064.

21 Pamela Ann Smith, *Palestine and the Palestinians 1876–1983* (London, 1985), pp. 117–20 and 144.

22 Segev, *1949*, p. 107.

23 Memorandum by G. Walpole, n.d. [April–May 1949], FO 371/75289.

24 Plascov, *Palestinian Refugees*, p. 36.

25 Jerusalem to FO, 30 September 1948, FO 371/68642.

26 Kirkbride to FO, 15 February 1951, FO 371/91808.

27 Walpole to Evans, 29 August 1950, FO 371/82723.

28 Plascov, *Palestinian Refugees* , p. 36.

29 Fritzlan (Amman) to State Department, 21 October 1949, USNA 890i.515/10-2049; Summary of events in Arab Palestine, October 1949, FO 371/75329; Kirkbride to FO, 27 July 1950, FO 371/82706; Transjordan economic report, 1 January–30 June 1950, FO 371/82721.

30 Smith, *Palestine*, p. 93.

31 Fritzlan to Secretary of State, 15 October 1949, USNA 890i.001/10-1549.

32 Burdett to State Department, 22 October 1949, USNA 890i.001/10-2449.

33 Major V. P. Rich to WO, 16 October 1949, FO 371/75333.

34 Amman to FO, 29 December 1949, FO 371/75287.

35 'The Incorporation of Arab Palestine in Transjordan,' enclosure in brief for the Secretary of State by B. A. B. Burrows, 18 August 1949, FO 371/75314; FO to Washington, 13 September 1949, FO 371/75287. The difference between American and British attitudes has best been described by Roger Louis in his recent book *British Empire*, pp. 562–3.

> Within the State Department . . . the belief prevailed that the Israelis could be relied upon not to impose an 'unjust' peace. This pro-Jewish attitude was reinforced by the quickness and the decisiveness of the Israeli victories, which seemed to indicate that in the future the Jews rather than the Arabs would be more dependable 'allies' . . . There was no reason, so far as the British were concerned . . . that the Jews would stop short of territorial annexations which the Arab states would find intolerable . . . That the British perceived their own power and prestige to be in jeopardy increased the dramatic tension.

36 Summary of events in Arab Palestine, January 1950, FO 371/82176.

37 The names and occupations of those elected can be found in Amman to FO, 14 April 1950, and Jerusalem to FO, 19 April 1950, FO 371/82705. Some dissident members were 'Abd Allah Na'was (Jerusalem) and 'Abd Allah Rimawi (Ramallah),

both Ba'thists, and Mustafa Bushnaq (Nablus), Anwar Nusayba (Jerusalem) and Kamil Ariqat (Jerusalem), who had formerly supported Hajj Amin al-Husayni.

38 Kirkbride to Furlonge, 4 April 1950, FO 371/82718.

39 Abdullah's justification for his recalcitrance was that if such a statement were made, the Anglo-Transjordanian treaty might not apply to the West Bank. (He may not have known it, but Britain had come to the conclusion that whether unification were formalized or not, Britain was liable to defend territory held by Transjordan.) The unspoken basis of his position, however, was a perfect understanding of the principle involved and a desire not to concede any point in the present which might work against him in the uncertain future. Iraq and Yemen abstained from the expulsion vote in the League, which needed unanimity in order to pass. The relatively mild response to unification may have been owing to the fear of League members that expulsion might push Abdullah into the arms of the Israelis. See FO to Cairo, 26 January 1950, FO 371/82715; Kirkbride to FO, 29 June 1950, FO 371/81933; BMEO to FO, 16 May 1950, FO 371/81931.

40 Kirkbride to FO, 30 November 1950, FO 371/82716.

41 Kirkbride to FO, 5 May 1951, FO 371/91789.

42 Fritzlan to State Department, 11 November 1949, USNA 890i.001/11-1149. In 1939 he had been dissuaded from enacting legislation making the veil mandatory garb for women. Report on the political situation for the month of February 1939, CO 831/51.

43 Record of a conversation with King Abdullah aboard the S.S. Highland Brigade at Tilbury, 3 September 1949, by Mr Cheke, and Madrid to FO, 15 September 1949, FO 371/75315; Monthly report on Transjordan, September 1949, FO 371/75273. See also King Abdullah, *al-Takmila*, in Madani (ed.), *al-Athar al-Kamila*, pp. 307–8.

44 He offered to send troops on condition that the United States indemnify Britain for the cost of expanding the Legion to take the place of the troops sent to Korea in the West Bank. Amman to FO, 19 August 1950, and FO to Amman, 29 August 1950, FO 371/82711.

45 Pappé, *British Foreign Policy*, p. 276.

46 Glubb, *Soldier*, p. 244; Note on the situation on the Israel–Jordan demarcation line by J. B. Glubb, 12 February 1951, FO 371/91385.

47 Amman to FO, 7 May 1949, FO 371/75387. *FRUS*, 1949, Vol. 6, pp. 980–2.

48 See for example Amman to FO, 8 June 1949, FO 371/75388, and 'The Situation in Palestine,' report from Arab Legion HQ, 15 June 1949, FO 816/147. See also Segev, *1949*, p. 40.

49 Glubb to Pirie-Gordon, 19 June 1949, FO 371/75388.

50 Novomeysky had seen Abdullah in London in August, when Abdullah had told him how to get in touch with him in Amman. A. M. Novomeysky, *Given to Salt*, pp. 30–1. Kirkbride to FO, 15 November 1949, FO 371/75287.

51 Information on the meetings between November 1949 and March 1950 comes from numerous letters and dispatches found in *FRUS*, 1949, Vol. 6, pp. 1512–14, 1516–20, 1540–41, 1545–46, 1558–59, and in FO 371/75277, 82177, and 82178.

52 Tel Aviv to FO, 1 March 1950, FO 371/82178.

53 Published in the Cairo daily, *Akhbar al-Yawm*, starting 18 March 1950. See also al-Tall, *Karitha Filastin.*
54 On the resulting Cabinet crisis in Jordan, see Kirkbride to Bevin, 6 March 1950, FO 371/82705.
55 BMEO to FO, 3 and 20 April 1950, FO 371/81933.
56 Amman to FO, 20 June 1950, FO 371/82178.
57 Kirkbride to Younger, 29 July 1950, FO 371/82179.
58 Amman to FO, 20 June 1950, FO 371/82178.
59 See FO 371/82203, 82204, 82205, and 82207. It was estimated that some 3,000 Arabs had been expelled from Israel to southern Jordan between 15 May and 15 October 1950. Monthly situation report, October 1950, FO 371/82703.
60 Amman to FO, 11 December 1950, FO 371/82179; Tel Aviv to FO, 13 December 1950 and Amman to FO, 18 December 1950, FO 371/82211; Amman to FO, 2 January and 15 January 1951, FO 371/91364.
61 'Proposed Jordan Plan,' communicated to Mr Shiloah by Samir Pasha on 15 March 1951, Shiloah to Rifa'i, 16 April 1951, 'Jordan Comments on the Note dated 16th April, 1951,' 30 April 1951, FO 371/91364.
62 The last meeting between Abdullah and Israeli representatives that I could find evidence of took place on 11 May 1951. The topic was Mount Scopus. Kirkbride to FO, 12 May 1951, and Tel Aviv to FO, 15 May 1951, FO 371/91364.
63 Kirkbride to B. J. Bowker, FO, 1 September 1951, FO 371/91368.
64 Knox-Helms to Bowker, 5 November 1951, FO 371/91368.
65 Kirkbride to Bevin, 6 March 1950, FO 371/82705.
66 For a recent discussion of the constitutional crisis see Bernard Avishai, *The Tragedy of Zionism* (New York, 1985), pp. 184–90.
67 Segev, *1949*, p. 14; Pappé, *British Foreign Policy*, pp. 345 and 359.
68 *FRUS*, 1949, Vol. 6, pp. 911–16.
69 Kirkbride to Furlonge, 14 July 1950, FO 371/82179.
70 Ankara to FO, 22 May 1951, FO 371/91838; FO minute by J. M. Hunter, 2 June 1951, FO 371/91820.
71 Baghdad to FO, 30 May 1951, FO 371/91703.
72 HM King Hussein of Transjordan, *Uneasy Lies the Head* (London, 1962), p. 2.
73 He had organized the so-called peace bands against the rebels in Palestine during the 1936–9 revolt. He was assassinated in Baghdad in 1941, presumably for reasons stemming from that time.
74 Jerusalem to FO, 20 July 1951, FO 371/92838; Jim Bell to *Time Magazine*, dispatch no. 126, 22 July 1951; King Hussein, *Uneasy Lies the Head*, p. 7; Nasir al-Din al-Nashashibi, *Man Qatala al-Malik 'Abd Allah* (Kuwait, 1980), pp. 28–32; Conversation with Hashim Dabbas, Abdullah's aide-de-camp who was with him when he was killed, Amman, 8 November 1978.

12 Epilogue

1 Jerusalem to FO, 21 July 1951, FO 371/91838; Jim Bell, dispatch no. 130, Beirut to Time Inc., New York, 23 July 1951.

2 Jerusalem to FO, 25 July 1951, FO 371/91838; Jim Bell dispatch no. 121, Beirut to Time Inc., New York, 21 July 1951.

3 Jim Bell dispatch no. 130, Beirut to Time Inc., New York, 25 July 1951.

4 Jim Bell dispatch no. 126, Beirut to Time Inc., New York, 22 July 1951.

5 Jim Bell dispatch no. 133, Beirut to Time Inc., New York, 25 July 1951.

6 Conversations with Princess Fawzi, London, 23 October 1978, and Ann Dearden, London, 18 October 1978; Jim Bell dispatch no. 121, Beirut to Time Inc., New York, 21 July 1951.

7 Kirkbride to FO, 25 July 1951, FO 371/91789.

8 Kirkbride to FO, 30 July 1951, FO 371/91839; Jim Bell to Don Burke, 24 July 1951.

9 House of Commons, 23 July 1951.

10 Kirkbride to FO, 24 September 1951, FO 371/91839.

11 M. T. Walker (Amman) to FO, 3 September 1951, FO 371/91839.

12 Kirkbride, *From the Wings*, p. 139.

13 Amman to FO, 20 August 1951, M. T. Walker to FO, 3 September 1951, Kirkbride to FO, 24 September 1951, FO 371/91839.

14 Conversations with Yousef Nawas, who was Musa al-Husayni's partner in the travel agency, New York, 2 September 1978, and Father Ibrahim Iyad, New York, 14 October 1981. Jerusalem to FO, 18 February 1949, FO 371/75329; Amman to FO, 20 August 1951, FO 371/91839.

15 Conversations with Father Ibrahim Iyad, New York, 14 October 1981, Dawud al-Husayni, Amman, 18 December 1978, and Jim Bell, Boston, 13 November 1983; Glubb to Lt. Col. R. K. Melville, 6 August 1951, FO 371/91839.

16 See for example the recently published *Man Qatala al-Malik 'Abd Allah* by Nasir al-Din al-Nashashibi. Musa and Madi implicated the Americans. See *Tarikh al-Urdun*, pp. 552–3.

17 Kirkbride to FO, 25 July 1951, FO 371/91789.

18 'Political Problems Created by King Abdullah's Assassination', n.d., Hamilton Fisher Papers.

19 See for example, FO to Baghdad, 22 July 1951, FO 371/91797; Amman to FO, 23, 24, and 25 July 1951, FO 371/91789.

20 Conversation with Jim Bell, Boston, 13 November 1983.

Bibliography

Archival sources

GREAT BRITAIN

Public Record Office, London
Foreign Office: FO 141 (Egypt)
    FO 195 (Constantinople and Consulates in the Ottoman Empire, Jidda)
    FO 226 (Beirut – Embassy and Consular archives)
    FO 371 (Political)
    FO 406 (Confidential prints – Eastern Affairs)
    FO 624 (Iraq from 1933)
    FO 684 (Damascus – Embassy and Consular archives)
    FO 686 (Jidda – Consular series)
    FO 800 (Private papers) Sir Gerard Lowther, Sir Gilbert Clayton, Professor Arminius
      Vambery
    FO 816 (Transjordan Consular series)
    FO 882 (Arab Bureau papers)
Cabinet: CAB 24, CAB 127
Colonial Office: CO 537 (Miscellaneous)
    CO 732 (Middle East)
    CO 733 (Palestine)
    CO 831 (Transjordan)
Defense: DEFE 7
War Office: WO 261

Private Papers
Middle East Centre, St Antony's College, Oxford
    'Arif al-'Arif, *'Amman Diary* (unpublished Arabic manuscript)
    Thomas Hodgkin
    R. F. P. Monckton
    H. St John Philby
    F. R. Somerset
    Sir Edward Spears
Sudan Archives, Middle East Centre, University of Durham, Durham
    'Abbas Hilmi II
    Arab Affairs File
    Gilbert F. Clayton
    Reginald Wingate

267

Bibliography

Imperial War Museum, London
   F. G. Peake

FRANCE

Ministère des Affaires Etrangères (MAE), Paris
   Guerre, 1939–45. Alger
   Gabriel Puaux Papers

Ministère de la Défense (MD), Service Historique de l'Armée, Vincennes
   Série: 7N, 16N

ISRAEL

Israel State Archives (ISA), Jerusalem
   2 (Chief Secretary's Office)
   65 (Abandoned Documents, 1920–48)
   Sir Herbert Samuel Papers

Central Zionist Archives (CZA), Jerusalem
   S 25 (Political Department)
   A 264 (Private papers: Felix Frankfurter)
   Z 4 (Zionist Organization, Central Office, London)

UNITED STATES

National Archives (USNA), Washington, D.C.
   867N., 890i. (Jordan)

Private Papers
   Jim Bell
   Hamilton Fisher

LEBANON

Private Papers
Institute for Palestine Studies, Beirut
   Yusuf Haykal, *Jalsat fi raghdan* (unpublished Arabic manuscript)

Official reports

Reports to the Council of the League of Nations on the Administration of Palestine and
   Transjordan (1920–38)
Report of the (Shaw) Commission on the Palestine Disturbances of August 1929, 30
   March 1930. Cmd. 3530
The Hope-Simpson Report, 2 October 1930. Cmd. 3686
Palestine Statement of Policy (Passfield White Paper), October 1930. Cmd. 3692

Report of the Royal (Peel) Commission, 22 June 1937. Cmd. 5479
Palestine Statement of Policy, 7 July 1937. Cmd. 5513
Report of the Partition (Woodhead) Commission, October 1938. Cmd. 5854
Palestine Statement of Policy, 9 November 1938. Cmd. 5893
Palestine Statement of Policy, 17 May 1939. Cmd. 6019

Newspapers and other periodicals

al-Ahram (Cairo)
Akhbar al-Yawm (Cairo)
Alif Ba' (Damascus)
Arab Bulletin (Arab Bureau, Cairo 1916–19)
La Chronique (Damascus)
Daily News Bulletin (Jewish Telegraph Agency)
al-Dustur (Amman)
al-Hilal (Cairo)
Manchester Guardian
Official Gazette (Amman)
Oriente Moderno (Rome)
Palestine and Transjordan (Jerusalem)
Revue du Monde Musulman (Paris)
The Times (London)
Umm al-Qura (Mecca)

Dissertations

al-Amr, Saleh [Salih al-'Amr], 'The Hijaz Under Ottoman Rule 1869–1914: The Ottoman, Vali, the Sharif of Mecca, and the Growth of British Influence,' Ph.D. dissertation, University of Leeds, 1974
Bailey, Clinton, 'The Participation of the Palestinians in the Politics of Jordan,' PhD. dissertation, Columbia University, 1965
Faddah, Muhammad Ibrahim, 'The Foreign Policy of Jordan 1947–1967,' Ph.D. dissertation, University of Oklahoma, 1971
Goldner, Werner, 'The Role of Abdullah ibn Hussain in Arab Politics, 1941–1951,' Ph.D. dissertation, Stanford University, 1954
Kazziha, Walid, 'The Emergence of the State of Jordan,' M.A. dissertation, University of London, 1967
Khoury, Philip S., 'The Politics of Nationalism: Syria and the French Mandate, 1920–1936,' Ph.D. dissertation, Harvard University, 1980
Mahmoud, Amin Abdullah, 'King Abdullah and Palestine: An historical study of his role in the Palestine Problem from the creation of Transjordan to the annexation of the West Bank, 1921–1950,' Ph.D. dissertation, Georgetown University, 1972
Nimri, Kamal T., 'Abdullah ibn al-Hussain: a study in Arab Political Leadership,' Ph.D. dissertation, University of London, 1977
Pappé, Ilan, 'British Foreign Policy Towards the Middle East 1948–1951: Britain and the Arab-Israeli Conflict,' D.Phil. dissertation, Oxford, 1984

Bibliography

Published sources

'Abd al-Hadi, 'Awni, *Awraq Khassa* [Private Papers], ed. Khayriyya Qasimiyya (Beirut, 1974)
Abdullah ibn Husayn, King, *Mudhakkirati* [*My Memoirs*] (Amman, 1945)
   Jawab al-Sa'il 'an al-Khayl al-Asa'il [*Answer to the Questioner about Thoroughbred Horses*], in 'Umar Madani, ed., *al-Athar al-Kamila li'l Malik 'Abd Allah* [*The Complete Works of King Abdullah*] (Amman, 1977)
   Man Ana [*Who am I?*], in 'Umar Madani, ed., *al-Athar*
   al-Mudhakkirat [*The Memoirs*], in 'Umar Madani, ed., *al-Athar*
   al-Takmila [*The Completion*], in 'Umar Madani, ed., *al-Athar*. (Published in English as *My Memoirs Completed*, London, 1978.)
Abidi, Hyder Hasan, *Jordan: A Political Study 1948–1957* (London, 1965)
Abu Jaber, Kamel S., 'The Legislature of the Hashemite Kingdom of Jordan,' *Muslim World* 59 (1969), 220–50
Abu-Manneh, Butrus, 'Sultan Abdulhamid II and Shaikh Abulhuda Al-Sayyadi,' *Middle Eastern Studies* 15 (1966), 131–53
Ahmad, Feroz, 'Britain's Relations with the Young Turks 1908–1914,' *Middle Eastern Studies* 2 (1966), 302–29
   The Young Turks (Oxford, 1969)
Andrew, Christopher M., and A. S. Kanya-Forstner, *France Overseas* (London, 1981)
Antonius, George, *The Arab Awakening* (New York, 1965)
al-'Arif, 'Arif, *al-Nakba* [*The Catastrophe*] (Beirut, n.d.)
Aruri, Naseer H., *Jordan: A Study in Political Development (1921–1965)* (The Hague, 1972)
Avishai, Bernard, *The Tragedy of Zionism* (New York, 1985)
Baker, Randall, *King Hussein and the Kingdom of the Hijaz* (Cambridge, 1979)
Barbir, Karl K., *Ottoman Rule in Damascus, 1708–1758* (Princeton, 1980)
Bashear, Suliman, *Judhur al-Wisaya al-Urduniyya* [*The Roots of the Jordanian Mandate*] (Jerusalem, 1980)
Baster, James, 'The Economic Problems of Jordan,' *International Affairs* 31 (1955), 26–35
al-Batanuni, Muhammad Labib, *al-Rihla al-Hijaziyya* [*The Hijaz Journey*] (Cairo, 1911)
Batatu, Hanna, *The Old Social Classes and the Revolutionary Movements of Iraq* (Princeton, 1978)
Bell, Gertrude, 'Turkish Rule East of the Jordan,' *The Nineteenth Century and After* 52 (1902), 226–38
Ben Gurion, David, *My Talks with Arab Leaders* (Jerusalem, 1972)
Berkes, Niyazi, *The Development of Secularism in Turkey* (Montreal, 1964)
Bernadotte, Count Folke, *To Jerusalem* (London, 1951)
Bolitho, Hector, *The Angry Neighbours: A Diary of Palestine and Transjordan* (London, 1957)
Bowden, Tom, 'Arab Rebellion in Palestine 1936–1939,' *Middle Eastern Studies* 11 (1975), 147–74

Brémond, E., *Le Hedjaz dans la Guerre Mondiale* (Paris, 1931)

Bullard, Sir Reader, *The Camels Must Go* (London, 1961)

Burckhardt, John Lewis, *Travels in Arabia* (London, 1824)

Burgoyne, Elizabeth, *Gertrude Bell from her Personal Papers 1914–1926* (London, 1961)

Busch, Briton Cooper, *Britain, India, and the Arabs, 1914–1921* (Berkeley, 1971)

Caplan, Neil, *Futile Diplomacy Vol. II: Arab–Zionist Negotiations and the End of the Mandate* (London, 1986)

Clayton, Sir Gilbert F., *An Arabian Diary* (Berkeley, 1969)

Cohen, Aharon, *Israel and the Arab World* (New York, 1970)

Cohen, Amnon, 'Political Parties in the West Bank under the Hashemite Regime,' in Moshe Ma'oz, ed., *Palestine Arab Politics* (Jerusalem, 1975)

    Political Parties in the West Bank under the Jordanian Regime 1949–1967 (Ithaca and London, 1982)

Cohen, Mendel, *be-Hatser ha-Melekh Abdullah [At the Court of King Abdullah]* (Tel Aviv, 1980)

Cohen, Michael J. 'Secret Diplomacy and the Rebellion in Palestine, 1936–1939,' *International Journal of Middle East Studies* 8 (July 1977), 379–404

    Palestine: Retreat from the Mandate (New York, 1978)

    Palestine and the Great Powers (Princeton, 1982)

Conder, Claude Regnier, *Heth and Moab. Explorations in Syria in 1881 and 1882* (London, 1883)

Cooke, Hedley V., *Challenge and Response in the Middle East. The Quest for Prosperity 1919–1951* (New York, 1952)

Crossman, Richard, *Palestine Mission: A personal record* (London, 1947)

Dann, Uriel, *Studies in the History of Transjordan, 1920–1949* (Boulder, 1984)

Darwaza, Muhammad 'Izzat, *al-Qadiyya al-Filastiniyya [The Palestine Problem]* (Sidon and Beirut, n.d.)

    Hawla al-Haraka al-'Arabiyya al-Haditha [On The Modern Arab Movement] (Sidon, 1950)

Davis, Helen Miller, *Constitutions, Electoral Laws, Treaties of the States in the Near and Middle East* (Durham, NC, 1947)

Dawn, C. Ernest, *From Ottomanism to Arabism* (Urbana, 1973)

Dearden, Ann, *Jordan* (London, 1958)

Djemal, Ahmad, *Memories of a Turkish Statesman, 1919–1922* (New York, 1922)

Doughty, Charles M., *Travels in Arabia Deserta* (Cambridge, 1888)

'Emir Abdullah the Smart Little Ruler of Transjordan is No. 1 British Pawn in the Middle East,' *Life Magazine*, 1 December 1941

Epstein, Eliahu, 'The Bedouins of Transjordan: Their Social and Economic Problems,' *Journal of the Royal Central Asian Society* 25 (April 1938), 228–36

Erskine, Mrs Steuart, *King Faisal of Iraq* (London, 1933)

Eytan, Walter, *The First Ten Years: A Diplomatic History of Israel* (New York, 1958)

Faddah, Mohammad Ibrahim, *The Middle East in Transition: a Study of Jordan's Foreign Policy* (New York, 1974)

'Fi Mudhakkirat Sulayman Shafiq Kamali Pasha' ['In the Memoirs of Sulayman Shafiq Kamali Pasha'], *al-'Arab*, June 1971, October 1971, January 1972

Flapan, Simha, *Zionism and the Palestinians* (London, 1979)

Fleming, Jackson, 'A Visit to Amir Abdullah,' *Asia* 38 (1938), 63–5

Forder, Archibald, *With the Arabs in Tent and Town* (London, 1902)

The Foreign Relations of the United States [FRUS], Vol. 5, part 2, 1948; Vol. 6, 1949

de Gaury, Gerald, *Rulers of Mecca* (New York, n.d.)

Ghuri, Emil, *Filastin 'Abra Sittin 'Am* [*Palestine Over Sixty Years*] (Beirut, 1973)

Glubb, John Bagot, 'The Economic Situation of the Trans-Jordan Tribes,' *Journal of the Royal Central Asian Society* 25 (1938), 445–9

　The Story of the Arab Legion (London, 1946)

　A Soldier with the Arabs (London, 1957)

　'Transjordan and the War,' *Journal of the Royal Central Asian Society* 33:1 (January 1945), 24–33

Goichon, A. M., *Jordanie Réelle* 2 vols (Paris, 1967 and 1972)

Gomaa, Ahmed M., *The Foundation of the League of Arab States* (London, 1977)

Gooch, G. P., and Harold Temperly (eds.), *British Documents on the Origins of the War, 1898–1914* (London, 1938)

Grafftey-Smith, Sir Laurence, *Bright Levant* (London, 1970)

Gubser, Peter, *Politics and Change in al-Karak, Jordan* (London, 1973)

Hacker, Jane M., *Modern Amman. A Social History* (Durham, 1960)

Haddad, William W., and William L. Ochsenwald, *Nationalism in a non-National State. The Dissolution of the Ottoman Empire* (Columbus, 1977)

Haidar, HRH Princess Musbah, *Arabesque* (London, 1944)

Harding, G. Lankester, "'Amman,' *Encyclopaedia of Islam*, new ed. (London, 1960), Vol. 1, p. 447

Harris, George L., *Jordan: its People, its Society, its Culture* (New York, 1958)

Hawrani, Hani, *al-Tarkib al-Iqtisadi al-Ijtima'i li-Sharq al-Urdun* [*The Economic and Social Structure of Transjordan*] (Beirut, 1978)

Haykal, Muhammad Husayn, *Mudhakkirat fi'l-Siyasa al-Misriyya* [*Memoirs of Egyptian Politics*] (Cairo, n.d.)

Hodgkin, Thomas, 'Antonius, Palestine and the 1930s,' *Gazelle Review of Literature on the Middle East* 10 (1982), 1–33

Hogarth, David George, *Hejaz Before World War I* (Cambridge, 1978)

Hourani, Albert, *Syria and Lebanon. A Political Essay* (London, 1946)

　Arabic Thought in the Liberal Age, 1798–1939 (London, 1962)

Hurewitz, J. C., *The Struggle for Palestine* (New York, 1950)

Hurgonje, C. Snouck, *Mekka in the Latter Part of the Nineteenth Century* (London, 1931)

al-Husri, Sati', *Yawm Maysalun* [*The Day of Maysalun*], new ed. (Beirut, n.d.)

Hussein of Jordan, HM King, *Uneasy Lies the Head* (London, 1962)

Huxley, Julian, *From an Antique Land* (London, 1954)

Ionides, M. G., *Report on the Water Resources of Transjordan and their Development* (London, 1939)

Jankowski, James, 'The Government of Egypt and the Palestine Question, 1936–1939,' *Middle Eastern Studies* 17 (1981), 427–53

Jarvis, Major C. S., *Arab Command. The Biography of Lieutenant Colonel F. W.* [*sic*] *Peake Pasha* (London, 1942)

Jaussen, Le Père Antonin, *Coutumes des Arabes au Pays de Moab* (Paris, 1948) et Savignac, PP, *Mission Archéologique en Arabie (Mars–Mai 1907) de Jérusalem au Hedjaz Medain-Saleh* (Paris, 1909)

Jbara, Taysir, *Palestinian Leader Hajj Amin al-Husayni Mufti of Jerusalem* (Princeton, 1985)

John, Robert, and Sami Hadawi, *The Palestine Diary* (Beirut, 1970)

Jordan, Ministry of Foreign Affairs, *The Rising Tide of Terror or Three Years of an Armistice in the Holy Land* (Amman, 1952)

Kayyali, A. W., *Palestine, a Modern History* (London, 1979)

Kazem-Zadeh, H., 'Relation d'un pèlerinage à la Mecque en 1910–1911,' *Revue du Monde Musulman* 19 (1912), 169–82

Kazziha, Walid, *The Social History of Southern Syria (Trans-Jordan) in the 19th and Early 20th Century* (Beirut, 1972)

Keane, John F., *Six Months in the Hijaz* (London, 1887)

Kedourie, Elie, *The Chatham House Version and Other Middle Eastern Studies* (London, 1970)
'The Surrender of Medina, January 1919,' *Middle Eastern Studies* 13:1 (1977), 124–43

Khalidi, Walid (ed.), *From Haven to Conquest* (Beirut, 1971)

Khalil, Muhammad, *The Arab States and the Arab League: A Documentary Record*, 2 vols (Beirut, 1962)

Khoury, Philip S., *Urban Notables and Arab Nationalism. The Politics of Damascus 1860–1920* (Cambridge, 1983)
Syria and the French Mandate: The Politics of Arab Nationalism, 1920–1945 (Princeton, 1987)

Kirkbride, Alec Seath. *A Crackle of Thorns* (London, 1956)
An Awakening (London, 1971)
From the Wings (London, 1976)

Kirk, George E., 'Cross-currents within the Arab League: The Greater Syria Plan,' *World Today* (January 1948), 15–25
The Middle East 1945–1950 (London, 1954)

Kisch, Colonel F. H., *Palestine Diary* (London, 1938)

al-Kitab al-Urduni al-Abyad [*The Jordanian White Book*] (Amman, 1946)

Kleiman, Aaron S., *Foundations of British Policy in the Arab World: The Cairo Conference of 1921* (Baltimore, 1970)

Konikoff, A., *Trans-Jordan, an Economic Survey* (Jerusalem, 1943)

Larès, Maurice, *T. E. Lawrence, la France et les Français* (Paris, 1980)

Lawrence, T. E., *Seven Pillars of Wisdom* (London, 1983)

Lias, Godfrey, *Glubb's Legion* (London, 1956)

Lorch, Netanel, *The Edge of the Sword: Israel's War of Independence 1947–1949* (New York, 1961)

Louis, William Roger, *The British Empire in the Middle East 1945–1951: Arab Nationalism, the United States and Postwar Imperialism* (London, 1984)
and Robert W. Stookey (eds), *The End of the Palestine Mandate* (Austin, 1986)

Luke, Sir Harry, and Edward Keith-Roach, *The Handbook of Palestine and Transjordan* (London, 1934)

Lunt, James, *Glubb Pasha: A Biography* (London, 1984)

Lustick, Ian, *Arabs in the Jewish State* (Austin, 1980)

Lyttleton, Oliver [Viscount Chandos], *The Memoirs of Lord Chandos* (London, 1962)

Bibliography

Mack, John, *A Prince of Our Disorder* (London, 1976)
MacKenzie, Marcus, 'Transjordan,' *Journal of the Royal Central Asian Society* 33 (July–October 1946), 260–70
al-Majali, Hazaʿ, *Mudhakkirati* [*My Memoirs*] (Amman, 1960)
Mandel, Neville, *The Arabs and Zionism Before World War I* (Berkeley, 1976)
Marsot, Afaf Lutfi al-Sayyid, *Egypt's Liberal Experiment, 1922–1936* (Berkeley, 1977)
Meinertzhagen, Colonel R., *Middle East Diary 1917–1956* (London, 1959)
Meir, Golda, *My Life* (New York, 1975)
Merrill, Selah, *East of the Jordan. A Record of Travel in the Countries of Moab, Gilead, and Bashan During the Years 1875–1877* (London, 1881)
Milson, Menahem (ed.), *Society and Political Structure in the Arab World* (New York, 1973)
Mishal, Shaul, *West Bank/East Bank. The Palestinians in Jordan 1949–1967* (New Haven, 1978)
Monroe, Elizabeth, *Britain's Moment in the Middle East* (London, 1963)
 Philby of Arabia (London, 1973)
Morris, Benny, 'Operation Dani and the Palestinian Exodus from Lydda and Ramle in 1948,' *Middle East Journal* 40:1 (Winter 1986), 82–108
Morris, James, *The Hashemite Kings* (London, 1959)
Mousa, Suleiman [Sulayman Musa], *al-Haraka al-ʿArabiyya 1908–1924* [*The Arab Movement 1908–1924*] (Beirut, 1970)
 Taʾsis al-Imara al-Urduniyya, 1921–1925 [*The Foundation of the Jordanian Amirate*] (Amman, 1971)
 (ed.), *al-Murasalat al-Tarikhiyya* [*Historic Correspondence*], Vol. 1, 1914–18 (Amman, 1973), Vol. 2, 1919 (Amman, 1975), Vol. 3, 1920–3 (Amman, 1978)
 al-Thawra al-ʿArabiyya al-Kubra. al-Harb fiʾl-Urdun 1917–1918. Mudhakkirat al-Amir Zayd [*The Great Arab Revolt. The War in Jordan 1917–1918. The Memoirs of Amir Zayd*] (Amman, 1976)
 'A Matter of Principle: King Hussain of the Hijaz and the Arabs of Palestine,' *International Journal of Middle East Studies* 9:2 (1978), 183–94
 Ayyam la Tunsa [*Days Not to Be Forgotten*] (Amman, 1982)
 and Munib al-Madi, *Tarikh al-Urdun fiʾl-Qarn al-ʿAshrin* [*The History of Jordan in the Twentieth Century*] (Amman, 1959)
Musil, Alois, *Northern Negd, A Topographical Itinerary* (New York, 1928)
al-Nashashibi, Nasir al-Din, *Man Qatala al-Malik ʿAbd Allah* [*Who Killed King Abdullah?*] (Kuwait, 1980)
Nasif, Husayn, *Madi al-Hijaz wa Hadiruhu* [*The Hijaz Past and Present*] (Cairo, 1930)
Naval Intelligence Division, *Western Arabia and the Red Sea*, Geographical Handbook Series (London, 1946)
Neumann, Emanuel, *In the Arena* (New York, 1976)
Nevakivi, Jukka, *Britain, France and the Arab Middle East 1914–1920* (London, 1969)
Nevo, Joseph, 'Abdallah and the Arabs of Palestine,' *The Wiener Library Bulletin* 31 (1978) 51–62
Nicolson, Harold, *Peacemaking 1919* (London, 1933)
Novomeysky, A. M., *Given to Salt* (London, 1958)
Ochsenwald, William, *Religion, Society and the State in Arabia* (Columbus, 1984)

Oliphant, Laurence, *The Land of Gilead with Excursions in the Lebanon* (New York, 1881)

O'Ballance, Edgar, *The Arab–Israeli War 1948* (London, 1956)

Owen, Roger, *The Middle East in the World Economy 1800–1914* (London, 1981)

Patai, Raphael, *Jordan, Lebanon and Syria: An Annotated Bibliography* (New Haven, 1957)

   The Kingdom of Jordan (Princeton, 1958)

Peake, F. G. 'Trans-Jordan', *Journal of the Royal Central Asian Society* 23:3 (1939), 375–96

   A History of Jordan and its Tribes (Coral Gables, Florida, 1958)

Philby, H. St. John, 'Trans-Jordan,' *Journal of the Royal Central Asian Society* 11:4 (1924), 296

Plascov, Avi, *The Palestinian Refugees in Jordan, 1948–1967* (London, 1981)

Porath, Yehoshua, *The Emergence of the Palestinian Arab National Movement, 1918–1929* (London, 1974)

   The Palestinian Arab National Movement, 1929–1939 (London, 1977)

   In Search of Arab Unity 1930–1945 (London, 1986)

Rendel, George, *The Sword and the Olive* (London, 1957)

de Reynier, Jacques, *A Jérusalem un drapeau flottait sur la ligne de feu* (Neuchâtel, 1950)

Rihani, Ameen, *Around the Coasts of Arabia* (London, 1930)

Royal Institute of International Affairs, *Great Britain and Palestine 1915–1945* (London, 1946)

   The Middle East: A Political and Economic Survey (London, 1950)

Rubin, Barry, *The Arab States and the Palestine Conflict* (Syracuse, 1981)

Ruppin, A., *Syrien als Wirtschaftsgebiet* (Berlin, 1917)

Ryan, Sir Andrew, *The Last of the Dragomans* (London, 1951)

Sa'id, Amin, *al-Thawra al-'Arabiyya al-Kubra* [*The Great Arab Revolt*] (Cairo, n.d.)

Sa'id, General Nuri, *Arab Independence and Unity* (Baghdad, 1943)

Sands, William (ed.), *Tensions in the Middle East* (Washington, DC, 1956)

Sayegh, Fayez [Fayiz Sayigh], *Arab Unity* (New York, 1958)

Sayigh, Anis, *al-Hashimiyyun wa Qadiyya Filastin* [*The Hashemites and the Palestine Problem*] (Beirut, 1966)

   al-Hashimiyyun wa al-Thawra al-'Arabiyya al-Kubra [*The Hashemites and the Great Arab Revolt*] (Beirut, 1966)

Seale, Patrick, *The Struggle for Syria, 1945–1958* (London, 1965)

Segev, Tom, *1949. The First Israelis* (New York, 1986)

Seton, C. W. R., *Legislation of Transjordan, 1918–1939*, 7 vols (London, 1931–9)

Shwadran, Benjamin, *Jordan: A State of Tension* (New York, 1959)

Sinai, Anne, and Allen Pollack (eds.), *The Hashemite Kingdom of Jordan and the West Bank* (New York, 1977)

Sluglett, Peter, *Britain in Iraq 1914–1932* (London, 1976)

Smith, Pamela Ann, *Palestine and the Palestinians 1876–1983* (London, 1985)

Snow, Peter, *Hussein* (New York, 1972)

Sofer, Naim, 'The Political Status of Jerusalem in the Hashemite Kingdom of Jordan, 1948–1967,' *Middle Eastern Studies* 12 (1976), 73–94

Sparrow, Gerald, *Modern Jordan* (London, 1961)

Stein, Kenneth W., *The Land Question in Palestine 1917–1939* (Chapel Hill, NC, 1984)

Stitt, George, *A Prince of Arabia the Emeer Shereef Ali Haidar* (London, 1944)

Storrs, Ronald, *Orientations* (London, 1937)

al-Tall, 'Abd Allah, *Karitha Filastin [Palestine Disaster]* (Cairo, 1959)

Tarbush, Mohammad A., *The Role of the Military in Politics. A Case Study of Iraq to 1941* (London, 1982)

Toynbee, Arnold, 'Arabia: Rise of the Wahhabi Power,' in *Survey of International Affairs* (Royal Institute of International Affairs), Vol. 1 (London, 1925)

Tresse, René, *Le Pèlerinage Syrien aux villes saintes de l'Islam* (Paris, 1937)

Tristram, Henry Baker, *The Land of Moab. Travels and Discoveries on the East Side of the Dead Sea and Jordan* (London, 1873)

Pathways of Palestine (London, 1881)

The Land of Israel: A Journey of Travels in Palestine Undertaken with Special Reference to its Physical Character (London, 1886)

Troeller, Gary, *The Birth of Saudi Arabia* (London, 1976)

Van Arendonk, C., 'Sharif,' *Encyclopaedia of Islam*, vol. 4 (London, 1934)

Vatikiotis, P. J., *Politics and the Military in Jordan* (London, 1967)

Vickery, C. E., 'Arabia and the Hedjaz,' *Journal of The Royal Central Asian Society* 10 (1923), 49–67

Walpole, G. F., 'Land Problems in Transjordan,' *Journal of the Royal Central Asian Society* 35 (January 1948), 32–65

Warriner, Doreen, *Land and Poverty in the Middle East* (London, 1948)

Wavell, A. J. B., *A Modern Pilgrim in Mecca* (London, 1918)

Weisgal, Meyer (ed.), *Chaim Weizmann, Scientist and Builder of the Jewish Commonwealth* (New York, 1944)

The Letters and Papers of Chaim Weizmann, Vol. 10, series A (Jerusalem, 1977)

Weizmann, Chaim, *Trial and Error* (Philadelphia, 1949)

Wilson, Arnold Talbot, *Loyalties Mesopotamia. Vol. II 1917–1920* (Oxford, 1931)

Woolbert, Robert Gale, 'Pan Arabism and the Palestine Problem,' *Foreign Affairs* (January 1938), 309–22

Yasin, Subhi, *al-Thawra al-'Arabiyya al-Kubra fi Filastin 1936–1939 [The Great Arab Revolt in Palestine 1936–1939]* (Beirut, 1961)

Yearbook of the United Nations 1947–1948

'Yadkhuru Sa'id al-Mufti' ['Sa'id al-Mufti Remembers'], six-part series in *al-Dustur* (Amman), beginning 21 February 1976

Zeine, Zeine *The Struggle for Arab Independence* (Beirut, 1960)

The Emergence of Arab Nationalism (Beirut, 1966)

Zirikli, Khayr al-Din, *al-'Alam; Qamus Tarajim li-Ashhar al-Rijal wa al-Nisa' min al-'Arab wa al-Musta'ribin wa al-Mustashriqin [Eminent Personalities; A Biographical Dictionary of Noted Men and Women among the Arabs, the Arabists and the Orientalists]*, 10 vols (Cairo, 1954–7)

Zirikli, Khayr al-Din, *Ma Ra'aytu wa ma Sama'tu [What I Saw and What I Heard]* (Cairo, 1923)

'Aman fi 'Amman [Two Years in Amman] (Cairo, 1925)

Zu'aytar, Akram, *al-Qadiyya al-Filastiniyya [The Palestine Problem]* (Cairo, 1955)

Zubyan, Muhammad Taysir, *al-Malik 'Abd Allah kama 'Araftuhu [King Abdullah as I Knew Him]*, Vol. 1 (Amman, 1967), Vol. 2 (Amman, 1977)

Interviews

Ra'uf Abu-Jabr	Amman, 15 December 1978
'Ali Abu-Nuwar	Amman, 27 December 1978
Sa'id 'Ala al-Din	Jerusalem, 16 January 1979
Musa al-'Alami	Jericho, January 1979
Amir 'Ali ibn Nayyif	Amman, 21 November 1978
Amira Wijdan 'Ali	Amman, 14 and 21 November 1978
Sulayman Saliba al-Armani (Abu Dawud)	Amman, 21 December 1978
Anton 'Atallah	Amman, 29 December 1978
'Adnan Bakhit	Amman, 7 November 1978
Sir Richard Beaumont	London, April 1979
Sir Harold Beeley	London, April 1979
Jim Bell	Boston, 12 and 13 November 1983
Lady Violet Bourdillon	Oxford, 30 August 1977
Khalil Budayri	Jerusalem, 16 January 1979
Lord Caradon	Washington, May 1979
Lady Cox	Chipstead, Surrey, 24 May 1978
Mr and Mrs Graham Cox	Chipstead, Surrey, February and May 1978
Hashim Dabbas	Amman, 8 November 1978
Abraham Daskal	Jerusalem, 12 February 1979
Fu'ad Debbas	Boston, 6 August 1979
Ann Edman Fisher	New York, April 1987
Eliahu Elath (Epstein)	Jerusalem, 8 January 1979
Mrs Every	Jerusalem, 5 January 1979
Princess Fawzi	London, 23 October 1978
'Akif Ibn Fayiz	Amman, 19 February 1979
Sir John Bagot and Mrs Glubb	Mayfield, Sussex, 14 June 1978
Mahmud al-Ghul	Amman, November–December 1978
Yehoshafat Harkabi	Jerusalem, 9 January 1979
Crown Prince Hasan	Amman, December 1978
Sharif Muhammad Hashim	Amman, 2 January 1979
Yusuf Haykal	Washington, 28 May 1979
Dollek Horowitz	Jerusalem, 14 January 1979
Sharif Husayn ibn Nasir	Amman, 18 December 1978
Sitt Amini al-Husayni	Amman, 15 December 1979
Dawud al-Husayni	Amman, 18 December 1978
Father Ibrahim Iyad	New York, 14 October 1981
Salma Jayyusi	Cambridge, Massachusetts, 22 June 1979
Juwaybir (Abu Ahmad)	Amman, 13 December 1978
Nayyif Kawar	Amman, 18 November 1978
Widad Kawar	Amman, November 1978
Walid Khalidi	Cambridge, Massachusetts, 27 July 1978
'Abd al-Rahman Khalifa	Amman, 26 December 1978
Angela Jurdak Khoury	Washington, 22 December 1980

Shukry E. Khoury	Washington, 22 December 1980
Sir Alec Kirkbride	Goring-on-Sea, Sussex, 6 November 1977
Dr ʿAli Mahafaza	Damascus, 28 November 1978
ʿAbbas Pasha Mirza	Amman, 19 November 1978
Wasfi Pasha Mirza	Amman, 21 November 1978
Saʿid Pasha al-Mufti	Amman, 21 December 1978
Sulayman Musa	Amman, November–December 1978
Yousef Nawas	New York, 2 September 1978
Anwar Nusseibeh	Jerusalem, 16 January 1979
Yehoshua Palmon	Jerusalem, 15 January 1979
Yehoshua Porath	Jerusalem, January 1979
Sir John Richmond	Durham, June 1979
ʿAbd al-Munʿim Rifaʿi	Amman, 19 February 1979
ʿAbd Allah Rimawi	Amman, 16 December 1978, 19 February 1979
ʿAziz Shihadeh	Ramallah, 14 February 1979
Fuʾad Shihadeh	Ramallah, 14 February 1979
Farhan Shubaylat	Amman, 15 February 1978
Freya Stark	London, May 1979
Sulayim ibn Jabir	Amman, 21 November 1978
Yasser Tabbaa	Boston, June 1984
Muraywid al-Tall	Amman, November 1978

Index

ʿAbadila (sharifian clan), 7
ʿAbd al-Hadi, ʿAwni, 50, 111, 220 n26,
226 n39; and meetings with Churchill,
51, 53; and Palestinian distrust of
Abdullah, 112
ʿAbd al-Hadi, Fakhri, 125
ʿAbd al-Ilah (Regent of Iraq), 14, 15, 156,
207, 210; Abdullah's rivalry with,
140, 143; and coup in Iraq, 133; and
Syrian throne question, 138
ʿAbdiyya bint Abdullah, 6
Abdülhamid II (Ottoman sultan), 12–13,
16, 19
Abdullah ibn al-Husayn (King of Jordan):
advocacy of Islam, *versus* communism,
166, 199; ambitions of, 2, 3, 33, 37,
38, 41, 59, 67, 101, 112, 134–40, 143–
4, 155; and Arab nationalists, 62–4,
67, 79; and Arab public opinion, 110,
123–4, 151–2, 166, 171, 174, 181,
184, 197, 201, 213; and Arab revolt,
28–9; armistice with Ibn Saud, 44;
ʿAsir campaign, 20, 21; assassination
of 112, 208–14; and assassination
plots, 124; background of 6–8, 14, 18;
battle at Turaba, 36–7; and British,
1–3, 23–4, 32, 44, 51–3, 64, 67–8,
72–4, 79, 88, 90, 102, 129, 153–5,
164, 173, 177, 183–4; calls for all-
Syria conference, 141, 158, 159;
character and personality of, 3, 33,
151–2, 154; and Committee of Union
and Progress, 19, 36; coronation of,
149; and creation of Transjordan, 48–
53; difficulties with Talal, 131, 132;
education of, 11, 13–14; and Faysal,
rivalry between, 32, 38, 40–1, 49, 67,
96, 102, 112, 135; financial difficulties
and manipulations of, 77, 85, 114,
121, 138; gifts and favors to Bani
Sakhr shaykhs, 77–8, 233 n66; and
Greater Syria, 134, 135, 139, 140–5; and
Hijaz, 25, 31, 101; and King Husayn
of the Hijaz, 15, 25, 31, 79, 88; and

intervention in Palestine (1948), 169–
81; and Iraq, 41–2, 49, 123, 207, 212;
and Jewish immigration, 120–1; as
landowner, 109, 112; and Lebanon,
139; lifestyle of, 29, 32–3, 61–2, 94–5,
113–14, 132; in London, 73–4, 112–
13, 195; in Maʿan, 48–9; marriage and
family, 14, 92–4, 131, 132, 210; and
Palestinians, 52, 112, 181, 190, 195;
and partition proposals, 122–4, 135,
160–3; and Philby, 70, 76–7, 82; and
profit on land sales to Zionists, 108–
10, 114, 242 n20; and return to Mecca
(1908), 16; and al-Rikabi, 83; rumors
of coup against, 189; siege of Medina,
32–6; siege of Taʾif, 28; and
Shahbandar, 138; sharing of power in
mandate, 91; and struggle for Syria,
34, 40–1; and succession, 62, 131–2,
207, 214; and talks with Israel, 200–7;
and Transjordanian independence,
147–9; in Turkey, 121–2, 200;
ultimatum from Clayton, 84; world
view of, 199, 206; yielding of land to
Israel, 188; and Zionism, 104–5, *See
also* Jordan; Transjordan
Abdülmecid (Ottoman caliph), 80, 81
Abha, 20, 21
al-ʿAbid, Ahmad ʿIzzat, 13, 17
Abramson, Albert, 62, 65, 66, 216, 230
n8; replacement by Philby, 68, 69
Abu Ghanima, Subhi, 111
Abu'l-Huda, Hasan Khalid, 83, 217
Abu'l-Huda, Tawfiq, 2, 91, 111, 130, 217;
mission to Egypt, 142–3; and
Palestine question, 2, 126, 127, 160,
166–7, 168, 171, 172, 180, 184; and
talks between Jordan and Israel, 203,
204
al-ʿAdwan, Majid, 110
al-ʿAdwan, Sultan, 78, 226 nn33, 38
ʿAdwan tribe, 54, 56, 57, 226 nn33, 36;
rebellion of, 77–8; rivalry with other
tribes, 58, 77; settlement by, 228 n68

279

Index

Palestine, *cont.*
164–5; Arab nationalists in, 72, 75;
Arab reaction to partition plans for,
123, 124, 162, 166, 177–8, 183, 197;
battle for Jerusalem (1948), 172–3;
borders with Transjordan, 103; British
high commissioners of, 216; British
proposal for partition, 122, 125, 143,
144, 160–4; disappearance of as
country, 198, 214; and Greater Syria,
136, 139, 143–4, 155; and Husayn's
bid for caliphate, 80; Jewish offensive
in, 168–70, 172; and Jewish
settlement in, 19–20, 45, 105;
massacre at Deir Yasin, 168; and
Negeb, 187; proposed constitutional
government, 127; rebellion in, 99,
124; and St James' Conference, 126;
shift in power to Jewish forces, 168;
strike (1936), 116–19; United Nations
plan for partition, 1, 160–4, 175; visit
of Philby and Abdullah to, 70; White
Paper on, 127, 128. *See also* British
mandate; Greater Syria; Israel;
Transjordan–Palestine relations;
Zionism
Palestine Administrative Council, 175
Palestine Conciliation Commission, 200–1,
207
Palestine Electric Company, 105, 205
Palestine Land Development Company,
106
Palestine Potash Company, 105, 202, 203
Palestinian(s): and Abdullah, 112, 181,
190, 195, 204; divisions among after
1948 war, 178–9; and Jordanian
citizenship, 194; in Jordanian
Parliament, 198–9; in mandate
bureaucracy, 91; refugees, 178, 179,
190–2; and St James' Conference, 126;
tension after Abdullah's assassination,
213
pan-Arabism: and Abdullah's ambitions, 2,
37, 59, 67, 101, 121, 135, 155, 159;
and British, 137; and failure of Syrian
revolt, 90; and Faysal's death, 111–12;
and hope for Arab kingdom, 27, 34,
42–3, 88; and Iraq, 123; and Istiqlal
party, 111; and partition of Palestine,
162; and Shahbandar, 138; Syria as
key to, 155; unity schemes, 140–1.
See also Arab League; Arab
nationalism; Greater Syria
Paris Peace Conference, 36, 39–40
Parliament (Jordanian), 214; composition
of, 197; elections to, 194, 196–7;

Kirkbride's view of, 199; opposition
to Abdullah in, 198–9. *See also*
Legislative Council
Parliament (Ottoman), 18–19
Partition Commission, 125, 126
Passfield White Paper, 105, 107, 115
Peake, Frederick, 66; and Arab Legion,
74, 75, 86; opposition to Abdullah,
83–4; and reserve force, 63, 65
Philby, H. St John, 68, 74, 216; and
Abdullah, 76–7; and Arab nationalists,
72; and constitutional government,
76–7; goals as colonial administrator,
69–70; replacement by Cox, 81–2
pilgrimage (*hajj*), 8, 25, 34; of Abdullah,
84; economic aspects of, 10–11, 87;
and Husayn, 16–17, 21; organization
of 9–10; and Ottoman Empire, 53
Plumer, Lord Arthur, 86, 216
politics: and Arab interests, 19; Committee
of Union and Progress, 14–15, 17, 19,
23; elections (in Jordan), 194, 196–7,
204; elections (in Ottoman empire),
18; elections (in Transjordan), 97,
130, 165; and Hijazi kingship, 31; and
opposition to Abdullah, 110–11, 238
n48; and Transjordanian
independence, 165. *See also*
Legislative Council

Qawz, 21
Qunfudha, 20, 21
al-Quwatli, Shukri, 137, 159, 173, 220
n26, 251 n35; and Arab unity, 141;
overthrow of, 189

railways, Damascus to Mecca, 13. *See also*
Hijaz railway
Ramallah, 182, 190
Ramla: Abdullah's request for return of,
201; fall of, 176, 177
Raslan, Mazhar, 50, 72, 217, 220 n26, 230
n7; and Arab nationalism, 62, 67, 226
n39
Red Sea, British presence in, 8
refugees: from Palestine, 178, 179, 190–2,
209; from Syria and Hijaz, 91
religious groups, 55–6
Renaissance party (*hizb al-nahda*), 195
Rendel, Sir George, 110
al-Rifaʿi, Samir, 91, 160, 217; and death of
Abdullah, 209, 210; and London
Conference, 161; and partition of
Palestine, 162; as prime minister, 204,
205
al-Rikabi, ʿAli Ridaʾ, 21, 217, 220 n26;

286